Ngaio MARSH

~ HER LIFE IN CRIME ~

Ngaio *MARSH*

~ HER LIFE IN CRIME ~

JOANNE
DRAYTON

HarperCollins*Publishers*

NOTE

Every care has been taken to ensure accuracy; however, inconsistencies in Ngaio's recollections and source material may result in some variation.

National Library of New Zealand Cataloguing-in-Publication Data
Drayton, Joanne.
Ngaio Marsh : her life in crime / Joanne Drayton.
Includes bibliographical references.
ISBN 978-1-86950-635-3
1. Marsh, Ngaio, 1895-1982. 2. Women authors, New Zealand
—20th century—Biography. 3. Authors, New Zealand—20th
century—Biography. 4. Women theatrical producers and
directors—New Zealand—Biography. 5. Theatrical producers
and directors—New Zealand—Biography. 6. Detective and
mystery stories—Authorship. I. Titles.
NZ823.2

First published 2008

HarperCollins*Publishers (New Zealand) Limited*
P.O. Box 1, Auckland

ISBN: 978 1 86950 635 3

Cover design by Matt Stanton
Front cover photograph: Alexander Turnbull Library, PAColl-8163-04
Back cover portrait: Vy Elsom
Endpaper and internal illustrations: costume designs by Jonathan Elsom
Internal text design and typesetting by Springfield West
Printed by Griffin Press, Australia

79 gsm Bulky Paperback used by HarperCollins*Publishers* is a natural, recyclable product made from wood grown in a combination of sustainable plantation and regrowth forests. It also contains up to a 20% portion of recycled fibre. The manufacturing processes conform to the environmental regulations in Tasmania, the place of manufacture.

Contents

For Suzanne Vincent Marshall

in memory of my father
Malcolm Drayton
(1933–2007)

and sincerest thanks to the staff of
Alexander Turnbull Library
and National Library of New Zealand

Acknowledgements

'Do you feel an uncomfortable heat at the pit of your stomach, sir? and a nasty thumping at the top of your head? . . . I call it detective fever . . .'

The Moonstone by Wilkie Collins (1868)

Like detection, the fever of research and writing is as exacting as it is rewarding. What keeps me going are people I meet along the way who share the fever with me, and make the journey worthwhile. To all those whose heads have thumped a little on my behalf, I thank you.

Our vision of Ngaio Marsh is as vivid as it is today because of the precious memories and memorabilia that her friends and family have kept and treasured. I have had the greatest privilege of meeting and working on this project with the following special people in Ngaio's life. I would like to thank them for their insights and unstinting support: Jonathan Elsom, Annette Facer, Gerald Lascelles, Elric Hooper, John Dacres-Mannings, Jean Crabtree, Roy Mannings, Richard and Ginx Fox, Barbara Webb, Bob Scott, Simon Acland, John and Rosemary Acland, Judie and Malcolm Douglass, Rosemary and Mike Greene, Joy Wilkinson, Deborah Walton, Anne and Harry Atkinson, Alistair Johnson, Marian Minson, Brian Bell, Donald Munro, Max Cryer, Shirley O'Connor, Libby and Denver Glass, Charlotte Wilson, Leslie Shaw, Marie Gaut, and Henrietta Garnett (whose conversation was the inspiration for this book). I would like to pay a special tribute to the vision of Lady Doris McIntosh, who gave to the nation one of the richest legacies — Ngaio's letters.

My research has been greatly assisted by the excellent scholarship of the following academics and writers. I am immensely grateful to Dr Margaret Lewis, Dr Bruce Harding, Dr Glyn Strange, Carole Acheson, Professor Howard McNaughton, Paul Bushnell and Dr Douglas Munro, and to my own superb lecturer in Shakespeare, Professor David Gunby. I am also indebted to Rowan Gibbs and Richard Williams for their very helpful bibliography.

'It was the fourth member of our family', Ngaio wrote of Marton Cottage; and it exists today because of the efforts of some outstanding and magnanimous people. To walk around the terraced gardens and then in the front door is to walk into Ngaio's life. For a biographer this is a dream, so I thank sincerely Ngaio

Marsh House and Heritage Trust members, Dr Bruce Harding, Colin McLachlan, Pamela and John Wilson, and Eve Harding, for their years of volunteer work to secure public access and preservation, and John Dacres-Mannings for his generosity in leaving so many of Ngaio's treasures intact.

In my research I have had been assisted by friends and significant people who have helped the project along the way. I would like to offer my heartfelt thanks especially to Linda Tyler for her vision and support over the years and of this project, to Suzanne Marshall, who shared my fever and researched tirelessly, to Patti Gurekian for her research in the United States, and to Dr Carole Shepheard, Dr Peter Lineham, Dr Mike Austin, Priscilla Pitts, Tonia Geddes, Brit Bunkley, Andrea Gardener, Susan Kano, Belynda De Mayo, Alison MacDuff, Mike Geraghty, Lorraine Shannon, Alison Gernhoefer, Sue McBride, Liz and Ian Rivers, Doug and Carolyn Ironside, Richard and Sarah Laycock, Julia, Philip and Richard Mottram, Mary and Barry Loe, Morrin Rout, Ruth Todd, Cilla McVeigh, David Harcourt, Steve Woodside, Dr Miriam Saphiro, Dr Richard Smith and Albert Chan, Cathy Hartles and Liz Nicolson, Sue Thompson, Sheryn Bennett, Ralph Knowles, Ann Rolinson, Leslie and Rick Land, Peter and Genevieve Packer, Graeme Ell and Sarah Hillary (who kept me running).

My thanks go to those who gave permissions, and to colleagues in libraries, galleries and educational institutions around New Zealand. I would like to extend my thanks especially to the Hon. Judith Tizard MP, Penny Carnaby, Margaret Calder, Chris Szekely, Phillip Rainer, Colleen Slater, David Colquhoun, Amy Watling, Cathy Bentley, Mary Cobeldick, Jill Goodwin, Linda Evans, Alison Laurie, Glenda Gale, Barbara Brownlie, Jocelyn Chalmers, Roger Swanson, John Sullivan, Joan McCracken, Diane Woods, Tania Connelly, David Jones, Susan Bartel, Emerson Vandy, Rachel Underwood, Rebecca Perkins, Amanda Brown, Tim Jones, Chris Bourke, Alison Lloyd-Davies, Jeny Curnow, Malcolm Ott, Matthew Wright, and Rob Osman. I would like to offer a special thank you, also, to Denis Welch, who put me onto some very fruitful *Listener* leads.

I am grateful to the staff of the following institutions for their cooperation and assistance in accessing archives, images and information: Radio New Zealand Sound Archives, Christchurch Art Gallery Te Puna o Waiwhetu, E.H. McCormick Research Library — Auckland Art Gallery Toi o Tamaki, Christchurch Polytechnic, Christchurch Public Library, Auckland Public Library, Wellington Public Library, Victoria University of Wellington Library, University of Sydney Library, National Library of Scotland, HarperCollins Archive

(Glasgow), British Library; BBC Sound Archives, British Theatre Library (Victoria and Albert Museum), British Theatre Museum, Mugar Memorial Library Boston, Princeton University Libraries, National Library of Scotland, University of Glasgow Archives, Wodehouse Library in Dulwich, Friends of the Alexander Turnbull Library, St Mary's College (Wellington), and Westlake Girls' High (Auckland). I would like to offer special thanks to the staff of St Margaret's College (Christchurch), particularly to Jillian Kerr, Geraldine Pickles, Diana White and Robyn Gosset, who were so generous in their assistance.

My grateful thanks goes to the administration, library and Long Black staff at UNITEC who have kindly supported me in my writing of this book. I am also grateful to Dr David Hawkins, Cassandra Barnett, Kathy Barry, Mary-Louise Browne, Dorina Jotti, Gina Ferguson, and Donna Salmon.

My warmest thanks to Lorain Day, for her vision in taking this project on, and to Kate Stone, Sandra Noakes, Shona Martyn and all the staff at HarperCollins working on this book, and especially to editor Anna Rogers — thank you for sure and steady support, and for your criticism, encouragement and inspiration. At HarperCollins in the London and Glasgow offices, I would like to thank, especially, David Brawn and Felicity Windmill.

Without the love and support of my family, this book would never have been written. Thank you for your patient acceptance of the sacrifices required. I would like to thank my mother Patricia Drayton, Paul Drayton, Chrissie Thomas and Guy Drayton, Megan Jamieson, and our children Jeremy Thomson and Katherine and Jason Lovelock.

My sincerest thanks to Johathan Elsom for permission to reproduce his wonderful costume designs for *Henry V* and *Hamlet*, and Vy Elsom's superb portrait of Ngaio Marsh, which is one of two pastels that were commissioned for *Black Beech and Honeydew*.

9

Chronology

1895	Born 23 April, Christchurch, New Zealand (birth not registered until 1899).
1910–14	Secondary education at St Margaret's College.
1915–19	Studied painting at Canterbury College School of Art, Christchurch.
1920–22	Toured with the Allan Wilkie Shakespeare Company and then with the Rosemary Rees Comedy Company.
1922–28	Painted, freelance journalist and began working with repertory companies and Unlimited Charities to produce amateur theatrical productions.
1928	Travelled to England.
1928–32	Lived with the Rhodes family first at Gerrards Cross, then in London. Wrote articles for the Christchurch *Press* under the title 'New Canterbury Pilgrim' and opened a design shop with Nelly Rhodes in Knightsbridge.
1931–32	Wrote first detective fiction novel, which was submitted to literary agent just before being called back to her mother's sickbed in New Zealand. Rose Marsh died 23 November 1932.
1932–37	Established herself as one of the four Queens of Crime; exhibited paintings with the Christchurch Society of Arts and The Group; and produced plays.
1937–38	Trip to Britain and tour of Europe with Betty Cotterill and Jean Webster.
1938	Returned to New Zealand and became a Red Cross ambulance driver during the war.
1943	Directed Shakespeare's *Hamlet* for the Canterbury University College Drama Society.
1944–45	Toured New Zealand with *Hamlet* and *Othello* under the aegis of Dan O'Connor.
1948	Awarded OBE for services to drama and literature. Henry Marsh died 4 September.

1949 — Toured Australia with *Six Characters* and *Othello* under the aegis of Dan O'Connor.

1949–51 — Trip to England. Collins threw 'Marsh Million' party to celebrate the release of her books. Gathered a company for the British Commonwealth Theatre Company tour, which toured Australia and New Zealand before disbanding.

1952–54 — Writing and directing in Christchurch.

1954–56 — Travelled to England on board the cargo ship *Temeraire*, which was the inspiration for *Singing in the Shrouds*.

1956–60 — Writing and directing in Christchurch.

1960–61 — Promotional tour of East Asia, North America and Britain, and lived for over a year in London.

1962–65 — Wrote libretto for *A Unicorn for Christmas*, which was performed in front of Queen Elizabeth II. Delivered the Macmillan Brown Lectures (1962), and was awarded an honorary doctorate of literature by the University of Canterbury (1962).

1966 — Travelled to England, and while there was awarded DBE. Delayed her departure to attend investiture at Buckingham Palace in November.

1968 — Stayed in Rome with Doris and Alister McIntosh. Tour of northern Italy with Pamela Mann, followed by five weeks in London.

1971 — Six-month stay in Britain, with promotional trip to Denmark and visit to Elsinore.

1974–75 — Six-month stay in Britain extended to 18 months by cancer operation. This was her last trip to England.

1976 — Directed last production — *Sweet Mr Shakespeare*.

1978 — Received the Grand Master of the Mystery Writers of America Award. Travelled to Australia to see John Dacres-Mannings and his family.

1982 — Finished *Light Thickens*, her 32nd novel, just weeks before dying at home on 18 February, aged 86.

CHAPTER ONE

A Cradle in a Grave

Rain beat incessantly against the window. All weekend she had been alone in her flat, immersed in books and distracted imaginings. The late afternoon light was almost gone as she reached decisively for her mackintosh and umbrella. She was ready, as ready as she would ever be. Up the basement steps she hurtled and onto the London street. The last stragglers of the day dashed purposefully past her, as she pulled the collar of her coat tight around her neck and bent into the weather. She moved swiftly, a tall, dark figure etched by streetlamps against unfolding blackness. Outside the local stationer's she hesitated for an instant before thrusting into the smell 'of damp newsprint, cheap magazines, and wet people'. She bought 'six exercise books, a pencil and pencil sharpener and splashed back to the flat'. Against the wind that threw itself at walls and fingered its way around cracks, she heaped the coal fire in the grate and drew her chair closer. With pencil posed, and exercise book in her lap, she was prepared — for murder.

It was in this cramped room on a wintry day that Ngaio Marsh committed her first crime to paper. *A Man Lay Dead* was written quickly in a burst of beginner's energy. She filled the exercise books in a matter of weeks, and when her mother returned from a motor trip with friends even she was forced to

13

accept that something remarkable had happened. 'I couldn't put it down,' she said. Up to this point, Rose Marsh's ambitions for her 36-year-old daughter had been theatrical, but in the deceptively clever intricacies of Ngaio's writing she glimpsed, if reluctantly, a new plot.

It was 1931, the Depression. The poor and unemployed queued for food and shelter in lines that grew longer by the day. But, in the cosseted circles of privilege, it was also the heyday of the flapper and the frivolous weekend murder party. Since her arrival in England more than two years earlier, Ngaio had been drawn into this world and it was the inspiration for her book. The people she met became models for her murderers and her bodies, and their haunts became her crime scenes.

On the hall floor at Frantock, Sir Hubert Handesley's country home, lies her first victim, with the blade of a ritual Russo-Mongolian dagger protruding from his back. The fortissimo bass voice of Doctor Tokareff singing Russian opera can be heard from an upstairs bedroom where he is dressing for dinner. Suddenly, the manor house is plunged into pitch blackness. In his room, handsome Fleet Street journalist Nigel Bathgate strikes a match, which gives him sufficient light to find the landing and grope his way downstairs. 'The house was alive with the voices of the guests, calling, laughing, questioning . . . The sudden blaze from the chandelier was blinding. On the stairs Wilde, his wife, Tokareff, Handesley, and Angela all shrank from it.' Here it is, the stuff of nightmares, waiting to unleash chaos among the sports-car-driving, dress-for-dinner, horsey set. Stunned guests collect around the body.

Motive for murder abounds. For in life the corpse was a womanizer, a good-looking, smooth-talking purveyor of envy. His girlfriend waited too long for their wedding; his mistress was an old school chum's wife. There will be few mourners at his funeral and even fewer who will find no silver lining in his coffin. But the measure of a man's character does not diminish the horror of murder. When a crime has been committed the perpetrator must be brought to justice, and few things galvanize the agencies of social control faster than a suspicious death. So the telephone call is made, and into this tight, almost claustrophobic plot walks the tall, distinguished figure of Chief Inspector Roderick Alleyn.

He arrives by chance. The local superintendent is down with an acute attack of gastric flu. Because of Sir Hubert's status and illustrious political career, the local office has been forced to appeal to Scotland Yard. Alleyn is thrilled to head the case.

'What's the matter with you?' Detective-Inspector Boys asked, noting his superior's enthusiasm. 'Has someone found you a job?'

'You've guessed my boyish secret. I've been given a murder to solve — aren't I a lucky little detective.'

Hurriedly, he assembles his 'flash' and 'dab' men — Detective Sergeant Smith with his Box Brownie and Detective Sergeant Bailey carrying his fingerprint apparatus; they head for a waiting car. Two hours later, Alleyn and his men are standing in the hall at Frantock.

The weekend party has assembled at Sir Hubert's manor house to play the Murder Game. Vassily Vassilyevitch, Sir Hubert's Russian retainer, was to give a scarlet plaque to whichever guest he chose to be the murderer. That person would have a day to hatch the heinous end of one of the guests by separating them from the crowd and saying, 'You're the corpse.' After the fatal words were uttered, the murderer would sound a primitive gong and turn the lights off at the main switch to symbolize the slaying. Darkness would last a minute or so before light and reason were restored in the form of a 'mock trial' with a 'judge' and a 'prosecuting attorney'. All of the party would have the right to cross-examine witnesses, including the murderer. But now the real corpse of Charles Rankin has been discovered with a blade driven into his heart. Shock overwhelms the party as they gather in the library the next day to hear Alleyn's words. He gives them strict instructions. No one is allowed to leave the grounds. 'I think the Murder Game should be played out. I propose that we hold the trial precisely as it was planned. I shall play the part of prosecuting attorney . . . For the moment there will be no judge.' He believes that playing the game will unravel the complexities of the crime and reveal its perpetrator. So the characters find themselves trapped inside a game inside a house until the murderer confesses.

When she arrived in England, Ngaio Marsh brought with her two chapters of a manuscript that she hoped would contain the genesis of the great New Zealand novel. She knew it was a literary challenge waiting to be taken up, and worked on it intermittently until London life lured her in a new creative direction. By the time she began her first detective novel, the genre was already well established. Its genesis was in Philadelphia in April 1841 when a young, impoverished editor named Edgar Allan Poe published an eerie tale called 'The Murders in the Rue Morgue' in *Graham's Magazine*. That year, Poe was invited to head the magazine's editorial staff on the condition that he controlled his drunken mood swings. Under his talented and more temperate stewardship, '*Graham's* became the world's first mass-circulation magazine, leaping in a few short months from . . . five thousand readers to an unprecedented forty thousand'. Poe's detective stories developed in the crucible of professional success and modest acclaim. The three tales he wrote with the Chevalier Auguste Dupin as his sleuth became a blueprint for the genre's evolution, and Dupin was a watershed character in Poe's writing because he represented the victory of the rational mind over Poe's usual theme of terror. Dupin's intellect was fired by the fusion of opposites that Poe most admired: he was at once a visionary poet and a rational logician.

The aristocratic and eccentric Auguste Dupin was introduced by an anonymous narrator who became his sycophantic sidekick. This unequal relationship set the pattern of the brilliantly omniscient detective dazzling his obtuse, slow-witted friend, who is the storyteller. Other conventions were established, such as the plodding constabulary who overlook all but the most obvious clues, the locked-room mystery, the innocent cast under suspicion, the elucidation of the criminal mind by appreciating the murderer's circumstances and motives, and the jaw-dropping dénouement that leaves everyone but the detective amazed. After solving the Rue Morgue murders, where, in a locked room, a corpse is discovered 'thrust head downward up a chimney', and an old woman's body is found frightfully mutilated, the subsequent crimes that perplex Auguste Dupin are smaller. In 'The Purloined Letter' he recovers stolen correspondence, and in 'The Mystery of Marie Rogêt' he establishes the fate of a murdered girl.

Poe set his detective stories in Paris, which encapsulated the Gothic and romantic traditions that inspired his work. Despite the notoriety that writing brought him, he remained a literary outsider in the United States, criticized for the blackness of his stories and for their European influence. He wrote out of ambition, but also to support his young wife, Virginia Clemm, who was dying of tuberculosis. She was his cousin, whom he had married when she was 13 years old. Stricken by grief and financial worry after her death, the destitute Poe drank heavily before dying prematurely in 1849. Ironically, when his own survival depended on the reason he so liberally instilled in Auguste Dupin, the archetypal sleuth vanished from his pages.

The Paris streets that stirred Poe's imagination also contained the germ of his great detective. In 1829, the autobiography of retired policeman François

Eugène Vidocq appeared on the city's bookstalls. He was a former criminal who began his career as a police informant in prison. This was not unusual: ex-cons were employed as detectives by La Sûreté Nationale, which began in 1812, by London's Bow Street Runners and by Scotland Yard following its founding in 1829. After 18 years working for the Sûreté, the 52-year-old Vidocq published his ghost-written four-volume *Mémoires*, containing a multitude of colourful anecdotes about the apprehension of an alleged 20,000 criminals. This fabulous concoction of fact and fiction became Poe's inspiration.

But Dupin was not a professional policeman like Vidocq: he was an amateur detective assisting local law enforcement with his powers of observation and logic. One of the earliest fictional detectives on the police payroll was created by Frenchman Émile Gaboriau who started out, in 1853, by writing halfpenny thrillers that he published in daily instalments to satisfy a burgeoning market. Urban, industrialized life demanded the rudiments of education from an increasing proportion of the population. For the enterprising Gaboriau, this translated into a sizeable readership hungry for serialized escape from the drudgery of everyday life. Gaboriau's Monsieur Lecoq (who appeared in his first novel in 1866) helped to rehabilitate the public image of the police detective by removing some of its criminal taint. His writing introduced the layered plot with its complex twists, turns and unexpected dénouements.

Across the Channel, Gaboriau's influence on the development of detective fiction was substantial. Although his stories lacked the monumental staying power of Poe's, they could be found on the bookshelves of such great English masters as Wilkie Collins and Arthur Conan Doyle. In fact, crime writer and critic Julian Symons believes Collins's superbly crafted *The Moonstone* may have been influenced by the Frenchman's three earliest crime stories, *L'Affaire Lerouge*, *Le Crime d'Orcival* and *Le Dossier No. 113*. Although *The Moonstone* was the first major detective novel published in English, the laurels for the first English detective go to Collins's colleague and close friend Charles Dickens, who created the ineffable Inspector Bucket of *Bleak House* in 1853. Like Poe and Gaboriau, Collins and Dickens responded to popular demand for spellbinding, affordable literature by serializing their work. And Dickens demonstrated his remarkable foresight not only for writing classics but for publishing them, when, as editor of the *All the Year Round* magazine, he serialized *The Moonstone*. The episodes began appearing early in 1868 and the three-volume novel was published in July. *The Moonstone* was innovative because it made detection central to a story conceived on an epic scale. Immediate critical response to the book was subdued, but posterity has judged it differently. 'Taking everything into consideration', wrote Dorothy Sayers in her introduction to *The Omnibus of Crime*, '*The Moonstone* is probably the very finest detective story ever written.'

Gaboriau was the inspiration for the 19th century's best-selling crime novel, *The Mystery of a Hansom Cab*, written by New Zealander Fergus Hume. It was his first novel. 'I tried to get it published, but every one to whom I offered it refused to even look at the manuscript on the ground that no Colonial could write anything worth reading.' Five thousand copies of the book were published at the author's expense in Melbourne in 1886; subsequently an estimated million copies have sold around the world. Hume moved to England and continued writing detective novels for more than 30 years, but never with the same blockbuster success.

The maturity of the genre came in a prolific golden age of short stories by Arthur Conan Doyle. Empty waiting rooms and a threatened medical practice inspired the Scotsman to begin writing about a super-sleuth based on the special deductive skills of consulting surgeon Dr Joseph Bell, at the Edinburgh Infirmary where he trained. Sherlock Holmes was given life in *A Study in Scarlet* in 1887. Over 40 years, through 56 short stories and four novels, he would become the world's greatest, and arguably most eccentric, detective. He was a cocaine addict, prone to 'scraping away' at his violin, and to prolonged periods lying prostrate on the couch in fits of depression. He was an alter ego to his creator, the huntin', shootin' and fishin' arch-philistine Conan Doyle, and an anathema to most conservative Victorians, yet his power to capture the popular imagination was phenomenal. His pyrotechnic displays of detection won him cult-hero status.

Conan Doyle's synthesis of existing approaches was superb. He adopted Poe and Gaboriau's admiring narrator, creating his own faithful retainer, Dr John H. Watson. He eschewed the terror of Poe's Gothic tales, but made high art of his conventions. His sleuth, an upper-class egotist like Auguste Dupin, was emotionally stilted, faintly misogynistic (if not misanthropic), and an amateur rather than a professional detective. He was an urban dweller living in a sleuthing *ménage* with his narrator. He observed the smallest clues, developed a psychological profile of the perpetrator, and drew on an awe-inspiring breadth of empirical knowledge. If Poe's Dupin gave shape to Sherlock Holmes, then the complex twists and turns of Gaboriau's stories suggested Conan Doyle's consummate puzzle plots. He remains one of the greatest and most original exponents of the intricately woven whodunit. With flair, he fashioned the conventions of the guessing game between writer and reader into rules. The diverse settings for his multifarious plots gave weight to the words of Sherlock Holmes in 'The Adventure of the Copper Beeches': 'It is my belief, Watson, founded upon my experience, that the lowest and vilest alleys in London do not present a more dreadful record of sin than does the smiling and beautiful countryside.' Crime could be close at hand; its location was in the complexities of human psychology.

Because public pressure foiled Conan Doyle's attempt in 1893 to kill off Sherlock Holmes by pushing him and his nemesis Professor Moriarty over a waterfall, the sleuth lived much longer than his creator ever intended. In fact, the short-story form was in decline by 1927 when *The Case Book of Sherlock Holmes* brought this famous career to an end. Conan Doyle's influence was immense, as was the part he played in a British-based literary lineage that included G. K. Chesterton, Edgar Wallace and others. In what could have been wasteland years between the two World Wars, the genre flourished, and, remarkably, the chief architects of this classical era of detective fiction were women.

On the surface the four Queens of Crime, as they became known, seemed to be conventional upper-class women with values rooted in the 'smiling and beautiful countryside' and lives untouched by their fetish subject, murder. But the conventions of the whodunit offered these very private women a perfect cover. When Agatha Christie introduced Hercule Poirot in *The Mysterious Affair of Styles* in 1920, she invested in the book little more of her private life than the knowledge of poisons she had gleaned from war work behind a hospital pharmacy counter in Torquay. There was even less of her in the wax-trimmed moustache-wearing, stout little Belgian with the egg-shaped head who became her dandified detective through 33 novels and 10 collections of short stories over more than 55 years. Death came easily to Agatha Christie, and Hercule Poirot irritated her intensely. She would have killed him off earlier, but he was the heir to Sherlock Holmes, a small man who became a superman in the public's imagination.

Hercule Poirot may sometimes have hovered perilously between cardboard cut-out and eccentric Holmesian cliché, but Christie transcended his weaknesses by constructing fabulously intricate problem plots. She was mathematical in her plotting, but also deceptive, and her killer instinct left no one exempt. In *The Murder of Roger Ackroyd*, which catapulted her into prominence in 1926, she treacherously breached detective etiquette by making the trusted narrator the murderer. This violation only enhanced her profile, beginning her reign as one of the world's greatest detective writers. Interestingly, her stories were local and almost over-brewed in their Englishness. They were set typically in rural English villages, like the fictional St Mary Mead, the home of Christie's other iconic sleuth, Miss Jane Marple. This was a world at risk from the emerging economies of the 20th century, but in the 1920s and 1930s a habitat still existed for the country squire, his family, servants and forelock-tugging gardeners and tradesmen. This was where the privileged Christie lived, and it was familiar to, or at least a desirable fantasy for, many of her readers. Miss Marple made her appearance in the midst of this cosy ordinariness, knitting and gossiping her way through the solution to her first *Murder at the Vicarage* in 1930. This elderly, mystery-solving spinster began as a bloodless archaism, severe, blue-eyed, frail and wearing a black lace cap and mittens, but she would update herself through 12 novels, becoming, warmer, wittier and more human. No other author has given so much snooping talent to a female figure of such advanced years, and created such a charismatic character.

Agatha Christie's writing followed the strict detective novel formula, with a tightly structured beginning, a middle that explored the possibilities of the plot, and an end that neatly tied everything up. This rigid form gave her absolute control. But in 1926 her own life was less conveniently scripted. In the wake of her much-loved mother's death and her dashing military husband's elopement with one of her acquaintances, she disappeared. Her car was found mysteriously abandoned in a chalk pit. She would be discovered 10 days later, at a Harrogate spa, checked into the hotel under the surname of her husband's mistress, Nancy Neele. The English press at the time accused her of orchestrating the event to promote sales of *The Murder of Roger Ackroyd*, her first book published by Collins. Although she began a new life with archaeologist Sir Max Mallowan, whom she married in 1930, the events surrounding her separation and divorce from Archibald Christie remained a mystery. Her autobiography describes the incident in terms of a mental breakdown or fugue, which seems a likely explanation for the disappearance of the intensely publicity-shy author. But publicity it did generate. The civilian response to police calls to mount a nationwide manhunt was almost unprecedented. Among the hundreds who searched for Agatha Christie was a young woman called Dorothy Sayers.

In 1923, *Whose Body?* introduced Sayers' foppish, monocle-wearing Lord

Peter Wimsey. Operating as an amateur detective with friendly Inspector Charles Parker of Scotland Yard and manservant Bunter, Wimsey would work out whodunit and how in 11 novels and 21 short stories. There was much of Dorothy Sayers in the make-up, or rather make-believe, of her detective, and this is probably why she fell so famously in love with him. He was a projection of her fantasies. Wimsey was hugely rich and it gave her pleasure to spend his money for him. 'When I was dissatisfied with my single unfurnished room, I took a luxurious flat for him in Piccadilly,' she wrote in 1936. 'When my cheap rug got a hole in it, I ordered him an Aubusson carpet. When I had no money to pay my bus fare I presented him with a Daimler Double Six . . . and when I felt dull I let him drive it.'

Wimsey began almost as a figure of farce, a caricature in his snobbish, over-mannered elegance, but he would evolve into an admirable man. He and Bunter were inspired in part by humorist and writer P.G. Wodehouse's bungling Bertie Wooster and gentleman's gentleman, Jeeves. But Sayers put existing models of the detective under a magnifying glass. Where his predecessors were mostly upper-class gentlemen, Wimsey was a blue-blooded aristocrat, the second son of the 15th Duke of Denver. He was educated at Eton, taking his degree, as Sayers had, at Oxford, where he received a First in history. His breeding was impeccable and his eccentricities refined to a high art. He was a talented musician, a collector of ancient books, and a connoisseur of fine wines, food, fashion and fast cars. Even his athletic prowess was consummate. At university he played cricket for Oxford, and when in sleuthing mode he dangled effortlessly from ropes off buildings. Only in visualizing his appearance did Sayers show restraint. Perhaps he could be called nondescript with his tow-coloured hair, beak-like nose and modest stature.

Wimsey's life was vastly different from that of his creator. Dorothy Sayers' first two detective novels were written during a difficult period. In 1921 she became infatuated with writer-journalist John Cournos, a man not prepared to return her love. She rebounded into an even less appropriate match with motorcar enthusiast Bill White, who, after a brief fling, left her pregnant and unmarried. Although she was a modern woman earning her living as a copywriter for Benson's Advertising Agency, she was also a conservative and ultimately devout High Church Anglican. She was the only child of older parents. Her father had been the chaplain of Christ Church, Oxford, and headmaster of the choir school. She felt unable to tell her parents, in their 70s, about the arrival of their grandson,

John Anthony, in 1924. As a result she kept the baby secret, fostering him with her cousin Ivy Shrimpton. Her relationships with Cournos and White were never made public, and neither was the fact that she had an illegitimate son. Even when she wed older Fleet Street journalist Mac Fleming in 1926, she lived a double life divided between her flat in London and country home in Witham. Mac, who left paid work because of illness soon after they married, was part of her provincial life and many of her London friends never knew he existed.

Unlike Agatha Christie, Sayers created her sleuth to pay the bills, and the same was true for another of the reigning Queens of Crime, Margery Allingham. Younger than her two co-rulers, and something of a prodigy, she came from a working literary family of writer-journalists and editors. She was eight when her first story was published in her aunt's magazine; her first novel, *Blackkerchief Dick*, came out in 1923 when she was 19. *The White Cottage Mystery*, her first story with a detective theme, was serialized in the *Daily Express* before it was produced as a novel in 1927, but it was not until *The Crime at Black Dudley* was published in 1929 that she had her first real success. It was in this book that she introduced her enigmatic Albert Campion. He began as a relatively minor figure, but when he captured the imagination and endorsement of her American publishers he was duly plucked from the chorus to become a star. There is more than a whiff of Wimsey and Wooster in Campion's demeanour, and he may have been created as a spoof of the archetypal silly-ass sleuth. His pedigree was the most illustrious yet, because of his connection to royalty, although his exact relationship to the throne was never made specific. In fact, very little about this slippery snoop's identity was specific. He had an assumed name, and there were other aliases. He was even physically ambiguous. His voice was described as idiotic and effete. A wiry albino-blond with buckteeth, he wore horn-rimmed spectacles and had a blank, unintelligent stare, but he was also heralded as a woman magnet.

Campion began as a modish young man-about-town with no serious intentions, but this was a smokescreen. In reality he moved easily between nobility and the criminal underworld to solve his crimes. Although a freelance government agent, and therefore seemingly on the right side of the law, his underworld connections were as close as his lugubrious valet, Magersfontein Lugg, who appeared first in *Mystery Mile*, in 1930. Lugg was a reformed cat burglar and borstal jail-bird, with a rich cockney accent and amusing turn of phrase. He would become the absent-minded Campion's minder and nanny.

Allingham wrote another 17 novels and 20 short stories with Campion as her hero-sleuth. Like Wimsey, he developed into a more complex and compelling figure as the novels progressed. Her plots improved along with her characters, but their strength remained in the element of risk rather than the intellectual puzzle plot. She created tension by evoking a sense of fear and foreboding that could be as disturbing as violence. Witchcraft and the occult were the themes in a number of plots. Her own connections to spiritualism began in her youth when she said *Blackkerchief Dick* was communicated to her at a séance. In her later years she was drawn to religion, studying sorcery and black magic with an interest intensified by the occult's long history in her local area.

Margery Allingham hoped she might make a career for herself on the stage. In 1920, she began an acting course at London's Regent Street Polytechnic. Speech therapy and drama classes cured her childhood stutter, but acting was not the profession for this shy woman who found speaking in public an ordeal. The theatre remained a lifelong passion, and introduced her to Philip Youngman Carter. The pair had their first date at The Old Vic theatre in London. Together they attended countless stage productions, became secretly engaged in 1922, and married in 1928. A love of the theatre linked all the Queens of Crime, but none loved it more than Ngaio Marsh, the last to join this criminal quartet. She may well have sat in the same West End productions as Margery Allingham, but this was not all they shared. Allingham's *The Crime at Black Dudley* bears the closest fingerprint to Ngaio Marsh's *A Man Lay Dead*. Before she began her murderous weekend's writing, Ngaio had been reading a detective novel from the local lending library. Later she remembered that it may have been an Agatha Christie or a Dorothy Sayers, but it was probably the residue of Margery Allingham's plot that stayed in her mind as she wrote.

In *The Crime at Black Dudley*, a homicide explodes the gaiety of a weekend party in a musty-dusty manor house in remote coastal Suffolk. After dinner, a bejewelled 15th-century Italian dagger is used in a ritual game that has ancient associations with the house. In a blackened room, the blade is passed between guests in a frenzied rite that combines the anxiety of a pass-the-parcel bomb with the sensory deprivation of blind-man's-buff. When light is restored, the host's invalid uncle, Colonel Coombe, is found murdered and an important document is missing from his papers; the house guests are held hostage by a criminal gang seeking the document's return. It is pathologist Dr George Abbershaw who uncovers the killer, assisted by the mysterious Albert Campion. Abbershaw was almost certainly intended to be Allingham's detective, but he was upstaged by the super-sleuth-spoof, Campion.

Although Ngaio and Allingham have similar plots, their execution is quite different. With each sinister ingredient, Allingham twists the tension of her story tighter. Her mansion is a rotting labyrinth of antique rooms and corridors connected by an ancient network of rat-infested secret passageways. Guests vanish through panelled walls, reappear behind fireplaces and are beaten up by Teutonic henchmen. Her host is a mask-wearing criminal mastermind, and his staff and associates some of Europe's most villainous thugs. The situation becomes combustible and burn the house nearly does, with the guests locked in an upper chamber. Salvation comes when their desperate choruses of 'view-halloo' attract the Monewdon Hunt. Ngaio's treatment, by comparison, is blander but more believable. Her suspense hinges on whodunit and how. Already her special talent for visualizing scenes is evident, as is her superb sense of dramatic timing.

In years to come Ngaio Marsh would cringe at the thought of her first novel, with its barely plausible storyline, shallow characterization and confined setting, but it was her entrée to crime fiction writing. In fact, both *A Man Lay Dead* and *The Crime at Black Dudley* exemplify the cosy detective novel form perfectly. Claustrophobic in every way, they unfold with a small group of characters, in a single main setting, over a short period of time. The exclusion of the outside world allows the writer to create a controlled environment where clues, red herrings, victims, innocents and villains can be paraded before the reader free of contamination. There can be no loose ends and no escapes. The isolated manor house is a favourite setting, but equally it could be a village, a train, a boat, a hospital, a theatre, or any discrete space that brings a hand-picked group of eccentrics together and locks the door. The cosy comes with a property box of stock characters. There is the prominent family with its multiple tensions, the vamp, the vicar, the rake, the student, the professor, the spinster, the young poseur, the doctor, the adventurer, the foreigner, the writer, the untouched young woman, and, of course, the murderer. For murder it mostly is, because the participants play for the highest stakes: the death penalty. Cosy plots are convoluted, so the reader is presented with a multiplicity of possible scenarios, each stopping at a dead end until the detective leads the way. The detective enters this amphitheatre of anxiety in a sanctified role to restore the balance of good over evil. He or she is neither judge nor executioner but high priest of order, exposing the wrongdoer, who is sacrificed to reaffirm society's rules.

In 1942, writer and critic Nicholas Blake described the detective as 'the Fairy Godmother of the twentieth century folk-myth'. Certainly this figure played a magical part in one of the century's favourite bedtime stories.

'I thought it would be fun to create someone who hadn't got tickets tied to him,' explained Ngaio Marsh in a 1978 radio interview for the BBC. She was talking about the genesis of her detective, Roderick Alleyn. She had visited Scotland and while staying with friends selected the popular Scottish name Roderick; and not long before she began writing she went to Dulwich College where her father had gone to school, and chose the surname of its founder, Elizabethan actor Edward Alleyn. So her detective was christened before he was born. His character was gestating in her mind as she tinkered with the coals in her London grate. She was thinking of a more ordinary man than the set of silly-assed sleuths who tweaked waxed moustaches, repositioned monocles or stared blankly over buckteeth. She wanted to create a believable professional policeman who could move comfortably between the lower echelons and upper-class circles where many of her stories would be set. He was to be an 'attractive, civilised man,' the kind, she later wrote, 'with whom it would be pleasant to talk but much less pleasant to fall out'. So Alleyn was born, 'tall and thin with an accidental elegance about him and a fastidiousness'. His hair is dark, his eyes are grey 'with corners that turned down. They looked as if they would smile easily, but his mouth didn't.' After a long look at her first detective, Sir Hubert Handesley's niece, Angela North, decides Alleyn is 'the sort they knew would "do" for house-parties'. He is the younger son of a landed family in Buckinghamshire, has been educated at Eton, employed briefly by the Foreign Office, and now works for the Yard. His brother is a baronet in the diplomatic corps, and his mother, Lady Alleyn of Danes Lodge, Bossicote, breeds Alsatians. His background is impeccable rather than impossible, and his worst habit is his irritating tendency to make banal comments and facetious jokes.

Like his sleuthing peers, Alleyn would mature, but not as much because he began more plausibly. There would be excursions abroad, but his natural habitat would remain the English hothouse cosy where traditional values were just a murder away from being restored. The anarchy of war, the devastation of pandemic, the General Strike of 1926, the Great Depression, and the rise of Communism and Fascism with their catastrophic episodes of genocide never properly enter his cloistered world where a single death can still be utterly shocking.

Explaining the extraordinary demand for the detective novel, Margery Allingham wrote: 'When the moralists cite the modern murder mystery as evidence of an unnatural love of violence in a decadent age, I wonder if it is nothing of the sort, but rather a sign of a popular instinct for order and form in a period of sudden and chaotic change [. . . .] There is something deeply healthy in the implication that to deprive a human being of his life is not only the most dreadful thing one can do to him, but also that it matters to the rest of us.' Faced with the flux of a rapidly changing world, readers sought intellectual escape in problem plots where sanitized death teased the minds of anyone from a housewife to a judge. While global war and economic slump eroded the class system and beat at the bastions of the family manor house, the detective novel offered fictional stability. Anybody with a stake in the restoration of traditional order was a potential reader. The detective novel portrayed a world of proscriptive hierarchies and reassuring ritual. It assumed a reasoned universe based on polarities of right and wrong where anarchy occasionally erupted but normality was always restored. And no one could be a more chivalrous representative of the status quo than that 'perfect specimen of English manhood', Roderick Alleyn.

As an orderly man in an ordered form, he required little personal revelation from Ngaio Marsh. Like the other Queens of Crime, Ngaio shunned uncomfortable publicity. She seemed largely conformist, from a conservative background, writing in an era when women were expected to behave conventionally. The crime novel kept up appearances by preserving her from the necessity of exploring difficult feelings. The genre exposed to public scrutiny her intellect and literary skills rather than her emotions. Ngaio was the most secretive of this very self-protective group. As crime novelist commentator Jessica Mann writes, 'she exemplifies in its most extreme form the reticence of the crime novelist . . . [she] never wrote anything which touched her emotions more deeply' and 'one senses withdrawal'.

Ngaio was the only Antipodean Crime Queen, and although she often left New Zealand's parochial fish bowl, she never escaped it. This made her, as she described it, 'a looker on in England'. But she was also something of an Anglophile outsider at home. Colonization creates cultural refugees and Ngaio was one of these, a wanderer between worlds, never belonging completely to any place or culture. But displacement does not explain the intensity of her need for privacy. In 32 novels written over nearly 50 years, she exposed countless villains, but never herself. She was a doyenne of concealment, knowing exactly what evidence was incriminating and who would point the finger. There are, however, clues to understanding this complex and elusive woman. Ngaio felt strong emotions. 'I guess I fell in love with them,' she said of the aristocratic family she stayed with in Britain, and love is as good a place as any to begin a mystery.

Ngaio's rusty freighter-cum-passenger ship steamed up the Thames, docking at Tilbury in the early summer of 1928. She was ecstatic about her first visit to England. 'We were bewilderingly gay,' she remembered, 'I got the tag end of a very ravished but very wonderful 1920s in London.' She went immediately to stay with her friends Helen and Tahu Rhodes, and their burgeoning family of five children. On her arrival at their magnificent Georgian mansion, Ngaio was greeted by a joke 'For Sale on Easy Terms' sign, which set the tone of her stay. Ngaio found the Rhodes family's theatricality, their irrepressible enthusiasm for practical jokes, for putting on costumes, for making up and acting up, irresistible. She would live with them on and off while in England; first at Alderbourne Manor near Gerrards Cross in Buckinghamshire, and later in London.

This would become a *ménage à trois* of sorts, held together by the infatuation of the two women. Helen, known as Nelly, was the eldest daughter of Lord Plunket, who had been Governor of New Zealand from 1904 to 1910. In 1916, she married her handsome soldier husband, Captain Tahu Rhodes, at an English church packed with wounded soldiers who had been driven to the service in Red Cross vehicles from the New Zealand hospital at Walton-on-Thames.

The pattern of Ngaio's weekend stays with the couple had begun when they returned to New Zealand at the end of the First World War. Tahu Rhodes, a childhood friend, owned Meadowbank, a large sheep station at Ellesmere, about 30 kilometres south-east of her hometown of Christchurch. Through her fund-raising activities in the theatre, Ngaio picked up the threads of her acquaintance with Tahu and was introduced to his wife, Nelly. The women's friendship became lifelong and binding.

In New Zealand, Ngaio had wandered listlessly from one touring theatre production to another, searching for something permanent and sustaining. She had acted in, written and directed plays; she had been to art school and produced paintings for exhibitions; she had written articles for the *Sun* newspaper. But after the Rhodeses' return to England in 1927, her enthusiasm for bit-jobs diminished in direct proportion to her desire to travel 'Home'. Much more than a literal home, England was for her a cultural pantheon presided over by her giant of literary gods, William Shakespeare. When it came, the invitation from the Rhodeses burst like a blaze of fireworks across a night sky. She was rapturous. Her parents were the only tug on her emotions. However, her doting bank-clerk father, Henry Marsh, and his economizing wife, Rose, magnanimously scrambled to pay their only child's passage to England. It meant a more spartan life than usual, but the opportunity for Ngaio to travel and stay with such illustrious friends abroad was impossible to miss.

Alderbourne, with its vast number of rooms and workforce — which included a butler, a footman, a full domestic staff, plus a nanny and a lady's maid — was a shock for Ngaio. The Rhodes family had returned to England to economize. They had found their big house, large staff and lavish life of weekend parties unsustainable in New Zealand. To Ngaio, however, Alderbourne Manor seemed luxurious. She waited for the ominous day when the Rhodes family 'bandwagon', as she called it, with its English 'rebore' and fresh 'coat of paint', lurched into another period of desperate insolvency. In the meantime, she took her seat.

A photograph taken on a Rhodes family holiday in Kent shows the easy comfort of the family group and their coterie of perpetual guests. Four high-spirited children, wearing swimsuits, sit in the front row with a favourite dog, while another is carried piggyback. Behind them are the adults, in soft suits that pull and pucker. On the far right, slightly apart, stands Tahu Rhodes. He was a captain in the Grenadier Guards, and there is still a trace of formality in the slicked-back black hair, prominent moustache and heavy-featured, swarthy good looks. Beside him is the crop-haired, trouser-clad, boyish figure of Ngaio. She was nearly 6 feet (1.8 metres) tall, and even in her 30s she carried the imprint of youth and a touch of the awkward teenager in her lanky stature. She was striking, with strong rather than conventionally beautiful features, a prominent nose, dark close-set eyes and tightly wavy dark hair. Toppy Blundell Hawkes stands open-faced and smiling between Ngaio and Nelly. He was a good-natured English farm cadet who became a favourite after staying with the Rhodes family in New Zealand. Nelly is squat and somewhat plain, but the warmth of her personality is evident in her face, which beams broadly. A 1920s hat is pulled down tightly on her head, and she is wearing a full-length, flecked dress-suit, which is comfortable rather than elegant. What is evident in the photograph is their delight at being together on holiday.

Ngaio joined the Society of Authors, and at Alderbourne Manor, in the midst of a noisy household of children, wrote syndicated accounts of her travels for newspapers in New Zealand. She hoped journalism would make her more independent of her parents' finances. The first of many articles, under the pen name 'A New Canterbury Pilgrim', was published in the Christchurch *Press* on 1 September 1928. She began by describing her departure from New Zealand. 'I know of no experience that compares with the adventure of setting out on one's travels . . . for me, at least, the office of Thomas Cook and Son, Christchurch, will always be the enchanted parlour whose doors open straight into Wonderland.' Like many creative colonial women of her generation, Ngaio felt travelling to Britain and Europe was like slipping into a magical parallel universe. New Zealand offered few opportunities in writing, art or the theatre, and, for women particularly, these were isolating, often desperate pursuits. Even after the First World War, remnants of Victorian provincialism hung like a miasma over cities such as Christchurch. Expatriate Australian artist and writer Stella Bowen described Christchurch's sister city Adelaide as 'a queer little backwater of intellectual timidity' which, 'isolated by three immense oceans . . . lies . . . prettyish, banal, and filled to the brim with an anguish of boredom'. This was what Ngaio felt she was leaving. It was also a chance to escape the confines of her relationship with her parents, to become independent — an adult even — and define herself as someone new.

Her first stop on the long sea voyage, which would take nearly eight weeks, was Sydney, where she witnessed a half-span of the harbour bridge going up. She saw a production of *Henry VIII* put on in Newton by her old actor-manager friend Allan Wilkie, and went to the city's 'grandiloquent' state gallery which stands on a hill flanked by giant statues of snorting steeds bearing symbolic figures of 'war and peace'. In the English section of the gallery, she was taken by the work of Impressionist Laura Knight, and in the Australian, by the Post-Impressionist Margaret Preston. 'They are brilliantly painted,' she wrote of Preston's still-lifes, 'they seem to reveal the very spirit of flowers without a touch of over-representation or sentimentality. Her sense of pattern is . . . inspiring.' In the colonies Ngaio's taste in art was modern, and her discussion of Preston perceptive, but in European centres that had wrestled with Cubist deconstruction, Dada nihilism and the psychosis of Surrealism, it was traditional. Her final visit was to the new Cabaret-Romanos, where she found heterogeneous humanity dancing cheek-to-cheek to the 'muted "Blues" of the best Jazz in Sydney'.

In Hobart, she shuddered at photographs of the 'dreadful instruments' of penal correction used in the former convict prison and noted the sad demise of Aboriginal culture in the face of English settlement. She found Melbourne cooler and more decorous than hot-blooded, sun-baked Sydney. Here she again visited the state gallery, noting the work of late 19th-century 'moderns' like idiosyncratic Symbolist Pierre Puvis de Chavannes, and the painting of French and English Impressionists such as Jean-Baptiste-Camille Corot, Frank Brangwyn, John Singer Sargent and Sir William Orpen. Again, her taste was conservative. The highlight of her stay was a lavish production, by the Melba-Williamson Grand Opera Company, of Puccini's unfinished *Turandot*. 'The audience at the opera in Melbourne is a very festive one and the gorgeous theatre coats made a brave show against the florid brilliance of the gilt walls. Many of the men wore tails and white ties.' Ngaio relished the rituals of class and culture and felt it gave the event dignity. She was naturally attracted to the theatrical, even camp accessories of upper-crust society, and this fascination lasted. Her observation of aristocratic manners was acute, and her belief in them shifted from born-again conviction to good-humoured scepticism.

The liver-coloured, coal-burning *Balranald* was making a last long sea voyage to the wreckers' yard, and Ngaio's berth was cramped, yet shipboard life appealed to her. She eagerly participated in deck games and dressing up for performances and parties, and delighted in the company of the other passengers. Already Ngaio was fascinated by the pursuit of people-watching, especially in a confined space. 'I have always had a vague and ill-informed interest in crowd-psychology, and never was there a better opportunity of studying it.' She could watch people with impunity — 'Australians who wanted to see the world, Americans who have seen it and insisted on telling you about it, Swedish, Greek, Armenians and Italian wanderers . . . South Africans' — and share her amusing observations with her Christchurch readers. It took three weeks to reach the coast of Africa, and by then much of the food on board was stale or bad. The water made people sick and, opening a folded slice of cold meat, she 'found it encrusted with small shells'. Ngaio decided 'to cut loose' and eat in Durban.

She was enchanted by the city's strangeness. 'The first excitement we [Ngaio and a fellow passenger] encountered was a row of Zulu rickshaw men with their amazing head-dresses of quills, feathers, and horns, their fur tippets and painted legs.' The rickshaw ride to the hotel through sunny streets that thronged with 'Hindoos, Kaffirs, Zulus . . . white people . . . [and] beautiful Indian women in ample robes of vivid blue and scarlet and cerise' was as colourful as it was exhilarating. On a hill, the driver drew himself onto the shafts of the rickshaw and 'we free-wheeled at an alarming speed while he rang his cow bell at the crossings'. They recovered from their ordeal by drinking coffee on the loggia of the hotel 'and looking on at the pageant of the streets'. Ngaio saw Sybil Thorndike, her husband Lewis Casson, and their small daughter in a revival of *The Liars* by Henry Arthur Jones, and in a packed Indian market she bought the food she had promised herself. For sixpence she filled a colossal basket with pineapples, oranges, pawpaws, succulent tangerines and gigantic grapefruit. Ngaio ached to paint the scene, with its bustle of humanity and kaleidoscope of costumes, produce, deeply shaded little shops and brilliant lengths of silk, but she had time only to take a photograph and make a quick sketch on the back of an envelope. She wrote about the market in her 'Pilgrim' article before she painted it. Increasingly she was capturing the world around her in words rather than paint, but she pictured it vividly with an artist's eye.

Durban's racism troubled her. She had qualms about taking a rickshaw ride, and described with contempt the treatment of a black man who 'ran in front of three sullen-looking Dutch youths, who turned on him savagely'. She concluded: 'I remember Mr J H Curle's contention that it is the under-bred white who, at bedrock, is responsible for the "colour question" ', and this is what she believed. Ngaio was sensitive about race and culture. As a Pakeha in New Zealand, she had seen the plight of Maori in the face of colonization, and she felt for their loss of culture, language and land. She saw pathos in the position of the 'aboriginals who have seen the coming of the English and the changing of their ways'. Ngaio was born a Victorian, her liberalism was flawed and limited, and her thinking sometimes straitjacketed by convention and class, but she despised racial prejudice. The final picture she painted of Durban was one that disturbed her. It was the fading image of 'a grinning kaffir boy' dancing on the wharf. He had made friends with children on the boat. ' "He's a nice nigger boy," said a little girl. "He does what I tell him, 'Dance boy'." He danced and waved his arms obediently . . . till we slid away and the children lost interest in him.'

From Durban, the *Balranald* sailed in heavy seas down the coast of Africa to Cape Town, where Ngaio met Uncle Freddie, one of Henry Marsh's six brothers. Their father, a tea broker in the days of clipper ships, had died suddenly leaving his widow in a small Georgian house near Epping with a family of 10 children to bring up. The sons, desperate for financial independence and opportunity, left

England for Canada, South Africa and New Zealand, adventurers out to make their fortunes. 'There seems to have been no thought of university or profession for any of them,' Ngaio later wrote. 'The Colonies, it was felt, were the thing.'

Henry learned Chinese at London University for a position in the Hong Kong-Shanghai Bank, but this plan was cut short by a bout of pleurisy and an invigorating year on the veldt of South Africa. A solution to his employment problem came from his father's eldest brother, who was Governor of Hong Kong. While this uncle was staying in New Zealand, he secured the offer of a good position for his nephew with the Colonial Bank. When Henry arrived, however, the unthinkable happened: the bank crashed and he was forced to take a humble clerk's job with the Bank of New Zealand. He remained in the same position for the rest of his life. Ngaio's Uncle Freddie, now permanent secretary to the Governor-General's Fund in Cape Town, was luckier. He and his family proudly escorted Ngaio around the sights of the city, which included the museum, the ancient colonial house of Koopmans-de Wet, the 'old Curfew bell that . . . call[ed] the slaves in from their work', and the 'ill-tailored statue' of former prime minister and colonizing magnate, Cecil Rhodes.

A sultry yellow sun beat unrelentingly down as they steamed along the Gold Coast. 'When the land breeze gets up it fans us with the accumulated heat of all Africa,' Ngaio wrote, 'but tomorrow we turn away towards Las Palmas, and sail out of the tropics.'

When she finally reached the silver-grey misty seas of England she could hardly believe it. 'Just before dawn the cabin steward made an isolated gesture. For the first time on the voyage he brought me a cup of tea. He said . . . the water had been filtered . . . I thanked him warmly and had drunk half the tea when I found the rest of the cup was full of a thick, viscid, grey silt.'

It was with a huge sense of relief and excitement that she met the Rhodes family on the wharf. They drove her through streets that were noisy monuments to history after the colonial outposts and cicada-serenaded towns she knew. She was infatuated. Her first excursions from Alderbourne Manor into London were dream-like. 'There is the same fascination here,' she wrote, 'as there was in the brilliance and heat of the Indian market in Durban.' One of the early stage shows she saw was Agatha Christie's *Alibi*, which was a 'detective drama, remarkable for the really brilliant acting of Mr Charles Laughton as M. Poirot'. She emerged afterwards onto warm summer-evening streets to see 'men in their evening dress, not wearing over coats or hats . . . [looking] exotic and important' and women with cloaks tied around their necks who seemed 'to move as though they are walking across a stage'.

London was a wonderland above and below ground. She was thrilled by the thronging Strand, and by Trafalgar Square, where humming multitudes of people pushed past iconic stone buildings and vast public sculptures. She delighted in Piccadilly Circus, where scarlet buses and black taxis hurtled. 'This, Londoners say, is the hub of the world, and it is here that I love to stand, my feet on London stones, in the very heart of that amazing labyrinth.' She relished the experience of diving down moving stairways, travelling through 'strangely scented warm tunnels' and coming out on subterranean platforms, to take the tube. 'As we gathered way, all these figures moved very slightly and spasmodically, for all the world like . . . masked jiggling puppets . . . As one does in the tubes, I sat idly speculating about my fellow travellers for three miles under the earth.' Mesmerized by people and places, she was looking at the city with the eyes of an outsider and it set her imagination on fire.

Ngaio was with the Rhodeses only a matter of months before the 'bandwagon' carried her off to Monte Carlo. She watched in astonishment as the family planned to spend a windfall given to them by Nelly's mother. Money worries hung over Alderbourne Manor, but Monte Carlo was chosen as an escape and a place where they could recover financially by making a fortune at the gaming tables. 'A domestic roulette was put into instant use.' They would take turns at spinning the wheel and record the patterns of numbers in order to devise a sensible and scientific system. Ngaio was sceptical. So, she suspected, were they. But they were having fun, and the fun was intoxicating. There were Nelly Rhodes, Ngaio, and Betty Cotterill, a student friend of Ngaio's who also stayed for a while with the Rhodes family. The Channel was 'grey and nasty and was covered with white horses' when they left Dover, but the boat was intriguing. She could observe again: 'Wondering about the nationality, private lives, and destinations of the people who are pouring up the wind-raked gangway on to the alarmingly small vessel that is to herd you all together.' Ngaio enjoyed the drama of arriving in Calais, which was like 'stepping on to the stage of an impromptu musical comedy'.

But it was the train beside the wharf that arrested her attention. It was 'the famous Blue Train,' she explained, 'cherished by all weavers of detective fiction on the Continental scale'. Already she was thinking of murder on an overnight express. The Blue Train carried them south from austere Paris past fields of vines and 'pointed ranks' of black cypress trees, through hills and heat-baked yellow houses to the Riviera. 'Monte Carlo is beautiful in a lavish carefree sort of way that rather took me aback,' she recorded. From the balcony of their adjoining rooms they looked down on a 'cheerful little street'. Subdued sounds of horses' hooves, church bells, motor horns 'and the endless lisp of quiet voices' drifted up in a muted haze of warmth and colour. The casino, by contrast, was a cacophony of Baroque flamboyance. Nude men supported shields; cornucopias spilled forth; voluptuous 'larger-than-life ladies' languished in pastoral landscapes. The colours were a muted confection of chocolate, ochre, 'baby blues and pinks that have gone off', and everything that could be gilded was. The extravagance of the roof and walls was an entrée to the hushed drama of the floor. 'Roulette in extremis is a disease,' announced Ngaio, after describing the many English *habituées* who came daily, their faces distorted by alcohol and drugs. She savoured the detail of hawk-like men and women who sat expressionless, watching their fortunes dance up and down on the back of an ivory ball.

'I usually start with a group of people,' Ngaio told a radio interviewer, explaining how she began a book. 'I get interested in a group of people . . . and think about them, their relationships . . . quite often, just start writing about them . . . Which of these people is capable of a crime of violence? . . . Under what circumstances would they be likely to commit it?'

At Monte Carlo, Ngaio was already looking for potential suspects.

She is over middle-age and . . . enormous. Her face, heavily enamelled, dangles in pockets from the bones of her skull. At three in the afternoon, when I first saw her, she was dressed in jonquil-coloured satin trimmed with marabou, and on her head was a golden cap covered in sparkling diamanté and garnished with an osprey about two feet high. In her claws she carried stacks of mills plaques worth more than £8-each, and in a few minutes she had trebled them . . . she gathered up her golden robes and swept over to the baccarrat [sic] table where she very quickly lost it all.

Ngaio's party nicknamed this 'enormous' woman's male counterpart 'Dolly', because he had minute hands and feet, a white moustache that looked as though it was stuck on with glue, and was 'rigidly tailored and tight-waisted to such a degree that he could only move in little mechanical jerks'.

There was also a third sex at the tables that was more memorable than

Ngaio was prepared to admit to 'Pilgrim' readers in 1928. It was not until she recalled the event in her autobiography *Black Beech and Honeydew* in 1966 that she mentioned a kind of woman that was 'entirely new to me. The croupiers referred to the most dominant of them as "cette monsieur-dame". She seemed to have quite a pleasant time of it, running her finger round inside her collar and settling her tie. She wore a sort of habit and was perhaps by [Christopher] Isherwood out of [Aldous] Huxley.'

The three women found the experience exhilarating. 'We chose a table and hit Monte Carlo with our system.' On the first evening they won so much that their purses bulged, but after a week they had lost nearly all their gains. A new tactic was devised. 'We separated and we spent ages waiting for long runs on the even chances.' They delighted in being together and free from restraints. In Christchurch, jealous rumours of an affair between Ngaio and Tahu Rhodes were whispered over teacups and behind theatre programmes, but it was the intimacy between Ngaio and Nelly Rhodes that was the glue.

Ngaio was captivated by her friend's languid, aristocratic ease. Nelly was sure of her place, and had a liberty of spirit that came from privilege. Luxury was assumed, and delicacies ordered and served before balance books were totted. She was vague about practicalities and self-indulgent, but generous to a fault with others whether family coffers were full or empty. Ngaio's childhood of genteel poverty was vastly different, and her social position more ambiguous. She could play the aristocrat, but she was not born one. For her the upper classes were a fiction, and travelling with Nelly to Monte Carlo was as full of wonder as waking up in Evelyn Waugh's *Decline and Fall* or *Vile Bodies*. What Ngaio brought to their relationship was her effervescent wit, her theatricality and the sheer energy of her excitement at being away. '[They] called us the "Ladies who Laugh",' she wrote, 'presumably because we were unable to manage the correct expressionless stare at the tables, and on the occasion when we disastrously lost all our plaques laughed helplessly until we cried.'

Nelly Rhodes and Betty Cotterill lost, then recovered to gain a little at the end. Ngaio was more fortunate. 'I suddenly found I'd won on 15 *en plein* and made enough to buy a coat and skirt.' In reality, the outfit she bought with her winnings was reminiscent of the *'cette monsieur-dame'* ensemble she later described in *Black Beech*. Whether Ngaio purchased this outfit to play fashionable-butch to Nelly's languid-*femme* is impossible to know, because she destroyed any intimate record of their relationship. In her 20s Ngaio began burning correspondence that would elucidate any deeply felt emotional or physical nuance in her relationships. However, a photograph survives of Ngaio in her '*cette monsieur-dame*' dress, suggesting not just modish chic but a theatrical delight in camping it up and testing the boundaries of cross-dressing.

They arrived back as white frosts were beginning to settle on the lawns at Alderbourne Manor. It was cold reality after the excitement of the Riviera, and the New Year of 1929 ushered in a bleak winter. 'We are in the middle of the greatest frost England has known since eighteen something,' Ngaio told readers. 'The woods, the fields, the streams are all frozen and silent, and this morning I found a robin – silent too, and stiff in the grass where he had fallen out of the dead-cold sky.' In London there were warnings in the press against skating on the Thames, which 'hundreds of these hardy English' did anyway, and in a quadrangle at Cambridge people flocked to see a frozen fountain. Ngaio ignored the biting cold and relished the sights: Westminster Abbey with its unearthly collection of sightless statues, and the Tower of London emerging from a 'thin morning mist' so that 'a turret shone out quite warm and clear while the underlying structure slipped away into a blue haze'. She drove through Windsor Park at sunset and watched the long, late 'rays of light touch trees and turf with the colours of heraldry'.

Later she visited art galleries and the spring exhibitions. Burlington House had a show of Dutch masters. She listened to a radio lecture about it by critic and art writer Roger Fry, and when she arrived to see the paintings the courtyard of Burlington House was 'crammed with rich cars and the rooms were thronged with rich people'. It was the people rather than the art that fascinated her. Two 'shrewdly critical Frenchwomen' captured her attention, then the 'modern' art students. 'They were very dirtily dressed in raincoats and trousers, and apparently little else. The prevailing fashion . . . [was to allow] their beards to grow to the "ten-days" lengths and then by a mysterious process, arresting their growth.'

She went in search of her roots, visiting the ancient Temple Church to find some trace of her great-grandfather who, according to family record, was the promised heir to a vast estate in Scotland. Unfortunately, the property owner (his uncle) died intestate, and the fortune was thrown into the Chancery. He was forced to take 'some extremely humble job in the Middle Temple and my grandfather went to the choir school of the Temple Church'. Ngaio had no luck. 'The verger, a grim man, had never heard of my ancestor.'

She lunched in style with the Rhodeses at such favourite places as the Ritz, the

Savoy and the Carlton, and quietly on her own at little back-street establishments that were not always as cheap as she expected. For a time she even captured a job as a mannequin in a small, exclusive fashion shop off Bond Street. She had the perfect figure, but not an ideal temperament. She felt like a 'richly turned-out automaton'. '[We] fell into lines, and, one by one, filed out of the door into the showroom, where we dropped into that curiously inhuman walk . . . we undulated backwards and forwards two or three times, stood in a half dozen modern attitudes, and strolled nonchalantly out of the door, the attendant nymphs fell upon us like automatic furies, switched dresses off . . . [and] on, and back we went into the queue again all silks and smiles.'

She was captivated, also, by the rituals of the Royal House, standing among crowds to watch the Trooping the Colour ceremony. She described the rich pageantry of uniforms, horses and foreign guests. 'The Sultan of Zanzibar arrived close by us, stepping from his car in an astonishing blaze of jewels and exotic robes, while the immaculate English aide-de-camps stood, silk hat in hand to usher his Midnight Extravagance to his appointed seat.'

Three 'Pilgrim' articles, published in September, October and November 1929, recorded another magical trip to France. Again, Ngaio, Nelly Rhodes and Betty Cotterill escaped, taking a hotel on the Rue des Capucines in Paris. The summer was sizzling hot, and when their train reached the 'environs of Paris the carriage next to ours actually caught fire'. Taxis flew past their hotel, tooting and adding thick vaporous exhaust fumes to the steaming boulevard. Ngaio sat out on the pavements, sipping coffee in a heat-induced dream state, while the city erupted around her. They visited Versailles and the Hall of Mirrors, which 'is the biggest room I have ever seen'. They ate at restaurants and visited nightclubs like the famed Folies Bergère where 'American voices, keyed up to their full siren pitch, cut the air into ribbons, French voices, with that soft, emphatic, rattle of words, burbled and eddied in a sort of conglomerate roar'. Paris was noisy, hot and expensive, but they loved it.

Once again, financial worries hit them when they returned to Alderbourne. In spite of their troubles, Ngaio helped Nelly Rhodes and her grandmother raise money for famine relief in India. Trestle tables were erected in the empty ballroom where they began painting. They decorated wooden cigarette boxes, tin wastepaper bins, trays, tables, lampshades, blotters and bowls, and made plaques with funny rhymes for bathroom and lavatory doors. Their 'artsy-craftsy stall' at the famine relief bazaar was a coup, realizing what seemed a small fortune.

It was not long before they decided that charity should begin at home. 'I have become a shopkeeper in London town,' Ngaio announced to her readers. 'My partner and I have rented these minute premises for October, November and December.' Their lock-up was in one of London's most fashionable areas and they planned to sell gift items over the Christmas period. In London it snowed so much that immediately before Christmas Ngaio stayed at The Rembrandt hotel opposite the Brompton Oratory so she could open the shop early in the morning. Remarkably, when they cashed up their business they had made a profit, even after the Wall Street crash the previous October, and it was too tantalizing to stop. They decided to follow up their entrepreneurial success by establishing a shop at a more permanent address on Brompton Road, in Knightsbridge. They called themselves Touch and Go, after a Christchurch entertainment group with which they had been involved, and their business flourished. They then moved around the corner to Beauchamp Place, before shifting again into a bigger shop in the same street, where they focused more on furniture and interior design.

Their salubrious address was a honey trap for the upper classes. When Touch and Go was asked to design the interior of a pet salon, Ngaio was disgusted. 'In respect of dogs I am a New Zealander'; at home, 'sensible dogs and sporting dogs' chased sheep or retrieved game birds. She found the dogs in Knightsbridge obscene and dirty. 'No amount of shampooing and twiddling will make anything but asses of them . . . when they were not defecating on the doorstep they were shivering in their mistresses' embrace.' In spite of her Antipodean scruples, the job was finished and work flowed in.

Sadly, unlike Roger Fry's avant-garde experimental Omega workshop in Fitzroy Square, which was supported by artists such as Vanessa Bell, Duncan Grant and Nina Hamnett, none of Touch and Go's objects or interior designs have survived. Omega had foundered in 1919, because of the war. Touch and Go was self-consciously commercial chic by comparison, and perhaps because of this it survived the Depression. For 18 months or more Ngaio was involved with the shop and would leave reluctantly. Her recipe for success: 'We became slightly less amateurish, never got on each other's nerves . . . and added to the staff largely from our circle of friends.'

Among Ngaio's circle of friends were many expatriate New Zealanders. A special person in this group was old childhood friend Dundas Walker, who had come to London years earlier in search of a professional acting career. Now that engagements had tailed off, he lived in genteel semi-retirement on a private income. With him, she visited print shops, junk shops, Portobello Road, and the bustling Caledonian market where hundreds of stallholders, 'raked by a cold wind', laid out their wares 'on frost-chilled cobble-stones'. With her artist friend Rhona Haszard, she talked art-school gossip. Haszard had left New Zealand in 1926, under a cloud of scandal. In 1922, she had married talented student and part-time art school tutor Ronald McKenzie. It seemed an ideal match, but then, in 1925, she met Englishman and ex-Indian Army officer, Leslie Greener, who enrolled in her classes. Their affair began almost immediately, and halfway through the year, after a hasty divorce, the couple eloped and then married at a Waihi registry office in December 1925. They were now resident in Alexandria, but Haszard was in London for specialist back treatment. Her split with the well-liked McKenzie had polarized their friends, so she was grateful to find Ngaio still warm and friendly towards her.

Between the wars, the West End throbbed with a racy theatrical life. In the late 19th century there had been a clean-up of brothels and seedy gin dens in the area, and fashionable plays by playwrights like Oscar Wilde and Arthur Wing Pinero began to appear. The area became a playground for the middle and upper classes, and foreign visitors poured in to savour the West End experience. During the 1920s, luxurious theatres like the vast 5,900-seat Roxy were built to cope with the crowds. The West End's leading performers — including Edith Evans, Cedric Hardwicke, Leon Quartermaine, Leslie Banks and Noël Coward — were international stars. Ngaio saw popular theatre with Nelly and Tahu Rhodes and Toppy Hawkes, and when she wanted something more discerning she went alone. 'I saw a dramatization of Christopher Morley's *Thunder on the Left*, and, later, the first of the Priestley "time" plays, Pirandello's *Henry IV* with Ernest Milton and a French tragi-comedy called *Beauty* with Charles Laughton . . . The first Shakespeare that I saw in the West End was John Gielgud as a very young, petulant and smouldering Hamlet', but it was Shakespeare at The Old Vic that she loved most. For her it had a raw immediacy that evoked Elizabethan theatre. The Old Vic audience included anyone from a policeman on the beat to 'students, labourers, tough elderly women, nondescripts, deadbeats, and characters who might have made bombs in their spare time'. Above them hung a haze of blue cigarette smoke. They drank, chewed, gave unsolicited advice, and when an actor dried up they shouted the lines.

Luigi Pirandello's *Six Characters in Search of an Author*, directed by Tyrone Guthrie at the Westminster Theatre, had a huge impact on Ngaio. When it opened in Rome in 1921, it caused a riot. The bare stage was booed, and a fight broke out in the boxes. By the end of the decade audiences were more accustomed to its avant-gardism. Ngaio was captivated by the uncompromising set design and the dramatic treatment. The arbitrary nature of perception was an important theme in radical theatre following the First World War, and Pirandello's play picked up this concept. In *Six Characters*, actors on stage rehearsing a Pirandello play are interrupted by a fictional family of characters who 'demand that the drama of their own lives be performed and thus given a reality denied them as the mere figments of their author's imagination'. They sketch out the scenes on stage for the actors to act. The supposedly ephemeral lives of the characters end up looking more convincing than those of the socially conditioned actors. The play challenges the relationship between art and life and the fictional roles played on stage and real roles played in life. The play would have continuing significance for Ngaio.

Theatre nights were late, and sometimes Ngaio, the Rhodeses and Hawkes were there to savour the 'smell of the West End in the early morning. Hot Bread. Coffee. Freshly watered pavements . . . Roses.' After the curtain went down, the crazed world of the fashionable club beckoned. They would usually go to more than one. ' "Uncles" was the smart night-club in those days and there one danced or inched at close quarters with poker-faced revellers . . . or sat and listened to Hutch [Leslie Hutchinson], a Negro entertainer whose popularity was supreme . . . Then there was the midnight floor show at the Savoy and a Tzigani band at the Hungaria.' It was the Hungaria in New Regent Street that they liked best because an ecstatic energy erupted after midnight. They heard Emilio Colombo lead the band, and watched as violinists threw their bows in the air while a tiny troll-like man 'went mad on the tzimbal'. The Hungaria was the habitat of high culture, of bohemians and the dissolute. It was the knife-edge of opposites Ngaio relished.

Sometimes the Prince of Wales was there and . . . alone, at a table just inside the door, sat a strange figure: an old, old man with a flower in his coat who looked as if he had been dehydrated like a specimen leaf and then rouged a little. No one ever accompanied him or paused at his table. He looked straight before him and at intervals raised his glass in a frog's hand and touched his lips.

One night we asked the restaurateur who he was.

'A poet,' said Signor Vecchi, 'and once, long ago I understand, a celebrated personage. It is Lord Alfred Douglas [Oscar Wilde's lover].'

It is in the Hungaria that Nigel Bathgate meets his girlfriend Angela North and waits for Roderick Alleyn in *A Man Lay Dead*. Alleyn has allowed them to leave Frantock briefly to help him track down a secret Russian brotherhood. Men from Scotland Yard are hiding in an empty shop opposite the house where members of the fiendish ancient sect are meeting. The signal for them to strike will come from the Hungaria. Nigel has been told the secret password: it is the name of a murdered Pole.

His heart is racing. He is alone on the street as he turns in and orders a table at the back of the restaurant because he is not wearing evening dress. He sits down. His hand shakes visibly as he takes out his lighter. He smokes three cigarettes and fidgets anxiously. The band is playing 'in the desultory manner that distinguishes the off hours in fashionable restaurants'. There are just three couples on the floor.

'Do you want to order, sir?' murmured Nigel's waiter.

'No thank you. I'll wait until my — I'm waiting for someone — I'll order when she comes.'

He lights another cigarette, wishes Angela were here, then loses himself in thoughts of Alleyn, and the agent, Sumiloff. Suddenly a voice from a solitary man at the next table cuts through his concentration. He wants to know when the Hungaria band will begin to play. Nigel is distracted and annoyed.

'Not until midnight.'

'That's a long time,' said the stranger, fretfully. 'I've come on purpose to hear it. Very good, I'm told.'

'Oh, frightfully,' said Nigel unenthusiastically.

'They tell me,' continued his neighbour, 'that some Russian is to sing here tonight. Lovely voice. He sings a thing called *The Death of Boris*.'

Nigel starts violently, then controls himself. He thinks he has been given the secret password. A thrill goes through him and he almost overflows with excitement. The information rushes out. He tells the stranger that the Russian brotherhood has been tricked into meeting at Alleyn's house, and that Sumiloff is waiting there now. With that, the stranger is satisfied and abruptly calls to the waiter for the bill. A few minutes later he passes Angela, who is just arriving at the door. Nigel Bathgate will become Alleyn's Watson, but not before he finds himself tied to a chair with a sharp blade being pushed under his fingernail. This is his apprenticeship, and he will learn the importance of passwords and getting them right.

Even though she was reading it in pencil from exercise books, Rose Marsh could hardly put *A Man Lay Dead* down. After her husband retired, by taking up 'a number of secretaryships' he had saved Rose's fare to England. They could not afford for Henry to accompany her, so Rose arrived alone at Alderbourne in 1930, to find her daughter distracted from writing and acting by working in a shop during the day and living the high life at night. She bitterly regretted the waste of Ngaio's talent and was not quiet about it. The situation gradually sorted itself out. The Rhodeses were tired of commuting and moved to London, where they took two big flats in Eaton Mansions, close to Eaton Square in Belgravia; some of the staff boarded out. Initially, Ngaio and her mother moved with them, but they stayed only long enough to find their own flat. In June or July, they shifted into a basement bedsit around the corner in Caroline Terrace. Nelly Rhodes was kind enough to make sure they were comfortably set up with excess furniture from the shop. Rose Marsh's arrival put the brakes on one of the most exciting periods of her daughter's life, but Ngaio could see why. She felt guilty that she had abandoned her New Zealand novel and had written only travel articles since she'd left New Zealand. Trips to the theatre became serious and critical, and fashionable nightclubs an occasional luxury. She started to think more seriously about writing a detective novel.

For Rose, the links Ngaio made with their own life and *A Man Lay Dead* were uncanny. In fact she had taken names, places and characters directly from real life. Most disquieting was Dr Tokareff, the Russian from Sir Hubert Handesley's embassy days in Petrograd. He not only shared the same name, but was obviously based on Peter Alfanasivich Tokareff, an unstable Russian *émigré* who had played opposite Rose in a production of George Calderon's *The Little Stone House* in 1914. Rose, a talented amateur actress and excellent acting coach, had invited him to practise at their home on the Cashmere Hills. They rehearsed endlessly, and the inevitable happened: Tokareff became enamoured with Rose, then Ngaio. On the evenings he visited them, they would hear him coming up the hill singing 'at the top of his formidable bass voice . . . My father, who found him noisy, would look up from his book and say mildly: "Good Lord, the Russian."' Henry and his wife were worried. Their daughter was the focus of their life and they did not want her to marry. Ngaio was flattered but not emotionally mature enough to handle the volatile relationship. After declaring his love for her, the rebuffed Russian disappeared. Rose Marsh recognized his singing and his accent intonations in the fictional Dr Tokareff's dialogue and mannerisms. The doctor was a suspect in the novel; Peter Tokareff, a victim of real life. On 28 October 1919, he was discovered dead in a Christchurch park. The unfortunate man had committed suicide.

In early 1932, Rose Marsh returned to New Zealand, reluctantly leaving Ngaio in England. She had hoped her daughter would come back with her, but did not feel she could push the point. Ngaio would only realize how much her return would have meant to her mother when it was too late. Really, there was no contest: her wild London life with the Rhodeses was infinitely more appealing than daughterly domesticity in sleepy Cashmere. With sadness, and a sense of guilt mixed with a certain amount of relief, she saw her mother off, then moved back in with the Rhodeses to immediately resume her old life. But it was only a matter of months before a worrying letter arrived from her mother. Rose was ill and it seemed her recovery would be protracted. Other letters came, and then a cable from her father that clutched at her heart. Three days later she sailed for New Zealand.

Frantic to depart, she barely had time to think about her book. Fortunately it had been typed and was left with Edmund Cork, a literary agent in London. On the wharf it dawned on her that her life was in two places half a world apart. She wondered if she would ever see her mother again, but also whether the Rhodeses would save her a seat in the English 'bandwagon' she had come to love.

CHAPTER TWO

The Theatre of Death

It was August 1932, the chill end of a stark Christchurch winter, when Ngaio returned. Her parents' bedroom at Marton Cottage was a hushed sickroom. There were silences and huddled out-of-sight consultations. Death could be only briefly contained, but to Ngaio, sitting by the bed watching, Rose Marsh's end was as 'cruelly and as excruciatingly protracted as if it had been designed by Torquemada', the most cold-blooded of the Dominican inquisitors. Rose's pain was managed so that they could whisper their parting words. The change in the woman Ngaio and Henry loved was terrible to see. She had been the family's mainstay; elegant, effervescent, always the driving force. As a child, Ngaio had watched in awe, believing her mother to be the most beautiful, talented woman alive. Rose had that special mixture of qualities that accelerated a child's imagination: she was both literary and theatrical, so life in her small family became a pantomime of castles and strange imaginary creatures.

Rose came from a family of conjurors, so it was only natural that she would add the magic. Her mother, born Esther Coster, taught her how to work hard, how to economize, and how to be a good wife; but it was her father, Edward Seager, who taught her how to perform, brilliantly. He was an Englishman who had arrived at the tiny settlement of Port Lyttelton in 1851. Behind the

44

fragile makeshift buildings of Lyttelton loomed the natural amphitheatre of the Port Hills, and close behind them was the settlement of Christchurch on the flat Canterbury Plains, stretching 40 miles (65 kilometres) across to the blue mountainous margins of the Southern Alps in the west. In England, Edward had been a poor schoolteacher, but he did not pursue this job in the colonies. At 24 years of age he became a sergeant, virtually in charge of the district police force. He designed a new police uniform, and within three years had tracked down and arrested James McKenzie, the notorious sheep rustler.

His job meant that Seager was in charge of both the prison and the asylum, because the colony made no distinction between the mad and the bad. At the time of his arrival, the Lyttelton prison housed 11 inmates in a room 14 feet (4.3 metres) square. Blankets crawled with lice. 'The roof leaked. There was no proper sanitation, no books, no indulgences, a diet that was not a diet, and hardly any furniture.' Seager lobbied for better conditions, and when in 1863–64, Sunnyside Hospital was finally built a few miles out of Christchurch, he moved there to become superintendent, and his wife, the matron. His treatments were both progressive and unorthodox. He improved diet, hygiene, and access to fresh air and exercise, but it was his commitment to cultural and mental stimulation that was almost unheard of. He called the patients his 'children'; he built a stage; he had a piano and organ installed; he gave magic lantern shows; circuses came; plays were performed; madness and fantasy mixed in a way that was medicinal.

His great love was conjuring. One of his favourite tricks was an act of levitation, where an appropriately sized daughter was 'crammed into a torturous under-suit of paper-thin jointed steel'. She would sit on stage reading a book with her chin propped pensively on her hand. Edward Seager waved his wand and turned 'a secret key in his daughter's back. The armour locked.' And, as Ngaio later recalled, 'Puck-like, Gramp snatched the stool from under her and there she was: suspended.' For encores, he would saw his daughters in half, or make them disappear in a magic cabinet. 'The patients adored it.' He was also something of a mesmerizer-cum-faith-healer: 'he would flutter his delicate hands across and across' the foreheads of difficult patients, and family and friends, until their headaches disappeared.

Rose emerged from her eccentric childhood as a quite 'extraordinarily talented' actress. She lived the parts she played and brought the characters alive in a way that was spellbinding. At just 19, she was chosen to play Lady Macbeth for a visiting company led by American Shakespearian actor-director George Milne. He wanted her to travel with the company, but she refused. When the English actor Charles Warner visited New Zealand, he offered to take her to England and launch her career. Again she declined, travelling with him and his wife only as far as Australia to get a flavour of the professional actor's life.

Rose found the makeshift bohemian existence of the travelling theatre unpalatable. The life was too untidy; the change, the uncertainties, the stress of opening to unknown audiences in unfamiliar centres too much for her. She returned to Christchurch, resumed her amateur acting activities, and on the stage met future husband, Henry Marsh. He was a tall, good-looking man like her father, theatrical and imaginative, with a dry wit and an idiosyncratic way of looking at the world that was unexpectedly funny. He wooed her with his humour and his make-believe. The chemistry between them on and off the stage was magnetic. They married in 1894, when Henry was 31 years old and Rose a year younger.

Ngaio described Gramp Seager and her father, Henry, as 'have-nots'. Christchurch was a cruel place in which to be a 'have-not'. The colonial vision for New Zealand was an egalitarian England reconstructed in an Antipodean Eden. It was to be a clean start: a post-industrial culture in a pre-industrial country. Community would stratify and flourish naturally without the artificial strictures or social evils of the Old World. In reality, class consciousness and social evils were packed in trunks along with the ballgowns, white ties and tailcoats.

In Canterbury, the founding charter was less egalitarian. The Canterbury Association Society, established to colonize the province, planned to transplant a perfectly variegated specimen of English society, complete with aristocracy and middle and lower classes. A good deal of the land surrounding Christchurch was sold off in huge farming blocks to wealthy English families who became the social élite. The city itself, laid out on a grid pattern with civic parks and gardens and, later, an elegant Gothic Anglican cathedral at its heart, was to be the service centre of the rich farmland that developed.

Christchurch's social stratification began with the first four Canterbury Association ships that landed in Lyttelton Harbour in December 1850. The well-heeled immigrants on board became the city's founding fathers, bequeathing to their descendants membership of an elect group. Since both sides of Ngaio's family had missed these social boats, there was only property ownership to distinguish them, and, as much as he was admired (and even romanticized), Gramp Seager was only a public servant and Ngaio's father a simple bank clerk. Thus, in Christchurch they were 'have-nots'.

Rose and Henry Marsh rented a small house in Fendalton — the best area they could afford — and kept a maid, which was almost beyond their means. Gramp Seager was a dreamer and a spendthrift, but still an ambitious man; Henry Marsh lived in a world of his own. From early days, Rose realized he would make a better father than provider. Their daughter, Edith Ngaio Marsh, was born on 23 April 1895. Henry's belated attempt four years later to register her birth created an official error, that Ngaio later used to claim she was born in 1899. (And this mistake was perpetuated in print many times.)

It was a perfect marriage of opposites. Henry's soft-centred fantasy combined with Rose's galvanized theatricality to create an imaginative wonderland for Ngaio that she never completely escaped. She was the centre of their world, and their world was a stage where life and drama mixed so seamlessly that the anxious, sometimes highly strung young Ngaio could not distinguish the difference. She was disconcerted when she saw her parents rehearsing a new script: suddenly they became strangers. In *The Fool's Paradise*, her mother was transformed into a wicked *femme fatale* who slowly poisoned her husband. The tension of the scenes was overpowering for the terrified child. Her horror of poison lingered, and was reignited when Rose Marsh took her to a production of *Romeo and Juliet*. The fighting scenes were incomprehensible. She buried her head in her mother's lap. 'They aren't really fighting, are they?' she asked desperately. 'Yes, yes!' cried Rose, consumed by the action on stage. And to add to the awfulness, 'there was Poison and a young girl Taking It!' This confirmed Ngaio's lifelong phobia about poisons.

But Rose's judgement was usually sound. She took Ngaio and her young friend Ned Bristed to children's plays like *Sweet Nell of Old Drury* and *Bluebell in Fairyland*, and when the vast International Exhibition opened in Christchurch in 1906, Rose took her daughter numerous times to see displays of paintings, go to concerts, watch the dazzling nightly fireworks, and take wild sideshow rides. She introduced Ngaio to literature that braced her mind and imagination. Between the ages of 11 and 14 Ngaio read *David Copperfield*, *Bleak House* and *Our Mutual Friend*. She was read to, and read herself, a kaleidoscope of different titles that included anything from *Peter Pan* to *Roderick Random* and *Tom Jones*, which her father recommended she read to find out about 'fast' girls.

Sexual looseness was tolerated by neither of her parents; nor did they accept breaches of etiquette or sloppy diction. Their uncompromising Victorian standards were rigorously policed, especially by her mother. It was a hothouse childhood Rose wanted for her daughter, and she was prepared to sacrifice having another baby to provide it.

Ngaio's first taste of the real world was a tiny, 20-student dame school run by Miss Sibella E. Ross for children between the ages of six and 10. Fitting in was an ordeal for Ngaio, who was the tallest in her class and had an astonishingly deep voice. Rose Marsh was anxious, but she realized that her only child must integrate. Ngaio made firm friends with two bristling boys in the class, and the bullying ceased.

Rose and Henry Marsh were in their early 40s by the time they had finally saved enough money to build their own home. They bought a steep section on the Cashmere Hills close to Christchurch, and employed Rose's architect cousin, Samuel Hurst Seager, to design a four-roomed bungalow with a large verandah, which they called Marton Cottage. A horse-drawn wagon was loaded with their belongings, and they journeyed from Fendalton to the Cashmere Hills, camping in bell-tents near the site for three months. They were so eager, they moved in before it was completed. 'From the beginning we loved our house,' wrote Ngaio. 'It was the fourth member of our family.' At last they were homeowners in a town that made property a criterion of status.

Marton Cottage was a brilliant piece of Marsh family foresight. At the time they bought the section, the Cashmere Hills were a blank canvas of heathery tussock, low bush, and the occasional stand of trees with an isolated homestead. As Christchurch grew, Cashmere became one of its most desirable suburbs. On a clear day, the view from the cottage across the city to the distant Southern Alps was breathtaking. But in the opening decade of the 20th century the city had not yet begun lapping at the edges of the honey-coloured hills, and the trip into town to Miss Ross's school involved a long walk and then a protracted tram ride. Rose took Ngaio each day. On the way home, they always got off a stop early and walked to save paying for another section.

When Ngaio became too old for the dame school, her mother struggled with lessons at home for a while before deciding to employ a governess, Miss Ffitch. Ngaio was more of a challenge now. The outdoor life of the Cashmere Hills had instigated a Huckleberry Finn phase. Her constant companions were boys: Vernon, who lived locally, and her cousin Harvey, and later there was

Ned Bristed. They made rafts and sailed them up the Heathcote River, they lit campfires, played primal games of hunt and chase across the tussock, and ran wild.

Henry Marsh did not exactly stem the tide. He secured Ngaio a succession of ponies, which were being broken in, so she could ride bareback along the beach. When she was still a young girl, he gave her a Frankfurt single-bore rifle. 'How superb were those sunny mornings when I was allowed to walk behind my father and Tip [the family dog] through the plantation where he and his friends went quail-shooting. On these occasions he was completely and explicitly himself.' It was Henry in his mellow easy moments with whom Ngaio identified; but it was Ned who taught her how to smoke:

> We bought a tin of ten 'Three Castles Yellow (strong)' divided them equally, retired into a wigwam we had built among some gorse-bushes, and chain-smoked the lot without evil results. Encouraged by this success, we carved ourselves pipes from willow wood into which we introduced bamboo stems and in which we smoked tea. We also smoked red-hot cigars made of pine needles and newspaper.

For a time Ngaio was out of control. 'I had become a formidable,' she later admitted, 'in some ways an abominable, child.' It was little wonder that Miss Ffitch chose to ignore the sight, from a bedroom window, of Ngaio under the trees with her head wreathed in pipe smoke. 'I encountered her gaze: transfixed, blank, appalled, incredulous. For a second or two we stared at each other and then her face withdrew into the shadows.' In addition to formal lessons, Miss Ffitch had the unfortunate job of dragging her reluctant charge twice a week to piano lessons with 'Miss Jennie Black, Mus. Bac.', a title Ngaio delighted in chanting 'because of its snappy rhythm'. According to Ngaio herself, she 'had a poor ear, little application and fluctuating interest', but at other marriage-worthy accomplishments she was even worse: 'I had and have, rather less aptitude than a bricklayer for sewing'. She was beginning to show real promise at art, but it was the shining light of Miss Ffitch's Shakespeare that first penetrated the smoky haze of Ngaio's adolescence. She began with *King Lear*. Despite the fact that it was a censored version with every possible sexual reference or innuendo removed ('just torture, murder and madness left'), and even though Miss Ffitch delivered it primly without 'a word of exposition' other than the notes (which she overused), Ngaio 'lapped it up'. She could understand it. She loved the poetry of its language.

It was probably with a sense of relief that Rose Marsh watched as 'Miss Ffitch said goodbye and bicycled down the lane for the last time': Ngaio was going to school. It would cost them a fortune for fees and the expensive uniform, but Rose felt certain that it would be worthwhile. Ngaio needed taming.

It was 1910, and St Margaret's College had just opened and was run by a strict order of Anglo-Catholic nuns. Only the best families could afford to send their daughters there. Rose would have to scrimp and save even more, but the school had the values and status she wanted. It was not that she was an avid Christian, or even a great snob; what impressed her most was the school's serious attitude towards young women's education. The curriculum was heavy in literature, history and the arts, but what they taught promised to be equal to that of any good boys' school. She knew Ngaio had potential and believed that Ngaio could realize it there. She was right. 'From the first day, I loved St. Margaret's.'

Ngaio swapped Huck Finn for High Anglicanism. 'To say that I took to Divinity as a duck to water is a gross understatement. I took to it with a sort of spiritual whoop and went in . . . boots and all.' St Michael and All Angels was the school's parish church. She adored its theatre: the sermons denouncing sin and promising retribution; the processions; the banners; the dressing-up — the stoles, the copes and the cassocks; and the 'drift of incense' mingled with the smell of waxed wood and coir matting. The vicar's children, the 'Burton sisters', became special friends. They were English and loved acting and the theatre. The other close friend was Sylvia Fox.

Then there was the drama of her English classes. 'Eng. Lit. with Miss Hughes was exacting, and absorbing, an immensely rewarding adventure . . . she gave me a present that I value more than any other: an abiding passion for the plays and sonnets of Shakespeare.' But Ngaio felt guilty about Miss Hughes. After winning a Navy League Empire Prize 'with an essay containing thirty-one spelling mistakes', she got the distinct impression that her teacher was not amused and would have liked to have read this, and other things her pupil wrote. Ngaio's diffidence about her work made it hard for her to ask for assistance. She was very independent, but also painfully shy at times.

However, Ngaio's interest in literature, creative writing, drama and art was fostered, so she distinguished herself, becoming head prefect in her senior year. This brought her into regular contact with her 'schoolgirl crush', the headmistress, Sister Winifred. They began swapping confidences, Ngaio trying awkwardly one day to express her wish to do something for the Church. 'To my amazement,' Ngaio recalled,

she opened wide her arms and, with a delighted smile exclaimed, 'You are coming to us!'

Nothing could have been farther from my thoughts. Never in my most exalted moments had I imagined myself to have a vocation for the Sisterhood. Immersed in the folds of her habit, I was appalled and utterly at a loss. It was impossible to extricate myself . . . I listened aghast to her expressions of joy and left in a state of utmost confusion. It was an appalling predicament.

But Ngaio did find a calling at St Margaret's. In fact, she found two: art and the theatre. While still at high school, she studied part-time at the Canterbury College School of Art, taking classes two afternoons a week in the antique room from 1909 to 1914. The results were encouraging. She believed art would become her occupation, and the theatre her leisure. In her lunchtimes, twice a week she went to the lower school at St Margaret's to entertain the small girls by writing stories and enacting them. This evolved into the play *Bundles*, which was deemed good enough by Sister Winifred (who harboured no hard feelings) to be performed at the end-of-year prizegiving.

Encouraged, Ngaio wrote a full-length play called *The Moon Princess*, based on a fairy story by George Macdonald. 'I showed it to my friends, the Burtons and they bravely decided to produce it on quite an imposing scale at St. Michael's.' Her mother agreed to take a leading role, as the witch. Rose played her heart out. She screeched the 'dark nights' curse so frighteningly that the neck of every small child in the house crawled with fear. Her big scene was with Helen Burton, who was director as well as star of the show. They gave it 'everything they had', transforming Ngaio's dialogue. Gramp Seager was there, too, and after the final performance he presented Ngaio with two precious heirlooms. One was a book called *Actors of the Century*, with his own emphatic annotations in the margins; the other was the 'tawny-coloured lush-velvet coat' of renowned actor Edmund Kean. This was his highest accolade.

Rose Marsh was a very proud woman that night. There were social engagements in Christchurch she could not attend because of the state of her clothes. She recycled her dresses, coats, hats and shoes so that her daughter could stay at school. Now, her sacrifice was vindicated. Ngaio was a work in progress. Through her, Rose could relive her own life and overcome the fear that had halted her development. There was much at stake.

Ngaio believed that her mother 'over-concentrated' on her. 'Is there such a thing as a daughter Fixation?' she asked in *Black Beech*. 'If so, I suppose it could be argued that my beloved mother was afflicted with it.' But how else could Rose realize her ambition?

After school finished, Ngaio's life became harder for Rose to control. When Ngaio met the Rhodes family in 1924, it was almost impossible. There were weekend parties at Meadowbank. 'In perpetuity' wrote Ngaio flippantly in their visitors' book after one of her stays. Her parents went to Meadowbank, too, and enjoyed it, but found the life of indolent luxury there something of an enigma. In England the Rhodeses were very kind to Ngaio, but Rose felt they had led her daughter astray. Her illness had brought Ngaio home.

Whatever I may write about my mother will be full of contradictions. I think that as I grew older I grew, better perhaps than anyone else, to understand her. And yet how much there was about her that still remains unaccounted for, like odd pieces of a jigsaw puzzle. Of one thing I am sure: she had in her an element of creative art never fully realised. I think the intensity of devotion which might have been spent upon its development was poured out upon her only child.

Rose Marsh died of liver cancer on 23 November 1932. She was 68 years old.

Three months after Ngaio's return to New Zealand, 'on a warm evening, my father and I faced each other across my old schoolroom table and divided between us the letters of sympathy that we must answer'. It would be a different future without Rose. Paradoxically, in spite of all that she had done to realize her daughter, it was in Rose Marsh's absence that Ngaio became herself. 'Most of us,' she wrote reflectively in *Black Beech*, 'could point to a time, often long after physical maturity has been reached, and say to ourselves: "it was then that I . . . grew up." My mother's illness . . . marked I think my own coming-of-age.' The Marsh household became orientated towards masculine things. Ngaio and her father bached together in a comfortable but less colourful life.

Then one day a note arrived from her literary agent Edmund Cork to say that he had placed her book with publisher Geoffrey Bles and that it would be released in 1934. It seemed nothing short of miraculous. Ngaio had hoped, but had hardly had time to give the book's progress a second thought. Geoffrey Bles offered her £30 in advance and a 10 per cent royalty. She worked on the proofs long-distance. When the book arrived, two months after it was on the shelves in England, Henry read it captivated, as Rose had, 'with his hand shaking and the pipe jiggling between his teeth when he came to the exciting parts'. The dedication was:

For

My Father

And in memory of

My Mother.

Nineteen thirty-four was a big year for the Queens of Crime.

Agatha Christie released her chilling *Murder on the Orient Express* with another remarkable dénouement that left readers rushing for the rulebook. Surely, it was not cricket to have everyone involved? After writing 29 novels, plays and collections of poems, Christie was reaching her zenith.

Then there was Dorothy Sayers, who was realizing her aim of integrating detective fiction with the novel of manners. In her eighth novel, *Murder Must Advertise*, published in 1933, she found her stride and so did Lord Peter Wimsey. He was less affected, and so was she. Sayers was writing about her own experiences working in an advertising agency. Her familiarity with the people and the settings gave the story conviction, making it her most successful and well integrated so far. *The Nine Tailors*, published in 1934, continued this process, providing readers with perceptive observations of church life and bellringing. By enriching the crime novel, Sayers expanded its market. Her interventions did not change the style or form, but they did rehabilitate it for a more sophisticated audience, ultimately broadening its readership.

The publication of Margery Allingham's *Death of a Ghost*, also in 1934, was another watershed. This was her first truly accomplished piece of crime writing. With her talent now tempered by the experience of writing six Campion novels, Allingham combined the dramatic tension of earlier books with more convincing characterization and plot to create a captivating story.

The Queens were in their prime when Ngaio began publishing, and their writing helped generate a huge interest in the genre. During the inter-war period — marked by the end of one catastrophic conflict and the anticipation of another — there was a seemingly spontaneous desire among readers to assuage fear of universal death by focusing on the particular. The demand for detective fiction burgeoned. But it was a difficult field to break into, and its exponents were well practised. Considering the context of its launch, Ngaio's *A Man Lay Dead* did remarkably well. Critics who had watched Christie, Sayers and Allingham develop seemed prepared to let Ngaio do the same, although there was confusion over the writer's race and gender. The *Times Literary Supplement* critic took a stab. 'Mr. Marsh's manipulation of motive and alibi is neat and effective and repays careful attention', but 'His methods of detection . . . [are] somewhat distracting', and Chief Detective Inspector Alleyn, a 'most superior person, expensively educated and a connoisseur of good living [is] rather tiresomely familiar'. This kind of criticism inspired Ngaio to develop her own individual approach.

She was working on a script that represented a new departure. *Enter a Murderer* drew on her knowledge of the theatre, 'trying to get the smell and feel of backstage'. *The Rat and Beaver* at the Unicorn is a play-within-a-novel, which echoes rather than explains the action. Roderick Alleyn is in the audience at the Unicorn Theatre, as a guest of Nigel Bathgate. The tension is palpable in the final fatal scene of *The Rat and Beaver*. Anger boils between cartel bosses the Beaver, played by Surbonadier, and the Rat, played by Felix Gardener. The intensity of their venom has brought the audience to the edge of their seats. Bathgate feels extremely uncomfortable because he knows the fury between the men is more than just acting: off stage they hate each other. Inspector Alleyn's eyes are riveted to the action. Nigel can see the tension in his face. The anxiety is almost unbearable.

This is the moment of truth when the infamous Rat is exposed as an illicit drug trafficker, traitor, Nazi spy, or hero of the British Secret Service. The Beaver's masterminding of the opium trade is well known. On stage he takes a revolver from his pocket and loads it, then addresses Gardener, the man who, in real life, has stolen his starring role and his lover.

'*So the Rat's in his hole at last!*'

'*Beaver,*' whispered Felix Gardener . . . '*You're not a killer, Rat,*' he said. '*I am.*'

Gardener raises his hands above his head, but then in the doorway stands Stephanie Vaughan holding a revolver pointed at Surbonadier. The Beaver has been outmanoeuvred by his cheating stage girlfriend (and real-life ex-lover). He drops his hand. The gun hangs limp in his fingers. Sneeringly, Gardener thanks Stephanie as he takes the revolver from Surbonadier. She taunts him. Suddenly Surbonadier snaps, grabs at Gardener's neck, and pushes his head back. Gardener's hand jerks. *Bang* goes the gun across the blackness. The sound is deafening. 'Surbonadier crumpled up and, turning a face that was blank of every expression but that of profound astonishment, fell in a heap at Gardener's feet.' Alleyn seems to know what has happened, even before the shocked usher finds him, seated on the aisle. He urges Nigel to get out as quickly as possible.

Someone has exchanged real bullets for fakes, breaching the boundary between illusion and reality. In the make-believe of the play, the Rat shoots the Beaver. In real life, Arthur Surbonadier is dead on the stage floor. There is no doubt that Gardener has killed Surbonadier, but did he murder him? It is in the slippage between illusion and reality that the ambiguity of the crime exists. The act of murder presupposes intent: the act of acting assumes pretence and therefore innocence. Is Gardener innocent or guilty? The answer is in his face when Chief Detective Inspector Alleyn tricks him into climbing up a ladder backstage beyond the ceiling cloth and into believing that a large sack hanging from a rope in the ceiling is the body of his second victim, Props.

> 'Alleyn!' he cried in a terrible voice, 'Alleyn!'
>
> 'What's the matter?' shouted Alleyn.
>
> 'He's here — he's hanged himself — he's here.'
>
> 'Who?'
>
> 'Props — it's Props.'
>
> His horrified face looked down at them.
>
> 'It's Props!' he repeated . . .
>
> 'Come down,' said Alleyn.

Gardener comes down, and within six rungs of the stage he turns and sees the men who are awaiting him. With an incoherent cry he stops short. His lips are drawn back, showing his gums. A streak of saliva trickles down his chin. He squints. 'And *how* do you know it is Props?' asks Alleyn. In that instant, the actor is unmasked to reveal the murderer, and his animal-like snarl is confirmation.

Felix Gardener is the face of deviance exposed. In Ngaio's closed world, he represents a temporary aberration in the fabric of normality. As in most Golden Age detective fiction, his psychology, his pathology, his reason for being what he is, is of less interest than the process of his identification and removal. The genre's focus is the restoration of order, and in the anxious decades of inter-war uncertainty this was immensely appealing.

The theatre provided Ngaio with the perfect place to stage a murder. It was a hermetic, hierarchical world where schedules and patterns of behaviour could be scrutinized and checked, and it was filled with sinister potential. Behind the stage was a labyrinth of backdrops, props and passageways; in front, when the lights went down, was a sea of blackness. Then there were the actors, their emotions heightened by the tensions of putting on a show and playing their parts. Among spectators, too, there was the buzz of excited expectation, and a tempting echo of crime novel readers, who were a parallel audience. It was an ideal backdrop against which to tease out issues. Ngaio was still intrigued by Pirandello's *Six Characters*, with its metaphysical exploration of illusion and reality: 'If you long above everything to be a director, this is the play that nags and clamours to be done.' She was not yet directing actors, but she could direct characters. What interested her was the melodramatic way actors play themselves in real life.

> 'Darling,' [Stephanie Vaughan] said, taking her time over lighting a cigarette and quite unconsciously adopting the best of her six by-the-mantelpiece poses. 'Darling, I'm so terribly, terribly upset by all this. I feel I'm to blame. I *am* to blame.'
>
> Surbonadier was silent. Miss Vaughan changed her pose. He knew quite well, through long experience, what her next pose would be, and equally well that it would charm him as though he were watching her for the first time. Her voice would drop. She would purr. She did purr.

Enter a Murderer had more dramatic pace and change of scene than *A Man Lay Dead*, and the dialogue was more compelling and implicit in moving action along. The characters were convincing and in sharper relief. The theatre was not just a venue for crime, it was the book's defining energy, creating a cohesive, vivid piece of writing.

Ngaio would write sunk in an armchair, mostly at night, with a favourite fountain pen filled with green ink in an exercise book or on loose-leaf foolscap paper in a hard cover resting on her knee. Only when the house lights went down did the characters come onto the stage of her imagination. The scenes would run through her mind almost complete, as if she were watching them. After she had written 1,000 words or so, the curtains were drawn and she would go to bed. She was disciplined and methodical, writing fluently with relatively few changes. Those she did make were written in the margins, above the line, or on the back of the facing page. The next day, what she had written would be typed by the woman she paid to handle her correspondence. She needed help and enjoyed her secretary's regular company.

Ngaio found the recovery from her mother's death 'agonising'. Her father became a constant companion. '[When] we built a hut in the Temple Basin above Arthur's Pass, he carried weatherboarding with the best of us up steep flanks in a nor'-west gale.' One of Henry's great gifts to his daughter was his spring of youthful energy. He gave her the ability to be physically and mentally young, long after youth usually lasted. In the latter part of his life he drew on it himself, tramping vast distances with her into the mountains. He played tennis, gardened, and continued his secretarial work. He was, in Ngaio's mind at least, a Peter Pan figure who immersed himself in a Neverland of late-night Lexicon games and mild-mannered drinking sessions with the boys. She felt almost parental towards him, but there was a cantankerous side that could suddenly rear up and remind her of their true relationship. At a point when she could have become independent, the tables were turned, and Ngaio the only child began caring for her only parent. It worked because of an arrested development in them both: he was not looking for another wife and she was not searching for a husband — or even a life substantially different from that of her childhood at Marton Cottage.

In many ways Ngaio was an orthodox person, yet her dress was startling for a woman in New Zealand in the mid-1930s. A photograph taken by her friend Olivia Spencer Bower in 1936 shows her seated on the back of a chair surrounded by fellow artists. She is conspicuous in her mannish slacks, tie and beret. Yet she wore her *cette monsieur-dame* dress to shock. Why? Was it to delineate herself as a modern woman? Was it to identify herself as a lesbian? Certainly, she knew it would signal both to some, and so this ambiguity may have been deliberate. But an androgynous persona was also commanding and theatrical, and more accurately perhaps expressed the woman she was. A person of independent means defined not by femininity, marriage or motherhood, but by her talent and skill as a writer and director. 'I think I'm one of those solitary creatures that aren't the marrying kind,' she would later write in her autobiography.

But this was only partly true, because there was a gregarious side to Ngaio that was satisfied by her women friends. She began picking up the threads of her old life. During the summer of 1933–34, she went on trips to the mountains with her Canterbury College School of Art friends. With her father's help they built a hut at Temple Basin so they could live and paint together. She loved the beauty and solitude of the magnificent ranges. On hot days the mountains became a suffocating crucible of stillness and heat, yet she found it cleansing. Olivia Spencer Bower painted Ngaio at her easel sketching the foothills of the Southern Alps on a dazzling Canterbury day, squinting into the brilliant sun, absorbed in her work, at one with the environment. Concentration on her painting and comfort in the company of old friends eased Ngaio's grief. Although Spencer Bower made a number of images of Ngaio working in the landscape, it was Phyllis Bethune (*née* Drummond Sharpe) who was her most constant companion, and other friends such as Evelyn Page (*née* Polson), and Rata Lovell-Smith (*née* Bird) travelled with her to paint in places like the Aclands' station at Peel Forest in South Canterbury, and the Mackenzie Country.

In the years immediately after the First World War, Christchurch had become the country's leading centre for the visual arts. Canterbury College School of Art was buoyant and had a reputation as one of the best art schools in the country, known for its painters, especially those who painted landscape *en plein air*. The city had an active exhibition culture. 'The Canterbury Society of Arts [CSA] was considered the most lively of New Zealand art societies.'

Ngaio and her friends were the cream of the art school. Ngaio had been enrolled there full-time from 1915 to 1919. Also attending had been Page, Lovell-Smith and Haszard; Spencer Bower had begun part-time study in 1920. Collectively, they represented a phenomenal blossoming of post-war female talent. Not only did they share the ambition to become professional painters, but they knew it was an unconventional role. 'Life at an Art School is considered by many to be Bohemian; this, to a great extent is true,' wrote Rhona Haszard. 'To people passing along Rolleston Avenue . . . we may certainly appear eccentric as we wander about in our paint-dabbed smocks, singing tuneful quartets.' As students, they ate meals together between classes, 'worked at anatomy, perspective and composition', and had parties there after evening session ended at nine o'clock. Leslie Greener remembered Haszard, 'a lithe, slim figure' among her studio friends, 'curled up in a chair strumming on a banjo while everyone sat round on the floor and crooned accompaniment'.

But heady student days gave way to the serious task of earning a living. In spite of her dramatic and literary successes, Ngaio had always seen herself making her living from art. 'It had never occurred to me that I would attempt to be anything else in life but a serious painter: there was no question of looking upon art as a sort of obsessive hobby — it was everything.' Her college years seemed to substantiate this dream. She practically paid her own way through art school with scholarships. She won the Pure Art Scholarship and Medal, worth £25, in 1917 and 1918, and two awards for figure composition in her final year. Art appeared to be her destiny. In order to establish her career, she exhibited with the CSA from 1919 to 1926, and also intermittently with the New Zealand Academy of Fine Arts (NZAFA) in Wellington and art societies in Auckland and Dunedin. However, even though she was mentioned positively in reviews, her receipts were modest.

As students, Evelyn Page and Ngaio had shared a studio, along with Haszard, Edith Wall, Margaret Anderson and Viola Macmillan Brown, and after leaving art school they kept it on. By 1927, it had become an established sanctuary away from the strictures of Victorian upbringings and families. They were delighted, not just to escape there, but also to assert their professionalism as artists. 'We rented a small room in Hereford Street,' recalled Evelyn Page many years later.

It was a *tiny* room . . . then I think it was Edith Wall who discovered the old *Press* building . . . right in the middle of Cashel Street, was vacant . . . and it was a whole top floor . . . it was brick and you had to go up a fire escape to get into it and . . . there were great big square windows all round so the lighting wasn't too bad but it was very cold so we had points put in and heaters, electric heaters. We couldn't afford too many of those so we had kerosene heaters as well . . . we thought we'd . . . have exhibitions . . . and we did.

They whitewashed the walls, and 'Ngaio thought instead of having tea and sandwiches' at the opening, that they should have 'a hock cup . . . or a claret cup'. So they pooled their money and bought a 'vast basin' of wine. They invited their friends, then 'we thought, we'd better invite some possible buyers . . . so we looked up the telephone book and rooted out all the wealthy old dowagers of Christchurch and invited them too and up they came, up the fire escape and had their hock cup and ran round buying indiscriminately — it was marvellous!'

In fact, this was a point of radical departure for art in New Zealand: the beginning of The Group. The exhibition, with its 'hock cup' and dowagers, was its inaugural show. Group members were looking for an opportunity to show their work outside the CSA's annual Edwardian clutter of pictures. 'There [was no] deliberate attitude towards the Arts of Christchurch,' said Ngaio of The Group's genesis. 'There were no politics. We were not a bunch of rebels, or angries, we were a group of friends.' They were discerning friends, though, Page remembered: 'We invited . . . only the newest, the most modern of our contemporaries.' The Group would become one of New Zealand's most important outlets for progressive painters.

Ngaio was a relatively pedestrian painter, and her talent glowed dimly in a constellation of stars. Page was beginning to realize her talent as a dazzling colourist who could apply Impressionistic brush strokes of impasto paint with a skill that looked effortless. Equally, Haszard was distinguishing herself, with pictures painted in the British Camden Town style composed of luscious paint-loaded mosaics of bold Post-Impressionist colour. Other talented painters — Spencer Bower, Rata and Colin Lovell-Smith, Rita Angus and Louise Henderson — were also establishing careers. In this context, many of Ngaio's Impressionistic scenes of New Zealand High Country looked staid and formulaic. They were competent but tepid: she laid down the bones of the landscape but not its heart.

By the time Ngaio joined her women friends (and two men, W.H. Montgomery and William Baverstock), in their new Cashel Street studio in 1927, she realized that art would never be more than an abiding passion. She showed with The Group in 1927 and 1928, then left for England.

Her friend Rhona Haszard had departed two years earlier, and many of their contemporaries followed. It was difficult for artists to establish themselves in New Zealand without the authority of overseas experience, so they were lured away. A few, like painter Frances Hodgkins, remained abroad, but most came back. The news, therefore, of Haszard's death after a four-storey fall from a tower in Alexandria, in February 1931, sent shockwaves through conservative

Christchurch. Many, already suspicious of her second husband Leslie Greener, believed he had killed her because of an affair she had while staying in London. Rumours abounded. His decision to bring his wife's paintings back to New Zealand and sell them reignited controversy. Ngaio almost certainly saw Greener's memorial exhibition, which he toured nationally in 1933, the year after she returned and began exhibiting herself. She showed with the CSA in 1933, and The Group in 1935, and continued to exhibit intermittently with The Group until 1947.

Among the paintings she showed at the CSA in 1933 was *Native Market, Durban*, taken from the photograph and quick sketch she had made on her voyage to England. Ironically, there is more visual interest in the bustling human energies and vibrant marketplace colour than she ever achieved in the remote Canterbury landscapes she loved to paint. The simplified forms of the figures and produce have a sculptural quality reminiscent of Paul Cézanne and his precept that Nature can be structurally reduced to the cone, the cylinder or the cube. She was influenced by work she saw in Europe, but also by Australian Margaret Preston's magnificent Post-Impressionist distillations of white-on-white: in *Native Market, Durban*, these are in the white folds and twists of turbans, veils and dresses.

Her painting *In the Quarry* was exhibited at the CSA in 1935. The subject is a group of local relief workers building a section of Valley Road close to her home on the Cashmere Hills. She looks down on the scene from above. The summer day is hot, and men work, sit, stand or laze lethargically in wheelbarrows. The work is a vivid communication of an ordinary scene. Forms are simplified and geometric. Captivating contrasts of work and repose, blazing light and deep shadow, and the warm cream of a dusty dirt road cut through lush green grass, activate the canvas. At The Group exhibition that opened in early September 1932, English *émigré* and Post-Impressionist Christopher Perkins showed four oils and a group of drawings. His hard-edged naturalism, with its simplified form and colour, pointed to a new direction in New Zealand art. Ngaio had seen the exhibition, and his drawing *Employed*, reproduced in *Art New Zealand* in September 1932. This almost certainly influenced her *In the Quarry*. She called it *Still Life* for the CSA catalogue, a pun as her novel titles often were. After the 'mistake' was pointed out by a literal-minded art society official, the painting was retitled and entered in the correct section.

But just as Ngaio was beginning to embrace modern ideas in painting, her writing career swept her off in another direction. *Enter a Murderer* was published in 1935, along with *The Nursing-Home Murder*, which was to secure her place as a leading crime writer in Britain. The year before she had suffered from gynaecological problems. 'I spent three months in hospital undergoing a series of minor operations and a final snorter of a major one.' As a result, quite devastatingly for her, she could never have children. While she was in hospital Ngaio began thinking of another story, about a murder that occurred, not on a stage, but on the table of an operating theatre. The parallels are obvious. It was a closed environment with distinct hierarchies and procedures, and the same kind of intensity of performance. But the stakes were higher and life routinely in balance. Imagine if the patient were the British Home Secretary, fighting for his life after a ruptured appendix, and everyone around the operating table had a motive for killing him . . .

Again, in *The Nursing-Home Murder*, a play within the novel becomes a metaphor for the action. In the sterile chill of the anteroom, nurse Jane Harden and Sister Marigold help the two surgeons into their white gowns.

'Seen this new show at the Palladium?' asked [assistant surgeon Dr] Thoms.

'No,' said Sir John Phillips.

'There's a one-act play. Anteroom to a theatre in a private hospital. Famous surgeon has to operate on a man who ruined him and seduced his wife. Problem — does he stick a knife into the patient?'

Phillips, deeply affected by Dr Thoms's description of the play, turns slowly to look at him. Nurse Jane Harden stifles an involuntary cry. Unable to contain himself any longer, he asks suddenly how the play ended. Dr Thoms replies, 'It ended in doubt. You were left to wonder if the patient died under the anaesthetic, or if the surgeon did him in. As a matter of fact, under the circumstances, no one could have found out.' As Roderick Alleyn will later point out, the operating theatre is 'the ideal setting for a murder. The whole place was cleaned up scientifically — hygienically — completely — as soon as the body of the victim was removed. No chance of a fingerprint, no significant bits and pieces left on the floor. Nothing.'

The Home Secretary, Sir Derek O'Callaghan, dies of a lethal dose of hyoscine administered on the operating table. Because she needed medical knowledge,

Ngaio took on her only collaborator, Irish surgeon Dr Henry Jellett. She also consulted Sir Hugh Acland. Both men were her specialists while she was in hospital, and friends of the Rhodeses. What is new about *The Nursing-Home Murder* is its sustained focus on the political rather than just the criminally deviant. 'Bolshie' Nurse Banks's impassioned speeches against capitalism introduce villainous ideology, which is any belief against the status quo. The veins stand out on her neck; her eyes bulge; she is fired with political fervour.

'And for that reason [Sir Derek's] the more devilish,' announced Banks with remarkable venom. 'He's done murderous things since he's been in office . . . He's directly responsible for every death from under-nourishment that has occurred during the last ten months. He's the enemy of the proletariat.'

Even Alleyn's generous helping of upper-crust pie does not escape her scrutiny. 'I know your type — the gentleman policemen — the latest development of the capitalist system. You've got where you are by influence while better men do bigger work for a slave's pittance. You'll go, and all others like you, when the Dawn breaks.' Although Nurse Banks is like a bad fairy at a Society wedding, she cannot be the killer: it is a golden rule of Golden Age crime that personal motive can never be superseded by the political.

After the book was finished, Ngaio decided to produce it as a play, *Exit Sir Derek*, with a group of local amateur actors. Once again, she called upon the expertise of Henry Jellett. He was a perfectionist, insisting on endless rehearsals. A stickler for detail, he made a 'startlingly realistic false abdomen with an incision and retractors'. He stationed a fully trained theatre sister in the wings to prepare the patient. He gave strict instructions to the cast that if a glove was dropped it must *not* be retrieved. The opening night audience was peppered with doctors, who came to see their colleague's collaboration. The last Act was set in the operating theatre. To make it realistic, Jellett released ether into the audience. The medical malpractice began when the assistant surgeon dropped a glove, and picked it up off the floor. (The audience laughed, especially the doctors.) Meanwhile, beneath the felt abdomen the actor writhed in muffled gasps of pain. In the wings, the overexcited sister had clipped his flesh rather than the felt with the retractors. The nauseating smell of ether plus the graphic unveiling of the felt incision was too much for the circle. An 'actress from an English touring company screamed and fainted' and, with difficulty, was carried out of the auditorium. In spite of initial hitches, the play opened to packed houses, and Ngaio considered sending the script to her agent, but decided it was too similar to another American stage play.

The rhythms of life at Marton Cottage were predictable and sedate, yet Ngaio's books were far from tranquil. In *Death in Ecstasy*, published in 1936, she faced her phobia: poison. 'The House of the Sacred Flame, its officials, and its congregation are all imaginative and exist only in Knocklatchers Row,' Ngaio wrote in her foreword. This was a touch of irony, because in Christchurch the story was instantly recognizable.

Forty years before, the fictional House of the Sacred Flame's flesh-and-blood forebears had existed in the town's Latimer Square. American Arthur Bently Worthington had taken the globe, spun it around and chosen the most far-flung outpost to escape to. He was one of life's real villains, a polygamist (with nine wives), a thief, a defrauder, a fake. Worthington, notorious in the United States for marrying wealthy women and taking their money, arrived in Christchurch in January 1890, with his 'soul mate', the already-married Mary Plunkett, international journal editor for the Christian Scientist sect, and her two children.

Worthington and Plunkett, renamed Sister Magdala, began a sect called the Students of Truth, based on a junket of beliefs that included pantheism and free love. By August 1892, with vast amounts pledged by the people of Christchurch, the sect built 'the imposing Temple of Truth, and next to it a "magnificent 12-room residence" for the Worthington family'. Worthington's mistake was to cross Sister Magdala, whom he banished with a splinter group to Australia when finances got low. She, and a collection of concerned Christchurch clergy, exposed Worthington in the press. The tide turned in September 1897, and at a series of revival lectures at the Oddfellows' Hall 6,000 angry people gathered in Lichfield Street to protest against Worthington; the crowd had to be forcibly dispersed. Ngaio's father, an arch sceptic and evangelizing atheist, chuckled over the episode until he nearly collapsed. His daughter was two years old when Worthington met his Armageddon, and Henry Marsh delighted in retelling the story as she grew up.

The version Ngaio tells in *Death in Ecstasy* is slightly different. Outside is blackness. The wind blows and rain beats against the temple roof as Sister Cara Quayne reaches a state of dishevelled ecstasy.

Her arms twitched and she mouthed and gibbered like an idiot, turning her head from side to side . . . She raised the cup to her lips. Her head tipped back and back until the last drop must have been drained. Suddenly she gasped violently. She slew half round as if to question the priest. Her hands shot outwards as though she offered him the cup. Then they parted inconsequently. The cup flashed as it dropped to the floor. Her face twisted into an appalling grimace. Her body twitched violently. She pitched forward like an enormous doll, jerked twice and then was still.

Ngaio's equivalent of 'Sister Magdala' was dead.

'To this day, on the rare occasions that I use poison in a detective story, I am visited by a ludicrous aftertaste of my childish horrors.' Ngaio must have spent some time exorcizing the after-image of Cara Quayne, 'eyes wide open and protuberant . . . At the corners of the mouth were traces of a rimy spume. The mouth itself was set, with the teeth clenched and the lips drawn back, in a rigid circle.' This was a death mask of rigor mortis brought on by the ingestion of cyanide of potassium.

Ngaio researched every aspect of her novels, especially the deaths. She knew police procedure and kept a diagram on her wall of the hierarchy of command at New Scotland Yard. Her shelves at home began to fill with books on poisons, medical jurisprudence, and forensic medicine. She consulted her medical friends and the reference section of the local library. Ngaio never wrote anything unless she investigated it before Alleyn. The vividness of Cara Quayne's ugly end, and its power as an image 'to linger in the memory', came from its authenticity, and from the fact that, as crime writer and critic P.D. James has said, 'Death is never glamorised nor trivialised in Ngaio Marsh.' In Death in Ecstasy, Ngaio harnesses the power of death to shock more fully than in her previous novels, and this she would refine further. Her fear of poison unlocked her imagination to explore the experience with a horror that was more than just intellectual.

Heroin was another substance she researched for her novel, because worshippers at the House of the Sacred Flame are hooked on more than just religion. Their highs come from heroin-laced cigarettes and a chalice of Le Comte's Invalid Port spiked with pure alcohol. The sect, inspired by the teachings of Father Jasper Garnette, Ngaio's Worthington figure, is broadly pantheistic, with Scandinavian deities Wotan and Thor mixed with a hint of free love between Garnette and his 'Chosen Vessel', Cara Quayne. 'Garnette seems actually to have persuaded her that the — the union — was blessed, had a spiritual significance,' announces Alleyn in disgust. Cara, a young, gullible neophyte, has made a £5,000 donation to the temple building fund. She is hypnotized by Garnette's religious prognostications and hooked on heroin, which, along with cocaine, was a favoured drug of 1930s detective fiction writers. Narcotics such as these were known as the abuse of the upper classes. It became fashionable to write about drugs and drug trafficking, along with blackmail, jewel robbery, embezzlement, trophy-wife snatching and will jumping. 'Pin-point pupils' were synonymous with high-society doping. Well-connected Arthur Surbonadier is shot at the Unicorn Theatre because of his drug connections. Wealthy Cara Quayne dies in an ecstasy of unwitting addiction. Drugs would become a regular theme in Ngaio's novels.

Death in Ecstasy makes teasing reference to Ngaio's colleagues in crime. She is playing with the reader and with other writers of detective fiction. It is halfway through the story and Alleyn and Nigel Bathgate are 'taking stock':

'Look here,' said Nigel suddenly, 'let's pretend it's a detective novel. Where would we be by this time? About half-way through, I should think. Well who's your pick [for the murderer]?'

'I am invariably gulled by detective novels [Alleyn replied] . . . You see in real detection herrings are so often out of season.'

'Well, never mind, who's your pick?'

'It depends on the author. If it's Agatha Christie, Miss Wade's occulted guilt drips from every page. Dorothy Sayers's Lord Peter would plump for Pringle, I fancy. [Freeman Wills Croft's] Inspector French would go for Ogden.'

This is a delicious irony, a playful piece of unconscious self-consciousness that underscores the real nature of Alleyn's and Bathgate's existence compared with their fictional colleagues. Ngaio's humour, her increased confidence as a writer, and her respect for practitioners like Christie, Sayers, and Freeman Wills Croft inspired this very public private joke. She also paid her respects to Arthur Conan Doyle. 'I receive facts . . . as a spider does flies,' announces Alleyn in Holmesian style, and Bathgate makes this slightly nauseating comment: 'I am your Watson, and your worm. You may both sit and trample on me. I shall continue to offer you the fruits of my inexperience.'

Ngaio would return to the theme of human gullibility in the face of religious sham, but never again with quite the same echo of reality. 'Damn, sickly, pseudo, bogus, mumbo-jumbo,' says Alleyn with great violence about Father Garnette, and those were Ngaio's thoughts. As an adult she was sceptical about all religion. She grieved for the loss of her adolescent fervour, wanted to believe in Christianity, but the leap of faith became a chasm.

Ngaio was the only agnostic Queen of Crime. Agatha Christie slept all her life with a crucifix by her bed; Dorothy Sayers was a theologian and a devout, if not always practising, Christian; and Margery Allingham became an avid follower of Christianity in her later years. Ronald Knox was the Roman Catholic chaplain at Oxford University when he formulated the precepts of Golden Age detective fiction in his 'Studies in the Literature of Sherlock Holmes', published in 1928. His precepts were steeped in Christian ideology. For the Queens of Crime, writing about murder was not a betrayal of Faith but an affirmation, the Christian theme of sin and expiation played over and over again. The murder victim was the sacrificial lamb, given up so that the agent of sin, the murderer, could be found out and exorcized. The detective was the high priest, the detective story a modern apocrypha. Ngaio may have lost faith in the Christian message, but she never tired of retelling its story.

In the evenings, when she began a new book, Ngaio wandered from room to room. In perpetual motion she formed the ideas, and it was often daybreak before they flowed freely. She slept, then waited again until nightfall to begin bringing her characters alive. Her nocturnal habits meant she rose late, but the rest of the day was free for the theatre and to paint. *Exit Sir Derek* reconnected her with repertory, which was lively in the city. Stepping onto the stage took her back to her beginnings. As a child she had written a play in rhyming couplets for a cast of six, called *Cinderella*, and at St Margaret's *Bundles* and *The Moon Princess*. It was the arrival of the Allan Wilkie Shakespeare Company in 1915 that rekindled her interest in writing for the theatre. She was transfixed, as if she was watching the progress of a miraculous comet across the sky. 'The opening night of *Hamlet* was the most enchanted I was ever to spend in the theatre.' English actor-manager Wilkie, his striking actress wife Frediswyde Hunter-Watts, and their travelling company played to audiences in the Far East, North America and Australasia. They were the remnant of a bygone era, but to a centre starved of professional theatre they seemed rare and illustrious. People queued for tickets, Ngaio and her student friends cut evening art classes, and for two weeks Shakespeare took Christchurch by storm.

Ghosts, gravediggers and Danes walked the ramparts of Ngaio's quiet nights. She went to *Hamlet* a number of times. The season ended too quickly, and as abruptly as it had arrived the company was gone. The experience had been ephemeral, like a shadow she wanted to pin down, so between the company's first and third visits to Christchurch she wrote a romantic regency drama called *The Medallion*. She hoped Allan Wilkie would cast a professional eye over it. Her mother encouraged her. Towards the end of 1919, they braved the ordeal of handing the script in at the theatre with a note, then seeing Allan Wilkie in person at the Clarendon Hotel. As always, Ngaio was tentative about her writing. The play was mannered and rhetorical, but her raw enthusiasm captured Wilkie's attention.

After art classes had finished one afternoon, Ngaio returned to her shared studio with her paint-box slung over her shoulder. She climbed the stairs, walked in, and there they were — Allan Wilkie and his wife. ' "I obtained the address," Mr. Wilkie said in his resonant actor's voice, "from your father. I have a suggestion to make . . . How . . . would you like to be an actress?" ' He thought that if she was going to write for the theatre she needed experience on the stage. She was speechless, stunned. It was as if Wilkie had opened a door through which she glimpsed her future. She had two hours to make up her mind. The Wilkies were leaving town almost immediately, but would employ her when they returned, if her parents agreed.

Ngaio's 'yes' was immediate, and her father's followed; Rose Marsh was harder to please. But Peter Tokareff's suicide was still fresh in her mind, and now there was a new threat. Her daughter had another besotted suitor, this time a middle-aged Englishman. Once again, Ngaio was flattered, but out of her depth.

'Your father,' [Rose] said, 'will speak to him.'
    And so he did and to some effect. 'I felt damn' sorry for the fellow . . . He made such a thing of it . . . He'll get over it, no doubt.'

But the Englishman began stalking Ngaio. 'One night, when I was alone in the studio, he came up the stairs and stood . . . in utter silence on the landing while I sat petrified and sick, on the other side of the door.'

Fear forced Rose to agree to Ngaio's touring with the Wilkies, plus the fact that she was greatly impressed with Allan Wilkie, who was a consummate charmer. Henry was amused: 'So you're off . . .with the raggle-taggle-gypsies, O.' Ngaio was ecstatic. Rose felt she had been painted into a corner. While she waited for the company to return to Christchurch, Ngaio took a relieving position as lady editor at the *Sun* newspaper. She wrote about clothes, society hostesses and 'concocted paragraphs to fill in the gaps'. Her anticipation mounted.

Ngaio was 25 years old and had never been out of the South Island. She would be living away from her parents and enjoying the pleasures of travel and adult life for the first time. 'On a warm autumn morning I reported at the Theatre Royal, walked under the ringing iron stairs I had so often climbed and went in at the Stage Door. The world of glue-size, canvas, dust and shadows engulfed me.' They played a season in Christchurch. The parts for Ngaio were limited. She had a deep contralto voice, which seemed odd in a woman, and was taller than the average leading man. As Wilkie remarked, 'Only I . . . am at liberty to take six foot strides on this stage.' To ensure she took demure steps, Ngaio hobbled her legs together above the knees with a stocking. The kindly Wilkie found her work in spite of this. She played a dubious 'Franco-Teutonic' maid in a spy thriller called *The Luck of the Navy*, where the main character was tied to a chair (like Nigel in *A Man Lay Dead*); an ex-WAAF, now housemaid, in *A Temporary Gentleman*; a vicious craggy crone in the farce *The Rotters*; and, in *Hindle Wakes*, yet another maid.

Rehearsals were arduous and Wilkie was a hard taskmaster, but Ngaio's energy and enthusiasm seemed endless. 'I learnt how actors work in consort,' she wrote, 'like musicians, how they shape the dialogue in its phrases, build to points of climax, mark the pauses and observe the tempi.' This was an apprenticeship she would draw on for the rest of her life. 'Without knowing it I laid down a little cellar of experiences which would one day be served up as the table wines of detective cookery.' The people she met in the company fascinated her. She tended to see them as types: the male heart-throb, his meltingly magnificent woman, the character actor, the juvenile, the straight man, and the comic. She relished the details that made the actors like the characters they played.

After Christchurch, there was a season in Auckland. They took the ferry from Lyttelton to Wellington, then a 14-hour train journey. Ngaio's senses were heightened by exhilaration.

I, however, persisted in my rapture. It was the first of many such occasions and I was to grow familiar with the look of my fellow-players in transit: the ones who read, the ones who stared out of the window, the ones who slept, the cheerful, the morose and the resigned. Mr. Wilkie and Pat Scully [the stage manager], their shoulders hunched and their heads nodding with the motion of the train, played endless games of two-handed whist. Mrs Wilkie read.

Through the winter they travelled up and down New Zealand with their four modern plays. Spring brought the end of a life she had come to love. Wilkie reformed a Shakespearian company in Australia, taking key players with him, but minor roles, especially maids, were dispensable. 'On a wet night in Wellington I said good-bye and returned alone in the ferry to Christchurch. One of the first things I did was to wrap up Gramp's book and sent it to Mr. Wilkie. In return I received a ring of which, he wrote . . . "It is a trifle of some reputed antiquity."' Ngaio, an only child, had tasted life with a carnival company of actors. Like a desert flower, the experience bloomed, then vanished. She would spend a lifetime trying to recapture its brilliance.

'It wasn't easy to settle down again: to return to a pattern, that, however freely designed, turned about a small house, one's parents and a circle of quiet friends.' Her sepia existence seemed drab by comparison. She painted with her friends and wrote for the *Sun*. But life was insular and restrained, until the Rosemary Rees English Comedy Company rolled into town and she was invited to tour again. Her mother was adamant that it would 'lead to nothing . . . Why do you want to do it? It's not the right kind of thing for you. *I know*.' But Ngaio was determined.

The tour was fraught from the beginning. The juvenile, who had no understudy, came down with scarlet fever. He had a big part and it was a disaster. Ngaio had an out-of-body experience: 'I heard myself saying that I thought I could play the boy, "Jimmy" ' — and she did. There were costume difficulties. She could fit Jimmy's fumigated suits, but cramming her long hair under a wig was torture. In desperation Rosemary Rees suggested she cut it. When Ngaio wrote to her mother, asking for permission, she received a 'snorter' of a reply by return post. Rees followed with a pleading epistle, but Rose Marsh was intractable. 'She was unable to discover,' Ngaio recalls, 'why it should be imagined the antics of a music-hall soubrette could reconcile her to the thought of her daughter masquerading in male attire in a third-rate company.' Rose almost ordered Ngaio home, but was tempered by her own fond feelings for the stage. If she had to abide her daughter playing a boy, there would be no haircut.

They travelled 'by buses, trains and coastal steamers'. The audiences were provincial and small, and the company lasted three months before it was disbanded. Rose had won a skirmish, but other battles were inevitable because Ngaio was not happy. Christchurch was claustrophobic and she was unsettled.

The bliss of touring was artificially prolonged when Kiore (Tor) King, a young woman Ngaio had become friendly with on the comedy tour, came to stay. Rose approved because King came from the right sort of family. Discussions with King about the theatre inspired Ngaio to write a piece called *Little Housebound*. 'My mother must have exercised superb self-control during this period . . . she did not discourage us: I was writing.' The play was almost a parody of Ngaio's life. It was about breaking free, taking risks and stepping out into the world. Perhaps Rose Marsh was too close to see the parallel.

They decided to tour it through provincial towns in the North Island. A recovered Jimmy from the Rosemary Rees company was roped in to play the male role and they were ready. 'Jimmy discovered that touring companies of five or more were allowed first-class railway accommodation at second-class fares.' The mothers were invited to boost numbers and, not surprisingly, they came. Ngaio's play, plus some sketches and recitations, was taken to Hastings and Havelock North. They had fun and made a modest profit. Ngaio was sad when the enterprise came to an end. Jimmy went to Australia to join the Marie Tempest Company, and Tor King to the Allan Wilkie Company. Once again, Ngaio was housebound.

<hr />

It was her first vivid sense of getting away with the Allan Wilkie Company that Ngaio captured in *Vintage Murder* in 1937. 'There were to be other tours with other companies,' she wrote in *Black Beech*, 'and many solitary train journeys in many parts of the world. In all of them, whenever I have found myself in a half-empty Pullman carriage I have re-peopled it with those long-remembered companions.' She dedicated the book to Allan Wilkie and his wife, 'In memory of a tour in New Zealand'. 'All the characters in this story are purely imaginary and bear no relation to any actual person,' she wrote in the foreword, but this was the convention. Many years later, in a BBC radio interview, she would admit that *Vintage Murder*'s Susan Max was based on an elderly Australian actress who was dresser for Mrs Wilkie. In the novel, Roderick Alleyn is in New Zealand on an enforced holiday for his health. In between sleeping and waking, he watches a group of dozing actors as his train hurries through the night.

> For the hundredth time he opened his eyes to see the dim carriage-lamps and the rows of faces with their murky high-lights and cadaverous shadows . . . Opposite him was the leading man, large, kindly, swaying slightly with the movement of the long narrow-gauge carriage, politely resigned to discomfort. The bundle of rugs in the next seat . . . was Miss Susan Max, the character woman. An old trouper, Susan, with years of jolting night journeys behind her, first in this country, then Australia, and then up and down the provinces in England.

Susan Max has toured for 45 years. Two years before, she had held the sobbing Stephanie Vaughan in her arms when Surbonadier was shot at the Unicorn Theatre. After that murder investigation closed *The Rat and Beaver*, she joined Carolyn Dacres Comedy Company, which is now touring New Zealand. It is the gorgeous Carolyn's birthday and they have planned a party for her on stage after the company's opening night in Middleton (a fictional mid-North Island town). Cast and crew are invited, plus select guests. A trestle table is set up, loaded with food. In the middle is a nest of maidenhair fern and coloured lights mixed with exotic flowers. At the crowning moment a massive jeroboam of wine is to descend on a crimson cord and settle in the centrepiece. Everyone is assembled. For impact, Carolyn Dacres delays her entrance. She looks fabulous as Alleyn presents her with his portentous gift of a 'he tiki', a Maori symbol of fertility. The moment comes: Carolyn cuts the cord.

> Something enormous . . . flashed down among them, jolting the table. Valerie Gaynes screaming. Broken glass and the smell of champagne. Champagne flowing over the white cloth. A thing like an enormous billiard ball embedded in the fern. Red in the champagne. Valerie Gaynes, screaming, screaming. Carolyn, her arm still raised, looking down. Himself [Alleyn], his voice, telling them to go away, telling Hambledon to take Carolyn away.

It is a horrifying spectacle: the bald head of actor-manager Alfred Meyer, squashed in the ferns and fairy lights under a huge jeroboam of wine.

Ngaio's imagination was gaining momentum. She would develop a reputation for sticky ends. Some would seem hardly plausible, but her skill at picturing them silenced most sceptics. As P.D. James has commented, regarding the ingenuity of her murder methods, 'Readers in the golden years demanded not only that the victim be murdered, but that he or she be mysteriously, intriguingly and bizarrely murdered . . . The method of death in a Ngaio Marsh novel tends to linger in the memory.'

While her ingenious murder methods became a trademark, Ngaio's police interrogations could be much drier. It was here that some of the brilliant momentum she created in setting scenes and introducing characters reached a plateau and on occasions even a frustrating hiatus. The unusual thing about *Vintage Murder* is that although the story depends heavily on police interrogation, it remains fresh. Perhaps the newness of New Zealand for Alleyn seals its vitality. Convalescent, as Ngaio had been, he is abroad for a complete break. For the first time in her writing they swap places: Alleyn is a foreigner in her country. Ngaio knew what it felt like. 'On my return to New Zealand after five years, I found myself looking at my own country, however superficially, from the outside, in.'

Ngaio could have chosen a more conventionally upper-class place for her detective to recuperate. He could have basked in the warmth of the Riviera, or enjoyed the buzz of the metropolis — Paris, Rome, Berlin — anywhere but the crisp stillness of a small mid-North Island town moving into winter. But although a murder mystery was traditionally pure entertainment, and not intended to be taken seriously, a clever writer like Ngaio had opinions, especially about New Zealand and its problematic relationship with Britain. *Vintage Murder* gave these their first proper airing. There is no Nigel Bathgate, so the central consciousness becomes Alleyn himself, and the story unfolds from his perspective. Whatever health breakdown he has had has transformed him: any remnant of silly-assed sleuth has gone. He is more considered, reflective and mature, but his seriousness is meted by a clever strain of humour that runs through the book. Alleyn is aware of his outsider status in relation to both Pakeha cultural cringe and Maori cultural difference.

His contribution to the case is welcomed by local police, because he knows the company of English actors involved. 'It looks as if it's an English case more than a New Zillund one, now, doesn't it?' says Sergeant Wade, sheepishly parodying his own accent. Alleyn is sensitive to the power dynamic. ' "I suppose," thought

Alleyn, "I must give him an inferiority complex. He feels I'm criticising him all the time. If I don't remember to be frightfully hearty and friendly, he'll think I'm all English and superior." ' Pakeha New Zealanders feel second-rate around Alleyn. In spite of his politeness, he makes them aware of their difference. They are changing and losing touch with their English and European roots as the Maori have with their indigenous heritage. Pakeha ambivalence comes from the fact that New Zealand will never be their place of origin. Ngaio lampoons the Pakeha dilemma. Young Detective Inspector Packer hero-worships Alleyn in language she loathed. ' "He looks like one of those swells in the English flicks," [Packer] afterwards confided to his girl, "and he talks with a corker sort of voice. Not queeny, but just corker. I reckon he's all right. Gosh, I reckon he's a humdinger." ' Parker's cringe is internalized, like Ngaio's, and the same applied to many Pakeha New Zealanders of this era.

The position of Maori is less complicated because they are the indigenous people, and in some respects Ngaio's treatment is more sympathetic. Alleyn is the first bicultural Golden Age detective. He attempts to understand the case according to Pakeha and Maori laws. It is Alfred Meyer who insults the sacredness of the he tiki on his wife's birthday, and it is his head that is pulverized almost as soon as he does. Alleyn asks his cultured Maori confidant, Dr Rangi Te Pokiha, 'Tell me, . . . if it's not an impertinent question, do you yourself feel anything of what your ancestors would have felt in regard to this coincidence?' He is trying to understand tapu and the meting out of consequences for its infringement.

The difficulties of colonization for Maori are also movingly explained by the Oxford-trained Te Pokiha, who has interrupted a promising academic career to train as a doctor. 'I began to see the terrible inroads made by civilization in the health of my own people. Tuberculosis, syphilis, typhoid.' But his comments on appropriation are even more revealing. 'The *pakeha* give their children Maori Christian names because they sound pretty. They call their ships and their houses by Maori names . . . We have become a side-show in the tourist bureau — our dances — our art — everything.' He is talking about Ngaio's parents, who named her after the white-blossomed native ngaio tree, and about the frenetic Pakeha search for 'signs' of New Zealand identity plundered from Maori culture.

Ngaio may have used popular fiction to explore social issues, but she never lost sight of the need to entertain. *Vintage Murder* encourages people to think about bicultural issues, but it does not unravel stereotypes. There is something still of the noble savage in Te Pokiha, and an inappropriateness in Alleyn's pompous thinking about him. In the dénouement, Te Pokiha almost comes to blows with the murderer. 'His lips coarsened into a sort of snarl. He showed his teeth like a dog. "By Jove," thought Alleyn, "the odd twenty percent of pure savage."' With that racist thought, Alleyn confirms his outsider status.

Three months later, his New Zealand holiday nearly over, Alleyn is sitting on tussock looking across Lake Pukaki to Mount Aorangi, the cloud-piercer, and thinking of home. He has three letters in his pocket: one from Carolyn Dacres announcing her pregnancy — the greenstone he tiki 'has fulfilled its purpose'; another from his assistant commissioner; and a final one from Inspector Fox, saying how glad they will be to see him back at the Yard again. Many of Alleyn's New Zealand insights occur in the form of correspondence with Fox. His letters home to England are an important narrative thread, and his thoughts in them private and spontaneous. Ngaio's letters to Nelly Rhodes were the same. After nearly five years in New Zealand, England seemed like a distant dream. Like Alleyn, she was ready to go back.

Chorus

CHAPTER THREE

Companions in Crime

It started off rather grandly with a printed invitation to Grosvenor House from the Detection Club,' Ngaio explained later. They ate in a private dining room, with the Chief Constable of Surrey as guest speaker, but the meal was prelude to a more significant event: the 1937 induction of E.C. Bentley as president of the Detection Club. The cream of crime was there: Dorothy Sayers, John Rhode, Anthony Gilbert and Freeman Wills Croft, to name a few. After the speeches, they withdrew to a private drawing room where the real business began. Dorothy Sayers was mistress of ceremonies. Her imposing figure, 'robust, round and rubicund', towered over her colleagues. She struck Ngaio as something of 'a cross between a guardsman & a female don with a jolly face (garnished with pince-nez), short grey curls, & a gruff voice'. Agatha Christie was not in attendance, but she would meet with Ngaio later that evening at the Detection Club rooms in Soho. In the meantime, Ngaio and her agent were seated in two chairs against an imposing rostrum. 'I should explain before I go any further that my agent is a man with an ironic turn of mind . . . & a most singularly loud laugh.' They were left alone in the room and suddenly the lights went out and there was blackness.

A door at the far end opened (as all doors in detective novels open) slowly. In came Miss Dorothy Sayers in her academic robes lit by a single taper. She mounted the rostrum. Judge my alarm when I saw that among the folds of her gown she secreted a large automatic revolver. She lit candles on her desk & . . . uttered some intimidating order. In came the others in a solemn procession bearing lighted tapers & lethal instruments. There was the warden of the blunt instrument — a frightful bludgeon, the warden of the sharp instrument — I think it was a dagger — the warden of the deadly phial, & last of all John Rhode with a grinning skull on a cushion. And there, in the middle of them, looking apprehensive, as well he might, was poor Mr Bentley.

With huge solemnity, Sayers administered the Detection Club oath to Bentley who promised:

under pain of every horror that every concoctor of crime fiction has ever invented to obey the laws of detective fiction. Never to conceal a clue. Never to leave a knotty point unravelled. To place before the reader every scrap of information that is relevant to the solution . . . He took the oath & then close to my ear & without the slightest hint of warning, in a private drawing room at Grosvenor House at about 11 p.m. on a summer evening Miss Dorothy Sayers loosed off her six-shooter. The others uttering primitive cries, waved their instruments, blunt sharp & venomous, & John Rhode, by means of some hidden device, caused his skull to be lit up from within. And to my undying shame my agent laughed like a hyena. The ceremony was practically over, which is perhaps the reason my agent escaped with his life.

Ngaio's writing had earned her a place in the inner sanctum of British detective fiction. Since her début with *A Man Lay Dead* in 1934, she had written four titles, and when she arrived in London in the spring of 1937 it was with the manuscript for her sixth, *Artists in Crime.* She was sufficiently esteemed to be invited to a Detection Club dinner. If she had lived in London she would have been a member, but the club requirement that members attend five or six meetings a year prevented her from joining.

She would dine out on stories of her Detection Club evening when she returned to New Zealand, giving speeches, broadcasts and press interviews, but in the meantime she savoured this and other experiences. 'I get a feeling coming back to London which I must confess I don't get coming back to New Zealand . . . something quite extraordinary happens,' she told a BBC interviewer. 'I always wonder perhaps it won't this time but it always does.' That familiar sense of ecstasy had returned and, to top it off, she discovered she was a celebrity among the many fans of crime fiction in Britain. In 1945, Edmund Wilson would write scathingly in *The New Yorker* of the sad addicts of crime fiction whose 'talk about "well-written" mysteries is simply an excuse for their vice, like the reasons that the alcoholic can always produce for a drink'. In 1937, this addiction was well established in Britain and the United States, and Ngaio Marsh was now a celebrated supplier of whodunits.

It was with some trepidation, therefore, that she contemplated a love interest for Alleyn. She had a winning formula with her monkish, bookish, aesthetic detective, and romance was a controversial issue among commentators. In 1928, S.S. Van Dine, writing under his real name of Willard Huntington Wright, had cautioned writers against involving their series detectives in romance. 'There must be no love interest,' he wrote in his list of 'Twenty rules for writing detective stories'. 'The business in hand is to bring a criminal to the bar of justice, not to bring a lovelorn couple to the hymeneal altar.' Perhaps as a consequence of this, when Dorothy Sayers introduced her sexually active Harriet Vane to Lord Peter Wimsey in *Strong Poison* in 1930, a critical outcry ensued. There was something not quite dependable about a detective who could be distracted from his crusade against crime by the sins of the flesh. Then there was reader distraction from the central problem of solving the murder, and the fact that detection was deemed a masculine pursuit. How could the puzzle be unravelled cleanly and fairly by a detective who was making romantic overtures to the opposite sex? Rationality must be ascendant in a genre with mind games at its core.

Ngaio's agent was dubious about her marrying Alleyn off. But there was a dilemma. Nigel Bathgate was young and shallow, and as a confidant he had worn thin; and Inspector Fox was like a huge, comfortable, slightly shabby armchair — just part of the furniture. Ngaio knew a wife would expose aspects of her detective that the men in his life could not. Marriage seemed the next logical step in his emotional development.

On the voyage from New Zealand to England, Ngaio had mixed the ingredients of romance. Initially they had fizzed and popped and threatened to separate, like two incompatible substances in a beaker. At the beginning of *Artists in Crime*, Roderick Alleyn is on board the *Niagara*, making the same trip back to England as Ngaio. It could almost be Ngaio whom he sees on deck when he looks up, startled by a female voice.

'Damn, damn, damn! Oh *blast!*' . . .

Sitting on the canvas cover of one of the [life] boats was a woman. She seemed to be dabbing at something. She stood up and he saw that she wore a pair of exceedingly grubby flannel trousers, and a short grey overall. In her hand was a long brush. Her face was disfigured by a smudge of green paint, and her short hair stood up in a worried shock, as though she had run her hands through it. She was very thin and dark . . . A small canvas was propped up in the lid of an open paint-box. Alleyn drew in his breath sharply.

Her canvas is a simplified, magnificent rendering of the wharf they have just left at Suva. Alleyn finds the sketch almost too painful to behold. Its creator, who is less sacrosanct about it, stares dispassionately at the work with an unlit cigarette between her lips. A distracted search through her trouser pockets for a match reveals only an old paint-smeared handkerchief. She runs her fingers through her hair in frustration.

'Blast!' she repeated, and took the unlit cigarette from her lips.
'Match?' said Alleyn.
[And with that . . .] She started, lost her balance, and sat down abruptly.

Agatha Troy's first encounter with her future husband is a bruising collision of egos. He is being his usual polite, slightly supercilious self, and she is being a professional painter with all the frustration and anxiety that this entails (and no one knew this better than her creator).

The view of the Suva wharf Troy is painting was a vision Ngaio had savoured on her return voyage to New Zealand on the *Niagara* in 1932. She treasured her impressions: the sultry day; the acid green of the banana leaves; the mop of dyed, 'screaming magenta' hair on the tall Fijian; and the brilliant sari of an Indian woman. She had wanted to paint them, but felt too inadequate. 'It was this feeling of unfullfilment [*sic*] that led me to put another painter on another boat-deck,' wrote Ngaio in her 'Portrait of Troy' for Dilys Winn's *Murderess Ink*. 'She made a much better job of it than I ever would have done.'

The naming of Troy seemed a more casual process than the naming of Alleyn. Ngaio wanted a plain, down-to-earth name, and thought of Agatha, and then the rather unusual surname of Troy. She signs her paintings 'Troy' and is known as Troy. Ngaio said there was no link between Agatha Troy and Agatha Christie.

Ngaio wove her whodunits out of the fabric of her own life. 'I always tried to keep the settings of my books as far as possible within the confines of my own experience.' For the make-up of her leading characters she looked to people she knew, and to herself.

If Alleyn reflected the almost fussily feminine, cultured, reserved side of Ngaio, then Troy was a projection of her truculently masculine, untamed artistic self. She was the painter in fiction that Ngaio longed to be in life. Ngaio could write about Troy's genius and her cleverly spontaneous response to the visual world, but seldom achieved this same untrammelled brilliance in her own canvases. In her painting, as in her detective writing, Ngaio looked for the golden section — for the perfect measure of ordered form, for the formula that made sense of the world and what she did. She wrote tellingly of her days at art school in Christchurch: 'I wanted to be told flatly whether things I had drawn were too big or too small, too busy or too empty. I wanted to know, when I failed completely, exactly where I had gone wrong and how I might have avoided doing so.' Ngaio could never be the wild soul she created for Troy. She was too busy searching for the rules to realize her own vision. 'It seems to me, now, that I never drew or painted in the way that was really my way: that somehow I failed to get on terms with myself.'

The parallels between Ngaio and her Pygmalion did not end there. They were uncannily alike in appearance. As the ship moved away, Agatha Troy 'stood for a moment staring back at Fiji'.

Her hands gripped the shoulder-straps of her paint-box. The light breeze whipped back her short dark hair, revealing the contour of the skull and the delicate bones of the face. The temples were slightly hollow, the cheek-bones showed, the dark-blue eyes were deep-set under the thin ridge of the brows. The sun caught the olive skin with its smudge of green paint, and gave it warmth. There was a kind of spare gallantry about her.

Ngaio and Troy were alike in their 'spare gallantry', cherishing good manners and discretion with a kind of masculine valour. They were hugely protective of their careers. They were self-contained, yet also shy and socially reticent. They shared the same mannerisms: the same boyishness; the same worried tousling of the hair; the same 'gruff stand-offish voice'; the same natural inclination to curl up their long legs and sit on the ground; the same addiction to smoking; the same long-fingered, tremulous hands . . . and the list could go on. Troy was made according to Ngaio's pattern.

Even in love, their paths were similarly rocky. The painter in Troy cannot resist Alleyn's good bones. She has to take his likeness. 'The subject,' she confesses in a letter to her artist friend Katti Bostock, in England, 'is a detective and looks like a grandee. Sounds like it, too — very old-world and chivalrous and so on . . . I'm rather on the defensive about this Sleuth — I was so filthy rude to him, and he took it like a gent and made me feel like a bounder. Very awkward.'

Alleyn finds it equally difficult: 'She bridles like a hedgehog . . . whenever I approach her'. And when she paints his portrait: 'it's a rum sensation when they get to the eyes; such a searching impersonal sort of glare they give you. She even comes close sometimes and peers into the pupils. Rather humiliating, it is. I try to return a stare every bit as impersonal, and find it tricky.' It is Troy's penetrating gaze that makes Alleyn self-reflective. In previous books he has openly regretted and loathed the more distasteful, invasive aspects of his job — the searching through 'under-garment drawers for incriminating correspondence', the opening up of private lives to public scrutiny.

He also abhors the carrying of guns and capital punishment. Fox says to him in *Death in Ecstasy*: 'I know how you feel about homicide cases. I'd put it down to your imagination . . . I'm not at all fanciful, myself, but it does seem queer to me sometimes, how calm-like we get to work . . . and all the time there's a trap and a rope and a broken neck at the end if we do our job properly.'

Alleyn is haunted by the consequences of a good result, but it is love, not death, that makes him really question his job. When they leave the ship at Southampton and find themselves tied up in the same murder case, with Troy as a suspect, Alleyn is full of qualms. He realizes she is appalled by the very aspects of his work that disturb him. Troy is running a small residential painting school at her home at Tatler's End when, in full view of the class, the life model is dramatically impaled on a dagger, wedged through the back of the wooden throne. Only one of Troy's pupils has pushed the model down onto the dagger, but everyone in the studio has a motive to kill her. The invasion of Troy's privacy and that of her pupils, when Alleyn begins his investigation, makes Troy angry, and she challenges him:

> 'Do you want to search our rooms for something? Is that it?'
> 'Not for anything specific. I feel we should just —' He stopped short. 'I detest my job,' he said; 'for the first time I despise and detest it.'

And if this is not disquieting enough for Alleyn, Troy is also worried about losing her independence and identity as a painter. He can see how she shies away whenever she imagines herself becoming subsumed by his job and their relationship. Through Troy, Ngaio communicates a modern woman's reluctance to sacrifice her career and her individuality to marriage; through Alleyn, she traces a modern man's waking comprehension of this. Theirs will be a marriage of equality, but getting to the altar will be fraught.

Not many of Ngaio's books are more biographically poignant than *Artists in Crime*. She knew the workings of the life room by heart. 'I enjoyed best the nights when we made time studies from the nude,' she wrote in *Black Beech*.

> The model . . . was Miss Carter, a dictatorial but good-tempered girl who had come to us from show business . . . She was a big fair creature. If a twist of the torso or pelvis was asked of her she would grumble professionally and then grin. The gas heaters roared and the great lamp above the throne held the motionless figure in a pool of light. When the door was opened the students hurried in to manoeuvre for places. In a semi-circle round the throne sat people on 'donkeys' and behind them easels jockeyed for vantage points. 'Have you see [*sic*] it from over there?' Mr Wallwork would mutter, with a jerk of his head and one would hurriedly shift into the gap he indicated. The room looked like a drawing from Trilby: timeless, oddly dramatic, sweltering-hot and alive with concentration.

Richard Wallwork took life classes at Canterbury College in the best of a very academic and staid tradition. But his talented students, and his inspiration as a teacher, made up for many of the progressive ideas that were missing. One of his cleverest students was Olivia Spencer Bower, a young woman freshly back, in 1919, from art school in Britain. She began classes at the end of Ngaio's time at Canterbury College. One day she remembered that 'the model hadn't turned up & Ngaio was doing the job'.

Mr Wallwork was pushing her around on the Throne mid gales of laughter. It was the personality which intrigues. Then one day I met her outside a painting shop in Colombo Street. She had on an enormous camel hair coat with high collar & great wide shoulders. I came home in rather shocked surprise & said to my mother — do you know she's beautiful.

Ngaio sat for her artist friends formally and informally. She knew what it was like to be manhandled by someone setting a pose. She could imagine the consequences of a dagger jammed through the back of the bench.

The tempestuous courtship of Alleyn and Troy continues unresolved through *Artists in Crime*, paralleling the police investigation, and just when the momentum of both is about to founder there is another murder, more hideous and haunting than any before. In Golden Age detective fiction, the horror of decay was usually mitigated by the narrow timeframe, and by makeshift shrouds and the sterile formality of mortuary vans, autopsy tables and coroner's inquests. But this body, that of free-living artist Garcia, waits days to be discovered, in a dusty garret-like studio in a semi-derelict warehouse in the East End of London. You can almost smell his putrefying corpse in the words she uses. Troy has warned Garcia about his lifestyle. 'While you're here you've got to behave yourself. You know what I mean? . . . I won't have any bogus Bohemianism, or free love, or mere promiscuity at Tatler's End. It shocks the servants, and it's messy. All right?' But Garcia cannot contain himself, and pays for his drug addiction and womanizing with his life.

Troy takes an orthodox stand on an issue Ngaio knew plenty about. Art studio life in Christchurch was bohemian. A sense of sexual freedom and fluidity reigned, and this was the *milieu* she sought out before and after her trip to England. But this repressed provincial bohemianism had to be circumspect to survive. Through the bedrock of Christchurch ran seams of liberalism, sexual licence, homosexuality and just plain eccentricity, which were known about but not usually discussed. Troy does not judge Garcia's behaviour; she merely tells him to keep it out of sight.

Artists in Crime was Ngaio's last title published with Geoffrey Bles. Her agent Edmund Cork negotiated a more favourable contract with Collins, who was also Agatha Christie's publisher. She left the company that launched her career with reluctance, but the advantages were undeniable. For the next four titles, she would receive an advance of £250 and 15 per cent royalties. From 1940 her American publisher would be Boston-based Little, Brown. In the meantime, Collins was wonderfully convenient because she was there in England to confirm arrangements and sign papers. Over the years, Ngaio established a close friendship with publishing magnate William (Billy) Collins, who in many ways resembled her dapper, well-mannered, well-meaning detective. Things were good for Ngaio. She was in a more lucrative stable with the promise of financial security, and England was an exciting place to be.

She began writing for New Zealand syndicated newspapers under the pen name 'The Canterbury Pilgrim Again'. Her exhilaration was clear in descriptions of her arrival in spring, which had more significance than New Zealand's. 'Here the trees are so long asleep, the fields hard with frost or sodden with the cold winter rains.' The English countryside was awakening, and she was thrilled to see 'the pricking of young buds', the soft blades of new grass like 'fine hair on the firm margins of hills', and yellow flowers in cottage gardens and cowslips in the hedgerows.

Her excitement was also there in descriptions of events leading up to the coronation of King George VI in May 1937. 'On the road outside Camberley we passed troops on their way up to London,' she told readers. 'When at last the roads turned finally into streets and scarlet buses joined the thickening stream of traffic, we saw banners hung out from all the windows.' London was alive with festive buzz and 'Hyde Park . . . turned into an enormous camp, with horse lines, tank lines, and rows and rows and rows of army tents'. Hazardous scaffolding was erected to clean huge civic monuments. 'All that strange bronze and marble population of London will be smartened for the Coronation,' she wrote. 'Only the rabbits and mice round Peter Pan's pedestal in Kensington Gardens have no need of spring cleaning, for they are polished . . . by small fat hands in woolly gloves . . . London, like a grand old dowager, puts on her royal colours with an air and prepares to welcome a king.' Set against this canvas of pomp and ceremony was her private pleasure at meeting the Rhodes family again. It was not long before their lives became enmeshed in the delights of London's debutante season.

Nelly Rhodes's daughter Maureen was presented, and Ngaio was invited to 'coming out' events that included a Royal Garden Party in June. These occasions provided fascinating slices of upper-class and aristocratic society. She sat with her friend in the chaperones' corner, a 'looker-on', and what she saw became material for another book. 'For *NELLY* to whom this book owes its existence,' she wrote in the dedication to *Death in a White Tie*, one of her most superbly crafted classic English whodunits. The flurry of debutante parties was a perfect setting for blackmail and high-society murder. Greed mixed with jealousy and aristocratic indulgence could conceivably transform the rituals of the mating game into the rituals of a murder game. And in London it could plausibly involve a small, overbred group. With Nelly, Ngaio heard the snatches of society gossip and learned the debutante rules, which were strict and established, but the idea for the murder had another source.

'The facts of the case are simply these,' wrote Fergus Hume in the opening chapter of *The Mystery of a Hansom Cab*. 'On the twenty-seventh day of July, at the hour of twenty minutes to two o' clock in the morning, a hansom cab drove up to the police station, in Grey Street, St Kilda, and the driver made the startling statement that his cab contained the body of a man whom he had reason to believe had been murdered.' The murderer wore an overcoat over his evening dress and a large soft felt hat that concealed his face. These clothes were identical to those of the victim. At the coroner's inquest, an expert witness confirmed that the victim had died from the inhalation of chloroform from a handkerchief held over his mouth. The victim's heart was flaccid with a 'tendency to fatty degeneration', and that accelerated the fatal result.

It was a brilliant concept — a hansom cab was so public and yet so private. Hume understood that it was the perfect place for a murder because the crime could be concealed from the driver seated outside, who was the only witness. Ngaio realized that a horseless cab driven in London in 1937 could be equally secluded. Lord Robert Gospell, known to his friends as Bunchy, is doing undercover work for Roderick Alleyn. Bunchy, an effete, aging, aristocratic party animal who minces his way unremarkably through London's upper echelons, has worked for Scotland Yard before. He is an ideal plant to bust a blackmail ring, and a personal friend of Alleyn's, so when he is discovered dead in a London taxi it gives the detective a terrible jolt.

Ring, ring, ring goes the telephone. He wakes up with a start. It is four o'clock in the morning and Alleyn has nodded off in his room at the Yard. He picks up the receiver and a disembodied voice says: 'There's a case come in, sir. I thought I'd better report to you at once. Taxi with a fare. Says the fare's been murdered and has driven straight here with the body.' Alleyn goes downstairs, thinking all the time of Bunchy and his blackmail ring. He cannot understand it: Bunchy was supposed to telephone and report in. Alleyn is greeted at the entrance by the uniformed sergeant on duty. 'Funny sort of business, Mr Alleyn . . . The cabby insists it was murder and won't say a word till he sees you.' Alleyn opens the door of the cab, turns on the dim roof light, and there is Bunchy, dead.

Alleyn reels in shock. When he recovers a little, he asks the cabby why he is so sure it was murder.

'Gorblimy, governor,' said the driver, 'ain't I seen wiv me own eyes 'ow the ovver bloke gets in wiv 'im, and ain't I seen wiv me own eyes 'ow the ovver bloke gets out at 'is lordship's 'ouse dressed up in 'is lordship's cloak and 'at and squeaks at me in a rum little voice same as 'is lordship.'

Bunchy has been asphyxiated with his cloak, and a consultation with Bunchy's doctor, Sir Daniel Davidson, confirms that Bunchy was ill: a healthy man might die in about four minutes, a man with a heart condition could take less than two, and Bunchy possibly died almost immediately.

The parallels between Ngaio's and Hume's murders are obvious, but beyond the basic framework of the killings, the stories develop differently. Hume's novel predated Conan Doyle's first Sherlock mystery by a year, and Simon Caterson, in his introduction to *The Mystery of a Hansom Cab*, argues that they spearheaded two very different directions in crime fiction. 'Where Conan Doyle concentrates on the establishing of the character of his protagonist, Hume's detectives Gorby and Kilsip are merely two players within an ensemble of actors.' Hume used his mystery to explore the world in which his characters lived rather than developing any one of them into a super-sleuth.

The Queens of Golden Age crime wrote in the Conan Doyle tradition, but in *Death in a White Tie* Ngaio broke away from the conventional model. This mystery was much more a commentary on human behaviour and social mores. It had a super-sleuth at its centre, but also a flavour of what Hume achieved with his anatomizing vision of society. Ngaio's criticism of the rhetorical aspects of the class system and her latent cynicism about the debutante process pushed boundaries. One of the most frequently made, and perhaps most valid, criticisms of Golden Age crime fiction was its class-consciousness and cultural bias. There can be no denying the fact that *Death in a White Tie* was a highly Anglo-centric detective novel, but it was also critical of the hierarchies that support class difference. Ngaio's attitude to snobbery was clear — she disliked it. Her least appealing characters are the most pretentious. General Halcut-Hackett is classic regiment. To meet him, Alleyn 'walked through a hall which, though it had no tongue, yet it did speak of the most expensive and most fashionable house decorator in London'. Halcut-Hackett's study is permeated by the smell of leather and cigars; his face is 'terra-cotta, his moustache formidable, his eyes china blue. He was the original ramrod brass-hat, the subject of all army jokes kindly or malicious. It was impossible to believe his mind was as blank as his face would seem to confess.' But of course it is.

Alleyn's first meeting with Sir Herbert Carrados is equally obnoxious. His opening response is to call on the old boy network. Immediately Alleyn and Fox are seated, Sir Herbert says, 'Your C.O. tells me you are a son of another old friend. I knew your mother very well years ago and she sees quite a lot of my wife, I believe.' Bunchy was murdered after attending Sir Herbert's debutante ball at Marsdon House. The superficiality of his reaction is breathtaking. After briefly bemoaning his friend's death, Sir Herbert comments, 'I cannot help thinking that my hospitality has been cruelly abused.' Alleyn is almost in disbelief: Sir Herbert seems to 'regard murder as a sort of inexcusable *faux pas*'. Selfishness, keeping up appearances and name-dropping are second nature to the worst examples of the upper classes, and their children are no better. Wealthy debutante Bridget O'Brien sets out her priorities for suitor, Donald Potter:

I suppose you think I'm hard and modern and beastly. I dare say I am, but I can't bear the idea of everything getting squalid and drab because we have to worry about money. A horrid little flat, second-rate restaurants, whitewood furniture painted to look fresh and nice. Ugh! I've seen these sorts of marriages.

Then there are the victims of the debutante meat market. In the character of Miss Birnbaum, the plight of the plainer debutante is followed to its isolated and lonely conclusion. Alleyn feels for her. He urges his mother to invite her over. Not to a fashionable party, he tells her, because they give her an inferiority complex. Miss Birnbaum, he explains, is one of the casualties of the season.

Ngaio uses her cosy collection of characters to expose the class system's flaws. Her aspiration was to write novels of social manners that included a puzzle plot. *Death in a White Tie* broke the rules. Its transgressions begin with the fact that the victim is a familiar and likeable character. Bunchy's end comes after the reader has viewed the debutante world from his perspective for some time. The reader knows his motives, has looked into his heart and knows his death will leave London a poorer place. He is someone to grieve over, and one of his pallbearers will be Alleyn himself. Bunchy's murder affects Alleyn as no murder has done before. To his friend's sister, Mildred, he vows: 'if it takes me the rest of my life, and if it costs me my job, by God! if I have to do the killing myself, I'll get this murderer and see him suffer for it'. This murder is personal, and so is Alleyn's desire for retribution. But then *Death in a White Tie* is intimate in many of its revelations. There is more agony for Alleyn over his job, as he tells Troy:

> If you painted a surrealist picture of me I would be made of Metropolitan Police notebooks, one eye would be set in a keyhole, my hands would be occupied with somebody else's private correspondence. The background would be a morgue and the whole pretty conceit wreathed with festoons of blue tape and hangman's rope.

His heightened feelings of despair come from Troy's complete horror of capital punishment. Confused, she tries to explain her feelings to him: 'I don't even know that I agree with the stock arguments against it. It's just one of those nightmare things. Like claustrophobia.'

Capital punishment was one of the serious social issues Ngaio tackled in her writing. Her scruples were exactly the same as those of Alleyn and Troy. Hanging by the neck has a long history in Britain. It was introduced in the fifth century by Anglo-Saxon invaders. During the reign of Henry VIII, an estimated 72,000 people were executed by methods that included beheading, burning, boiling, and hanging with the possibility of drawing and quartering. It was hanging that survived. In 1810, the 'Bloody Code' listed an astonishing 220 crimes punishable by death. An 1832 Act reduced the list by two-thirds. In 1957, it was six. It was not until 1930, and again in 1938, that a five-year experimental suspension of capital punishment was recommended, first by a select committee, then by a clause in the Criminal Justice Bill: one was ignored, and the other postponed by war. Between 1900 and 1949, 621 men and 11 women were executed in England and Wales. The last two executions in England occurred simultaneously on 13 August 1964.

Troy confesses to Alleyn that as a child she adored the *Ingoldsby Legends*. 'One day I came across the one about my Lord Tomnoddy and the hanging. It made the most extraordinary impression on me . . . I used to turn the pages of the book, knowing that I would come to it, dreading it, and yet — I had to read it.'

> *My Lord Tomnoddy jump'd up at the news . . .*
> > *'But to see a man swing*
> > *At the end of a string*
> > *With his neck in a noose, will be quite a new thing!'*

'*Death in a White Tie* might have been called *Siege of Troy*,' wrote Ngaio. Against the backdrop of Bunchy's death, Alleyn woos his future wife. In a heated moment, Donald accuses his uncle Bunchy of being a bloody 'Edwardian relic'. He could have said the same thing about Troy. Although she has modern expectations of career and marriage, her ideas about sex come lukewarm from a Victorian priory. 'I've always been frightened of the whole business,' she tells Alleyn. 'Love and so on . . . The breaking down of all one's reserves. The mental as well as the physical intimacy.' And, perhaps by way of an explanation, she says, 'I don't understand physical love. I don't know how much it means. I'm just plain frightened, and that's a fact.'

Alleyn, often described as monk-like, is no more worldly-wise. In desperation, Lady Alleyn takes her 43-year-old son aside and tells him the facts of life. 'Arrogant masculinity . . . attracts ninety-nine out of a hundred' women, she explains. Alleyn is appalled. 'Do you suggest that I go to Miss Agatha Troy, haul her about her studio by her hair, tuck her under my arrogant masculine arm, and lug her off to the nearest registry office?' No, replies his mother, to the nearest church, 'if you please'. So Alleyn dons a bearskin and demands Troy marry him. He kisses her hard on the mouth, then says, 'And don't think I shall ask you to forgive me . . . You've no right to let this go by. You're too damn particular by half, my girl. I'm your man and you know it.'

Theirs will be a marriage of profile careers. Troy makes a comfortable living from her painting and is famous, as well known in artistic circles as Alleyn is in his. Ngaio writes knowledgably about Troy's work. She paints in a simple, high-keyed late Post-Impressionist style. Her wharf at Suva is an interpretation of a scene rather than a rendering. It is 'an expression of an emotion,' Alleyn thinks, as he admires it, 'rather than a record of a visual impression'. In the real world of contemporary art practice and criticism, what Troy paints may be fashionable in 1937, but it is certainly not avant-garde. However, this is fiction, and the 'private viewing' of her show at the Wiltshire Galleries in Bond Street is a notable social event of the Season. She 'pulled her smart new cap over one eye and walked' in.

> It always embarrassed her intensely to put in these duty appearances at her own exhibitions . . . She became gruff with shyness and her incoherence was mistaken for intellectual snobbishness. Like most painters she was singularly inarticulate on the subject of her work. The careful phrases of literary appreciation showered upon her by highbrow critics threw Troy into an agony of embarrassment.

Like Troy, Ngaio came closest to marrying when she had aspirations to being an artist. While she was at art school, Peter Tokareff proposed to her, and a little later, her middle-aged English stalker also wanted to get married. Both were unlikely candidates, assiduously warned off by her parents. Ngaio never asserted her feelings for these men the way she did when, infatuated, she wanted to follow Allen Wilkie onto the stage or the Rhodes family back to England.

More, however, can be said of her fairytale fiancé, Ned Bristed, who died in Belgium in December 1917. He was the friend of her childhood who later took her to the theatre. Edward Griffith Bristed was a year older than Ngaio and he grew up to be a shepherd. When he enlisted in 1915, and left with the First Battalion of the Canterbury Regiment in the New Zealand Expeditionary Force, he was just 20 years old. He was blue-eyed, fair-haired and, at 5 foot 6 (1.67 metres), of modest height. In June 1917 he was promoted to platoon commander. The comment on his army file read: 'this officer is keen but requires more experience as an officer'. He was killed in action less than a month later.

Although 19-year-old Ngaio towered over Ned, he was a perfect escort. Like her, he enjoyed theatre and the outdoor life. They had a youthful romantic attachment, and probably an engagement. She kept his ruby ring all her life, and this relationship was undoubtedly significant. Ngaio was one of many women whose husbands, lovers or fiancés were killed in the First World War, and they remained single. There was an assumption in Ngaio's circle, partly fostered by Ngaio herself, that Ned's tragic death prevented her from marrying. However, there seems also to have been a distinct lack of drive on Ngaio's part to pursue sexual relationships with men. Although a frightening number of the males of her generation were buried on battlefields and in military graveyards, many also returned. Throughout her life Ngaio had close relationships with men — older, younger, married, homosexual — but she did not, it seems, sleep with them. Sexual reticence was a trait she shared with Troy.

Ngaio continued to write for *The Press* as 'Canterbury Pilgrim' while she worked on *Death in a White Tie*. Her articles included tales of the voyage from New Zealand to England with friends Betty Cotterill and Jean Webster, plus a colourful two-episode account of a remarkable three-month road trip through Europe.

Their journey took them through Belgium, Luxembourg, Germany, Austria, Northern Italy, and France. Towards the end of June, Ngaio, Betty and Jean took off in a car they christened 'B.F.'. 'We said at the beginning that we would not give our car a pet name,' she wrote. 'When . . . our engine and chassis numbers both began with B.F. we felt the dice had been loaded against us.' Their 1934 Ford was the type 'still used by the British police for . . . traffic control'. After crossing the Channel, they drove through Belgium's Flanders fields where Ned Bristed was buried. Ngaio had lived 20 years longer than her fiancé, and almost unbelievably there was the threat of another war; many believed it was only a matter of time.

'All towns look their best by twilight,' wrote Ngaio of Bruges. She watched lamps being lit by people returning home from work to 'houses still warm with the day's sun'. Their drive along the canal was a journey into the past. 'Peasants turned homewards,' she recorded,

and they were by Jean François Millet to a peasant. The waters of the canal were filled with a golden translucence, the long rows of trees stood dark and still, the air was filled with the smell of unshed rain. Along the banks stood single ranks of small flat houses . . . They were houses that might have been drawn by a child with an unerring sense of the decorative.

For a time they were tourists, drinking in a different world. In Bruges, they took a room at the Le Panier d'Or, a tiny hotel kept by two elderly women. 'They led us up stairs as crooked and worn as those of a fairytale [and] into a low room whose windows opened on the square.' Across the cobbled market square scurried nuns escorting schoolchildren, a soldier on a Flanders horse, and three priests. They could just make out 'Breidal and de Coninc', two bronze battle heroes on plinths, and against the skyline the three-tiered shape of Nôtre Dame's famous bell tower. In midsummer warmth, they sat outside a café and 'drank Burgundy and black coffee in glasses with their own filters. Then, before it had grown quite dark, we took a walk through the crooked streets.' They were lulled to sleep by the soporific chime of Nôtre Dame's 49 bells.

The following day they saw Memlinc's and Jan van Eyck's paintings and Michelangelo's *Virgin and Child*, and after lunch set off for 'ancient Ghent', where they marvelled at 'the tall turrets and the pointed towers', then drove across Flanders Plain to Brussels where, suddenly, the traffic converged. Driving on the right-hand side of the road was a challenge. 'Jean read aloud instructions from our admirable A.A. tour; Bet ventured boldly into the heart of lurking traffic; I sat bemused in the back seat.' They crossed Brussels, found the Chaussée de Wavre, which took them to the Forest of Soignes, and on 'into an upland country and our road passed through cornfields where poppies were in bloom'. They saw half a house. 'It was curtained and there were flowers in the window-boxes', but it had been bombed. This sight, the scarlet poppies and the 'great many soldiers' reminded Ngaio of the war. 'In Flanders they are everywhere,' she wrote, 'stocky, workmanlike soldiers going about their business in everyday uniforms. There is something disturbing in this constant reminder of a standing army.'

It was seven o'clock on a hot evening when they drove into Namur, where they dined at a wayside café near the town centre. 'It is difficult to order from Belgian menus,' Ngaio explained. The only word they felt confident to say in French was *poulet*, and they had eaten 'three poulets in as many days'. They were determined to eat something different. Scanning the menu, they spotted *Jambon d'Ardennes* — 'Ham!'— only to find, when it was delivered, that it was 'sliced pig, heavily salted, but otherwise quite raw. In a ghoulish sort of way we rather enjoyed it. The salad, as usual, was excellent.'

Their journey took them deep into Belgium. 'The young forests on the mountains were half-veiled in a delicate smoke. The river's surface was a sliding mirror.' The countryside was old; the smell of new-mown grass and honeysuckle captivating; the fireflies in the orchard a spectacle from their *pension* window. They slowed their pace to savour the trip. At Profondeville, on a brilliant day, Ngaio attempted to paint a sweeping vista of the Meuse River valley with its 'procession of young trees'.

Before long a large Belgian bull, two Flanders draught-horses, and the bull's five wives all gathered about me, sighing heavily . . . Before we left, Monsieur told us how this same valley had been cut down by shrapnel after the battle of Dinant in August 1914. Over and over again he made a violent gesture with his hands. Coupé! Coupé! C'était terrible! Coupé!

That is why all the trees in the valley of the Meuse are so young.

Ngaio's last 'Pilgrim' article ended in the Meuse Valley with the words 'to be continued', but there would be a five-year gap.

It was not until she wrote the script for a series of radio broadcasts in 1942 that she continued her account of the road trip, taking up their story in the Duchy of Luxembourg. Ngaio's description of the countryside was vivid and sensual, her picture of roadside cottages infused with sensitivity. 'There are glimpses . . . into lighted rooms where families gather for their evening meal,' she wrote, 'glimpses that are arresting & dramatic because the lamplit figures are unaware that outside in the dusk there is a stranger who sees them so briefly & so intimately.'

At a corner inn they stopped the car and took instructions from three tipsy men. 'I shall always be grateful to them', Ngaio recalled, for they directed the travellers up the road to the enchanting medieval village of Esche-sur-Sûre. They drove on until they came to a tunnel. 'The only way into Esche-sur-Sûre was by the Rip-van-Winkleish, the Peer Gyntish, the altogether goblin-like way of a hole in the hills. Dank walls closed about us & at the far end there was a dazzling little medieval landscape.' The Sûre River they had been following looped at this point, turning the village, with its fortified castle, into an island. Daylight was disappearing as they drove through the streets and stopped outside an inn directly above the river where it 'widened into a millpond'.

They were given one huge room with three feather beds. 'It was a three-bears sort of apartment with windows that opened above the water.' That night they feasted on chicken *pâté*, a variety of spicy sausage, a mixed salad and a glass of rough wine. 'Our lodging for the night in this pleasant inn cost us about 5/-,' Ngaio explained. 'But then three months' travel in Europe in 1937, including our shares in the car cost each of us only £40, & what richness we found on our journey.'

Before bed they explored the village with its 'round towers, pepper-pot roofs and loophole windows'. Ngaio tried to make a sketch but found herself surrounded by a crowd, first of children, then of adults — all eager to communicate. By the time they finished their pantomime of gestures interspersed with broken French, German and English, it was too dark to paint. Ngaio looked up again at her fairytale subject. Through the blackness, on the castle battlements, she could just make out, 'of all extraordinary things, a monkey in a skyblue coat, chattering at me. He ran up & down on the battlement shaking his chain.'

That night the heat and humidity precipitated a massive thunderstorm. Everything rumbled as they sat up and listened. The next day Ngaio was up early to paint. She thought her work was insipid, but kept it as a reminder of an adventure that would otherwise seem 'more like a dream'.

But the dream had a darker *doppelgänger*. At Wasserbillig they crossed the border into Nazi Germany. 'Lots of people thought it was wonderful,' she remembered. 'Even the humblest tourist saw only the fine rooms in the Herrenvock house. The Bluebeard cupboards were kept tactfully locked.' But not at Beilstein on the Mosel River, where they were delayed three weeks while Betty Cotterill recovered from pleurisy. If they had moved on they would have missed the dark side of this picturesque town.

'Think of the nicest woodcut . . . in the oldest book you have ever seen,' Ngaio wrote. Imagine a town with a castle, with houses with rooftops 'crazily joined together', 'where hay is stored in the attic rooms & the cow lives in the basement', and you have pictured Beilstein. The sound of singing and the hospitable clink of glasses lured them up twisting stairs to a wine garden owned by the widow Lippmann and her son. It was with the Lippmanns that they stayed. During the day the village emptied of all but the youngest children and crones, who would 'lean out of their windows & screech amiably across the square'. At sunset, the able-bodied peasants returned from sweltering vineyards 'dyed from head to foot, in cerulean blue' from copper sulphate sprays.

It seemed an idyllic existence until they took a walk in hills behind the castle, and discovered a carefully concealed Jewish graveyard. 'The headstones bore the symbol of interwoven triangles & carried among them most of the familiar village names.' Nearly 100 years before, a vine-growing nobleman had introduced Jewish workers to the district and they had settled and inter-married. Almost everyone was touched by this legacy, especially Frau and Herr Koppel, 'an old couple, the man disabled, who bore very clearly, the physical signs of their mixed ancestry. They were terribly poor & eked out a livelihood by selling sweets & screws of tobacco & faded postcards in their room on the market square.'

The sound of jackboots on Beilstein's cobblestones heralded a new era. While Ngaio sat on the castle battlements writing letters, she watched three Gestapo arrive by river raft. Disturbed by what she saw, she joined her friends in their room overlooking the square. 'All over the little town there was the sound of slamming doors. Followed by complete silence', and then the sound of Gestapo boots as they went around the houses. Before departing they pinned up a notice in the square. That evening a bell was rung to gather townspeople in the square. Leaflets were distributed and the mayor read a proclamation.

'The people of the town were warned that they would no longer be considered true Nordic citizens if they continued to patronize the tiny shop kept by the old couple . . . or communicate with them in any way.' Ngaio saw the Koppels once more a few nights later. It was stiflingly hot, the early hours of the morning, and she was awake and restless. She got up and went to the window that looked over the square. In the moonlight she caught sight of something unexpected. It was the old woman standing 'stock-still'. 'Her hands were folded in a shawl, her heavy face up turned to the light. She had dared to come out for a moment.' Beyond her in deeper shadow was her husband. 'I felt myself an intruder & I drew away from the window. But I couldn't help listening.' For a long time there was silence, then the faint tinkle of a shop bell. They had gone indoors — they would be gone for good. The scene was ominous, and Ngaio knew it. 'It seemed to me that the little town was threatened with madness, that a great surge of lethal insanity was rolling up the Mosel like a tidal wave & that these peasants with their little dram of Jewish blood were doomed.'

Ngaio wrote when she could during the day and late at night. She sat out on the battlements or in the Lippmanns' terraced garden among carnations and 'night-scented stocks' and worked on *Death in a White Tie*. They savoured the delights of the wine cellar. They paddled and swam in the Mosel River and collected strawberries from the nearby woods, where one afternoon they met a young New Zealander who proclaimed the wonders of Nazi Germany. But all the time there were signs that something heinous was happening. Ngaio saw a group of small schoolboys on holiday with their teacher. All day he drilled them. 'They even bathed to orders bobbing up & down in routine & morning & evening they recited a sort of creed ending with their drawn out cry — "Heil Hitler".' A vitriolic denunciation of the Jews was nailed to cottage doors in Beilstein. The people were frightened, and their fear was infectious. As soon as Betty Cotterill was well, the New Zealanders left.

Their 'journey through 6 realms' would take them 'from London to Vienna', but sadly the rest of their itinerary was unrecorded. Ngaio met up with Nelly Rhodes in October and they holidayed in Monte Carlo. Unlike the publicly documented road trip, this was a private meeting of close friends. During her 1937–38 English visit, Ngaio spent a considerable amount of time with the Rhodes family. She stayed with them for a while in an old schoolhouse, and at country residences. It is likely Ngaio was with Nelly when she toured Devon and Cornwall in early 1938, and stayed in the fishing village of Polperro on the Cornish coast. Ngaio developed a great affection for the Rhodes children, who were getting older and more interesting, and during this visit she illustrated 'Over the Edge of the Earth', a children's story written by Eileen, the eldest Rhodes daughter. The slightly stiff pen-and-ink illustrations have a redeeming, surreal quality that is intriguing. Unfortunately, the enthusiastically conceived joint project was never published.

In 1938, Ngaio had the thrill of seeing a pair of titles published that represented the fruition of nearly two years' hard work. *Artists in Crime* and *Death in a White Tie* were well received by British and American critics. There was a sense that her stature had not yet been fully recognized. 'Miss Marsh is a novelist of variety as well as an expert craftsman of crime,' wrote the critic for *Punch* in February 1938. 'She deserves to be much better known.' There was an appreciation, too, of her ingenuity and sheer brilliance at evoking a grisly scene. The critic for the *Church Times* described the second murder in *Artists in Crime*, as 'probably the best bit of crime writing of the year', and, in the opinion of *The Observer*, Ngaio Marsh specialized in 'cunning and novel modes of inflicting death' and had a 'bold and happy gift of portraiture'.

The reception of *Death in a White Tie* a little later in the year was equally enthusiastic, although, as Edmund Cork had predicted, there were mixed responses to the introduction of Alleyn's love interest. '*Death in a White Tie* is the best type of detective story and well up to Miss Marsh's previous high standards,' wrote the reviewer for *The Times Literary Supplement*, in September.

[It] has only one serious defect. The chief inspector is made to pursue his love affair . . . It would be a pity if the example set by Miss Sayers with Lord Peter Wimsey of entangling her detective of seemingly settled and delightful bachelor habits in a serious-minded love affair were to be regularly followed by all writers of detective stories . . . romance is not Miss Marsh's metier, and some of the dialogue leaves one a bit hot under the collar. It is hoped, with all due respect to Miss Sayers, that when Alleyn is next confronted with a corpse it will not be in the course of his honeymoon.

For many enthusiasts, and even crime fiction reviewers, the introduction of a series wife to partner a series detective was corrosive of conventions designed to secure the purity of the puzzle.

Although this thinking was laced with implicit misogyny, it was not an exclusively male argument. Agatha Christie found love 'a terrible bore in detective stories' and felt that it belonged more appropriately in romance stories. 'To force a love motif into what should be a scientific process went much against the grain.'

Christie was safe in making these assertions because her detectives were not obviously marriageable material: a heart-stopping romance was not expected of Poirot or Miss Marple. Wimsey, Campion and Alleyn, on the other hand, were youngish, red-blooded males with assumed sexual needs. As Jessica Mann points out, 'a series hero who is allowed to mature in other ways must either prove to be a selfish bastard' — like James Bond who played the field — '[or] fix his affection on one particular girl and . . . marry her'. Without some degree of sexual and emotional development, these detectives would be stunted. Series romance and marriage fitted also with their authors' shared aspiration to raise the detective novel above the level of a puzzle plot. If their sleuths were to become more psychologically complex, they needed a third dimension — an emotional life.

Harriet Vane had simmered away as a potential long-term liaison for Lord Peter Wimsey since her trial for the murder of former lover, Philip Boyes, in *Strong Poison* in 1930. Wimsey is transfixed at their first meeting. She will face the hangman's noose if he does not find the real killer. Vane and Boyes have been living together as lovers. Boyes has been an opponent of marriage, so when he turns around a year later and proposes, she is angered by his hypocrisy and leaves. When he is found dead from arsenic poisoning, Vane has both motive and method because she is a crime writer researching this very subject for a new book. All the clues point to her. Certainly Sayers drew on her own life when she created Vane. Like Sayers, Vane is a first-generation woman graduate from Oxford. At heart she is an intellectual attracted, like Sayers, to academia.

Vane's relationship with bohemian-scrupled Boyes is like that of Sayers with John Cournos, and with Bill White. Like her creator, Vane lives in a bedsit in Mecklenburgh Square, Bloomsbury, socializes with artists and writers, and makes an independent living from her crime fiction writing. She has similar experiences as a writer, and holds similar views. Vane refuses Wimsey's proposal, even after she is acquitted of murder on his evidence. Gratitude, she believes, is no basis for marriage. Like Agatha Troy, Vane is reluctant to give up her freedom, and she finds Wimsey shallow and overbearing. Wimsey pursues his sweetheart, finally marrying her in *Busman's Honeymoon* in 1937.

In keeping with the swashbuckling flavour of her writing, Margery Allingham's love interest for Campion is adventurous — the Amelia Earhart-style Amanda Fitton. Campion first meets her, aged 17, in *Sweet Danger* in 1933. Her parents are dead and she lives in the crumbling mansion of Pontisbright Mill in Suffolk, with her brother and sister. They are poor, and to make ends meet the ingenious Amanda works out a way of powering an electric car from a local watermill. This is an aphrodisiac for Campion, who has been called in to establish the ownership of Averna, a tiny oil-rich principality on the Adriatic. The Fittons are claimants, and Campion is charged with protecting them from thugs hired by an unscrupulous developer. At the end of the novel, Amanda asks Campion to take her into partnership and hints that 'in about six years' time she may be ready to marry. In *The Fashion in Shrouds*, published in 1937, Amanda reappears as an aircraft engineer. To distract attention from an awkward investigative moment, she announces her engagement to Campion. The super-sleuth is shocked, but warms to the idea. After a party to celebrate the breaking-off of their fake engagement, the jilted Campion argues with Amanda and throws her in the river. Somehow she manages to see this as a demonstration of his affection and at end of the novel they become properly engaged.

These romantic liaisons in detective fiction prove to be ideal marriages, the sort the writers would have wanted for themselves. They are pairings of equality, where a super-sleuth's match is an equally capable wife, who makes no career compromises. Amanda Campion's work takes precedence over housekeeping, and Peter Wimsey is emphatic that Harriet's writing is not to be interrupted by domestic trivia. Within the conventional institution of marriage, the Queens of Crime tackled a tricky modern problem that did not necessarily reflect the views of the status quo. Women's equality in the workplace and at home was not a social assumption like the hierarchies of class, culture and religion. For many it was controversial. The Queens were not flagrant feminists or subversives, yet it was revolutionary in a genre that was assumed to reflect society's established mores, to portray a marriage of equality as the norm.

In *Overture to Death*, published in 1939, but inspired by Ngaio's experiences in 1938, Alleyn writes a letter to Troy, committing himself to a modern marriage. In it he admits that his profession makes him 'a chancey sort of lover . . . A fly-by-night who speaks to you at nine o'clock on Saturday evening, and soon after midnight is down in Dorset looking at lethal pianos.' He makes a pledge:

My dear and my darling Troy, you shall disappear, too, when you choose, into the austerity of your work, and never, never, never shall I look sideways, or disagreeably, or in the manner of the martyred spouse. Not as easy a promise as you think, but I make it.

While Wimsey, Campion, and Alleyn were either engaged or honeymooning, Hercule Poirot was safely single and holidaying aboard a paddle steamer on the Nile.

In 1937, Agatha Christie was in the Middle East with her husband Max Mallowan, who was leading an archaeological expedition to Tell Brak in Syria. Christie photographed and recorded finds at the site, and during her spare time began *Death on the Nile*, a novel set in Egypt where they took a break. She uses love mixed with greed as the motive for her crime. Simon Doyle and his rich heiress wife, Linnet, are on a luckless honeymoon, tracked down and stalked relentlessly by the thwarted Jacqueline de Bellefort, Simon's former fiancée and Linnet's former best friend. Linnet is eventually found shot through the head, with the letter 'J' drawn in blood on the wall to incriminate Jacqueline. Christie uses this romantic triangle to generate one of her cleverest plots. The novel was one of her favourites, and certainly, she thought, one of her best 'foreign travel' books.

Death on the Nile was well received by critics, some of whom were rapturous. 'She has excelled herself,' wrote the critic for the *Evening News*, '. . . must call for unqualified praise.' Even *The Times* reviewer admired the complexity: 'Must be read twice, once for enjoyment and once to see how the wheels go round.' Agatha Christie was at a peak.

Hercule Poirot remains untouched, however. He never faces the complications of sharing his life with anyone and never changes to accommodate it. Christie puts romance at the heart of her plot, but not in the heart of her sleuth. To her, the novel of social manners was another genre. The most she expected of her principal characters was that they seemed 'real and alive', and this is what she felt she had done with aplomb in *Death on the Nile*. She also cleverly evoked the Middle East. Christie shared Ngaio's passion for travel and her most interesting settings were taken from her real-life experiences. 'To Sybil Burnett who also loves wandering the world' she wrote in the dedication to *Death on the Nile*.

Writing was a portable occupation that an upper-middle-class wife could do while she accompanied her husband. Remarkably, Christie always saw Mallowan's profession as an archaeologist as more important than her own as a writer. She was openly mercenary about what she did: she wrote now to make money. Mallowan's archaeological digs were expensive and at times financed from their own pockets. But she believed that her role as a wife was her principal occupation. Perhaps this is why she never floated Hercule Poirot's paddle steamer with anything more than murder.

For Ngaio, the English country village had some of the same sense of strangeness that the Nile had for Christie. *Overture to Death* came out of her time with Nelly Rhodes in the wintry south of England. 'The upland air was cold after the stuffiness of the car. It smelt of dead leaves and frost.' Alleyn notes the physical presence of winter as he steps out of the car in the Vale-of-Pen-Cuckoo, just as Ngaio would have noticed it at the tail end of her 1937–38 trip.

He has been called in to investigate a most unlikely murder, which has occurred at a Pen-Cuckoo fund-raising performance of a well-known West End play. The greying Idris Campanula is called upon at the last moment to stand in as pianist for her aging rival for the vicar's affection, Eleanor Prentice, who is distraught. The victorious Campanula sits down at the keyboard to begin her *pièce de résistance*, Rachmaninoff's 'Prelude in C'. She holds her bony left hand in the air. Then down it comes. 'Pom. *Pom*. POM. The three familiar pretentious chords.' Then she puts her left foot on the soft pedal, and it happens.

The air was blown into splinters of atrocious clamour. For a second nothing existed but noise — hard racketing noise. The hall, suddenly thick with dust, was also thick with a cloud of intolerable sound. And, as the dust fell, so the pandemonium abated and separated into recognisable sources. Women were screaming. Chair legs scraped . . . the piano hummed like a gigantic top.

Miss Campanula slumps forward and her face slides down the sheet of music. She has been shot between the eyes by a 'Heath-Robinson-style-gadget' rigged inside the piano. It is a childish prank of village bad-boy Georgie Biggins, who has set up an ingenious system of strings and pulleys to fire a water pistol at one of the unsuspecting spinsters. But the murderer has exchanged the child's water pistol for a Colt 32.

The tension that holds this English cosy together is 'jealousy rooted in sex'. Eleanor Prentice is a thin, bloodless, bucktoothed woman of about 49. Idris Campanula, her buxom foe, is a large-framed, hot-flushed, wire-haired woman of equal antiquity. One is sanctimonious, the other arrogant, and they are rampant for the vicar, who holds them at bay with holy conversation which, on one horrible occasion, in a private moment with Idris Campanula, abandons him completely. As the vicar explains to Alleyn, she misunderstands his silence.

The next moment she was, to be frank, in my arms. It was without any exception the most awful thing that has ever happened to me. She was sobbing and laughing at the same time. I was in agony. I couldn't release myself.

Ngaio knew exactly how awkward that experience could be because she'd had it in the headmistress's office at St Margaret's. 'It's beastly for you,' says Alleyn, 'but I'm sure you should tell me', and he is right, because this is the trigger for the murder. It is Ngaio's vivid picture of the sexual tension between two spinsters that gives this novel its bittersweet pull. Although they are caricatures in their grotesqueness, dependent on readers' internalized misogyny and fear of aging, they are recognizable people. The stalking spinster is easily visualized in Dinah's words of warning to her young fiancé, Henry. 'She creeps and creeps, and she's simply brimful of poison. She'll drop some of it into our cup of happiness if she can.'

The critics loved it. 'Although I would have considerable difficulty in pronouncing Miss Ngaio Marsh's first name,' wrote the reviewer for the *Daily Mail*, 'I have no difficulty at all in pronouncing her *Overture to Death* a first-rate murder novel thoroughly justifying its selection by the Crime Club.' The critic for the *Irish Independent*, writing in June 1939, was equally ecstatic. 'Ingenuity is only one of the author's assets.'

> She draws very clearly the characters of the half-dozen members of the village 'upper ten' who are suspects of the murder. She describes the procedure of police investigation as authentically as if she had served for years in the detective branch of a police force. Above all, she seems a natural storyteller with a gift for concise and dramatic writing. The hall mark of first class is stamped large over this book.

Commentators were now consistently identifying the qualities that set Ngaio apart from the plethora of other detective writers: her characterization, her narrative ability, her ingenuity, and especially her humour, which 'performs the important function of making them more palatable'. The writer for *The Times Literary Supplement* thought it 'well written' and enjoyable, but expressed relief that Alleyn's 'romance, which figured so prominently in Miss Marsh's last novel, is mercifully thrust into the background'. Only the *Daily Herald* had a problem with her treatment of older women. 'Spinsters are having a tough time in detective fiction just now. And it is the women writers who are responsible.'

Ironically, Ngaio was unmarried and 44 years old herself when she concocted this bleak picture of spinsterhood. She knew the clichés perhaps better than her colleagues, and feasted on them unmercifully for her inspiration. Christie had been more sympathetic in her creation of Miss Marple. In *Overture to Death*, Ngaio's spinsters are contrasted with an attractive, young, newly engaged couple and a straw-blonde *femme fatale*, who has lured the local doctor away from his invalid wife. And there is Alleyn's love letter to Troy: ' . . . shall we have a holiday cottage in Dorset? . . . high up in the world so that you could paint the curves of the hills . . . Shall we have one? I'm going to marry you next April, and I love you with all my heart.' Ngaio offers a polarity that suggests either romantic companionship or sexual frustration and doom. But this is conventional light fiction, untrammelled by political correctness, and Ngaio is equally hard on her geriatric men.

> Mr. Saul Tranter was an old man with a very bad face. His eyes were no bigger than a pig's and they squinted, wickedly close together, on either side

of his mean little nose. His mouth was loose and leered uncertainly, and his few teeth were objects of horror. He smelt very strongly indeed of dirty old man, dead birds and whisky.

Ngaio was a superb creator especially of cameo characters, who had about them a whiff of the stage, which tipped them occasionally towards the 'stock'. On the whole, the people she created satisfied rather than challenged readers' established prejudices. Ngaio's spinsters were as many in mainstream society imagined them to be: sick and frustrated.

Interestingly, Nigel Bathgate makes one of his last appearances in *Overture to Death*. Alleyn is not pleased to discover that Nigel is in Pen-Cuckoo and is less willing to take him into his confidence. When he and Fox are going over 'the facts', Alleyn suggests that Nigel is out of the loop:

We are, as might be . . . two experts on a watch-tower in the middle of a maze. 'Look at the poor wretch,' we say and nudge each other, 'there he goes into the same old blind alley. Jolly comical,' we say, and then we laugh like anything. Don't we, Fox?

In the next novel, Alleyn and Troy are already married and she will increasingly take over Nigel's role of detective's stooge, although she remains an ancillary character. She introduces a new dynamic around which some of the future plots will turn. But it will be a cerebral relationship. Commentators complained that their pillow talk was stilted. The critic for *The Times Literary Supplement* was not alone in thinking romance was 'not Miss Marsh's metier' and that some of the dialogue left 'one a bit hot under the collar'. Romance writing was not Ngaio's strong suit, and she kept it to a minimum. But perhaps it was her restraint that made her love scenes alluring — for alluring they often were — and decades of subsequent books groaning with sex have probably done nothing to alter their appeal.

But Alleyn's most consistent and long-serving companion in crime is neither Troy nor Nigel, but Inspector Fox, whose role in investigations grows after his first appearance in *Enter a Murderer* in 1935. He is the huge, lumbering, gentle giant, a counter-balance to the highly-strung, fine-boned, fast-moving Alleyn, who is regularly likened to a cat or a faun. They complement each other. It is an attraction of opposites. As writer Kathryne Slate McDorman points out,

'Fox represents what most of the upper and upper-middle classes of the early twentieth century would have regarded as the best of working-class virtues'. He is solid, steady and unshakable in his loyalty to his superior; he can be sensitive or brutish; he is immune to social snobbery. Fox is Alleyn's secret weapon with the working classes. Alleyn's own social background sets him in upstairs amber, but Fox has the flexibility to move between floors, questioning anyone from the butler to the scullery maid with impunity.

Alleyn and Fox's partnership is tested in the last novel directly inspired by Ngaio's sojourn in south England. While in Cornwall she stayed in the fishing village of Polperro, which was the model for Ottercombe in *Death at the Bar*. Fox is poisoned in an attempt by the murderer to foil the investigation. In an excellent sherry, Fox ingests a near-fatal dose of a cyanide-based rat poison. As he desperately tries to save Fox's life, Alleyn touchingly realizes what his colleague means to him.

Alleyn scarcely knew he had a body of his own. His body and breath, precariously and dubiously, belonged to Fox . . .

'Fox,' said Alleyn. 'Fox, my dear old thing.' Fox's lips moved. Alleyn took his handkerchief and wiped that large face carefully.

Overture to Death was dedicated to 'The Sunday Morning Party: G.M.L. Lester, Dundas and Cecil Walker, Norman and Miles Stacpoole Batchelor and MY FATHER', and *Death at the Bar* was based on pub culture around a dartboard, and a lethal game of cyanide-tipped darts. This was reminiscent of the Marton Cottage dartboard, and her father and his buddies who gathered around to play.

'On the whole ours was a masculine household,' Ngaio remembered in *Black Beech*. 'For days on end the only other woman in it was our much loved housekeeper, Mrs Crawford, who looked after my father when I was away . . . by and large it was a male establishment with the emphasis on my father's generation rather than my own.' On Sunday mornings and evenings, and on Tuesday nights, Dundas and Cecil Walker, Henry Jellett, an uncle by marriage known as Unk, and other friends met at Marton Cottage to have dinner and play Lexicon and darts with Ngaio's father.

She was thinking of home and her obligation to her father, and these novels, published in 1940, reflect that orientation. By April 1938, Ngaio was back in

New Zealand. Filial obligation had overpowered her desire to travel. As she would write in the introduction to a radio talk, broadcast in 1943:

The itch for travel is a chronic disease — incurable, insistent, sometimes flaring up, sometimes more or less quiescent . . . The cure is at best temporary, the treatment curious. For a comfortable home, a rational existence, an ordered routine, & a chosen circle of friends; the patient must substitute a jolting train, a heaving ship, a muddled surge of complete strangers, & an incoherent mode of life . . . Tormented, during treatment, by blistered heels, lost luggage & a perpetual search for somewhere to lay his head, why does this odd creature desire so ardently the renewal of all the uncomfortable conditions?

The itinerant existence was one she loved, especially with the Rhodes family, who enjoyed a particularly indulgent version of it. Moments of 'arrival' made the ordeals of travel melt away. 'For the incurable & unrepentant traveller; a landfall, a foreign port, the great white lights of a foreign city still unexplored, or the modest lamps of a strange village at the end of a darkling road — these things are happiness.' But this was happiness she would not experience again for many years. Her father was old and increasingly dependent, and in her travels she had witnessed the seeds of the Jewish Holocaust and the rise of the Nazi Party's machine in Germany. The Second World War, which began in September 1939, would change Europe's frontiers to frontlines. It would stop elective travel and force New Zealanders, other than military personnel, to remain at home.

'It can't be explained,' Ngaio wrote of the addiction to travel. 'It can be appeased in peace time only by indulgence; or in these bad days of war by some such counter-irritant as hard work.' To stem her desire to travel, Ngaio would work in the theatre and on her books. New Zealand amateur and repertory theatre, thrown back on its own resources, would prove fertile ground.

Ironically, too, although the war interrupted so many things, it did not affect the ascendancy of the detective novel. People continued to read crime fiction while bombs rained down and vast casualty lists were posted. Special pocket-sized editions of detective novels were produced for easy reading in bomb shelters, and lending libraries posted crime sections close to bunker entrances. The demand for intriguing puzzle plots would soar.

Constable
of France

CHAPTER FOUR

Death Down Under

D on't pretend to be so *feeble!*' cries Roberta in a fury at Henry's
acquiescence.

'But it's true,' Henry explodes with equal vehemence.

We are feeble. We're museum pieces. Carryovers from another age. Two
generations ago we didn't bother about what we would do when we
grew up. We went into regiments, or politics, and lived on large estates . . .
Everything was all ready for us from the moment we were born . . . Now
look at us! My papa is really an amiable dilettante. So, I suppose, would I
be if I could go back into the setting, but you can't do that without money.
Our trouble is that we go on behaving in the grand leisured manner without
the necessary backing. It's very dishonest of us, but we're conditioned to it.
We're the victims of inherited behaviourism.

Roberta Grey and Henry Lamprey are standing on a tussock-covered ridge in
South Canterbury's Mackenzie Country. They have walked up through bush
to the lower slope of little Mount Silver, where there is a view over Deepacres
sheep station and across the paddocks, roads and shelter belts that stretch as far

106

as the eye can see. Henry's father, Lord Charles, has bought Mount Silver Station on a whim and renamed it after the family estate in Kent. He has brought his family out to New Zealand and farms the rough unrelenting landscape like a country squire, with a butler, maids, a nanny, and a governess and a French tutor for his six children.

Lord Charles has failed in his attempt to become a runholder. His efforts to assimilate have been so extreme that Henry believes his father has used sheep-dip on his hair. He has proved hopeless, especially with the dogs. He bought four at the exorbitant cost of £20 each, and when he sat on horseback his whistle was so feeble that his mount gazed blissfully into space, the dogs went to sleep and the sheep stood and stared at him in 'mild surprise'. When he swore and shouted at them, he lost his voice. Henry feels their coming out to New Zealand was a mistake.

Only child Roberta has been drawn into the Lamprey circle since meeting Henry's sister Frid at boarding school. When the winter holidays came, she stayed at Deepacres, and from then on at weekends and during the long summer break. Enchanted with the Lampreys, she has stayed regularly for two years. But in the midst of this idyllic existence is the sense of impending disaster. They are running out of money. Lady Charles has begun economizing: they will no longer take *Punch* or the *Tatler*, and will dispense with table napkins to save laundry bills. A second, cheaper, car is purchased to save taking out the Rolls so often. Of course, they are shocked when these strategies prove insufficient. The decision is made to return to England.

The memory of her 1937–38 stay with the Rhodes family was still vivid as Ngaio wrote *Surfeit of Lampreys* in 1939. By the end of that year, she realized that she was trapped in New Zealand by the war, so the novel may have been inspired by her need to revisit and pay tribute to the family who had changed her life. By fictionalizing her friends she could relive cherished experiences. In the quiet hours of the morning she mixed real life with fiction to create one of her most acclaimed pieces of writing, and the most personally revealing of all her novels. 'There can be no doubt,' wrote Ngaio many years later in *Black Beech*, 'however much we may disclaim the circumstance, that fictional characters are pretty often derived, sub-consciously or not, from persons of the writer's acquaintance.' She was writing about the Rhodes family, whom she also called the Lampreys in her autobiography. Things were changed in the novel, and a murder or two added, but these people were based on the Rhodeses, and

Ngaio's connection to them had begun before she was born.

The Pakeha settlement of the South Canterbury High Country started with George Rhodes and his brothers in 1851, when they drove a flock of 5,000 sheep south from Banks Peninsula to a tract of land that would become The Levels. This station covered a huge area of 150,000 acres (60,700 hectares), between the Opihi and Pareora rivers, and from the snow-capped Southern Divide to the sea. Within four years the flock was increased to 24,000 sheep.

The Levels' far-flung boundary lines were subject to sheep rustling. James McKenzie was a poor Gaelic-speaking Scottish immigrant who was found with 1,000 of the Rhodeses' sheep, which he had rustled. He and his border collie, Friday, proved an elusive pair, slipping through the hands of a posse sent to apprehend them. Even when he was caught, McKenzie escaped. A £1,000 reward was offered for his capture, and it was Sergeant Edward Seager, Ngaio's grandfather, who arrested him in Lyttelton and was a witness at his trial. As Seager remembered, 'the only time Mackenzie [*sic*] showed any emotion was when the dog was produced in court and tried in vain to reach her master'. The giant ginger-haired sheep-stealer broke down. 'Poor lassie! They've got you too!' he is reputed to have cried. A Rhodes family album contains a photograph of a border collie inscribed 'Yours faithfully Friday', and she is said to have ended her days on The Levels as a favourite dog.

George Rhodes died at 47, of a chill he caught dipping sheep, but his family continued, and one branch moved to Fendalton in Christchurch, where young Tahu Rhodes and his sister Marie played with Ngaio before the Marsh family moved to Cashmere. The Rhodes family lived across the lane in a very large house, with a long drive and a lodge at its gate. They had 'carriages and gigs, a motor, grooms, servants and a nanny'. Ngaio's friendship with the fairytale family continued at St Margaret's, where Marie Rhodes was also a pupil. Ngaio visited the Rhodes farm at Tai Tapu on a school trip, which she wrote about for the school magazine.

But it was not until after Tahu Rhodes had been injured at Gallipoli, married Nelly Plunket and had three children that they met again. It was in Christchurch, in June 1924, when Ngaio was directing an Unlimited Charities production of her childhood favourite, *Bluebell in Fairyland*, and two of the Rhodes children were in the production. 'After the final performance I went dancing with the Lampreys,' wrote Ngaio in *Black Beech*. 'In the early hours of the morning we drove to their house, twenty miles away in the country. Its doors opened into a life whose scale of values, casual grandeur, cock-eyed gaiety and vague friendliness will bewilder and delight me for the rest of my days. If one can be said to fall in love with a family I fell in love with the Lampreys. It has been a lasting affair.'

After the Rosemary Rees tour, and her own of the North Island with Tor King and Jimmy in 1922, Ngaio had settled in Christchurch, producing plays for amateur societies, and teaching drama at the newly founded Wauchop School of Drama and Dance. At this time an organization called Unlimited Charities began in the city to produce a large annual show for charity. Ngaio and her parents attended the inaugural meeting in rooms above a piano shop. There she met the Honourable Mrs Rhodes, and their friendship began. As a child, Ngaio, the daughter of a bank teller, had been taken to a public procession where she had glimpsed her young contemporary, Nelly Plunket, daughter of the Governor, in an official carriage with a crown on the door. Socially, the friendship was unequal, but time and talent would tie their lives together. Nelly Rhodes became the patron of Unlimited Charities, and her children delighted in the *Bluebell in Fairyland* production, which was an extravaganza of choreographed dancers, orchestral music and magnificent costuming. Ngaio's sedate existence was suddenly technicolored. At last she had found the magic ingredient of romance.

The Rhodeses' weekend parties at Meadowbank, which Ngaio attended, were prominent social occasions. The family 'lived on a scale probably unmatched in any other New Zealand establishment except Government House'. When the Duke and Duchess of York visited New Zealand in 1927, Meadowbank was on their itinerary, although the duke came alone as his wife had tonsillitis. He dined with the Rhodeses, and the next evening attended one of their charity cabarets. The royal visit to Meadowbank was 'typical of a Lamprey occasion'. Both Ngaio and the family were 'grossly unmusical', yet a nursery song around the piano seemed to entertain their eminent guest. 'I can only suppose that he too was unmusical or that we were bad enough to be funny: I know we were bad.'

But these were the glowing embers of a dying way of life. In reality, the Rhodes family lived a precarious existence based on inherited wealth and family remittances. There was always a feeling that it might not last. This did not, however, stop the Rhodeses from being great philanthropists. Life had been generous to them and they were open-handedly generous to others. 'While the Lampreys did not seem able to earn anything for themselves,' Ngaio remembered, 'they were enormously successful in raising princely sums for good causes.' The Rhodes family sponsored a cabaret and amateur vaudeville group called Touch and Go, which Ngaio produced and toured. Altogether, she estimated the Rhodeses' earnings for charity at £12,000. Their way of life, though, was difficult to maintain in New Zealand, and then there was the children's education to consider: as they grew older, English schools were deemed essential. Ngaio's 'Brideshead' days of charity drama mixed with astonishing luxury lasted little more than two years.

Like Roberta Grey, Ngaio was desolate at the Lampreys' departure. It felt as if summer had gone forever and every day from now on would be a hoar frost. An invitation came for Ngaio to stay with the family in England and she would write a detective novel. A similar invitation comes for Roberta and she will become involved in a murder. Before she began writing *Surfeit of Lampreys*, Ngaio, at dinner with her surgeon, Sir Hugh Acland, enquired about the quickest and cleanest way of dispatching a victim. He recommended a sharp instrument, perhaps a skewer, pushed through the eye socket into the brain. 'For Sir Hugh and Lady Acland with my love,' she wrote in the dedication to the novel. 'For the one since he has helped me so often with my stories and for the other since she likes stories about London.' Not only had the Aclands given her advice and encouragement, but their extensive South Canterbury property at Mount Peel was the model that helped her to visualize Mount Silver Station. The plot would revolve around a sudden financial crisis into which the Lampreys had lurched.

After returning to England, Lord Charles goes into business with a man horribly in debt who promptly commits suicide by shooting himself through the head. The Lampreys are left to pay his bills. Roberta Grey arrives in London on the eve of a begging request to Lord Charles's brother Gabriel, the Marquis of Wutherwood and Rune, for a 'permanent loan' of £2,000. He and his wife Violet are to visit the Lampreys at their double flat in a building known as Pleasaunce Court Mansions, on the corner of a fictitious street linking the real Cadogan Square, in Brompton, with Lennox Gardens. The Rhodeses' double flat had been in a similar building a few blocks away at the back of Sloane Square, on the corner of Cliveden Place and Bourne Street. The newspaper agent where Ngaio bought her exercise books was on Bourne Street; the basement flat where she had written *A Man Lay Dead* was around the corner in Caroline Terrace. Roberta is living with the Lampreys in the heart of Ngaio's London. As a sweetener, the Lamprey children have been instructed by their parents to perform an impromptu charade for the marquis and his wife. Interestingly, Roberta is of the Lamprey children's generation, not their parents'. This circumvents any difficulties implicit in the *ménage* that developed between Ngaio, Nelly and Tahu. Roberta can and does fall in love with Henry, the Lampreys' son and heir. In his parents' generation, whom would she have fallen in love with?

The charade, an ugly echo of what is about to happen, is an unmitigated disaster because it completely fails to impress, as does the ancient Chinese pot offered to Gabriel as a gift by the Lampreys' youngest son, Michael. After their improvization is finished, the family, including Gabriel's wife, Violet, retire to various rooms, leaving Lord Charles and his brother closeted together. Lord Charles makes his supplication, but the miserly Marquis of Wutherwood and Rune is intractable. He storms out of the room, shouting loudly for his wife to join him in the lift. When she arrives, she discovers him dead. The plated-silver skewer used by the Lamprey children in their charade is protruding from Gabriel's eye. The fur-lined motoring gloves they also used are covered in blood and lying under the chair where the marquis is slumped. Violet screams and screams and screams.

Ngaio provided readers with a map of the two third-storey flats, joined by a landing that housed the lift and the stairwell. This was common detective fiction practice — to provide some piece of empirical evidence that might hold a key. She included the charred fragments of a note in *Death in Ecstasy*, and a map of Pen-Cuckoo village in *Overture to Death*. In 1930, writing in conjunction with Robert Eustace, Dorothy Sayers followed this logic in *The Documents in the Case*, to the extent that the book was a collection of letters and documents: all the evidence required for the armchair detective — the reader — to solve the crime. Lord Wimsey's services were not required.

But Ngaio was too interested in her characters to allow the problem to take over. In fact, it is in *Surfeit of Lampreys* that Alleyn makes a comment that parallels her own attitude to crime writing. He admits that he gets heartily sick of the monotonous routine of investigation, but people fascinate him and homicide is all about people. Each person is secure inside their psychological 'bomb-proof shelter' until the 'holocaust' of murder blows their world apart. It is Alleyn's job in *Surfeit of Lampreys* to cast an objective eye over a collection of characters who are based on Ngaio's friends. He summarizes his findings for Nigel Bathgate who, by complete coincidence, is a personal friend of the family's.

'Boiled down to a few unsympathetic adjectives they came to this: "Charming. Irresponsible. Unscrupulous about money. Good-natured. Lazy. Amusing. Enormously popular." Do you agree?'

'Nobody knows better than you,' said Nigel, 'that people can*not* be boiled down into a few adjectives.'

Alleyn remains sceptical of the Lampreys, calling them, at one point in the investigation, 'that collection of certifiable grotesques'. His practical, puritanical side will not allow him to embrace their surfeit of self-indulgence. Yet he quietly admires the tenacity of the young colonial, Roberta Grey, who uses her ingenuity to fabricate a story to protect her friends. More than once he describes her as a 'courageous little liar'. And Alleyn is not the only one to see her as resourceful. The Lampreys are in awe, too, and convinced of her aptitude by vague notions of 'pioneering hardihood' that deem colonials robust and therefore less accustomed to 'nervous strain than their English contemporaries'.

Surfeit of Lampreys explores the tension between the capable colonial of the new world and the addled aristocracy of an old, but now changing world. Ngaio was a colonial who worked prodigiously. Each book she wrote was 60,000–80,000 words long, and with *Surfeit of Lampreys* she had published 10 novels in seven years. It was an extraordinary output, which she worked hard to maintain with an aging father and household to support. There was more than a little of Ngaio's mother in Alleyn's view of the Lampreys. He has evolved from the same privileged stock, but he is a professional policeman, working hard to solve crime and earn a living. That is why, like his creator, he never approves of that aspect of the Lampreys.

The Lampreys' flat is the perfect cosy fit for murder, a cramped stage for a confined number of characters. One of the more colourful is Violet, the Marchioness of Wutherwood and Rune. She is involved in spiritualism and 'sits in the dark' with what the Lampreys' Aunt Kit describes as 'a set of very second-rate sort of people'. But Charlot Lamprey corrects her: 'Not spiritualism, darling, . . . Black magic.' Violet is a necromancer. Her interest in the occult echoes a key reference through the book to Shakespeare's *Macbeth*, which provides an ominous backdrop of foreboding and analogous action. Violet is likened to the three weird sisters on the blasted heath, and to the medieval witches Marguerite Loundman of Gegweiler and Anna Ruffa of Douzy. 'Is it so very unusual among women of her age, restless by temperament, to become hag-ridden by the bogus-occult?' asks Dr Kantripp of his colleague Dr Curtis.

The themes of *Macbeth* haunt the pages of Ngaio's novels like Banquo's ghost. 'Don't quote from Macbeth. It couldn't be more unlucky,' Dinah warns her fiancé in *Death in Ecstasy*, and in *Surfeit of Lampreys* it is Henry who sounds the alarm. In theatre circles, he explains, it is considered bad luck to quote from *Macbeth* off stage. Ngaio consistently uses dramatic language, metaphors, references, stage superstition and actors to give her writing structure, humour, verve and intellectual vitality.

Perhaps it was always impossible that a Lamprey could commit murder. In the wind-up to *Surfeit of Lampreys* they inherit Gabriel's title and money and are saved the pain of a difficult lesson. Roberta cannot believe it as the family sit and make plans for the future, having averted disaster without even trying. They now have two enormous properties and an income of £30,000 a year. She is even more astonished that they still feel poor.

'It's been a bit too much for all of us,' said Charlot . . . 'I think it would be such a good idea if we all crept away somewhere for a little holiday before the trial comes off or war breaks out and nobody can go anywhere . . . I don't mean anywhere smart like Antibes or the Lido but some *un-smart* place . . . where we could bathe and blow away the horrors and have a tiny bit of mild gambling at night.'

This is the fecklessness that Ngaio found so charming yet also reprehensible. She was not long back from a reckless trip with Nelly Rhodes to Monte Carlo, and the Rhodeses had survived another financial crisis while she was there. Ngaio could be puritanical about their work ethic and extravagance, but deep down the daughter of a mother who walked miles to save a tram fare could not help but be impressed. Love is not rational, and there is always hope for the next generation — as there is at the end of *Surfeit of Lampreys*, when Alleyn tells Nigel that 'Henry's been talking about a job'.

'Good Lord! Not the little New Zealander['s influence]?'
'I think so.' Alleyn grimaced. 'I told you she was a courageous little party,' he said.

Surfeit of Lampreys was released in the United States in 1940, under the title

Death of a Peer, and in Britain at the beginning of 1941. Reviews on both sides of the Atlantic were glowing. 'There is no doubt that Miss Ngaio Marsh is among the most brilliant of those authors who are transforming the detective story from a mere puzzle into a novel with many other qualities besides the challenge to our wits,' wrote the critic for *The Times Literary Supplement* in January 1941. The reviewer for *The Observer* rated the novel as her best so far, describing it as 'a brilliantly readable drawing room detective story . . . [The h]igh spot is lavish, very cunning characterisation of vague, charming, dotty family of bankrupt peer.' *The Sunday Times* called it 'capital': 'gruesome crimes, light relief, sprightly characters, good plot, resolute and broad-minded detective'.

A negative, but perhaps justified, criticism was made in the *Sketch*. Overall the reviewer endorsed the book, but 'some of the Lampreys show a tiresome tendency to become stage characters, and there are moments when the sound of the raising curtain becomes almost audible'. Ngaio's characters were occasionally stagy and affected, and sometimes her novel of manners became mannered. By making Roberta Grey a contemporary of the Lamprey children she slyly escaped any deep psychological analysis of her characters. Roberta is the book's central consciousness and she is only 20 years old.

Critics could see potential for Ngaio, both as pure novelist and as a writer for theatre. 'Her strongest card is dialogue,' wrote the critic for *Punch*; 'when the theatre comes to life again after HITLER'S funeral it will be surprising if Miss MARSH does not make a new name for herself.' On the other side of the world, and in spite of the war, that was what Ngaio was doing.

In July 1941, she produced *Outward Bound* at the Little Theatre in Christchurch. Early that year a small delegation of Canterbury University students had ventured up to her house on Valley Road to ask her if she would produce their annual play. The title had already been selected so it was something of a *fait accompli*, but she agreed anyway, 'for the hell of it'. She was hungry for young company and loved the idea of working with students bristling with intelligence and a raw, untapped energy. This was talent she could mould as she could the characters in her books. She brought all the resources she had to her production of *Outward Bound*. Evelyn Page's husband, Frederick, wrote the music and she began to use her old friend Dundas Walker to give maturity to the acting. The good-natured, gaunt, sometimes cadaverous-looking Walker became a regular feature in her productions.

The following year, for the Canterbury Repertory Society, she produced Harold

Hobhouse's one-Act play, *Lonesome Life*, and also Noël Coward's *Blithe Spirit* for the Canterbury and Wellington repertory companies. Theatre production used skills that had lain relatively dormant in her renaissance repertoire of talent, and provided a life richly textured with people, passion and intellect.

Her own personal performances were confined largely to speeches and radio broadcasts. In 1940, she travelled to Wellington to be part of a gathering of writers in the Women's Section of the Centennial Exhibition. While she was there she made recordings with the National Broadcasting Service (NBS), which included three travel talks, the story of the initiation of E.C. Bentley at the Detection Club dinner in 1937, and a reflection on detective fiction writing, which was published in the *New Zealand Listener* in August 1940.

She would become a broadcasting celebrity. Her immaculately delivered, elegantly styled, thoughtful, rather romantic reflections on faraway places most New Zealanders only read about or saw on newsreels and in films were highly sought after. Her deep contralto voice was compelling and authoritative, and thousands listened in. Ngaio Marsh became a household name, not just because of her crime writing, but because of her vivid recollections of London and the Continent, now sealed off by war. Her talks were broadcast on 3YA in June and July of 1940, and again in January 1943. A delightfully apt Russell Clark cartoon of Detection Club writers, titled 'Miss Marsh is Detected . . .', was published in the *Listener* to advertise one of the broadcasts. 'Miss Marsh called her talk "The Queerest Party",' the caption read.

Ngaio's radio talks were so successful that before *Surfeit of Lampreys* came out negotiations were in full swing to broadcast it, and the rights were secured. 'Not only will this detective novel be broadcast simultaneously with publication,' proclaimed the *New Zealand Listener* triumphantly, 'but the author herself will be the broadcaster.' *Surfeit of Lampreys* was played to 2YA listeners in February 1942, in a series of 20 readings, each about 20 minutes long.

In December 1942, an elegant full-page portrait photograph of Ngaio graced the front page of the *Listener*. The caption underneath read: 'a new series of talks for the NBS, and the producing of a Noel Coward play for the Wellington Repertory this week must make her one of the busiest women in New Zealand'. The production of Coward's *Blithe Spirit* was 'the reward I allowed myself for finishing my last detective story,' Ngaio explained to the interviewer in an accompanying article. 'I always give myself some sort of break before I start on the next.' This was the gap between the publication of *Death and the Dancing*

Footman in 1941 and *Colour Scheme* in 1943. During this period she had also written a book for 'The British Commonwealth in Pictures' series entitled *New Zealand*. Ngaio was astonishingly busy. She worked like a machine, and much of what she did, in her diverse fields, was remarkably clever.

⊏■▮❪▭❫

Ngaio felt her most recent writing was her best. '*Death and the Dancing Footman* is Miss Marsh's favourite among her own books,' the *New Zealand Listener* journalist told readers. It was published in the same year as *Surfeit of Lampreys*, yet it contained far less personal material. It was almost as if Ngaio were trying to create a plot that would give her perfect form.

Death and the Dancing Footman was her most suspense-ridden murder to date, because almost all her cosy cast of characters have good reason to fear they may be the victim, and the murder does not occur until late in the book. In the first chapter, called 'Project', Jonathan Royal introduces his monstrous scheme for a weekend party at Highfold Manor in Dorset. He has orchestrated a real-life drama, that will be played out by people who hate each other, in front of poetic dramatist Aubrey Mandrake, who is the unwitting audience. Royal is producer-director, and *Death and the Dancing Footman* a foretaste of the nightmare of reality television. He hand-picks his guests on the basis of their acrimony. There is a German surgeon, along with the woman he mutilated in a botched facelift 20 years earlier; the woman's sons, who hate each other; an ex-fiancée and her current lover; plus two bitter business rivals in the beauty business. The only person without an axe to grind (or in this case a Maori mere to swing, because this is the murder weapon) is their host, Jonathan Royal, and Aubrey Mandrake, whose darkest secret is that he changed his name by deed poll from Stanley Footling.

It is beginning, thinks Jonathan Royal, who almost hugs himself with pleasure when Aubrey Mandrake arrives before the other guests, so he can outline his ugly plan. It seems to him, he explains, that:

> 'given the limitations of an imposed stage, some of my acquaintances would at once begin to unfold an exciting drama . . . I would set my palette with human colours, and the picture would paint itself. I would summon my characters to the theatre of my own house, and the drama would unfold itself.'

> 'Pirandello,' Mandrake began, 'has become quite —'

'But this is *not* Pirandello,' Jonathan interrupted in a great hurry. 'No. In this instance we shall see not six characters in search of an author, but an author who has deliberately summoned seven characters to do his work for him.'

Ngaio is playing with Pirandello's idea, but the Existentialism has been removed and the conceit twisted so that what remains is the result of bringing together characters who despise each other. That catalyst for action in Royal's human drama is hate. Pirandello's ideas still held an appeal for Ngaio, and *Death and the Dancing Footman* was an opportunity to see them played out in a different way. She was fascinated by the role of director in controlling actors and characters, and, like Royal, she often played host.

Selecting guests for dinner parties at Marton Cottage became a familiar ritual as her involvement in theatre increased and her celebrity status grew. Ngaio loved giving parties and they became a phenomenon in Christchurch. They were meticulously planned, lavish events catered by housekeeper and cook Mrs Crawford (Crawsie), and on special occasions the table was waited on by the gardener, Crawsie's husband Andy. It was a joke they all shared — a playing of roles, an aping of parts. 'Dinner is served, Ma'am,' Crawsie would announce in her plummiest voice. 'Come on, dear.' And Ngaio would smile wryly. On cue, the guests would file into a warm wood-panelled dining room and sit at a round table gorgeously laden with silver and crystal.

Ngaio's friends and colleagues remembered these as wonderful occasions. She was a generous host, and food, wine and whisky flowed freely. The laughter was riotous, and the talk animated and intelligent. Ngaio was a great facilitator. She fed but never dominated conversation. 'She was a strong woman, but never overpowering.' Ngaio read the nuances of her guests' behaviour and anticipated their needs. Always, at the end of the meal the women retired, and the men would sit smoking and drinking double-fingered whiskies. Even though she was excluded, Ngaio was a stickler for Old World protocol.

Jonathan Royal's dinner party is a dogfight. As he dresses, Aubrey Mandrake wonders where Jonathan will place his guests at the table. On sheets of Highfold notepaper he tries to work out a seating order that will keep the most acrimonious apart, but it is impossible. Jonathan Royal, on the other hand, has set himself the completely different task of devising a seating plan that will create the greatest friction. He has 'the long dining-table . . . replaced by a round one', then threads the enemies together one after another like beads on a necklace. There are just two seats left, which belong to the last guests to arrive. 'Both were extremely pale and, when they found their place-cards, seemed to flinch all over: "Like agitated horses," thought Mandrake.' Jonathan has also carefully judged the alcohol requirements of some of his guests, but intoxicates others. The best part of the evening for all of them, except Jonathan, is bed.

The next day, a case of mistaken identity results in Aubrey Mandrake being pushed into the swimming pool. In any other season but deepest winter this might not have been a problem, but the club-footed Aubrey is pulled from the water bedraggled and hypothermic. It begins to snow unrelentingly: a quiet, insidious build-up of impenetrable white. There is a murderer at large at Highfold Manor and the house party is snowbound. It is a brilliantly constructed plot. Fear dogs the footsteps of the guests until one of them is murdered. Terror creates the dramatic tension that makes this novel such a success.

In the United States, the consensus was that this was an exceptional novel. Kay Irwin, writing for *The New York Times*, was the most perceptive in her assessment of strengths and weaknesses:

Although the puzzle is intricate, the appeal of *Death and the Dancing Footman* is almost as much that of a novel as of a murder mystery. The movement of the plot is deliberate at the beginning and rather arbitrarily slowed down at the end. But the interest of character is brilliant and unflagging, both incident and conversation are alive with wit.

The artificial slowing-down in the plot is caused by the arrival of Alleyn. Slow, plodding police detection kills the suspense and pace which make the beginning of the novel so engrossing.

Alleyn would arrive late in many of Ngaio's future novels. The fascinating way she developed her characters in the lead-up to his entrance would leave commentators wondering whether the detective element was even necessary. What impressed her critics most was not the relentless interrogation of the puzzle plot by the super-sleuth, but the canvas of human foibles and frailties against which it was played out. Her ambition to write crime fiction that doubled as a novel of manners left her characters free to take on a life of their own, and sometimes they became so interesting that they challenged the detective's domination. Because her literary ambitions were contrary to the essential precepts of the genre, tension developed between the life of the early part of the novel and what came after Alleyn's arrival. Some critics found this division so extreme that they described her novels as containing two separate books.

In England, critics widely acclaimed the novel's cleverness. The reviewer for *The Observer* applauded the 'prolonged suspense over who is going to be the victim' and the 'good surprise finish', which was 'based on a complicated but neat alibi system'. In a book that was 'lively and entertaining', the 'ultra rational motives' compensated for the 'heavily artificial situation'. The *Tatler* described it as a 'detective *novel*, not [a] detective story. Her *Death and the Dancing Footman* is a fit and not disappointing successor to her brilliant *Surfeit of Lampreys* — can I say more?'

But there was also the faintest note of negative criticism. Some commentators were beginning to find the cosy tired and limiting. 'We have met this setting before,' wrote the *Sunday Times* critic; 'there are no characters to command our affections and no places to make us linger over the view,' said *The Times Literary Supplement*. It was not that Ngaio had failed — it was that the Golden Age detective novel was beginning to lose its power. In 1944, American detective novelist Raymond Chandler would write his famous criticism of crime detective fiction for *The Atlantic Monthly*. He debunked A.A. Milne's *The Red House Mystery* and E.C. Bentley's seminal *Trent's Last Case*, but his most cutting criticism was saved for the Queens of Crime, Agatha Christie and Dorothy Sayers.

In the introduction to her *Omnibus of Crime*, Sayers had made a distinction between 'literature of escape' and the more lofty 'literature of expression'. She believed that the conventions of crime detective fiction made them mutually exclusive. Chandler, who represented a new form of detective fiction writing, was incensed: 'there are no dull subjects, only dull writers,' he jeered. 'I think what was really gnawing at Miss Sayers' mind was the slow realisation that her kind of detective story was an arid formula which could not even satisfy its own implications.' He saw stereotypical characters and plots as more dead than their victims. 'It is the same careful grouping of suspects, the same utterly incomprehensible trick of how somebody stabbed Mrs. Pottington Postlethwaite III with the solid platinum poignard just as she flatted on the top note of the "Bell Song" from *Lakmé* in the presence of fifteen ill-assorted guests.' Ngaio was not specifically mentioned in the article, but this was certainly a reference to her plots. 'The English,' he concluded, 'may not always be the best writers in the world, but they are incomparably the best dull writers.' Chandler advocated the new style of 'hard-boiled' authors like American Dashiell Hammett. This writing, he claimed, was authentic because it was based on fact. 'Hammett took murder out of the Venetian vase and dropped it into the alley,' he announced. His novels were about realistic crime and the realistic people who committed it. It was frugal and his scenes 'seemed never to have been written before'. Aficionados would have recognized the validity of what Chandler said, but they would also have known that he was a disaffected English-born writer of the hard-boiled school and, therefore, not exactly objective.

The war that played a cursory role in *Death of the Dancing Footman* was more immediately present in Ngaio's real life. She donned a uniform and fortnightly drove a Red Cross transport bus that ferried wounded soldiers home from Lyttelton. Feeling New Zealand's isolation and her own helplessness to make a contribution to the war effort, Ngaio thought that this was the least she could do. She was intensely patriotic, as was her father. As soon as he recovered from a life-threatening perforated appendix operation, he joined the Home Guard and 'ran about the hills hurling hand grenades and throwing himself flat on his face until his doctor forbade it'. After that, an abortive attempt at making camouflage nets ended in his falling out with the authorities over the type of knot he used, and he spent much of the rest of the time digging and perfecting a 'funk-hole' in their garden. His brush with death was sobering for Ngaio. 'I could see, to my terror, that everybody except Sir Hugh [Acland] expected my father to die', and the thought was too awful to contemplate. Henry Marsh played tennis until he was 80 years old, and Ngaio kept his mind and interest in life alive by involving him in her productions. 'He played two small character parts . . . I used to walk round the set every night just before his entrance and there he would be, listening, with his ear at the door, for his cue.' Their eyes would meet, they would share a knowing glance and he would walk onto the stage.

Ngaio's knowledge of New Zealand and her patriotic zeal made her an ideal choice to write the *New Zealand* title of 'The British Commonwealth in Pictures' series, put out by Collins in 1942. She co-authored it with historian R.M. Burden, but the text was unmistakably hers.

A key ambition of the project was to affirm New Zealand's link to the Commonwealth united in war against Germany. 'Why have they left their small farms, their shops, their offices, and their native villages?' she wrote of the thousands of New Zealanders who had enlisted. 'It seems that one must say of these young men that they are about to fight for an ideal, and that this ideal is freedom, the freedom of a commonwealth of nations.' Apart from its jingoistic purpose, the publication was also designed to dish up a slice of New Zealand to a principally British audience. It began with a look at the 'New Zealand people', Pakeha and Maori, then considered 'Social and Political' policy, gave a brief 'Survey of New Zealand History', and ended with a look at 'The Landscape' in the North and South Islands. This was achieved in just 48 heavily illustrated pages. It was a book written for the lay reader, offering personal perspectives highly coloured by the colonial attitudes of the time:

When white-skinned men came to this country they found a people living in a Stone Age. To-day the Maori has so far assimilated our ways that members of his race are to be found in most professions and trades in New Zealand. This process of acquiring in a century habits and usages which the white man has taken a thousand years to develop, may be likened to forcible feeding, and it is not surprising if at times the Maori has suffered from a sort of evolutionary indigestion.

Ngaio's view was that of colonizing Pakeha, who justified the appropriation of Maori land and culture by seeing themselves as humane usurpers. 'The strong have dispossessed the weak either violently or peacefully,' she wrote. 'But seldom in history have the conquerors shown such concern for the welfare and perpetuation of the conquered race.' This was the Euro-centric cliché trotted out by many liberal Pakeha New Zealanders in the 1940s and 1950s. More conservative Pakeha attitudes were worse.

Ngaio saw the country as young, in terms of European settlement, when the clock arrived and Pakeha time began. When she spoke of the people generally, she spoke of Pakeha. 'In some ways New Zealanders are still mid-Victorian Englishmen of good heart,' she wrote of a population she described as the most homogeneous of any British colony. Her long-term prognosis was that Pakeha and Maori would inter-marry until they became indistinguishable. She saw New Zealand as being in a time warp created by the county's far-flung isolation from the land of its European conquerors. 'New Zealand stands like a cranky little coda, at the bottom of the world. Its isolation is extreme.' Her New Zealand was a white male world where women, deprived of leisure, were the harassed helpmeets of the runholders, cockies, stock and station agents, and small businessmen who made up the backbone of the country.

Today, this mainstream piece of feel-good propaganda for New Zealand and the war effort may seem bigoted and contrived. It stands as a record of its time, but if anything redeems it, it is Ngaio's love of New Zealand and her anachronistically slanted, but nevertheless absolute, commitment to biculturalism. She respected Maori, and was pressingly aware of the huge price they had paid for colonization. This was a constant theme in her New Zealand-based fiction. Her affection for her country was based on her love of the land. New Zealand may not have restaurants as good as those of English or American department stores, or thermal regions as dramatic as Yellowstone, or alpine vistas as picturesque as Austria and Switzerland,

> but Pohutukawa trees grow above bays of enchantment only in New Zealand, and nowhere else have I found an equivalent to the clear spaciousness of our mountain plateaux, or heard bird song as deep and moving as that of the New Zealand bush. This is a country so young that it impinges on the very ancient, and its clear and primordial landscape reaches back to emotions that have nothing to do with civilisation, but its spell — once felt — is not easily forgotten.

These emotions reached back to her childhood, when she was overwhelmed by the presence of the bush. In the summer of 1912, when she was still at high school, her parents and a group of friends made the long trip to Glentui in the foothills of the Southern Alps. They caught a train from Christchurch to Rangiora, then another along a branch line to Oxford. There in the sweltering heat they lunched at a pub, then picked up two horse-drawn farm carts loaded with stores and camping equipment. It was an 8-mile (13-kilometre) amble among hills and across the Ashley River to Glentui, where they went up the valley to find a campsite.

The carts juddered over the rough track while younger members of the party raced ahead to find the ideal clearing among native beech trees. The men cut manuka tent poles, Ngaio's mother cooked in a camp oven ingeniously rigged up by Cecil Walker, and Ngaio collected water in a 'clanking Kerosene-tin bucket' from a river that lulled them to sleep at night in their hay-stuffed sleeping sacks. Bellbirds were the soloists in a magnificent dawn chorus of birds. Ngaio woke early and was flooded by a sense of ecstasy. This was a defining moment of youthful rapture. 'I experienced . . . absolute happiness: bliss.' And she shared the emotion with someone special. 'My father was magnificent on these occasions. He was in his natural element and seemed to give off a glow of profound satisfaction.' There were others, too, whom she enjoyed: her actor friends the Burtons, plus Aileen's and Helen's fiancés; her friend Sylvia Fox; and Dundas Walker and his brother Cecil. Her world of intimate association was complete.

During blazing hot days of dazzling sunlight, they revived in the chill mountain waters of a swimming-hole they made by damming the river. In the seclusion of their private beech-fringed glade, 'the girls could rid themselves of their neck-to-knee bathing clothes' and swim and exult in the soft 'springing pleasure of young grass' as they sunbathed. 'One day we climbed the mountain to Blowhard and looked across a great valley into the backcountry: range after naked range with a glittering of snow on the big tops. "My country," I thought.'

In this landscape Ngaio felt a connection and a sense of belonging that was never extinguished. England was the home of her ancestors, but New Zealand was her turangawaewae. The land of her birth always drew her back. Like many Pakeha — or 'newcomers', as she called them — she felt the dilemma of protest against and disillusionment with the Old World, of a truncated history, of the anomalies of colonization and land ownership. 'I do not know if other New Zealanders are visited by this contradictory feeling of belonging and not-belonging,' she wrote in *Black Beech*, 'but it came upon me very vividly when I first looked into the high-country from the top of Blowhard and it has returned many times since then. It is a feeling that deepens rather than modifies one's attachment to New Zealand.'

The Burton girls' fiancés were both Anglican curates, and on Christmas Day at Glentui they celebrated Holy Communion at dawn. Henry Marsh, the ardent atheist, spent Christmas Eve fashioning an altar made out of manuka poles in a clearing by the river. Ngaio was at her religious zenith and probably still smarting from the loss of a confirmation cross and chain which had been spirited away from her tent by a thieving weka who crept across sleeping bodies to steal it. Henry, who allowed each individual their belief, built the altar for his daughter. He carefully positioned the structure between two trees so that the sun would rise behind it, but was not present at the service the next day. He was magnanimous again later, when one of the Burton fiancés, a union supporter, was involved in the Waterfront Strike of 1913 and Henry was a government-appointed special constable. He was conservative in his political principles, yet he let others have theirs. The Marsh family enjoyed several more Christmas camping holidays at Glentui before Ngaio left school and her friends drifted off like dandelion seeds on a gust of autumn wind. It was natural that they would go their own ways, but Dundas Walker and Sylvia Fox would remain constant throughout Ngaio's life.

Glentui formed part of the backdrop to Ngaio's writing in *New Zealand*, but other outdoor experiences were equally charged. The book included 12 colour plates of landscape paintings documenting New Zealand's settlement and scenery, from *Captain Cook Arriving at Queen Charlotte's Sound, February 10th, 1777* (by J. Clevely) to Elizabeth Wallwork's more recent *Wind in the Larches*. Ngaio included two of her own mountain landscapes, and one by her friend Olivia Spencer Bower. It was the borrowing of the Wallwork painting that would have brought back a host of memories. Elizabeth and Richard Wallwork had been Ngaio's teachers at Canterbury College. Richard was the life-room lecturer, but he and his wife were also devotees of landscape painting, and part of a wider Canterbury School who selected raw, often South Canterbury vistas of rivers, rolling plains and mountains as their subject matter. The more progressive painters sought to convey the arid bones of the landscape in simple dramatic forms. They shunned the picturesque and the iconic in favour of the simple and the ordinary: the quiet railway siding, the isolated mountain hut, the meandering shingle road crossed by a ramshackle bridge. The human scale was insignificant. Ngaio expressed it perfectly: 'our presence here was no more than a cobweb across the hide of a monster'. These were subjects that visualized how it felt to be overpowered by Nature. The artists of the Canterbury School painted outdoors in front of the subjects that inspired them. The itinerant camping life, the sand in the oils, the mosquitoes in the watercolour water were all part of the ritual. Their landscapes were a groping, instinctive statement of nationalism.

After she had been at art school for a year, Richard and Elizabeth Wallwork invited Ngaio, her mother and a young cousin on a painting trip to the West Coast. This was the rich, dark, brooding, primordial balance to the dry, open plains of the east. Their train left at 8am, and by noon foothills loomed on either side and they were climbing, hurtling through scree and tussock until they reached the mountain tunnels. Ngaio and her cousin stood outside in the blackness as the platform surged and bucked beneath their feet. Sooty cinders burned their lungs and the noise of the train in the tunnel was deafening, but they were exhilarated. The railway line stopped at Arthur's Pass, so the final stage was taken by road. Their party was among the last to take a Cobb and Co. Royal Mail Coach, before the Otira Tunnel was opened in 1923. Women sat inside the coach and men on the top, but Ngaio slipped past convention and climbed up into the box seat.

We were plunged into a region of wet forest and dark mountains. We looked into a chasm where treetops were no bigger than green fungi . . . It opens with a series of hairpin bends. I am badly affected with height vertigo . . . On the outside seat one seemed, literally, to overhang the edge. I gripped a ridiculously small curved rail . . . Nobody spoke. From time to time the brakes screamed and stank.

Passengers were paralysed with fear until the going finally became calmer and the coach pulled up in the sleepy West Coast settlement of Otira.

There they found 'a straggle of huts, a large pub and a little station' that was the West Coast railroad terminus. At the pub, which was coming alive after the day's hibernation, they ate cold mutton, yellow pickles and a loaf with butter and black tea. The smell of beer mixed with the smell of pungent bush. That night they slept on blanket-covered bracken in tiny two-bunk logging huts standing in a row overlooking a railway bridge at Te Kinga. Richard Wallwork had to commandeer a railway jigger to carry their gear. The rent was 5 shillings a week. At dawn they were woken by the sound of logging teams leaving for their camp deep in the bush. They were invited by the timber men to visit the camp, and watch gigantic tree trunks being winched out. At the mill at Te Kinga, they saw the logs thundering down the skids. 'I did a painting of this and would have liked to call it "Too Bloody Big," for that was what the mill-hands said repeatedly of the giant we had seen felled.' In the mornings and evenings they painted with great concentration. 'We learned about the behaviour of trees, about the anatomy of mountains, how to lay out the ghost of a subject and then, at the fleeting hour of sunset, seize upon it.' The afternoons were free to take expeditions into the bush.

During her art school days, Ngaio returned three times to Westland. Each visit gave them a reminder of the region's cruelty. There was the timber man's snigger horse, blind in one eye from the whiplash of a bush; the farmer's three young sons drowned in the cruel waters of Lake Brunner; and the thin, refined hermit woman who lived in a shack near Lake Kaniere. They stumbled across her hut one day in a clearing. She was dressed in rags and ruined workingman's boots, but still she invited them in. As she poured the tea, they noticed the faded photographs on the wall behind her. One of them was of a 'very pretty woman in full Victorian evening dress'; another of a group of three children with a boy in an Eton suit. As they were leaving, Rose Marsh said, 'Did you recognise the photograph on the wall? . . . She must have been lovely as a girl.'

This was remittance country, and when remittance men and women ran out of money Nature was unforgiving. It was on the West Coast that Ngaio and her fellow student Phyllis Bethune encountered the drunken revellers who became the subject of 'The Night Train From Grey', her first piece of professional writing for the *Sun*, under its progressive editor Edward Huie, who was also president of the Canterbury Society of Arts. The rugged, New Zealand landscape and its solid, self-contained, sometimes bush-crazed people were an inspiration for Ngaio.

Her own paintings in *New Zealand* were dry east coast scenes typical of the Canterbury School. In *Mount Goldie*, three singlet-clad athletic stockmen stand looking across a rural landscape dotted with sheep to the etched forms of distant foothills. It is a cleverly composed but conventional picture, ideally suited to its illustrative purpose. Ngaio began her *New Zealand* story like one of her novels, introducing the various groups of people attending an agricultural fair. 'To find such a slice of local colour a stranger would do well to visit one of the cities during a carnival week. These festivals take place in the spring, and, in most towns at this time, a race-meeting coincides with an agricultural . . . show.' The first people mentioned were the runholders, described as the 'squattocracy' of New Zealand.

New Zealand also contained reproductions of 19th-century engravings and a selection of contemporary black-and-white photographs. The initial batch of the latter, sent to London to be included in the book, were lost at sea, and the colour film that was to be used instead could not be processed, but this did not mar the experience for English critics, who were enthusiastic in their praise. Reflecting on all the Commonwealth titles produced to that point, the reviewer for *Time and Tide*, writing in April 1942, stated: 'I confess it was Miss Ngaio Marsh's *New Zealand* which caught my attention most of all. And here perhaps it was partly by means of the pictures.' Ngaio's slice of New Zealand was an affirming rather than provocative view of the empire and colonization. 'Most

English people . . . have the feeling that New Zealand is a kind of business-like fairyland, and Miss Marsh left me with the conviction that most English people are right,' wrote *The Observer*.

⊂▬▮◻▭⊃

It may have been the *New Zealand* book that shifted Ngaio's focus to Rotorua and *Colour Scheme*, but how could she explain Alleyn's presence Down Under? Then it occurred to her.

The Japanese attack on Pearl Harbor in December 1941 brought war to the Pacific. On 19 February 1942, Japanese aircraft bombed Darwin, in the first of about 100 air raids against Australia carried out between 1942 and 1943. In that first attack, the Japanese dropped more bombs on Darwin than they did on Pearl Harbor. It was a huge psychological blow, not only to Australia but also to New Zealand. These were countries stripped of able men — over 140,000 New Zealanders were fighting in Europe and North Africa — and now there was the possibility of a homeland invasion. New Zealand's isolation did not automatically make it impregnable.

A spy theme could justify Alleyn's being in New Zealand and give the novel a contemporary flavour. Ngaio gathered her characters around a health spa owned and run by the Claires at fictional Wai-ata-tapu Springs near Rotorua. The vague and incompetent Colonel Claire, his wife, and two children, Simon and Barbara, are English emigrants who have lived here for 12 years, just long enough for the Antipodean dream to fade and curl at the edges. The money has gone, and their energy is as dilapidated as the flyblown posters that hang by a single drawing pin on the notice board.

As he approaches the spa by road, renowned Shakespearian actor Geoffry Gaunt thinks it is a dosshouse. Gaunt and his secretary Dikon Bell are guests, along with Mrs Claire's brother, retired London doctor James Ackrington. Gaunt hopes he will find a cure for the ravages of the stage in the murky thermal waters of the spa. In his spare moments he is dictating his autobiography to his secretary. Thermal activity seethes around the Claires' jaded bathhouse, producing pyrotechnic displays of geysers, gas and steam, and pools of scalding mud. Close by is the Maori village of Te Rarawas, and behind it, looking across the fictional Harpoon Harbour, the extinct volcanic cone of Rangi's Peak. Two miles (5 kilometres) off the coast from Harpoon Inlet, a fully laden warship has been torpedoed. A seemingly coded series of flashing lights from Rangi's Peak seemed to have precipitated the attack, and espionage is suspected. Who in the Wai-ata-tapu Hot-Springs Spa is a spy?

Dr Ackrington decides to report these strange events to Roderick Alleyn, who is in New Zealand looking for leaks of classified information. Alleyn disguises himself as the elusive Septimus Falls: bent, but still good-looking and lean, seeking treatment for a bogus case of lumbago. The leading spy suspect is the gauche Maurice Questing, who holds the Claires' hot pools to ransom over an unpaid debt. His disappearance, and subsequent reappearance as a boiled skull bubbling in the briny waters of a mud pool, lays the case wide open. Who is the murderer? Who is the spy?

This thin plot is brilliantly thickened by Ngaio's investigation of two cultures undergoing dislocation and change. The most ravaged and therefore sympathetically presented is the Maori facing the consequences of colonization. It is not a flaky liberal, but cantankerous old Dr Ackrington who explains the 'criminal imbecility' of the Pakeha to Geoffry Gaunt:

We sent missionaries to stop them eating each other and bribed them with bad whisky to give us their land. We cured them of their own perfectly good communistic system . . . We took away their chiefs and gave them trade-union secretaries. And for mating-customs . . . we substituted . . . disease and holy matrimony.

Through the character of Eru Saul, Ngaio explores the dilemma of the young Maori 'half-breed' caught between cultures — a 'bad Pakeha and a bad Maori' — trouble for both peoples. She saw the loss of Maori language, beliefs and values as destabilizing and tragic, and despised the exploitation of Maori culture through merchandising and appropriation.

Maurice Questing is a speculator whose programme of enhancing the tourist value of his property includes organizing groups of 'poi girls' and young Maori children who dive for pennies, and the sale of curios. He is the least likeable character in the book. It is Questing who violates the laws of tapu when he climbs Rangi's Peak and desecrates a Maori burial ground by removing the magnificent adze of great chief Rewi, grandfather of aging rangatira Rua. And Questing who comes to one of Ngaio's stickiest ends. His scream across the blackness of the night as he boils echoes the sad end, years before, of a young Maori woman who inadvertently ate food near her grandfather's grave and broke tapu. She crept back to her village at night, fell into the boiling mud of

Taupo-tapu, and her blood-curdling scream was heard across the village. The next morning, all that the pool would relinquish was her dress.

Is Questing's end the judgment of Tane, protector of Rewi's adze, or a cover-up for espionage? Perhaps it is a bit of both. In both *New Zealand* and *Colour Scheme*, Ngaio describes Maori as being like the easygoing generous Scottish Highlander or Irishman. They are tribal like the Celts, family-orientated, war-like at times yet extremely hospitable — and they have their own mysticism and law, which she respects. In *Black Beech*, Ngaio wrote of her mother's ability to sense things, to anticipate events, to see into the future: if she had been a Highlander, it would have been called second sight. Ngaio was never the complete sceptic that her father was, and there was always room in her imagination for the unknowable.

What grates for modern readers, though, is Ngaio's representation of Maori as the noble savage. All her most admirable Maori characters, such as Dr Rangi Te Pokiha in *Vintage Murder* and chief Rua Te Kahu in *Colour Scheme*, have a European crust of education, manners, breeding and dress, beneath which seethes their essential savagery, waiting to erupt like the plume of a geyser. As well as her usual 'Cast of Characters' routinely listed at the beginning of her books, in *Colour Scheme* she included a list of Maori words so readers could understand them in context. Ngaio was hoping the novel would promote an interest in Maoritanga overseas.

The Claire family represents another cultural group under siege. They came to New Zealand for vague and misguided reasons. Their business has languished because of their incompetence and the tough conditions. Colonel Claire puffs and procrastinates over bad manners and bad form, but does nothing. His heyday was his time in the Indian army. Mrs Claire's hands are calloused and stained, as are her daughter's. For years God's Own Country has delivered the slimmest margins, and now they are in debt to a charlatan property developer who has possibly committed treason. Isolated in New Zealand by their old-fashioned Edwardian ideas, they turn away dubious guests in order to maintain standards that have no relevance in the New World. The Claires have run out of money and hope, but it is the next generation who will pay the proper price of their misplaced idealism.

Like Eru Saul, their son Simon is caught between two cultures — he is neither a proper Englishman nor a proper New Zealander. Simon has become introverted and uncouth. He is aggressive and speaks with an unpleasant twang.

Ngaio, with her superb ear for spoken dialogue, delights in putting the most banal sayings and brutal slang into his mouth. His sister Barbara, who has escaped her brother's state school 'education' at Harpoon High, has not integrated like her brother. Without her parents' background, she has become shy and awkward, the unsophisticated product of a genteel poverty that is becoming less genteel by the day. Geoffry Gaunt observes her deprivation with such sympathy that he secretly instructs his secretary to order a new black dress from a fashion store in Auckland. It arrives with an anonymous Shakespearian quotation written in green ink. There are shoes, gloves, and stockings to match — even underpants, because Gaunt shudders to think what the old ones were like. In England, the Claires had the class system to tell them they had something and were something. In New Zealand, they merely survive.

Ngaio understood the difficulties of biculturalism, and knew that it was permeated with prejudice on both sides. The night Questing is killed there is a village concert. Guests from the Claires' Wai-ata-tapu spa, plus the locals, cram into a medley of seats in the meeting house. 'It became very hot and the Maori people thought indulgently that it smelt of *pakeha*, while the *pakehas* thought a little less indulgently that it smelt of Maori.' Ngaio saw the relationship between Maori and Pakeha as a partnership, if unequal and flawed. She also acknowledged that colonization created victims. For both Maori and Pakeha, cultural and geographical displacement had truncated the historical and social roots that defined people's place and identity.

Colour Scheme explores this in an entertaining and thought-provoking way. In the dénouement of *Colour Scheme*, Ngaio brings attention to a piece of New Zealand legislation she thought long overdue. As Dikon Bell says of the book's murderous spy, 'It's no good asking me to work up a grain of sympathy for him . . . There's no capital punishment in this country now. He'll spend the rest of his life in jail.' On 17 September 1941, the Labour government abolished the death penalty for murder, commuting sentences to life imprisonment with hard labour. To Ngaio, this seemed a substantial humanitarian victory, and she did not miss the opportunity to point this out.

Colour Scheme was generally well received by critics, the only major difficulty being the implausibility of the spy theme. The reviewer for *The New York Times* commended Ngaio for her 'marvellous sense of comedy' and gift for 'crazy characterisation', and went on perceptively to identify the book's major strength and its central problem:

Alas for my desires, however: I never will know the destiny of the Claires, for Miss Marsh just had to make *Colour Scheme* into a mystery story, and the establishment of the Claires is just so much background for a spy hunt. But I, for one, would like to see Miss Marsh write a real book about the Claires.

In some respects, Ngaio was too successful in her efforts to create realistic characters experiencing the real consequences of colonization. She gave them an imaginative life that made them linger longer in the reader's mind than the circumstances of the death. The murder was resolved, but their lives were not. They were still there like a haunting after-image. What happened to the truculent Simon and his shabby sister, Barbara, or to Eru Saul and his girlfriend? The perfect exorcism would have been a serious New Zealand novel, but Ngaio steadfastly resisted the challenge. The structure of detective novel was too appealing and she was too successful to give it away.

Ngaio's next novel, *Died in the Wool*, published in 1945, was also set in New Zealand. But this time it was located in the South Island High Country where issues of cultural displacement and integration were less central to the plot. Overpoweringly present in this novel is its sense of brooding landscape, in the awesome amphitheatres of treacherous mountains. Visions of *Died in the Wool*'s grizzly murder steal along the dark passages of the imagination to the primal depths of horror. The suffocation and subsequent rotting of Florence Rubrick in a wool bale echoes the chilling claustrophobia of the setting. Everyone is a suspect and everyone feels trapped in this mausoleum of frozen rock.

Flossie Rubrick is attending an auction of Mount Moon's wool clip. She is in her late 40s, with dyed blonde hair; is short and finely built, but clumsy in her movements. In fact, everything about Flossie Rubrick is rough and abrasive. She is not supposed to be there, yet she forces her way backstage so she can look into the faces of the buyers. She is ecstatic when her Japanese friend, Kurata Kan, buys Mount Moon's clip. 'Top price!' she shouts shrilly, to the mortification of her husband, Arthur Rubrick, who is sitting politely in the audience.

It is one of those stinking-hot nor-west days in February 1942, when wool buyer Sammy Joseph and the storeman set about checking the bales. There is a terrible smell. They wonder if it is dead wool, but that smell usually diminishes over time. Sammy Joseph thinks it is more likely a dead rat. The storeman, wearing a canvas glove, reaches an iron hook into a large cut they have made in the offending bale. When he draws the hook out, it is covered in rust-coloured gore and a strand of metallic-gold hair. The stench is unbelievable, but not a whiff is left when Alleyn arrives at Mount Moon to investigate the murder in May 1943.

He is still in the country chasing spies. Flossie Rubrick's unsolved murder alone would not have drawn him into the mountains. She was a member of parliament and much too free with her wartime information. There has been a leak through a Portuguese journalist that has been traced back to Mount Moon, where Flossie's nephew, Douglas Grace, is working with Arthur Rubrick's nephew, Fabian Losse, on the development of a secret magnetic fuse for anti-aircraft shells. The fuse is designed to explode when it approaches anything metallic. Was Flossie Rubrick a German spy? Has she been killed to cover up the activities of a double agent? These are the questions Alleyn is hoping to answer 15 months after Flossie was murdered, bound in the foetal position with ropes, and pressed into a wool bale. This is Alleyn's first cold case.

Ngaio had never used a timeframe of recollection that went so far back; nor had she had a victim dead in the first few pages of the book. Almost every aspect of Flossie Rubrick, and the events of the night she died, is remembered by suspects at Mount Moon. Alleyn refers to the group's need to unburden itself about Flossie as 'verbal striptease'. 'You are using this room as a sort of confessional,' he tells them, 'but I'm bound by no priestly rule.' There is very little action in the present until close to the end of the book, when it becomes suspense-ridden and the criminal is caught in the act of cleaning up the woolshed after a second murder attempt. Vivid recollections of the unpalatable Flossie Rubrick save the narrative from suffocating in its own inertia. Once again, Ngaio's set of characters take on lives that are fascinating in their own right.

Perhaps it was the relevance of some of the issues to Ngaio's own life that gave the story its potency. Like Flossie, Ngaio felt the lack of a son and heir. In 1943, she had travelled to the North Island to stay with her Aunt Edith, whom she called Aunt Amy. This was her father's eldest sister, who had immigrated to New Zealand with her husband Frederick Baker and five adult children in 1924. Aunt Amy now lived in Tauranga with Lill and Hal, her unmarried children. While Ngaio was staying with them, they drove to Hamilton to meet Aunt Amy's daughter Stella, her husband John Mannings, and their children Jean, John and younger brother Roy. It would prove to be a life-changing visit. Lack of family in her life was something Ngaio felt keenly, and she always regretted not having children. In Stella she found the closest thing she would have to a sister and a ready-made family. Ngaio was drawn to the Mannings children whom she came to see as surrogates for her own. The boys captivated her, especially John, the more sedate and contemplative of the two brothers.

John was a well-mannered 'Etonian' boy, already suited to her notions of an upper-class son. As a child he was happy to sit at the piano while Roy, nicknamed Bear, 'rough-and-tumbled and got grubby outside'. Ngaio really only saw the boys: '[Hers] was very much the Edwardian psyche even though she was a woman herself,' remembers Jean Crabtree, Stella Mannings's daughter. Blood relationships meant a lot to Ngaio, and she was generous to all her extended family, but 'she definitely took a shine' to John. For the Mannings children, Ngaio was something of a bombshell with her deep voice, international chic, and odd eating habits. She 'produced a salad for lunch with oranges and garlic in it . . . she wiped the bowl with garlic'. This was extraordinary cuisine for Hamilton in the 1940s.

Later, the Mannings would stay with Ngaio in Christchurch, and in the early 1950s they lived at Marton Cottage for a number of years. When they stayed, Ngaio would take Stella on shopping expeditions to town and drag her into men's clothing shops to buy shirts and jerseys. With her unusually long arms, Ngaio claimed these were the only things she could find to fit her. Stella Mannings was a self-taught typist, and when she stayed she translated Ngaio's handwritten pages into typed manuscript. Ngaio loved the comforting buzz and activity of family life, but also the freedom to isolate herself and write. Stella became a confidante and source of practical assistance and advice. Ngaio was naïve about money. 'Anyone could take her down and they did,' Jean Crabtree recalled. She 'lived for months with a huge hole in the kitchen' when the workman just took off. 'If she ever got anything done, she paid through the nose for it.'

Having seen the potential of Stella's son John, Ngaio decided to foster it. She wanted a surrogate son who could benefit from the money she had made and in return give her affection and respect. In 1945 there was much heated discussion, particularly between Ngaio and Stella's husband, John, about Ngaio paying for young John to go to high school at Christ's College in Christchurch. In the end it was decided that John (whom she called 'Johnny') would become a boarder at the élite boys' school, and he was enrolled in 1946.

Ngaio derived a huge amount of pleasure from knowing that young John was in Christchurch. He came for regular Sunday visits, biking over from Christ's College and working in the garden while strains of music wafted from the windows of the sleepout or 'whari', where John was allowed to play Ngaio's state-of-the-art gramophone. They enjoyed each other's company. Like her father, Ngaio was capable of moving easily between generations. Cecil and Dundas Walker were often there until 1pm on Sundays, when they departed to return in the evening for a game of Lexicon. Ngaio would pour drinks, and inevitably some excellent apple cider would find its way into John's glass. His bicycle ride back to Christ's College for Evensong, Compline, and bed was anything but steady.

Ngaio, the indulgent, mild-mannered rule-breaker, was the perfect patron for a teenage boy. But John's experiences at Christ's College were not as positive as Ngaio had hoped. The school, with its internationally trained staff, opened a window for him on the world — 'When you took literature, your teacher actually knew T.S. Eliot' — but the emphasis was academic and sporting, rather than cultural. It was a macho atmosphere with well-bred trappings. John Mannings, musically inclined and from the provincial north, was out of step. Although he was joined at Christ's College, and in his Sunday excursions to Ngaio's, by his brother Bear in 1949, this did little to alleviate his sense of isolation.

It is the dark side of surrogate parenting that Ngaio explores in *Died in the Wool*. Flossie enrolled her farm manager's son, Cliff, at the equivalent of the best English public school in New Zealand. Cliff's father, Tommy Johns, raised objections and there were ructions at home, but eventually it was settled. Cliff's precocious appetite for the piano and writing would be nurtured in the best learning environment money could buy. Cliff, 'a full-sized enfant prodigé [*sic*]', was taken out of his own environment to satisfy Flossie's need for a child. She wooed him with books, a gramophone with specially selected records, and her Bechstein piano, but away from Mount Moon he faced the realities of life outside the familiar woolshed world of rouseabouts. Flossie planned a big future. Cliff was to go to university and, at the end of the war, to the Royal College of Music in London. But Cliff was miserable at school, and he and Flossie quarrelled. At the age of 16 he wanted to enlist and fight in the war. At 47, she wanted him to remain her protégé and to succeed. She was the parent-figure he rebelled against to become a man. Like a financial investment, Flossie tallied up her losses and railed against him. Her love was not unconditional. He owed her a huge debt. Flossie was bludgeoned and suffocated to the sound of Cliff playing Bach on an old piano in the shearers' quarters. Or was he?

The links to Ngaio's life are fascinating. It is almost as if she is teasing out potential scenarios fictionally, before the possibilities are unleashed in reality. The relationship between real life and her fictional creations is never in any way precise, yet she has a clever way of identifying and exploring the essential issues. Flossie is a dictator (Ngaio was not), so many more than just Cliff have a motive to kill her. As Fabian Losse observes about Flossie's spouse, Arthur Rubrick, 'it takes a strong man to be a weak husband. Matrimonially speaking, a condition of perpetual apology is difficult to sustain.' Flossie's life is littered with people unable to transcend her suffocating ego. Her husband, her ward, her nephews, and her surrogate son all have a stake in her death. She is likened to one of the weird sisters in *Macbeth*, because there is something uncannily clever about her ability to manipulate people. Flossie is ruthless to succeed. The 'ambitious type' is how Markins, manservant and special agent, describes her. 'You see them everywhere. Very often they're childless.' Her political endeavours are insincere. When asked to contribute an article for a weekly journal, she explains: 'I want to stress the sanctity of women's work in the high country'. But her best platitudes 'faltered before the picture of any cocky-farmer's wife, whose working-day is fourteen hours long and comparable only to that of a man under sentence of hard labour'.

As writer and detective fiction commentator Carole Acheson points out, Mount Moon symbolizes 'the multiple role the sheep station has played in New Zealand's history: bringing settlers to the secluded hill country; making sheep the backbone of the nation's economy; and creating a new landed gentry out of the wealthy station owners'.

Cliff's generation will tackle the creation of a New Zealand National Identity in the arts, and his symphonies will capture the quintessence of the landscape and its history. In the meantime, though, this is a mystery and the murderer revealed at the end of *Died in the Wool* is a young man indoctrinated by a Nazi 'youth training scheme' with supremacist ideas. In a letter to Fox, Alleyn explains: 'He was one of a clutch of young foreign Herrinvolk [sic] . . . who did their worst to raise Cain when they returned, bloated with Fascism, to their own country.' Ngaio drew on her own experiences to create her killer, weaving into her plot threads of experiences in Germany in 1937. She was remembering the New Zealander who extolled the virtues of the Nazi Party, and the boys that shouted 'Heil Hitler' as they bathed with their master in the Mosel River. What kind of men would they become, and what would they be capable of?

Alleyn is thinking increasingly of home. As he builds up the fire in the study, he is caught 'on a wave of nostalgia'. He has been away from his wife and London life for three years. He longs to be back in his own country and with his own people. His salve at Mount Moon has been the overpowering presence of the landscape, a presence that even at midnight comes through the windows and sends a shiver of excitement down his spine. But for Alleyn it is time to go.

From this point on, Ngaio would discuss the New Zealand accent, manners and cultural identity in newspaper and *Listener* articles, in letters to the editor and on the radio, but never again in such depth fictionally. It was hard to justify her detective's presence in New Zealand. 'Well I can't keep on lugging old Alleyn out to New Zealand for this reason or that,' she explained to a radio interviewer in 1978. The war had given her an excuse, but Japan surrendered in August 1945, and the fighting was over.

Died in the Wool was criticized for its slow plod through repetitious reminiscences. On the whole, though, critics commended it for its psychological insights and marvellous evocation of the High Country landscape. The most cutting criticism came from the reviewer for the *Time and Tide*. It was overly harsh, but there was an element of truth:

> *Died in the Wool*, though competent, is heavy and, let's face it, dull. The first half of the book is aptly described as 'a verbal striptease before an investigating officer', and before it is over one has long ceased to care which, if any, of these tedious characters is a Nazi agent. Nor are the technical details of New Zealand sheep-shearing very exciting to a layman. The whole thing lacks grip. Come back to England, Miss Marsh; you've been wool-gathering long enough.

The two-year gap between the publication of *Colour Scheme* and *Died in the Wool* was her longest so far. Between these books she entered a new phase in her life that would make detective fiction pale by comparison. In 1941, when the young drama students from the Canterbury University College Drama Society (CUCDS) had cycled up to her home and asked her to produce *Outward Bound*, she had agreed, on one condition: that the next year's production was *Hamlet* and she would be the director.

Dauphin
as for Battle Scenes

CHAPTER FIVE

A Stage Set for Tragedy

A midnight bell tolled as the curtain rose. The stage was simply lit and spartan. High contrasts of light and dark created long silhouettes that played across the plain backdrop. This was the freezing cold battlement of Elsinore Castle in Denmark.

'Who's there?' cried Bernardo, stepping onto the narrow rampart.

'Nay, answer me. Stand and unfold yourself,' challenged Francisco.

'Long live the King!' exclaimed Bernardo.

It was August 1943, and the opening night of a student production of *Hamlet*. Because it was wartime, 'Long live the King!' had a patriotic echo that reverberated around the room. The Little Theatre in Christchurch was packed to capacity. More tickets had been sold than there were seats, and as people's eyes grew accustomed to the darkness the unseated overflow emerged, draped over beams and electrical boxes, and standing leaning against the stage. They crept into place as the lights went down to watch a spectacle, a cultural awakening that would keep Christchurch transfixed for six nights. This was the first time since Allan Wilkie had toured *Hamlet* over 20 years before that *Hamlet* had played to Christchurch audiences. The student players had been reluctant to do it and the audience reaction was impossible to predict. Staging *Hamlet* was a risk.

Francisco, the sentinel, was dressed in an army-issue greatcoat and tin hat. Under his arm he carried a service rifle with a fixed bayonet. The play programme warned audiences that the actors would be wearing modern dress, but the austerity of the stage, its eerie blue lighting, plus the costumes' contemporary poignancy, gave the production a chill impact that few could have anticipated. Bernardo was also dressed in army uniform, and the two men loomed larger than life on the tiny stage. What began in those opening moments would keep the audience spellbound for nearly two hours. They watched Dundas Walker as King Hamlet's ghost standing in bloodcurdling conversation with his son; they watched the young Hamlet, racked by fear and grief, crawling across the stage steps towards the spectre.

'Revenge his foul and most unnatural murder,' the ghost commanded his son.

'Murder!' cried young Hamlet.

'Murder most foul, as in the best it is, but this most foul, strange and unnatural.'

'Haste me to know't,' replied Hamlet, 'that I, with wings as swift as meditation or the thoughts of love, may sweep to my revenge.'

Jack Henderson was perfect as Hamlet. Dark-haired, sallow-skinned, seething and slightly petulant, he had stage presence before he opened his mouth. Henderson, who was 19 when rehearsals began, was the son of Justice Henderson, a High Court judge in Calcutta. He had been attending Westminster School in London when war broke out, and his parents arranged for him to finish his schooling at Christ's College and continue on to Canterbury University. He had previous acting experience and planned to leave shortly for England to study at The Old Vic. Even then, Ngaio and Dundas Walker spent hours with him going over lines so that he got the timing, intonations and breathing correct. They spent a whole afternoon on the first 10 lines of his opening soliloquy. For a time he even stayed with Ngaio at Marton Cottage. Exhausted after rehearsals, they would creep in late at night and cook bacon and eggs, whispering so that they did not disturb Ngaio's father. She thrived on the camaraderie and loved the intellectual exercise of translating the play script into dramatic action. Henderson, however, struggled to find his form. He had to learn how to speak in blank verse and hold some of his energy in reserve so that he could build to a climax. He found it hard to texture the delivery of his lines. At times, he unleashed emotion with an intensity that was as exhausting for those who listened as it was for him. But there was a power in his passion that would ultimately rivet the audience, and leave it marvelling that a young, relatively inexperienced actor could bring so much fire to one of Shakespeare's most turbulent roles.

Some of the play's impact came from the changes Ngaio made to the script. *Hamlet* was presented in prose rather than verse. This made it seem more immediate and accessible, and stopped students from falling into the pattern of reading it like a poem that paused 'at the end of each line of verse, regardless of sense or punctuation'. The Christchurch audience was provincial; a purist version of the play could not be staged. It was imperative to capture and hold people's interest, and the rhythms of the staid city must be considered. Ngaio cut the play with the precision of a surgeon, reducing it to 17 scenes with a shortened interval so that the theatre emptied before the last tram left Cathedral Square at 10.30pm. This distilled the action so everything that remained contributed to the dramatic climax. She kept the structure tight and the timing precise. In rehearsal she ran through the scenes, timing them so that they had speed and economy of delivery.

The script she worked from was heavily annotated and had illustrations of characters and action in the margins and on facing pages. She mapped the stage out in models to visualize how the production would work. The Little Theatre stage was tiny, and the challenge was to make it seem expansive enough to cope with the epic aspects of the play. The space easily evoked the intimacy of the soliloquy, but a grander canvas was harder to suggest.

Ngaio brought a degree of professionalism to student drama, and it was infectious. She took the productions seriously and she communicated her seriousness so that students felt compelled to rise to her expectations. Young people excited her. She loved their untried, easy confidence, and their willingness to learn. Ngaio, although flattered at being put on a pedestal, made sincere efforts to climb down from it. The play gave her a reason to be in the company of a generation who could have been her children, but always the work stood between them and close personal intimacy. It protected this shy, reserved woman from the glare of uncomfortable sentiment and youthful exuberance, but occasionally it was an unfortunate barrier to something more meaningful and revealing. Acting brings raw humanity before the gods. Its instrument is the human body and voice, and few things test people more than live performance. Inevitably, emotions are heightened and intense, and added to this were bristling juvenile egos, hormones and alcohol. Most single women of 48 would have blanched at the prospect, but Ngaio thrived. She had found her *métier* — another passion, another great love, a second life.

She stepped into the hurly-burly with her firm way of handling the cast. She was never gratuitously cutting or cruel, but she had an awesome presence that riveted young actors to the spot, sending a ripple of discomfort down their spines when they were not on the mark. Her voice 'boomed like a bittern', she gestured extravagantly, and she could leap onto the stage with an agility that left no one out of her reach. Physically, she was still young, able to flick her leg up behind her with flamboyant flexibility. To the students, she seemed as extraordinary in life as she was in print. Even the engineering students who shambled into rehearsals to do the lighting stiffened to her cue. She made them believe in something bigger than themselves: the play, the playwright and the production. All of these were more important than the individual, and the cast's collective responsibility was to make it the best production possible.

Ngaio had the perfect psychology: she set high standards and encouraged people to reach them. The stick was not a rod but a carrot, and the energy to reach it was the actor's own self-motivation. Ngaio led from behind. Interestingly, she hung back from putting her name to her first Shakespearian production. In the programme the producers were given as Jack Henderson and Marie Donaldson, but *Canta*, the student magazine, recognized her shadowy presence:

> 'Hamlet' — in modern dress — is the most ambitious production the Drama Society has attempted for many years. In fact, were it not for Ngaio Marsh continually in the background (for she refuses to be called 'producer', only 'godmother', on the grounds that she has insufficient time to devote to the play), the society would indeed be rash to attempt it.

Ngaio was determined to make *Hamlet* a success. She may have been too humble, or too cautious, to put her name to the play, but in every other way it carried her stamp. She coached the cast in voice projection. Ngaio was less concerned with the Kiwi accent than with clear speech that reached the back of the room. In the Little Theatre, empty, this was easy, but when the theatre was crowded it was more of a challenge.

It was also her idea to use modern dress, which could be justified on the grounds of war rationing and expediency, but in reality was a covert experiment.

Christchurch had a literati and a university at its heart, and Ngaio wanted to challenge and impress them. *Hamlet* brought something of the urbane West End avant-garde to an Antipodean garden city. In 1938, Tyrone Guthrie had produced *Hamlet* in modern dress at The Old Vic, and memories of this were still vivid in Ngaio's mind. So parents' cupboards were raided for the sake of art. Except for the sentinels, the men wore everyday suits and overcoats, the women evening gowns and housecoats. Hamlet and Claudius were a yin and yang pair. Ngaio's father commissioned his tailor to make a dashing black suit for Hamlet, and Claudius was dressed in a white suit made out of nappy fabric stiffened by shoe whiting. Regular applications of the latter were required to maintain its pristine appearance.

Modern costuming was matched by the minimalism of a modern stage. The clutter of scenery and props was kept to a minimum by the use of the cyclorama, lit for outdoor scenes and curtained for inside. It was a brilliantly simple concept that became a Ngaio trademark.

Music was another addition. Frederick Page recommended the talented Douglas Lilburn to write the incidental music. He had returned to Christchurch in 1941, from the Royal College of Music in London where he had worked under Vaughan Williams, and was keen to build on his repertoire and experience. The play was due to 'open on a Monday night [and] Lilburn only began work after attending a rehearsal the preceding Wednesday'. By the dress rehearsal on the Sunday he had written and rehearsed with his three violins and a tubular bell-ringer. It was a scramble to produce and practise the music, so Lilburn must have been relieved when the results were rapturously received. 'The good Ngaio,' he recalled many years later, 'always made me feel that whatever I realised for her was just what she had been wanting.' Lilburn's music was perfectly placed. His violins evoked 'the very breath of the cold night air at Elsinore,' wrote Ngaio, and his finale, a funeral march, where the dead Hamlet was carried out on the shoulders of four soldiers, left a lingering sense of solemnity that underscored the prince's tragic end.

When the final curtain came down, the crowd clapped wildly. The actors took their bows. The star of the show was undoubtedly Jack Henderson, but there was also Paul Molineaux, a young law student, who played an excellent Laertes, and accomplished performances from Yvonne Westmacott as Ophelia and Marie Donaldson as Gertrude. In fact, the cast of *Hamlet* had held the audience captive and they were reluctant to break the spell and go home.

News of the show's success spread like wildfire around a city tinder-dry for serious theatre. Ngaio was elated. Everywhere she went it was the topic of conversation. Newspaper reviews of the show were very positive. Its simple stage, and skilful editing, pace and execution were commended. 'I would praise the good diction, rapid ease and smooth timing of the spoken lines, which, throughout the play, retain the exciting nature of spontaneous dialogue and involuntary out pouring of thought,' wrote the *Press* critic. The queues that formed to buy tickets for the next performance were so long that the company received complaints from the police about the obstruction of the pavement. The play continued to open to packed houses. There was demand for an extended season, but it was impossible to extend it much longer because of the end-of-year examinations. A compromise was reached and it was decided that *Hamlet* would run again after examinations in late November–December.

This was the human involvement and public recognition that Ngaio Marsh had always longed for. Writing detective novels was an introverted experience. She wrote in isolation to focus her mind, and her real fame overseas was now vicariously experienced through reviews and letters from her publisher and English and American agents. New Zealanders read her books, but few people fully appreciated the enormity of her achievement abroad.

All the detective books she had written had never brought this kind of local acclaim. It must have seemed ironic that a student play should generate so much fuss, but she relished it, because in that relationship she glimpsed her dream of a Shakespearian renaissance in Christchurch. 'This was the beginning of an association that has lasted for twenty years,' Ngaio wrote in *Black Beech*. 'For me it has been a love affair.' Between *Hamlet* and the following year's production of *Othello*, Ngaio wrote *Colour Scheme*. She was still writing when rehearsals for *Othello* began, and some nights she would return home exhausted, but somehow found the energy to attend to her book. Increasingly, she tried to write during the day. Sometimes she even dictated sections to her secretary to relieve the strain of handwriting.

The rehearsal period for *Othello* was six weeks. Paul Molineaux was cast as the Moor and Jack Henderson as Iago, but a new leading lady was required to play Desdemona. Auditions were a serious matter, and students now lined up for the honour of playing a part in a Shakespearian drama directed by Ngaio Marsh. From this point on, the pretence of student producers was dropped and Ngaio's name featured boldly on the programme. Barbara Reay (now Webb) auditioned on the stage of the Little Theatre for the part of Desdemona.

> I wasn't very good at reading . . . I remember her saying 'I didn't want to give you the part.' It was so frank and so sweet (I don't know who else auditioned but they probably weren't very good) . . . It wasn't said with any animosity and we both laughed.

Ngaio called the students by their nicknames, and Reay's was Bubs. Well coached by Ngaio, she improved. 'She would take every part . . . I'm five feet and she's six feet [tall] and she played my part beautifully.' A great respect developed between director and cast. '[Ngaio] was controlling . . . in a very charming sort of way . . . She got us doing things we never dreamed we could do.' All the time she was directing her actors, Ngaio was thinking of how the audience would respond. She wanted them to experience Shakespeare as she had, so she made momentum and dramatic action paramount. 'Othello strangling poor little Desdemona . . . well, it was murder,' Barbara Webb remembers.

> As she was a [detective fiction] writer she had a great sense of drama and excitement . . . I think she produced these two tragedies like thrillers. Which were very watchable and very presentable. She really presented Shakespeare back to Christchurch . . . when I was throttled everyone used to scream.

Ngaio had considered the possibility of staging both *Romeo and Juliet* and *Julius Caesar*, but she had such strong male leads in Paul Molineaux and Jack Henderson that it seemed a waste of their talent not to cast them in roles of equal complexity in *Othello*, with its central struggle between good and evil.

Ngaio enjoyed working with young men. In Shakespeare's plays, they had the most dramatic and complex roles, and it was this that attracted her as much as the people who played them. She spent hours in private sessions going over their lines. This 'coterie of young men . . . became real friends of Ngaio's. They used to go up and have suppers on Sunday nights.' There was nothing overtly sexual in these relationships, but they contained a degree of flirtation. Ngaio was much older, and her infatuation was with the work and the challenge, but the titillation of being surrounded by good-looking men was undoubtedly a boost to her ego. It seems perhaps odd, then, that Ngaio dressed as she did. 'She always wore trousers and usually a scarf and a three-quarter coat. She always looked mannish.' Although these were comfortable clothes that allowed her to move easily and stay warm on a draughty stage in the middle of winter, they were still a curious choice for a woman in the 1940s. As was her hallmark habit of chain-smoking cigarettes without flicking off the ash, so that students took bets on how long it would defy gravity and curl before it fell, usually down the front of her dark-coloured top.

Douglas Lilburn was again invited to write the music, and Ngaio's cousin Samuel Marsh Williams designed the set and costumes. Modern dress could not be repeated, so, at the height of rationing, wardrobe mistress Margaret Westmacott was charged with the responsibility of finding velvets, satins, lace and the fabric to make Tudor ruffs and cuffs. Ngaio and the drama society's confidence had been bolstered after the previous year's success. There was no need to make the play seem so contemporary. *Othello* would be the Elizabethan spectacle that *Hamlet* was not. They felt sure that the audience would make the leap and see its modern relevance, in spite of the antique dress.

Before the curtain rose on a Venetian street, the audience could hear the cries of a gondolier over the strains of Lilburn's opening music. The flavour of a foreign scene was set. 'Just imagine you are a couple of old Venetians,' Lilburn had told his musicians, who were to become 'part of the drama'. A courtly piece then heralded the arrival of the duke and senators. The scenes changed easily to ones of courtly splendour. 'We had three acting levels,' Ngaio explained, 'with the stage arranged so that acting was continuous — one scene going on in one quarter of the stage while a new scene is set up — as quietly as possible — behind curtains on another part of the stage.' In its own way, *Othello* was as experimental as the modern-dress *Hamlet* had been.

Ngaio's staging technique made the Little Theatre seem more spacious, and her costuming gave it a rich visual texture. Desdemona was a splash of sumptuous colour against a sepia-toned wartime audience. Her *pièce de résistance* was a gown made of rose pink satin with a cloak of deep green velvet and a black headdress embroidered with pearls. She was breathtaking, and so was the performance. When the curtain came down on the first night, the audience clapped madly as they had a year before. According to a *New Zealand Listener* article, 'seats for the whole season were sold out before it opened'. It seemed destined for success, but could it reach *Hamlet*'s benchmark of critical acclaim? Allen Curnow's review in *The Press* was an enthusiastic endorsement. He thought Jack Henderson made a worthy Iago to Othello, but:

the Moor himself, deserves the highest praise. Mr Molineaux was emotionally 'possessed' by the part . . . His clear capacity for actual suffering in the tragic role both startled his audience and really touched those nerves of experience which tragedy must touch if it is to be more than the name . . . Barbara Reay's Desdemona was appealing, though her love for Othello might have been less romantic.

Curnow also praised Lilburn's music, which he thought distinctive, yet at the same time 'submissive to the meaning of the play, and perfectly in place'.

Othello was a coup, and once again 'the whole town was a stir', as Ngaio noted in an interview a few months later.

I was walking through town one day and I went past a tailor's shop. The tailor came dashing out with a piece of tweed over his arm when he saw me, and said he had taken his son five times, and could I possibly get him seats again . . . exactly the same thing happened with an electrician.

What thrilled Ngaio most was that her play had been a democratic success, appealing to the 'man in the street' as well as to the literati. This, she believed, was Shakespeare's intention — to communicate on all levels to all people — and she had achieved it. The models for her approach began with Allan Wilkie. His theatre was constantly on the move, so props and settings were kept to a minimum. His costumes, more easily transported, were lavish and considered. According to theatre commentator Paul McGuire, 'he stepped up the tempo of speech and action and reduced the scene changes, to reach something like the pace of Elizabethan playing'. There was also the avant-garde Pirandello with his bleak stages, and Constantin Stanislavsky, whom Ngaio described as 'the G.O.M. [Grand Old Man], as it were, of the Russian theatre'. From Stanislavsky, she took his method of 'complete muscular relaxation and natural-looking movements' and seamless scene changes. Nothing Ngaio did was entirely unique, but the combination was her own.

Ngaio's greatest achievement was her ability to pull together talent. She had that rare ability to see and realize potential in others. This was the skill of a 'looker on' who watched and assessed people just as she weighed up the strengths and weaknesses of her characters. She wanted to draw the best from her actors. As a result, when the *Othello* cast party died away and inebriated students climbed on their bicycles to weave their way home, there was a huge void.

Ngaio saw the disbanding of this group as a loss. She had aspirations to create a national theatre company in New Zealand and she believed her student players might form a nucleus or at least the pattern for a professional theatre. Ngaio was already a member of a select group, which included cousin Sam Marsh Williams, George Swan and Arnold Goodwin, that was planning to tour professional actors in plays around the country. However, it was not this group but a pair of young students who kept the cast together and put Ngaio's players on the road.

In July 1944, Lyall Holmes and Colin Allan suggested that the university drama society tour *Hamlet* and *Othello* around New Zealand. The idea was enthusiastically embraced, but the cast failed in its first attempt to find a backer. Unannounced, a delegation of promoters led by John Farrell arrived at the Little Theatre, expecting to watch an impromptu taste of *Hamlet* and *Othello* to assess whether they would invest. Without make-up and costumes, the cast lurched nervously through their lines. Harold Bowden, general manager of theatrical company J.C. Williamson, was not convinced. It seemed the dream would founder. But Farrell, moved by the students' disappointment, suggested they try Dan O'Connor, a theatrical manager and impresario in Auckland. In the end, Allan travelled all the way to Auckland to convince O'Connor to come down to Christchurch to see a matinée performance of *Othello*. O'Connor, a great lover of Shakespeare himself, agreed and was convinced.

In early September, Ngaio confirmed publicly that a student tour was planned. 'Some friends are coming to light with the necessary backing and ideas, and suggestions on the business side,' she explained to an interviewer. 'Of course there are all sorts of things that will have to be dovetailed in, and there will be transport and manpower difficulties, too, but you might see us tour, all the same, in the summer.'

No one was naïve about problems of touring a wartime company of students, least of all Ngaio, but perhaps no one realized quite how difficult 'difficult' could be. Rehearsals began after end-of-year examinations, and one of the first obstacles was to free six of the young men from compulsory military training over the summer. Ngaio's name, in association with that of Dan O'Connor — who had toured Yehudi Menuhin, the Vienna Boys' Choir and pianist Wilhelm Backhaus — was enough to convince the military authorities, but the pair had less luck with the railways. There were restrictions on non-essential travel, and bookings were at a peak over the Christmas period. The railways were reluctant to move a cast of 32 (plus hangers-on), let alone the massive amount of gear that accompanied them. They were denied discount fares, but negotiations continued until it seemed transport to Dunedin, before Christmas, and Auckland and Wellington in the New Year, had been secured. The transition from the Little Theatre to the much larger His Majesty's Theatre in Dunedin had to be carefully considered. Suddenly, action and scenery on a tiny stage had to convey the same intensity in a much bigger space, and such props as Desdemona's bed had to be made to move.

Their itinerary was in such flux that the programmes were printed in Dunedin, rather than, as usual, by the Caxton Press in Christchurch. When the company arrived in Dunedin there was the worrying issue of accommodation. The women were quickly billeted, but 15 of the men were homeless until a dilapidated house in George Street called The Chookery was found and they crammed into it. It was a party powder-keg, and Ngaio knew it. She could only hope that the fuse would not be lit until after the final curtain. Wild rumours abounded about what went on in The Chookery, which became the company's hub. *Hamlet* opened on 16 December 1944, and once the *Star* critic got over the fact that modern dress meant overcoats, felt hats, beer bottles, guns and uniforms, the reviews were good. The *Otago Daily Times* looked beyond individual performance to Ngaio's creative direction: 'Miss Marsh's imagery is striking, and the play's manners and action retained unspoiled . . . Those who do not feel the beauty and force of it can hardly be alive to artistry and imaginative direction.'

Othello was equally well received. 'Miss Barbara Reay as Desdemona achieved a perfect contrast to the turbulent Othello,' wrote one commentator. While another, on a more negative note, identified:

a propensity on the part of some of the actors to unduly raise their voices in the more passionate passages, and in two cases at least this ranting was rather a distressing note. But the performance as a whole was a vivid, colourful one and met with the enthusiastic approval of a fairly large audience.

This accusation of 'ranting' was not new. Although newspaper response in Christchurch was almost unanimously positive, a student review in *Canta* magazine had been critical, especially of Jack Henderson, who was described as mannered and conceited. There was an air of tongue-in-cheek tease in these reviews and articles, but also an element of truth. At moments of climactic action, the acting could lose the contours of Shakespeare's language and emotion and became an unrelenting tirade. Ngaio impressed on her actors that they needed to be larger than life on stage to communicate with an audience separated by their place in the mob and the shroud of darkness. Sometimes, however, this strategy was applied too literally and they overcompensated.

This, did not, however, dampen the ardour of Dunedin audiences. The season lasted six nights, finishing two days before Christmas. The reviews were good, the house sizes and returns reasonable, and in due course The Chookery powder-keg went off. Fish and chips and beer were the party staples for a group of students who arrived back in Christchurch fatigued and slightly hungover. Ngaio was relieved to get home. Crawsie, her housekeeper, had been left with the responsibility of looking after her father who was getting increasingly cantankerous as his health deteriorated. 'He could be a tyrant and very difficult at times.'

The New Year brought yet another separation. The journey to Auckland involved a ferry journey and a long train trip. As Ngaio sat with her company of young actors, memories of her own tour with Allan Wilkie jogged back. When she travelled by train she repeopled the carriage with those 'long-remembered companions'. 'It was the first of many such occasions and I was to grow familiar with the look of my fellow-players in transit,' she wrote in *Black Beech*, 'the ones who read, the ones who stared out of the window, the ones who slept, the cheerful, the morose and the resigned.' But this time Ngaio was the actor-director in charge.

In Auckland, the travelling troupe was welcomed by a mayoral reception. In her address, Ngaio took the opportunity to promote the need for a better infrastructure of performance venues throughout the country to foster the development of actors, playwrights and a national theatre. She unapologetically used the public platforms that her drama activities and celebrity status gave her to uphold the value of theatre and argue for more state investment in its promotion.

The theatre they were forced to use in Auckland was a case in point. In the January heat, the tiny auditorium became an oven. Opening doors and windows simply changed the oven to fan-bake and, worst of all, let in the thundering noise of trams and an electrical generator that rumbled away to supply power to the stage. The stage props and furnishings were sent by sea. 'When the coffin made its way from the wharf perched on top of a lorry, hats were reverently doffed.' Sets and scenery were assembled in the heat. At night there was some relief, but the matinées were a sauna. In spite of the conditions, they played to packed houses. 'For fully five minutes after the final curtain the hall rang with continuous applause in appreciation of a production of outstanding merit,' wrote the reviewer for the *Herald*.

Accusations of ranting vanished. 'Miss Marsh is to be congratulated,' said the *Auckland Star* critic, 'on the way in which she had trained her cast to take Shakespeare's declamatory speeches in their stride, giving oratory the full power of their voices, but dropping to ordinary conversational rhythm for the more casual lines.' Once again, Ngaio's directing received accolades:

for the handling and grouping of her cast and the smoothness of the production. Her talent for unusual effect, together with the skill of Marsh Williams, who designed the scenery, produced striking settings by the aid of drapes, cyclorama and pillars. Lighting was given varied play; and the period costumes were attractive.

The two-week Auckland season was a box-office success, grossing £1,115 and making 'an enormous contribution to the expenses of the tour'. To keep costs down, most of the cast were billeted, but the management and stars, like Desdemona, stayed in hotels. 'They thought they were doing well by me,' recalls Barbara Webb. 'I was put in the Railway Hotel . . . [and each night] one of those young men used to walk me home . . . [but] a creepy man used to go up in the lift with me every night and I had to run to my bedroom . . . I would have rather been billeted.'

Any individual anxieties were soon overshadowed by the collective disaster of a rail strike. They expected to open in Wellington on 24 January 1945, but there was no way of getting there. At the last minute, the strike was averted and the cast were retrieved urgently from Mission Bay beach and herded onto the train. Their props and scenery were delayed in Auckland until the beginning of the next week, so they arrived empty-handed. Ngaio, Dan O'Connor and tour manager, Colin Allan, were frantic. Amazingly, the Wellington season opened with sets and costumes borrowed from local repertory societies and hotels. The stress took its toll on everyone. By this stage an estimated 12,000 New

Zealanders had seen the plays, but none of them like this. In Auckland, they gave 17 performances; in Wellington, it was six.

A storm of controversy broke out over critic Harcus Plimmer's *Hamlet* review in *The Dominion*. His snide comments that modern dress was no novelty as 'it was done in like manner in Berlin 30 years ago' could be overlooked, but his attack on Jack Henderson caused outrage.

It was difficult for instance to be deeply impressed with a melancholy Prince who, from time to time lit a cigarette, and on one occasion puffed smoke into the face of his father's murderer . . . Mr J. Henderson, a small man with uncertain legs, who has the gift of velocity of high vibrancy.

It was the remark about the young actor's legs that was the trigger, because Jack Henderson had been crippled by polio. One of his legs was significantly shorter than the other and he walked with a pronounced limp. When he was tired on stage he staggered under the exertion of the part, but he had done such a good job that critics had failed to pick, or were too polite to mention, this flaw in his performance.

People flew to his defence. 'Even to the most unobservant, it is apparent that Mr. Henderson is handicapped by a physical disability. He is to be congratulated rather than jeered at' stated one of many letters to *The Dominion's* editor. The battle between opposing forces got so heated that Ngaio finally stepped in with her own letter to the editor.

Sir — Some of your correspondents suggested that we resent your critic's review. On the contrary we welcome it as salutary. None of the players has taken part in this correspondence; all feel that if New Zealand can get angry about a Shakespearian production there is still hope for the theatre in this country. As for Jack Henderson's lameness, it is easy to believe that your critic failed to notice it.

Ngaio raised the tone of what had become an acrimonious debate. She graciously accepted criticism of her directing and modified her practice, and knowing that she might eventually receive criticism for having a lame leading man, she had gone ahead regardless. She was a director who learned from her mistakes and took risks, and this was the admirable standard she set for her players. The controversy brought crowds flooding in. It was the best piece of free publicity the actors had received all tour. They played again to packed houses, and at the end of their season were given a public reception at the Alexander Turnbull Library.

On their return to Christchurch in early February 1945 the players received another civic welcome, and played a final season in the Radiant Hall. Allen Curnow revisited *Hamlet* in a review that summed up its director's achievement.

> Miss Ngaio Marsh's *Hamlet* does make the magic work. It is living Shakespeare: it is able to release those feelings of pity, wonder, and horror, which in our times of screen-fed theatre-going we are liable to forget . . . It works; it is alive to every part; the 17 scenes bear the action forward with faultlessly managed continuity . . . Miss Marsh's company must soon largely disband . . . But the greatest loss and the saddest waste are of something intangible — the spirit in this company, the imagination and devotion.

The tour made a national icon of Ngaio Marsh. In New Zealanders' minds, she became synonymous with Shakespeare and the theatre. Her popular approach broadened its audience. She made Shakespeare appealing and proved that, in spite of difficult conditions and a small-scale economy, a tour was not only possible, but could be deemed a success. An estimated 20,000 people saw Ngaio's *Hamlet* and *Othello*. London's West End theatres had a huge audience in their backyard; Ngaio's troupe had to carry Shakespeare around the country to capture theirs. The great 18th-century actor, David Garrick, wrote in his prologue to *The Clandestine Marriage*, in 1766:

> But he, who struts his hour upon the stage;
> Can scarce extend his fame for half an age;
> Nor pen nor pencil can the actor save,
> The art, and artist, share one common grave.

The imagination and devotion that Ngaio collected together in this band of players on this extraordinary tour would dissipate and only the shadow of memories would remain. But she had established a style of production and a stable of talent that could live again in new incarnations, and she had highlighted the need for what Curnow referred to as a 'national theatre enterprise' in New Zealand.

⊂▦▮▭⊃

In the meantime, there was a gap. Perhaps as a consoling gesture, *Canta* published the shows' comic out-takes. Even the anxious moments and the accidents now seemed fun.

> For who in the cast will forget the complete collapse of Desdemona's bed in the final scene of *Othello*, when the grief-stricken Moor throws the gentle lady down on the bed, and how she disappeared from view, folded between the two halves . . . like meat in a sandwich? . . . Or when Horatio missed his entrance . . . [or] Cassio . . . had such 'poor and unhappy drain for drinking'. What shall be said of the dagger that flew into the front stalls . . . the footlight broken by a foil, and the foil broken by the duel.

It was widely known that Jack Henderson planned to leave almost immediately for London to begin training at The Old Vic, so the cast assembled for one last occasion and Dan O'Connor kindly sponsored a charity matinée performance, which raised £100. The cheque was presented to Henderson with the best wishes of the cast. Then, a massive shockwave rocked the foundations of conservative Christchurch society: Jack Henderson was not leaving alone, but with Dan O'Connor's wife, Trixie.

This confounded Ngaio. He was her actor, but O'Connor was a close friend and a cornerstone of her productions. Ngaio's allegiance was split, but she was quite clear about the ethics of the scandal. O'Connor had been betrayed and so had she, and she never quite trusted Henderson again. The affair cast a pall over winding-up arrangements. The charity cheque was returned, and Henderson and Trixie O'Connor made a very public elopement. Trixie was younger than O'Connor and older than Henderson. The plan was that she would help him promote his acting career in England, but Henderson never acted again: his final moments in the castle of Elsinore were his last on stage. One of the great sadnesses for Ngaio was that Dan O'Connor had embraced the idea of a national theatre, and now, surely, his allegiance to the concept would be compromised.

She returned home to her routine. Maybe the future would be brighter now the end of the war seemed inevitable. Reviews of *Died in the Wool* had begun appearing in British newspapers as the tour was drawing to an end. On the

152

whole they were positive, but she took to heart the *Time and Tide* comment that it was time for Alleyn to go home. The setting for the next novel would be British.

Ngaio kept alive her passion for the theatre in the wake of the tour by spending hours in animated conversation with Dundas Walker. He resumed his Sunday visits and they talked about the latest overseas shows, directors and actors. Dundas had toured with Ngaio and the student players, and was a constant companion at rehearsals and during productions. 'He was a very nice gentleman,' remembers Barbara Webb. 'He was tall and very skinny with dyed black hair.' Walker, who was homosexual, had a close and supportive, but platonic, relationship with Ngaio.

They mulled over what the next student production should be, and in the end Ngaio recommended Shakespeare's *A Midsummer Night's Dream* to the drama society. A comedy would contrast with the two previous tragedies and reflect New Zealand's ascendant mood now that victory in the war seemed close. (Germany surrendered in May.) The production was conceived on an epic scale, from the tiny elves co-opted from a local ballet school, to the fantastic fairy court of King Oberon and Queen Titania. Wind, rain and fiercely cold temperatures battered rehearsals at the Little Theatre, while snow lay on the ground for the show's opening night at the Radiant Hall in July 1945.

Henderson was overseas and Molineaux was following the demands of a legal career, but not having strong male leads was a strategy. The dominance of men in *Hamlet* and *Othello* had been noted and challenged by members of the drama society. *A Midsummer Night's Dream* was more even in its weighting of male and female roles. This choice would give young women a chance to hone their acting skills in a way that the tragedies had not. Without the star quality of Henderson and Molineaux, however, the topography of talent and acting in *A Midsummer Night's Dream* was much flatter. The infant elves sometimes came close to stealing the show, and what did dominate was the raucous acting of the rude mechanics, especially Hugh Ross as Nick Bottom, Mervyn Glue as Francis Flute, and Jim Erikson as Robin Starveling, who were described by the *Star-Sun* as 'gems of pure comedy'. Douglas Lilburn's music, 'specially composed' for the show, was commended for contributing much to the 'mood of the comedy'.

The point was made, in a collection of reviews published in *Canta* magazine, that the costuming was evocative of the sinister rather than the magical side of fantasy. A Tolkienesque quality to the wardrobe and make-up made them positively frightening. This was a dream with nightmarish elements that offered a fascinating insight into the dark side of Ngaio's imagination. As a child, she had been captivated by grotesque fairytales and the black-humoured Victorian limericks of authors such as R.H. Barham. It was only natural, when she brought this vision to the stage, that it would contain more than a little of the macabre. According to John Pollard, writing in *Canta* as 'Friar Balsam', the characters had:

> Great green eyebrows, greenish clothes and faces, and a hairdressing making coiffures resemble dingy dish clouts, all combined to produce beings that looked more like mossy corpses than airy sprites, while Oberon, with his ghastly face and sinister pokings, pointings, and rolling of eye-balls, was reminiscent of 'Frankenstein' filmed in Gruesome Technicolor.

This chilling interpretation of Shakespeare's comedy was undoubtedly the result of Ngaio's direction, and in some respects it came close, in spirit at least, to the Elizabethan mind that conceived it. If Ngaio's ghoulish visualization of *A Midsummer Night's Dream* was a mismatch in Christchurch, in 1945, it would certainly not have been out of place in Shakespeare's time. Fifty years later, Peter Jackson would bring similar imaginative elements to the screen in *Heavenly Creatures* and the *Lord of the Rings* trilogy.

A Midsummer Night's Dream was not toured, and nor was Ngaio's production of *Henry V* which was staged in December of the same year. After his marriage break-up, Dan O'Connor had gone overseas, so the encouragement and financial impetus of a leading impresario was missing. The casts were huge, and to justify a tour of this size the productions had to demonstrate a precocious talent and flair that they never realized. Rehearsals for *Henry V* began after end-of-year examinations and the season lasted three nights. The houses were full, partly because Allen Curnow's *Press* review encouraged people to see the production. In spite of the short rehearsal period, and 'heavy cuts', he felt Ngaio had 'caught the spirit of the play'. His negative criticism was an old albatross. 'As before, in the Drama Society's Shakespeare, one could have wished for more to be said and less to be sung or ranted.' The play was staged in the Little Theatre, and this would be Ngaio's last production there. *Henry V*'s huge heraldic scenes looked bizarre in the tiny space, and the power for lighting was supplied by a single socket, which blew during performances. Each night the battle on stage was matched by a battle behind the scenes to ensure the power board was not overloaded. At one point, when the fuse blew, Max McGlashan had to jam his screwdriver into it to complete the circuit. The Little Theatre was becoming too cramped to accommodate Ngaio's dream.

In 1946, Ngaio staged *Macbeth*. This was the play, along with *Hamlet*, that she mentioned so often in her novels, and the Scottish Highland setting excited feelings of family history. *Macbeth* was also supposed to be unlucky, and she loved the idea that the play was jinxed. 'The Scottish play' also satisfied the continuing call for strong female leads. Lady Macbeth is one of Shakespeare's most dynamic and complex women. The lynchpin in her husband's downfall, she is torn apart by warring motives and emotions. It is this psychological and spiritual journey from normality to madness, and from grace to damnation, that must be portrayed convincingly on stage. The challenge for Ngaio was to find a young female actor of sufficient calibre to carry the role. When the tall, contralto-voiced Maryrose Miller marched into the auditions, Ngaio could not believe her good luck. Miller's deep voice gave her acting a range of intensity that suggested someone much older. The show opened in July. People flooded in to watch Norman Ettlinger, a returned serviceman, and his wife, a second-year student, destroy themselves on stage. Ngaio had advertised for ex-soldiers to audition. This was a new source of acting potential, as were the refugees and immigrants who came to Christchurch to escape the catastrophic consequences of the war.

Macbeth played for seven nights. Douglas Lilburn's haunting Highland pipes set the scene, and Ngaio's now-established formula perfectly captured the bleakness of the heath. Things were distilled and dramatic. In *Canta* magazine reviews, there were gripes about ranting and an overall sense that the actors had not quite fulfilled their roles. For the play to be successful, sympathy for the thane and his wife has to survive a convincing portrayal of their slide into madness and moral degradation. This is a fine balance even experienced actors struggle to achieve. The production was also criticized for its cheap costuming and stingy props. The most unconvincing were the toy swords and Macbeth's *papier-mâché* head on a broomstick, which, according to one critic, 'deserved the hearty laugh it received'.

Student reviewers were always among Ngaio's harshest critics. They reserved the right to offer an independent view, which was often jaundiced and bubbling with bravado. They were the radical voice and Ngaio represented the establishment, but sometimes they got it right. Lukewarm criticism was not matched by the popular response. The show played to capacity crowds and was a huge financial success. Dan O'Connor was back in the country, so the decision was made to tour *Macbeth* over the summer break. Ngaio made changes to the cast, costumes, shields, swords, backcloth — and *papier-mâché* head — in preparation for their seasons in Auckland and Wellington.

The *Auckland Star* raved: 'Settings almost stark in their simplicity, splendid use of lighting, imaginative costuming and drapings all reveal her outstanding talent in this field.' The changes she had made seemed to have hit the mark. A *Herald* review had one main reservation: 'When Macbeth's soliloquies are spoken as though they had nothing like absolute values of their own, they lose their power to sweep the listener.' A letter to the editor from poet and academic A.R.D. Fairburn took the reviewer to task.

The custom of lifting soliloquies out of the action of the play and treating them as 'purple passages' is one that has marred generations of Shakespearian acting. [Macbeth] and his colleagues are, I think, to be commended for the way in which they maintain a strict unity of the dramatic and literary elements in the play, letting the poetry 'come through'. I felt that they brought us very close to Shakespeare, and a long way from the 19th century 'drawing room reciter'.

Ngaio saw Shakespeare's soliloquies in the same way. In fact, it was in 1946 that Ngaio published her *A Play Toward: A Note on Play Production*, a handbook that collected her thoughts on theatre production. 'These notes, too slight for dedication, carry my thanks to those members of the Canterbury College Drama Society with whom I shared the experience of Shakespearean production,' she wrote on the dedication page. There was nothing slight about her thoughts at all, and the book became a classic.

Ngaio covered play production from a variety of angles. There was the director's perspective, then those of the actor and the audience. Her ideas had been honed by recent Shakespearian productions. She did not mention Shakespeare's soliloquies specifically, but made it clear that she saw the plays as integrated entities. The actors were like dancers, whose voices pulsed with the words of the author. Their contribution was integral to a greater choreographed pattern of players, which must be 'rhythmic' and work together as a 'team'.

Dramatic dialogue was not a series of speeches delivered by individual actors but a 'series of spoken movements, each with its own form and climax, carried out by a group of players'.

Ngaio analysed the relationship between actors and their audience. Each performance was a completely new experience and was 'infinitely variable, hazardous and incalculable'. A good actor played his audience like a musical instrument, shaping and controlling their 'emotional response to his work'. The actor achieved a 'fusion of himself with his role'. 'This process is brilliantly set out by Stanislavsky,' wrote Ngaio. The actor 'should seek not so much to "lose himself in his part" as to find his part in himself'.

Ngaio provided a working methodology for directors and small amateur groups in what she called New Zealand's 'renaissance of flesh-and-blood theatre'. She outlined a process that began with the director spending several weeks becoming familiar with the script. 'The producer's script should leave plenty of room for notes. A typed script on one side of foolscap pages, bound horizontally, with wide margins is none too big.' Her own prompt book was a blueprint of minute detail. To get a sense of scale and movement, she suggested making an accurate cardboard model. She advocated acting on different levels to help composition and flow, and the addition of stairs for dramatic variation. Her regime of rehearsals included individual and group work with actors, so that they fused with their parts and acted seamlessly together. 'Don't snap,' was her comment on discipline. 'There are only three legitimate excuses for blackguarding your cast; unpunctuality, talking off stage and failure to memorise.'

What she offered readers was her recipe for success, plus some basic philosophy. It was the actor's responsibility to be heard, and the director's to be understood. 'If you can't make an intelligent play intelligible then you had better not attempt it,' she pronounced. Part of making a complex play comprehensible was communicating its basic message. 'Many an attempt at a serious play has been lost by a kind of ingrained genteelism . . . If the production of . . . a play is healthy it will probably err on the side of coarseness.' Underpinning all this was Ngaio's fundamental assumption that New Zealand must have its own national theatre.

Ngaio offered directors a tightly structured approach. She had a clear idea herself about what she hoped to achieve from a production, and was unambiguous about how she realized it. There was not much room in her approach for spontaneity or intuition. Her methods have been described as autocratic and tyrannical, but they were underpinned by a wit and humanity that won most people over. She was glamorous and talented, and this made her something of a cult figure to a younger generation hungry for international insights.

Her ideas were a conglomerate of things she had seen and read overseas. From William Poel, she discovered the open stage. It was similar to 'the kind . . . on which Shakespeare's plays were first performed. The playing area was a permanent space . . . There was no attempt at illusion of place because there was no scenery, and the plays were allowed to charge forward, one scene overlapping another.' It was Edward Gordon Craig who introduced her to the concept that the stage was an atmosphere and not a physical space, and the German director Leopold Jessner whose productions prompted her to use stairs. Her greatest model was Stanislavsky, who encouraged actors to find qualities in themselves that connected with their roles.

She believed in the authenticity of a specific approach. Plays were 'real objects possessing an absolute set of meanings, prone to damage by careless direction or acting. To her, the director was like a curator, charged with revealing the play's absolute value to the audience in the clearest possible light.'

Her handbook was published by the Caxton Press, whom Ngaio used, whenever she could, to print her programmes. Like her stage sets, Caxton's typography was spare and in keeping with the play. As she distilled the play's message, so they expressed it graphically. Often she provided the illustrations, either her own, or those of a friend. First-night programmes became collectors' items, because they were all individually signed by Ngaio. (This tradition continued until her last production.)

Her handbook marked the end of a fervent few years of theatrical production. She had been away from her novels, which were her bread and butter, and her publishers were anxious for another book. She told the drama society she was unavailable for 1947, which must be kept free for another murder mystery. Her work in the theatre and the recent tour with *Macbeth* had given her a wealth of ideas, but picking up the threads was a challenge.

Ngaio lived her life in compartments. She had her life as a writer, as a director, her life in New Zealand and abroad, and her private life, often lived with different people in separate spheres that occasionally overlapped. The complexity of her life allowed her to move with seamless ease from one project to the next. She directed her life as she directed a play, filling each fresh scene with a new set of actors; only she was privy to the prompt book. She had become a very public figure but few people had access to the compartment that was her private life.

It was often in her dedications that Ngaio's public and private lives coalesced. *Final Curtain*, published in 1947, was dedicated to Cecil Walker and his sister, Joan. There was substantial private money in the Walker family, and Dundas, Cecil and their sister lived in an overgrown rambling old villa with high ceilings and dark corridors. Eccentricity abounded. Joan was a Miss Havisham-style recluse, and her brothers both bohemian and homosexual. All three were part of Ngaio's inner circle of friends.

In *Final Curtain*, the threads of Agatha Troy and Roderick Alleyn's lives are woven together again after their long separation. At the beginning of the book, Alleyn is still chasing spies in New Zealand and Troy is in England, making maps and 'pictorial surveys for the army'. The war has taken its toll. She is fragile and tense. It is a grey day, and bitterly cold, as Troy walks up the path from her studio to her Buckinghamshire house. She is thinking of her husband thousands of miles away.

'Suppose,' Troy pretended, 'I was to walk in and find it was Rory. Suppose he'd kept [his return] a secret and there he was waiting in the library. He'd have lit the fire so that it should be there for us to meet by' . . . She had a lively imagination and . . . so clear was her picture that it brought a physical reaction; her heart knocked, her hand, even, trembled a little as she opened the library door.

There is no Alleyn waiting in the library, but into that waiting space of anticipation slips an opportunity: a commission from Millamant Ancred inviting Troy to paint her father-in-law, Sir Henry Ancred, in the character of Macbeth. One of the grand actors of pre-war West End productions, he has moved audiences for years, particularly by his rendition of Macbeth. The picture is to hang in the entrance hall at the splendid Gothic-styled Ancreton Manor. Troy is even given the specifications: it is to occupy a niche 6 feet by 4 feet. She turns the commission down immediately — she is no made-to-measure Society portrait painter — but the Ancreds, a flamboyantly dramatic family with an acting pedigree that goes back to the Norman Conquest, interpret her refusal as provocation to persist. A family envoy, Thomas Ancred, is sent, and

Troy, already tempted to paint the elderly tragedian's handsome, well-formed head, caves in. She is to stay at Ancreton Manor for a week and paint. She and Sir Henry will have their sittings in what the family calls the 'little theatre'. Sir Henry sits for her in his Macbeth costume. The background is a painted backcloth of the wasteland before Forres Castle.

Troy is riveted at their first meeting. She has seen Sir Henry on stage and knows what a powerful actor he is. At their fourth sitting in the 'little theatre', suddenly Sir Henry breaks the silence with Macbeth's words:

> Light thickens, and the crow
> Makes wing to the rooky wood . . .

And so he continues. Troy's hand jerks and she stands transfixed until he has finished. His performance has shaken her and 'she had the feeling the old man knew very well how much it had moved her'. Over the next few days Troy will meet the whole 'larger-than-life' Ancred family, whom she regards as 'two-dimensional figures gesticulating on a ridiculously magnificent stage', especially the 'loathsome blond', Miss Orrincourt, a gold-digger with pretensions to becoming the next Lady Ancred.

The scene is perfectly set for murder, not of a Scottish king, but of a Shakespearian actor. The unveiling of Troy's painting is to coincide with Sir Henry's 70th birthday. The premier event of Sir Henry's birthday parties is a reading of his current will. 'He has always made public each new draft. He can't resist the dramatic mise-en-scène,' his grandson Cedric explains to Troy. The family members jockey like Derby horses to finish in the money. Each new reading is a fresh race, and now Miss Orrincourt, a rank outsider, is in the lead. Sir Henry announces their engagement before the family assembles in the little theatre for the portrait unveiling. They file into their seats in anticipation. When the cloth is drawn dramatically back, there is the sombre head of a legend — and 'flying against a clear patch of night sky, somebody had painted an emerald green cow with vermilion wings' dropping black bombs. Someone has graffitied the nation's painting. In shock, Sir Henry retires to bed. The next morning he is discovered dead in his room. The death certificate says heart failure brought on by a severe gastric attack, but his room has been scrupulously cleaned so there is no evidence to the contrary, and no autopsy.

The matter would have rested in the family crypt along with Sir Henry,

Ngaio Marsh in dame school uniform with her spaniel, Tip, and with dolls, c. 1900.
St Margaret's College (SMC 1-4e)

Ngaio as head prefect at St Margaret's College, Christchurch, c. 1914.
St Margaret's College (SMC 1-4e)

Ngaio's mother, Rose Marsh, c. 1910.
St Margaret's College (SMC 1-4e)

Ngaio Marsh with Allan
Wilkie, c. 1920.

St Margaret's College (SMC 1-4e)

Ngaio Marsh reclining in a chair, c. 1933.

Photograph by William Sykes Baverstock, ATL, PAColl-0326-09

Ngaio Marsh with the Rhodes and Plunket families on seaside holiday in Birchington, Kent. Nelly Rhodes is at the centre, with Toppy Blundell Hawkes, Ngaio Marsh and Tahu Rhodes to her right. In front are Denys, Teddy, Eileen and Pam Rhodes, c. 1930.

ATL, PAColl-9232-08

Ngaio Marsh's painting *In the Quarry*, c. 1935, featured on the front cover of *Art New Zealand*, Number 78/Autumn 1996.

Ngaio Marsh's painting, *Native Market, Durban*, c. 1933.

Christchurch Polytechnic Institute of Technology

The 1936 Group Exhibition in Christchurch, Ngaio in the centre, wearing tie and beret. Left to right: Rata Lovell-Smith, Phyllis Bethune, Mr Bethune, Dr Lester, Billy Baverstock, Margaret Anderson (holding Toss Woollaston's *Figures from Life*), Mr Henderson, Rosa Sawtell, Louise Henderson.

Photograph by Olivia Spencer Bower, Collection of Christchurch Art Gallery Te Puna o Waiwhetu

Mannings family photograph (right to left): Stella, John, John (senior), and in front Jean and Roy with Pekinese dogs Misty and Chee-Chee, c. 1946.
Collection of Jean Crabtree

Ngaio with her father Henry Marsh, still playing tennis on his 80th birthday in May 1943. St Margaret's College (SMC 1-4e)

Cast members from *Othello* (right to left): Dundas Walker, Barbara Reay, Paul Molineaux (Othello), Ngaio, (unknown woman), and Jack Henderson (Iago). ATL, PA1-q-173-73-2

Ngaio Marsh's first proper meeting with Agatha Christie at a Crime Writers' Association 'prize winners party' at the Savoy, London, 1962.
St Margaret's College (SMC 1-4e)

Ngaio as guest of honour at the 'Marsh Millions' party given by Collins and Penguin, with author and critic, Ivor Brown (left), and William Collins (right), London, 1949. St Margaret's College (SMC 1-4e)

Ngaio Marsh with George Baker in the role of Chief Detective Inspector Alleyn on the set of *Vintage Murder*, 1977. ATL, PAColl-0957-01

A quiet moment for Ngaio while directing.
Collection of Annette Facer

Set designed by Tom Taylor for *Julius Caesar* produced in the Great Hall of Canterbury University College, Christchurch, 1953.
Collection of Annette Facer

Ngaio and Gerald Lascelles in rehearsals for the inaugural production of *Twelfth Night* at the Ngaio Marsh Theatre, Christchurch, 1967. Collection of Annette Facer

Ngaio directing *King Lear,* with Annette Facer, David Hindin, and Mervyn Glue (Lear) in the background. Collection of Annette Facer

David Hindin (Earl of Kent) and Annette Facer (Cordelia) in *King Lear*, 1956.
Collection of Annette Facer

Elric Hooper as the Fool in *King Lear*, 1956. ATL, PA Coll-0285-1-042

Jonathan Elsom in *Sweet Mr Shakespeare*, 1975. He also wore this costume as Chorus in *Henry V*, 1972. Collection of Jonathan Elsom

Ngaio, 15 April 1936. ATL, ½-046800-F

Sylvia Fox, c. 1930.
Collection of Richard and Ginx Fox

Ngaio in the 1940s. ATL, ½-144512-F

Dame Ngaio Marsh, Buckingham Palace, 1966.
St Margaret's College (SMC 1-4e)

if anonymous letters suggesting that he had been murdered had not begun circulating. The final straw comes when the stiff body of white-saddled Carabbas the cat is found in the garden. The murderer has inadvertently killed twice. When Barker, the butler, had taken in Sir Henry's morning tray, Carabbas had fled from the room. Barker thought Sir Henry had forgotten to let him out, and was surprised that the cat had not woken him. But it was too late to wake either Sir Henry or Carabbas, because both had been poisoned. Into this double homicide walks the unsuspecting Chief Detective Inspector Alleyn, for a touching reunion with his wife and an instant immersion in English murder. The novel makes constant references to the play Ngaio had just finished directing. There are mentions of a 'little theatre' and lines quoted from *Macbeth*. The play would continue to simmer in her novelist's imagination.

Final Curtain was well received in Britain and the United States. 'Another of Ngaio's delightful who-dun-its,' announced the critic for *The Sunday Times* in April 1947. '[Sir Henry] and his curious family are such good company that you would be quite content to read about them without any murder-mystery at all.' *The New York Times* identified exactly what Ngaio's writing offered 'whodunit maniacs':

Ahead of them lie certain assured items of perfection. There will be excellent craftsmanship applied to the everyday matter of crime detection. There will be civilized human beings making good conversation which relies on wit rather than gore. There will be full-bodied characterization and murder proceeding quite naturally out of some small frustration uncomfortably like one's own pet neurosis.

Only one newspaper hinted at a debate that had raged through the newspapers and had recently reached the misty shores of New Zealand: Golden Age detective fiction's relevance in the post-war era. 'What will happen to the detective story,' asked the *Daily Sketch*, 'now that so many country houses are being nationalised, and week-end parties, the detective's happy hunting ground, may soon be a thing of the past? We shall be denied such a story as *Final Curtain* in which Miss Ngaio Marsh is at her best.' Was there a place for stylized murder in a world that had experienced Auschwitz and the atom bomb?

In September 1945, the *New Zealand Listener* printed sections of an article by critic Edmund Wilson, published in January in *The New Yorker*. His title, referring to Agatha Christie's 1926 best-seller, was 'Who Cares Who Killed Roger Ackroyd?' Wilson was vitriolic in his attack on Golden Age crime writers. His criticism of Sayers' *The Nine Tailors* was bitter; Ngaio's *Overture to Death* fared even worse:

> It would be impossible, I should think, for anyone with the faintest feeling for words to describe the unappetizing sawdust which Miss Marsh has poured into her pages as 'excellent prose' or as prose at all except in the sense that distinguishes prose from verse. And here again the book is mostly padding. There is the notion that you could commit a murder by rigging up a gun in a piano, so that the victim will shoot himself when he presses down the pedal, but this is embedded in the dialogue and doings of a lot of faked-up English country people who are even more tedious than those of *The Nine Tailors*.

He found Margery Allingham's *Flowers for the Judge* wooden and unreadable. The characters were flat and stock, and the circumstances of the murders unconvincing. 'How can you probe the possibilities of guilt among characters who all seem alike because they are all simply names on the page?' he asked. Wilson's aggravation continued unabated until he reached the conclusion that the readers were addicts and the 'reading of detective stories is simply a kind of vice that, for silliness and minor harmfulness, ranks between crossword puzzles and smoking'.

Ngaio found it disturbing to be pilloried. There were heated rebuttals overseas as well as at home. The *New Zealand Listener* published a defence of detective fiction. The author accepted some of Wilson's more moderate claims, but disagreed adamantly with his comments about Sayers' *The Nine Tailors*, and was enthusiastic about Ngaio's New Zealand novels. 'The local colour in these books is excellent. I am much less interested in the mystery of *Died in the Wool* than in the character-drawing and the fine pictures of McKenzie Country landscape.' Ngaio wrote book reviews for the *Listener* and letters to the editor on pronunciation and the Kiwi accent, but was not drawn into the whodunit debate until October 1947, when she was invited to comment on the question: 'Is the Detective Story Dying?' 'I think that the character of the detective novel is changing,' she responded, and changing very markedly. Many readers who, ten years ago, devoured the purely two-dimensional piece, depending entirely upon its interest as a puzzle, now demand from their detective novels a very much more solid affair. They want three-dimensional characters, and psychological as well as intellectual problems . . . the entirely mechanical detective novel is yielding to the longer, more elaborate and less conventional plot.

For her own sake, Ngaio hoped the decline would be gradual and 'that the thing itself may merge almost imperceptibly into a changed form'.

⊂▬▮▮⊃

The revenue from the sales of Ngaio's books was essential to keep her life going. Often over the past few years she had dug deep into her own pockets to assist the drama society, contributing to wardrobe costs and financing anything from post-production parties to the construction of purpose-built wooden property boxes. Much of her discretionary income went into the theatre. Her professional career as a writer subsidized her vocation as a director, but there were also everyday costs that were demanding. Her father's health was rapidly failing. The Crawfords were there to help him when Ngaio was away, but his care was getting too much even for them. Henry had been active all his life and a sedentary deteriorating existence was more than he could abide. Ngaio could see his death coming and, with it, the end of an irreplaceable connection to her past. He was the surviving parent of an intense adult-and-only-child union, a last connection to her childhood and to her mother.

In March 1948, Ngaio sat Henry down in the garden at Marton Cottage, with the vista before him of the city that he had watched grow. She propped a folio of foolscap paper on his knee and urged him to record his life, for her and for posterity. It was a struggle for him to hold the pen. His mind wandered along the corridors of distant memories. He remembered stories of his father and the clipper ships that brought tea from the New World to the Old. This was a time of wealth for his family, then decline, and the untimely death of his father at 51 years of age. Henry was at school at Dulwich College with his brother Edward when the news came. Dulwich had been chosen specially, because it was a public school with a good reputation but without the huge fees of Eton or Harrow. P.G. Wodehouse described his years at Dulwich as 'six years of unbroken bliss'; Raymond Chandler had also been a pupil. It was a good school, but the Marsh boys had to leave, because there was no money to keep them there. Knocked off-course, Henry tried banking, but became ill with pleurisy.

It was while recovering on the vast plains of South Africa's veldt that he discovered one of his great loves: Nature. 'I fairly took to the country and found its appeal very strong being exceedingly keen on animals, natural history and field sports . . . I simply adored the life and the surroundings.' He reluctantly returned in England in July 1884. For about two years he worked in a leather factory office, before another opportunity surfaced and he ended up in New Zealand in 1888. Forced to take a position with the Bank of New Zealand in Dunedin, he was in Dunedin for two years before moving to nearby Palmerston for a year, and then to Christchurch. It was a lonely life of single-men's boarding establishments, punctuated by the highlight of amateur theatre. Henry began acting in Dunedin and continued it in Christchurch where he met Rose Seager. 'I married as fine a woman as any man could deserve, and although poor were very happy and blessed with our child a daughter who was the pride of our life.' Often during his memoir he drifted onto the subject of his wife and daughter.

Henry's potential was never realized in New Zealand. Poverty was always near, but Rose stoically made so much of what they had and did not complain. She was his great source of pleasure, and Ngaio was 'brightness itself . . . A most intelligent child a keen sense of humour and always drawing or writing stories as soon as she could do anything and of course we thought the world of her.' His wife was the authority figure; Henry was the fun. A fervent atheist, he believed the Church was a scourge. 'Why can't there be a religion of universal brotherhood & ethics and rules for the whole of mankind expedient & suitable for the life of communities without all the fictitious dogma of the different religions which have been the curse of humanity?'

Henry's instinct was to do the best for his family, so when he lost everything that might have put them ahead he was broken. Because he was in charge of his till at the bank, he was responsible when one day a shortfall was discovered — and not just a small amount, but £500. Henry knew who the culprit might be, but could never prove it. The missing cash was nearly 10 years' income for a housemaid; Henry himself earned not much more than a pound a week. It was a fortune to find; his fortune, as it turned out, because he repaid the money with a family inheritance that could have settled his future. Henry never recovered. It was hard on the family because there were rumours and rumblings, but worse still was the fact that he could not forgive himself for being so trusting or, perhaps, absent-minded.

When his father-in-law, Edward Seager, was in his 90s he used to stay with them at Marton Cottage, look out over Christchurch and shake his fist at the city for which he had done so much but which had forced him to retire ignominiously from Sunnyside Hospital in favour of a man with qualifications. He had spent his last years as a court usher. His son-in-law came to understand his anger.

Although it haunted him still, Henry chose not to mention the missing money in his memoir. What he did highlight, however, was his great foresight in buying on the Cashmere Hills. The family were free now from chest infections and Christchurch's lowland epidemics and, like his daughter, he rejoiced in the outdoor life. 'I travelled on a bicycle the 2 or 3 miles from town carrying most of our supplies and as soon as I got home I got into rough working clothes and worked hard with pick, shovel and wheelbarrow and got as hard and strong as a horse.' He was proud of his wife's strict upbringing of Ngaio, because he felt she had given Ngaio the best values and opportunities to succeed — the right things to read, the right schools, the right acquaintances — and look how it had paid off. He could not have been more pleased.

He mentioned Ngaio's early days playing with Tahu Rhodes, but not the disaster of her 10th birthday party. Henry had added the sparkle to an otherwise flat life, and his ginger-beer brewing was a case in point. The family's gardener had made it when Henry was young in Essex, and he bragged about how good it was. His mother sent out the recipe, and in preparation for his daughter's birthday he laid down a ginger-beer brew in the cellar under the verandah. He bought 'half a used brandy cask' and all the ingredients, and pungent fumes wafted through the rooms of Marton Cottage. For weeks he eyed the bottles in anticipation. By the time Ngaio's birthday came round they were ripe for the popping. Gramp Seager was there, playing the piano, and all the myriad aunts, uncles, friends and relations. Henry disappeared into the garden and arrived back with a tray laden with fizzing glasses. It was a super-brew, they all agreed. Then suddenly everyone was screaming with laughter while 'children, unreproved, tacked about the room, cannoned into each other, fell, threw cream cakes or subsided on the floor in a trance'. No one could remember quite how it ended. Henry was adamant. 'It's no good you thinking it was my ginger-beer,' he told his wife. But these were famous last words, because on a second sampling Rose and Ngaio were left comatose on the carpet, staring at the ceiling for an afternoon. In the end, Henry decided the impregnated brandy cask was to blame.

It was something of an enchanted life, and letting go was harder than he expected. He warded off the boys who hung around Ngaio. He and Rose had ambitions for her, and a male on the horizon was a threat. They could not face Ngaio going away. Allan Wilkie became a great friend, as did the Rhodes family, but both parents expected these relationships would enhance her life rather than separate her from them. 'Ngaio was invited to spend a weekend at Meadowbank the end of it was Nellie Rhodes and she became such great friends we could hardly get her home sometimes,' he remembered. 'I can never feel grateful enough for the chances they gave her to meet interesting people & people of note and their experience & knowledge of different kinds of fellow beings and varied surroundings.' And that was where his memoir ended. His health had deteriorated so much that he struggled to write.

Henry was 85 years old in May 1948, and slipping, although not so fast that he did not take great pleasure in Ngaio being awarded the Order of the British Empire in the Queen's Birthday Honours List in June. He was delighted and so was she. She had won the award, not specifically for her crime writing, but more it seemed for her services to the theatre. She had worked tirelessly over the past decade, directing, writing about directing and the stage, and pushing vigorously for a national theatre. He knew she deserved it. But he would have taken special pleasure if there had been more mention of her detective novels, because he was the inspiration for these. Ngaio knew he 'was keen on detective stories', and one day she said, 'I'll write you one.'

Success followed success, so that Henry found it hard to share his famous daughter. He did not think much of young John Mannings, whom Ngaio seemed to have adopted as a surrogate son. He came to the house too often. Henry, jealous and irascible, persecuted the boy when he could do so out of sight. Old age made him angry. John's sister, Jean, remembers 'Uncle Harry' just before he died. She was passing through Christchurch on the way to an inter-provincial hockey meet in Dunedin:

Ngaio left me in charge looking after Uncle Harry who was bedridden.

[There was a] booming voice from the bedroom: 'Girl . . . Girl . . . get me a whisky.'

'How much do you have?' I asked him. So he showed me on a glass. I poured out that much whisky.

'*Girl*, it's neat!' he cried in frustration, and died two or three days later. He probably shouldn't have had it.

Henry died at St George's Hospital in Christchurch on 4 September 1948. Ngaio 'missed him dreadfully'. Her grief was palpable, and close friends knew it cut her to the core, 'but there was no bitterness' in his death. He was old and ready to go, and his passing was the end of a relationship that had satisfied them both.

Ngaio barely had time to grieve before life swept her off in another direction. Dan O'Connor had a stunning piece of news. In association with the British Council, he was promoting a tour of The Old Vic Theatre Company to Australia and New Zealand, and the stars of the show were Sir Laurence Olivier and his wife, Vivien Leigh. The visit seemed almost impossible to comprehend when there were other more strategic destinations like the United States and Canada. 'Why are you, the greatest actor in the world, making a tour of Australia of all places?' asked an astonished Sam Goldwyn, who was one of Olivier's friends. Leigh's 1939 *Gone with the Wind* was legendary, and Laurence Olivier was internationally renowned for his renditions of Shakespeare's greatest roles, especially Richard III, but also Hamlet, Henry V, Othello and Macbeth on stage and film. His 1944 film version of *Henry V* won him an Oscar nomination, as did his 1948 *Hamlet*. He had been made a Knight Bachelor in 1947, and in 1948 he was on the board of directors of The Old Vic. To raise money for the theatre, Olivier had decided to tour the Antipodes. As well as being a money-raising venture, 'the tour was a grand gesture of showing the flag, in an empire that still just existed'. They were coming to Christchurch, so Dan O'Connor wanted Ngaio involved. It was an extraordinary opportunity.

In Australia, the company performed Shakespeare's *Richard III*, Sheridan's *The School for Scandal,* and Thornton Wilder's *The Skin of Our Teeth.* The actors were treated like royalty, with media coverage and civic receptions wherever they went. After six exhausting months, the company flew from Brisbane to New Zealand, arriving in September 1948 for the last six-week stint of their tour. On paper printed with the letterhead 'The Old Vic tour of Australia and New Zealand', Vivien Leigh crossed out the word 'Australia' and wrote 'Over, God be praised'. Their Australian tour had left them shattered. 'You may not realise it,' Olivier told a New Zealand reporter, 'but you are looking at two walking corpses.' The continuous grind of performances, sometimes two a day, and often in mediocre venues, was exhausting. By the time Olivier reached Sydney, he had limped his 'club-footed' way through so many performances of *Richard III*, that his knee gave way on stage, permanently damaging the cartilage. In Christchurch, he was in so much pain that he was forced to perform on crutches.

Three weeks before their arrival in Christchurch, Dan O'Connor sent Ngaio a telegram, asking if she would put on supper and an evening of entertainment for the company at the Little Theatre. Leigh and Olivier were recruiting for The Old Vic: this was an opportunity to showcase New Zealand talent. In spite of her grief over her father's death, Ngaio applied herself to the problem of what to present. The evening was set for 27 September, at 11.30pm, after The Old Vic's performance of *The School for Scandal*. Ngaio gave in to her 'obsession', choosing *Six Characters in Search of an Author*.

As always, she worked shrewdly with the talent she had. There was a big new star — Brigid Lenihan — to match the calibre of her men. Lenihan, breathtakingly beautiful and a dancer, moved across the stage with elegance, and, although her voice was not epic in strength, she could capture the nuance and equivocal intimacy of experimental theatre brilliantly. She was perfect for *Six Characters*, in which she played the Stepdaughter. Other talent had emerged during previous student productions. There was the gifted Pamela Mann, who had proved her skills as a producer of William Congreve's *The Way of the World*, and, with Bernard Kearns, as joint producer of Jean-Paul Sartre's *Les Mouches (The Flies)*. Both were clever actors: Mann played the Mother and Kearns the Father in *Six Characters*, along with William Scannell as the Son, Rodney Kennedy as the Boy, and Beth Wilson as the Child.

The Old Vic tour had pushed Leigh and Olivier's relationship to its limits. They were already a volatile personality mix. For years Leigh had suffered from bipolar disorder, and her mood swings and nights of manic insomnia took their toll. Immediately before going on stage in Christchurch the stars argued violently, creating a backstage scene when, according to local accounts, Leigh, refusing to go out, slapped Olivier across the face and he slapped her back. For the local cast and crew it seemed too amazing to be true: silver-screen sexual tension happening in Christchurch.

But the fraught relationship did not dampen the post-production performance of *Six Characters* or the reception at the Little Theatre. Ngaio, her players and crew had worked and 'rehearsed as if the devil was after' them. They would be performing in front of the most acclaimed actors in the world and were understandably nervous. 'The entire power for the stage lighting [still] came from a single wall socket' and the stagehands worried it might overload. 'There was a rumour — possibly apocryphal,' remembers crew member Alistair Johnson, 'that for this performance, Max McGlashan, the stage manager, climbed up the electricity supply pole in the street just outside the Little Theatre, to "strengthen" the fuse to prevent an unexpected blackout.'

'At the end [of the performance] there was warm applause from the audience, and . . . drinks were served,' recalls Harry Atkinson, who was a violinist in the play.

Everyone gathered around the seated Olivier (and Vivien Leigh). I was somewhat shyly standing apart from the main crowd: but then, in a gap between several people, I suddenly saw Vivien looking straight at me with the most beautiful blue eyes. I looked back — and wonder Oh wonder, she beckoned me over, reaching out her hand towards me and saying: 'It's so *very* good to see you!' Well! We talked a little . . . and after the party I went back to my college room walking on air!

Ngaio and Dan O'Connor introduced young New Zealand players to the world of the West End, and the experience was unforgettable. A private party afterwards at Marton Cottage celebrated, early, Vivien Leigh's birthday, which would take place on the ship, and Ngaio presented Olivier with Edmund Kean's ancient coat, given to her by her grandfather so many years before. Ngaio described the students' performance as 'rough but not too bad' and was quietly pleased that her famous guests were so encouraging.

At the end of their week-long season in Christchurch, Olivier went into hospital for a knee operation. He was still there the day before their boat was due to leave for England. Unable to move, he was placed on a canvas stretcher and hoisted by crane onto the boat. 'I soared into the sky,' he wrote to a friend, 'smoothly floating over the side of the ship and gently down.' It was an ignominious end to an internationally acclaimed tour.

Their legacy in New Zealand was considerable. Not only were Pamela Mann and Robert Stead, from the Unity Players in Wellington, offered places in The Old Vic's production course, but Brigid Lenihan was given a huge endorsement. She was so good, according to Olivier, that there was no point in her attending drama school. 'She has star quality. Let her sweat it out in Rep,' he announced. But the stellar outcome of their visit was impetus for an Australian tour. Dan O'Connor, struck by the talented acting he saw in *Six Characters*, suggested a two-play tour of Sydney, Canberra and Melbourne over the summer break. Ngaio's superb Othello, Paul Molineaux, was available, so that was her Shakespearian selection to companion Pirandello's play.

The tour represented a pinnacle for Ngaio. She had worked hard to build the acting, directing and technical experience in Christchurch to carry off such a venture. It was a crowning achievement, and she was delighted. But she knew it was an immense challenge, so the moment the end-of-year examinations finished, rehearsals began. They were daily and rigorous, and she spent hours with principal characters going over their roles. The actors were clever and eager to be involved, so Ngaio's direction became more of an exchange of ideas rather than a prescriptive approach. She modified her methods accordingly.

This was the first New Zealand theatre company to tour abroad, and with the prospect of international exposure and acclaim the University of Canterbury offered Ngaio an honorary lectureship in drama. Her appointment, 'greeted by prolonged applause', was announced at a special reception. This was belated recognition, but Ngaio accepted it graciously. There was no time, anyway, to calculate grievances or rest on laurels. They had just seven weeks to rehearse two plays; then 24 student players, plus 2 tons of scenery and props, had to be shipped to Australia for the opening of *Othello* at the Sydney Conservatorium on 10 January 1949. Everything had to be ready.

They arrived in Sydney to a celebrity-style welcome, with reporters boarding the *Wanganella* before they came ashore. Ngaio's international reputation as a mystery writer attracted immediate attention. Before opening night, however, a burglary left the company seriously rattled. Costumes, traveller's cheques and a recording of Douglas Lilburn's music were stolen from one of the dressing rooms.

The first night of *Othello* only suggested the magic and momentum the production would assume as the tour progressed. Paul Molineaux grew into his character. Initially, his Othello was a little too admirable to be a convincing anti-hero, but he would find the despot as well as the deceived. When *Six Characters* switched from afternoon rehearsals to evening performances a week later, it was an instant success. Brigid Lenihan's Stepdaughter had the depth Olivier had predicted. She had exactly 'the right air of soiled allurement, defiance, smouldering spite and wretched self-loathing', wrote the critic for *The Sydney Morning Herald*. Her Desdemona was initially a little too confident.

Reviews reached a fever pitch of enthusiasm the longer the company toured.

In Canberra, they were complimentary; in Melbourne, they were ecstatic. Ngaio's production of Shakespeare was likened to that of The Old Vic. Her tempo, simple stage settings, and subtle lighting were highly commended. An English company of Stratford Players, also performing *Othello* in Melbourne, at the Prince Theatre, were negatively compared with Ngaio's company. According to the Melbourne *Herald*, the students were 'far more interesting and compelling'. To avoid competing with the Stratford Player's *Othello*, Ngaio alternated her plays in three-day blocks. This meant there was no clash. In the end the English production made hers look better.

It was the freshness of her *Six Characters*, though, that took Melbourne by storm. This Existential play, with its impromptu dialogue and unexpected psychological twists and turns, was rapturously received by audiences, and the critics fell in love with Lenihan. Her playfulness, youth and glamour kept them enthralled. 'People sat in Collins Street throughout the night to get tickets to see Vivien Leigh — here is one who is easily her equal. To my mind, she is the better actress', wrote Frank Murphy for *The Advocate*.

The tour was a triumph. But in its wake, as she had done before, Ngaio watched the talent disappear. Brigid Lenihan left directly for England from Australia, and when they returned to New Zealand in early March, Bernard Kearns married and began teaching, and Paul Molineaux involved himself in his career. As a group they had found a momentum that could not be maintained.

O'Connor made a suggestion to Ngaio: why not create a company that would take in the best actors from the British Commonwealth and tour them? It seemed a logical extension of what they had begun. Ngaio was thrilled with the idea, and began plotting almost immediately. Her long-term hope was that a British Commonwealth company might form the basis of a national theatre in New Zealand.

In the short term, she planned to return to England. The war was over, the responsibility of looking after her father was over, and her energy for student theatre was depleted. She had been away too long from her agent and publisher, and there was exciting news about a multi-million-dollar promotion of her books. She longed for England, and for her friends the Rhodes. Pamela Mann, who had been living with Ngaio for a year as her secretary, was about to travel to take up her place at The Old Vic. On 1 June 1949, the pair left Lyttelton. The future seemed full of promise for them both.

King Henry V —
Battle- Scenes

CHAPTER SIX

The Marsh Million Murders

Almost as soon as she stepped off the boat, Billy Collins threw a massive cocktail party to celebrate Ngaio's amazing success. It was July 1949, and, in conjunction with Penguin Books, Collins released 10 of her novels simultaneously, with a print run of 100,000 copies per title: a million books by Ngaio Marsh came onto the international market. The only other writers given this distinction were George Bernard Shaw, H.G. Wells and Agatha Christie.

As she stood elegantly sipping her drink, Ngaio knew she had made it. She had come fresh from the Antipodes to England to discover she was a star. The experience was like slipping through the back of the wardrobe in Narnia, into another world, a world that appreciated her as a writer. 'So it was astonishing, this time in England,' she wrote reflectively in *Black Beech*, 'to find myself broadcasting and being televised and interviewed and it was pleasant to find detective fiction being discussed as a tolerable form of reading by people whose opinion one valued.' She was fêted for something that was almost an embarrassment in New Zealand.

I am always asked to write articles saying what I think about [the theatre] *now* and even, on exceptional occasions, what I think about William Shakespeare, but seldom what I think about crime stories . . . Intellectual New Zealand friends tactfully avoid all mention of my published work and if they like me, do so, I cannot but feel, in spite of it.

So far as Collins was concerned, Ngaio had become an industry. Back in 1943, the publisher had brokered a deal with the Doubleday Dollar Book Club, which had chosen *Colour Scheme* as its December selection. In a memo to Ngaio, Collins explained: 'They guarantee 175,000 copies and pay $8,750, which will be split between Little Brown and the author.'

Billy Collins was a personal friend as well as a business associate, and the pair exchanged regular letters, always with warmth. He admired her writing, and delighted in promoting her books. 'I have read your new MS *Died in the Wool* and enjoyed it immensely,' he had told her in August 1944.

We are planning to publish in January 1945, with the biggest first edition we have yet printed of your books. We will probably be printing it in Canada at the same time, to fit in with the American edition . . . I do not expect you have any plans yet for after the war but I wonder if there is any chance of your coming over here. I hope there is.

He had ended with a startling piece of news: 'Our Pall Mall office was bombed earlier in this year and this is our temporary office.' All records relating to Collins's publication of Ngaio's and Agatha Christie's books were destroyed in the air raid. Ngaio had responded, in October:

Here in New Zealand we feel almost apologetic about our immunity from air raids. Your laconic sentence about your own offices in Pall Mall having gone is typical of so many English letters. One usually regrets very sincerely that one has not been there during the last four cataclysmic years. I hope very much to get home before long, but as you probably know, all permits to travel have been refused since the war.

Now Ngaio was finally here, but the London she returned to was bomb-scarred and depressed. She felt a difference in the people. There was an acquiescence she had never seen before. The wild inter-war period, with its theatre traffic and riotous night-life, had all but gone, to be replaced by tiredness and indifference.

The BBC chased her for an interview, which was broadcast in September 1949. What were her impressions of post-war London? What could she say, she responded, but that something was missing in the theatre she saw, and in the city's streets? Her rich, velvety voice faltered when she came to the final words of her 'London Revisited':

What can a New Zealander have the cheek to say about the wastelands behind St Paul's? Only that one turns away from them with a kind of astonishment that a people who suffered this nightmare outrage should be as they are, in good heart after all. What an impertinence to say that one finds them a 'little tired'.

In the midst of the rubble and rationing, Ngaio was experiencing the glamour of celebrity, as the launch of her 'Marsh Million' was accompanied by a massive marketing drive. Howard Haycraft, in his seminal book *Murder for Pleasure: The life and times of the detective story*, published in 1942, estimated that in the United States at the beginning of the 1940s 'the average sale of the ordinary crime novel — as nearly as may be gauged from the cautious statements of the publishers — lies somewhere between 1,500 and 2,000 copies'. Best-sellers were rare, he claimed, and the greatest to date were those of S.S. Van Dine who '*averaged* only 30,000 copies per title'. But he was an exception. 'An entire year may pass in which no crime story tops the 10,000 mark.' He estimated 'that a maximum of 600,000 new copies are *sold* in the United States yearly', and that the whole detective writing industry grossed 'little more than a million dollars' annually. In Britain, less than a decade later, Collins and Penguin were releasing a million books by just one author. It was a calculated risk, but still a risk. The distribution and marketing implications were huge. Ngaio was obliged to assist Collins in every way she could.

There were radio and newspaper interviews, and now even television, which had been commercially obtainable in Britain from the late 1930s and by 1950 was widely available. In New Zealand, radio still reigned, so when Ngaio was invited to appear as a guest on BBC television shows it was a novel experience. But radio remained her *métier*. She broadcast on the Home and World Services and on Light Programmes. She spoke with a precision and allure that challenged any BBC voice, and her sometimes sycophantic colonial sentiments were balm to a wounded empire. During her 20-month stay in Britain she was involved in radio programmes like *Talk Yourself Out of This*, *Woman's Hour* and *London West Central*. She was a quick-witted, humorous and popular guest, but she was also something more. Ngaio represented nostalgia in a post-war limbo period before Britain found its feet. The colonial that she was, the Golden Age of the detective novel that she was part of: both belonged to a pre-war era. She could talk convincingly of Britain as 'Home', and people still avidly read her books, but change was in the air.

It was a tremendous asset that, at heart, Ngaio, although a shy and private person, was a natural performer. Collins knew they could put her in any public situation and she would attract the right kind of attention. Agatha Christie was much more reclusive and found public exposure an ordeal. In public, in England, Ngaio was glamorous and fashionably dressed; there was a gorgeous sealskin coat for which she was renowned. She still had the elegant mannequin's figure of her early years in London, and could carry off exquisitely cut long skirts, hats, bags and high-heeled shoes. Her *pièce de résistance* of dazzling eccentricity was to walk through Knightsbridge with her Siamese cat Ptolemy in a blue jewelled collar on a lead. She loved cats, and in London she acquired Ptolemy as a kitten. Because there was not much room in her small flat, she exercised him in the street. Tastefully dressed and walking together, Ptolemy and Ngaio turned heads.

Another equally attention-grabbing purchase was Ngaio's cream Mark V Jaguar. She bought it almost immediately after she arrived in London, and took it back to New Zealand when she returned. In a world of shortages and rationing, it was a breathtaking piece of extravagance. Ngaio loved driving fast cars and this was the opportunity to indulge her passion. She was conscious of status symbols and image, but this social awareness was tempered by her puritanical upbringing. Her indulgences were never absolutely excessive, and she was always very generous with her possessions. Numerous people drove her car, including young John and Bear Mannings, and she often reached into her own pocket to help friends. And suddenly money was there in bigger amounts than ever before. The shops were full of Marsh novels and the cash registers rang.

But British post-war taxes were inordinately high. Britain used its people on the battlefields of the Second World War, and when the killing ended they were used again to make good the nation's debt. Ngaio was taxed under these conditions, so what could have been a vast income was dramatically reduced. Terry Coleman quotes taxation figures related to incomes of Laurence Olivier and Vivien Leigh, which demonstrate the huge increase. The standard rate of income tax in 1939 was 22.75 per cent; by 1940 this had risen to 35 per cent, and to 50 per cent by 1945. Income tax on the first £2,000 earned was set at 50 per cent, and after that a surtax was added: the highest rate possible was 'an absurd 97.5 per cent'. Ngaio also faced further levies in New Zealand. Not long before he died, Ngaio's father calculated that on some of her income she was paying 'one pound and seven pence in income tax for every pound earned'. But she loved nice things, fine food and a life edged with flamboyance, and this was expensive to maintain in Britain, so the incentive to keep writing remained.

Ngaio fiercely protected her private life, away from the media and the streets of Knightsbridge. For much of her time in London she lived with Pamela Mann in an unfurnished flat above a clock shop. '[We] are sharing this flat with two New Zealanders — Elizabeth & Bob Stead,' she wrote to friends in Christchurch. Bob Stead was attending The Old Vic with five other 'ex-student-players'. 'We like our flat & our Georgian street so much that we want all of you to hurry Home & visit us. I'm writing hard & doing quite a bit of Broadcasting.' The address was 56 Beauchamp Place, just a few doors down from the second Touch and Go shop she and Nelly Rhodes had taken 20 years before. It was *déjà vu*, but now she was a successful author.

Her nights were alive with the sound of clocks from below. 'I could hear minuscule chimes, single tinkling bells, a gong, musical-box confections and the punctual wheelhorses observations of a dependable grandfather. There was a French clock that tootled a little silver trumpet.' London was a fantasy world for Ngaio, and her imagination was caught up again in its history and literature. 'It was like the setting for a Victorian fairy-tale' she said of the nights she lay awake in her flat, picturing the clocks below. She bought food from Harrod's around the corner, but the flat was furnished 'from junk picked up in or near Fulham Road'. Ngaio loved luxuries, but she was a pragmatist when it came to life's rudiments. When she wanted extravagance there were the fashionable shops of Brompton Road and Sloane Street, and the busy markets. After 12 long years away she was thrilled to be back.

Pamela Mann was an ideal companion for Ngaio, who delighted in showing her the wonders of London. She bought her a smart imitation ocelot coat, elegant armoury against the chill of London's winter. Together they attended theatre in quantities that could be described as compulsive. They both kept a record of the shows attended, and Ngaio pasted each programme into her scrapbook, commenting on all the productions and ranking them. Between July 1949, when she arrived, and September 1950, when she stopped keeping a record, Ngaio saw 'sixty-two productions, sometimes two a day'. Although Mann was a student player, one of Ngaio's protégés, it was her attendance at Ngaio's production courses that probably began their intimate association.

In 1947 Ngaio had run production workshops at Canterbury College and, in January 1948, a Theatrical Production residential workshop at Wallis House in Lower Hutt. At the summer school Ngaio was the 'director and instructor in production', actor and voice teacher Maria Dronke taught 'speech craft', and Sam Marsh Williams 'décor' design. Pamela Mann was one of many promising Canterbury College students, including Brigid Lenihan and Bernard Kearns, who attended these workshops. Lenihan dazzled everyone at breakfast on the first morning at Wallis House. 'She was late and she made her entrance down a big staircase. She filled the room,' according to artist and drama tutor Rodney Kennedy. Mann, less ostentatious, steady, intelligent and interested in the production side of theatre, appealed to Ngaio, and they began a close working relationship. Ngaio's young male stars, who came to stay with her for one-on-one acting instruction, left before the show ended, but Pamela Mann stayed on. Ngaio had status and experience to offer her; Mann had skills a director and writer could use.

Ngaio developed intense emotional bonds with women, and this was one of them. Mann had moved up to Marton Cottage as Ngaio's live-in secretary until their departure for London. She typed correspondence and manuscripts while Ngaio directed Congreve's *The Way of the World*, and they went to rehearsals and toured Australia together with the student players. It was an ideal arrangement, and when Mann gained a place in the production course at The Old Vic it seemed the perfect time for them to leave New Zealand. It was Mann who helped Ngaio in Christchurch with *Swing, Brother, Swing* (published in the United States as *A Wreath for Rivera*), which came out in April 1949, and Mann who assisted her to write as much as she could of *Opening Night* before they arrived in London. Mann was with Ngaio through the difficult time of her father's death, compounded by The Old Vic visit and the disruptions of the Australian tour, which took their toll on her writing.

Swing, Brother, Swing was a formulaic book. Ngaio fell back on what she knew to produce something that bordered on the hackneyed. The plot is familiar: another death on stage in front of an audience that miraculously includes Chief Detective

Inspector Roderick Alleyn. This time, the setting is one of the jazz nightclubs that filled Ngaio's early days in London with electrifying colour, although she makes the band's style more contemporary. The Breezy Bellair's Boy-band is gimmicky and offbeat like American Spike Jones and His City Slickers, whose radio programmes were broadcast around the world from the mid-1940s. Jones was known for his satirical renditions of popular songs, punctuated by the sound of whistles, bells, Goonish snatches of lyrics, and gunshots. In Breezy Bellair, Ngaio creates a similar iconic band leader and this lively conceit could have created an upbeat piece of writing, but she peoples her nightclub with tired old aristocratic characters.

The members of the upper-crust Pastern and Bagott family find themselves embroiled in the not-so-unfortunate murder of a philandering piano-accordion player called Carlos Rivera. Lord Pastern and Bagott's Toad-like fixation with percussion instruments inspires him to convince Breezy Bellair and his boys to let him join them on stage. For their first public appearance together at the Metronome in London, Pastern suggests a promotional prank that involves the fake firing of a gun across stage at Rivera, who is to feign death. A wreath will be laid on his chest and he will be carried out on a stretcher by pallbearers to the mock strains of a funeral dirge: pure Spike Jones.

Predictably, the blank cartridge is replaced, almost unbelievably, by a lethal parasol tip, and when Pastern fires the gun Rivera slumps down dead. Drug dealing and its co-dependent companion, blackmail, make a thin appearance, as does a 'bolshie' Australian Communist called Skelton. These are old themes that have not appreciably developed, but it is the aristocracy that takes the cake. Pastern is an irritating, quarrelsome peer whose eccentricities fail to redeem him. Even Ngaio's humour falters in the face of his selfish stupidity. His wife, Lady Pastern and Bagott, calls him 'A madman, except in a few unimportant technicalities', but it is his niece Carlisle Wayne who has the insight:

There's really a kind of terrifying sanity about him. He's overloaded with energy, he says exactly what he thinks and he does exactly what he wants to do. But he's an over-simplification of a type, and he's got no perspective.

Pastern is an anachronistic comic cliché straight out of Ngaio's property box of 1930s stock characters. Before the war there had been nostalgia value and shared humour in this aristocratic type, but that cosy familiarity had disappeared somewhere in the grey daily grind of casualty lists. There is no place in post-war Britain for Pastern's hedonism. The wreath for Rivera is really Pastern's, and the only news in *Swing, Brother, Swing* is that Nigel Bathgate is leaving for good and Troy is expecting a baby. Alleyn drops the bombshell casually, to maximize its impact. 'Did you know you were going to be a godfather, Br'er Fox?'

Although Ngaio was out of date and out of touch, her writing retained a vibrancy that still made it creditable. It was testimony to her professionalism that, in spite of her intense workload and personal loss, she produced a book that sold well. There was more of Ngaio's life caught in the pages of her next novel, begun on the *Orion* on her way to England. In the mornings she and Pamela Mann would work on the book, but after this they were at liberty to participate in games and shows and mix with the passengers. For the first time in years Ngaio was free from constant commitment, and she found the rolling, empty sea of relaxing space creative. She drew on her recent experiences in the theatre to write *Opening Night*, published in the United States in 1951 as *Night at the Vulcan* and released in Britain in the same year. The dedication was 'To the Management and Company of the New Zealand Student Players of 1949 in love and gratitude'. Her central character, a young New Zealand girl who travels to London to follow an acting career, could have been Biddy Lenihan, who was already looking for work in English repertory, or perhaps Pamela Mann, or even Ngaio herself as a young woman — certainly there is a little of all of them in Martyn Tarne.

Martyn Tarne's circumstances are fraught by comparison. She is penniless and desperate for work because her money has been stolen on the boat. It is a damp, dark evening and Martyn is lingering in an alleyway outside the Vulcan Theatre. She has missed the audition. An overpainted, large-faced woman wandering away from the stage door stops to talk. Martyn had met her that morning. 'You've had it, dear. I gave you the wrong tip at Marks's. The show here, with the part I told you about, goes on this week. They were auditioning for a tour.' Martyn is so hungry and the news is so bad that she staggers under the weight of her disappointment. What can she do? She remembers the church back in the Strand. She has been told you can sleep there: perhaps there is even a soup kitchen. She picks up her suitcase, suddenly heavier than before, and walks towards the entrance of the alleyway. Half a dozen huge raindrops plop ominously in a puddle. People hurry by, looking up and unfurling umbrellas. She approaches the front of the theatre, which she thinks is locked. A wedge of light from a plate-glass door that is ajar cuts across the blackness. Two people are talking in the office behind it. They are in dire straits. Helena Hamilton, star of the stage and silver screen, is opening in a new show, *Thus to Revisit*, and she has no dresser. Martyn steps forward: 'I believe . . . you are looking for a dresser.'

A door has opened, literally and figuratively, and this is the beginning of a three-day roller-coaster ride that will end in Martyn performing Gay Gainsford's key role on stage on the opening night. Murder occurs late in the book, so the investigation is reduced and the machinations of the theatrical world take centre stage. Ngaio's characters are convincing because they are influenced by people she knew. Helena Hamilton and her ex-lover Adam Poole are megastars recently back from a tour of Australia and New Zealand. It is hard not to see the parallel between these characters and Leigh and Olivier. Before she left, Martyn had queued many times to see them, and all of Adam Poole's films had been shown in New Zealand. They were 'famous faces'. Inspired by their example, Martyn had joined an English touring company in New Zealand a year before and travelled to Australia. The pay was quite good, and she supplemented it with broadcasting. From there she sailed directly to England.

Ngaio cleverly explores Martyn's deep sense of anxiety before going on stage, and her experience, once there, of connecting with her part. It is a kind of nirvana on stage. 'That perfection of duality for which actors pray and which they are so rarely granted now fully invested her. She was herself and she was the girl in the play.' This was pure Stanislavsky. Ngaio fictionalizes her theatrical philosophy in *Opening Night*. 'Reflect upon the minuteness of Edmund Kean,' says Jacko Doré, designer and assistant to Adam Poole:

upon Sarah's one leg and upon Irving's two, upon ugly actresses who convince their audience they are beautiful and old actors who persuade them they are young. It is all in the mind, the spirit and the preparation.

Like Ngaio with her players, Jacko has watched the magic happen. And are these Ngaio's own views about the voice?

Martyn had formed the habit of thinking of people's voices in terms of colour. Helena Hamilton's voice . . . [was] golden, Gay Gainsford's pink . . . Adam Poole's violet. When Alleyn spoke she decided . . . [it] was a royal blue of the clearest sort.

Once again the action on stage echoes real events in the lives of the actors in the book. In the play, one of the leading men kills himself off stage. The actors and the audience hear the gun go off and Adam Poole explains to Alleyn: '[Then] I come in, shut the door, go up to Helena, and say: *"You've guessed, haven't you? He's taken the only way out."*' In real life, five years before when the Vulcan was known as the Jupiter, Helena's husband was found immediately after the show, asphyxiated by a gas heater in his dressing room. Then it was 'homicide dressed up to look like suicide'; now lightning has struck again.

Opening Night is a more successful novel than her last. The characters are credible, and the action tight and convincing. Ngaio even manages to weave in a thread from *Surfeit of Lampreys*. One of the young constables handling the case was PC Lord Michael Lamprey, grown up and doing what he had watched Alleyn do a decade before at his parents' double flat in Pleasaunce Court Mansions. Life has come full circle, as had Ngaio, who had returned to the company of the Rhodeses as soon as her boat berthed at Southampton.

Two of the Rhodes children, Denys and Teddy, were there to meet Ngaio and Pamela Mann. Ngaio was absolutely delighted to pick up this connection after so many years of separation. The youngest Rhodes children were adults, and three were married. The new arrivals were transported by car to the Rhodes family home at Mount Offham in Kent, to be greeted by pandemonium, excitement and confusion. It was the village fête. The local band was playing and children in fancy dress were chasing each other through the crowds. The Rhodes family was assembled to meet an overwhelmed Ngaio. 'We've invited a few people to meet you,' said the now not-so-young Eileen Rhodes. 'Hope you don't mind.' It was a delight to see them all, and it was as if Ngaio and Nelly had never parted. They laughed together like a mischievous pair of schoolgirls, and made a pact to see as much of each other as they could. Whenever Nelly came to town she visited, and when Ngaio could escape to Mount Offham she did.

It was an exhilarating time, and one of the highlights of Ngaio's visit was a trip in October to Monte Carlo. Nelly Rhodes's family, the Plunkets, had rented an old converted Saracen castle at Eze in the hills behind Monte Carlo. The ancient stronghold, hewn in parts out of the sheer cliff face, was both an engineering marvel and a spectacular example of medieval Islamic architecture in the most sumptuous Mediterranean setting. From almost any vantage point there were startling vistas of countryside and dazzling turquoise sea. '[Nelly] and I joined [a] house-party there for a fortnight and then, since the alpine atmosphere did not agree with her came down to our old hotel, and, for a few days, revived old goings-on.' It was wonderful, although not the same as their young days in London because 'our old quartette was now only a pair'. Sadly, Tahu Rhodes had died prematurely in 1947, and Ngaio's escort and the Rhodes farm cadet, Toppy Blundell Hawkes, had died even earlier, in 1935.

The Monte Carlo visit inspired another book, which Ngaio began when she returned to London. *Opening Night* was submitted to Collins in August 1949, and by November Ngaio was already shaping her experiences in a Saracen castle on the French Riviera into ideas for *Spinsters in Jeopardy*. Somewhere in the fictional space between *Opening Night* and *Spinsters in Jeopardy*, Alleyn and Troy have had a baby boy called Ricky, who is already six years old when he makes his first appearance. The family is thinking about a holiday in Roqueville in the Alpes Maritimes. Alleyn will be on a mission in conjunction with the Narcotics Bureau, the Sûreté and MI5, to bust an international drug ring. Troy is curt. 'You can't go round doing top-secret jobs . . . trailing your wife and child. It would look so amateurish. Besides, we agreed never to mix business and pleasure.' She would have been better sticking to their resolution, but the lure of the Riviera and temptation to meet her distant cousin P.E. Garbel, a chemist who lives in Roqueville, is overwhelming.

On the overnight train to Roqueville, Troy and Alleyn catch a fleeting glimpse through a castle window of what turns out to be a murder. The train grinds momentarily to a standstill as it struggles to climb the oppressive alpine grade, and across a distance of about 100 yards they see the figure of a woman fall against a blind, releasing it so it springs up. In the room beyond the woman is a man in a long white robe.

'And in his hand——?'

'Yes,' Alleyn said, 'that's the tricky bit, isn't it?'

Neither Troy nor Alleyn has time to make out what is in the man's hand before the train lurches forward into a tunnel of concealing blackness. As serendipity would have it, an aging spinster on the train becomes seriously ill with a ruptured appendix, and Troy and Alleyn, with Ricky in tow, make a mercy dash to the Château de la Chèvre d'Argent, where the only doctor not attending an out-of-town medical conference is staying. As they approach the castle by road, they see, on their right, 'a cliff that [is] mounted into a stone face pierced irregularly with windows. This in turn broke against the skyline into fabulous turrets and parapets.' It was in one of these windows that they saw the woman from the train.

Its clever manipulation of tension makes *Spinsters in Jeopardy* more of a thriller than a mystery. Ricky is kidnapped in the book's opening section, and Ngaio leads readers through a sensitive portrayal of a child's terrifying separation from his parents and a mother's angst-ridden search for her son. '[Troy's] heart rammed against her ribs . . . sweat poured between her shoulder-blades and ran down her forehead into her eyes. She was in a nightmare.' To this tension is added the sinister drug culture and strange satanic sun practices of a house party up at the ancient Saracen castle. Alleyn breaks in and disguises himself in a cowled gown to join a secret ceremony held in a white-stone room with a window and a pentagram on the floor. He finds himself surrounded by similarly dressed, drugged cult members, all making 'small feral noises' and occupying one of the points of the pentagram. They are awaiting the high priest's sexual sacrifice of a young female initiate. *Spinsters in Jeopardy* is a return to *Death in Ecstasy*'s mix of drug taking and religious euphoria, but the handling is more sophisticated and the issues are better explored. 'By and large [drugs are] probably the worst thing apart from war that's happened to human beings in modern times,' Alleyn explains to Troy in his narcotics monologue. 'The addicts were killing themselves in studies, studios, dressing-rooms, brothels, boudoirs and garrets; young intellectuals and misfits were ruining themselves by the score.'

There is also a tract of pure Henry Marsh on the pitfalls of organized religion. The case of the satanic sun worshippers at Roqueville reminds Alleyn of his earlier one in Knocklatchers Row in London. For centuries, intelligent people have subjected themselves to the ordeal of reciting senseless chants and liturgies, to the indignity of bizarre practices and the ghastly fear of punitive retribution. They have 'starved, frightened and exhausted themselves . . . got themselves racked, broken and burnt', and it is all so senseless. By contrast, Alleyn and Troy are incarnations of sublime sensibleness. 'You're almost pathologically normal, aren't you?' Alleyn says proudly to Troy. 'Forgive me if I bolt back to my burrow, the glare is really *more* than I can endure.'

Ngaio barely had time to relax and enjoy Monte Carlo before she was due back in London for another radio interview. On the return journey, she and Nelly Rhodes stopped in Paris to meet Ngaio's French agent, Marguerite Scieltiel. 'We breakfasted at her flat and then I signed a contract and was photographed in the act.'

Ngaio returned to the problem of replacing her secretary, as Pamela Mann had begun her course at The Old Vic. An ideal substitute was found in Rosemary Clark-Hall (now Greene), a young New Zealand figure skater who had come to London after the war to train. Ngaio knew Greene from her days as a student actor, when she had played Katharine in the 1945 production of *Henry V*. Ngaio rang her up and they agreed that she would come over to Ngaio's flat at Beauchamp Place three afternoons a week. On her visits, Roses, as Nagio called her, was introduced to the owner of the clock shop, whom Ngaio had nicknamed Mr Tick Tock. 'He was tall and thin and wore small steel-rimmed spectacles,' Rosemary Greene remembers. One day, Ngaio found herself locked out of her flat and was forced to appeal to Mr Tick Tock for assistance. His professional skills came to the rescue, and Greene was duly 'sent down to the shop with a thank-you present'. It was one of Ngaio's books, with the inscription: 'To Mr Tick Tock who is also a pick lock'.'

One of Ngaio's great public coups was the paper she delivered in December 1950 to the Royal Society of Arts, on the subject of 'The Development of the Arts in New Zealand'. For this she was awarded a silver medal, and in April 1952 she was made a Fellow of the Royal Society of Art, which was a considerable honour. Ngaio worked day and night to meet her many public commitments, but there were private ones that were also consuming because of their personal importance. Her old friend Allan Wilkie invited her out for lunch and asked her to write a preface for an autobiography he hoped to publish with Faber and Faber. She read the manuscript with pleasure. It brought back memories of a touring company with a talented, autocratic actor-manager. In her preface, she recalled her first defining experience of Wilkie.

With a group of fellow art-students, I sat in the front row of the gallery . . . since three o'clock, [we] had waited on an iron staircase in a cold wind for the early doors to open. The play was *Hamlet*, the house was full and the Dane was Allan Wilkie . . . What one would think now if one could re-visit that glimpse of the moon?

She described Wilkie as 'a bit larger than life': 'a bullet head, a large frame, a drooping cigarette and a voice of peculiar resonance . . . letting forth streams of a particularly inventive blasphemy'. She endorsed his story because it was 'about the living theatre' and the strength of a man's vision to tour players across the world. Sadly, T.S. Eliot, who received the manuscript, turned it down and it was subsequently lost.

Meeting Wilkie again must have been a poignant experience for Ngaio, who was working on preparations for the launch of her Commonwealth theatre company with Dan O'Connor. This was partly why she attended so many theatre productions. She was enjoying herself, assessing the state of post-war theatre in London, and looking for talented actors initially to tour Australia and New Zealand, with the possibility of more Commonwealth countries in the future. Allen Curnow explained the venture in a letter to John Schroder, who was the literary editor for *The Press*, a leading broadcaster and, according to Ngaio, 'an accomplished letter writer'.

She is talent-scouting & otherwise prospecting for her own & D. D. O'Connor's big British Commonwealth theatre project — U. K. & Dominions, season & season about — which is to come into being some time next year. She is also busy on a new book, hoping to get it done before the curtain goes up. She talked me into delivering my play [*The Axe*] (reconstructed from the Christchurch prototype) up to Alex Clues *in* the West End if not exactly of it . . . the more I think of it the less I can imagine it on any other stage than the one it was written for.

Ngaio greatly respected Curnow's work, especially his *Axe*, the experimental play with a quasi-indigenous theme which he had staged in Christchurch, with John Pocock as producer, in 1948. That year, Ngaio was immersed in writing her book but still found time to help with the production. Pocock rode his bike from one side of Christchurch to the other to consult her over details of design and production. She thought Curnow's clever concept could have been the beginning of more local playwriting and production, and was eager to encourage it. Her support of talented New Zealanders like Curnow meant that her London flat became a hub of expatriate activity. Her old art-school friend Evelyn Page, and her husband Frederick, who had composed Ngaio's early theatre scores, were visitors, along with school friend Sylvia Fox, Biddy Lenihan and her fiancé John Knight, John Pocock and others.

Ngaio delighted in their company: 'Allen Curnow comes in quite often & is in terrific form,' she told the Schroders. But not all theatrical projects received the same endorsement.

D'Arcy Cresswell turned up with the final draft of his play in verse. It's extremely good, but is an apologia for homosexuality [and] it's destination will probably be a not too delicious private theatre. Pity in many ways. These things always cause one to end with the most churlish abruptness as I do now.

Curnow wrote to Schroder about the same episode:

It struck me as strange that this was a surprise to Ngaio; she had not read 'Present Without Leave' where D'Arcy makes no secret of [his homosexuality]: in any case it is always a slight jolt when the internal & external evidences merge suddenly into proof. D'Arcy (I have this from Ngaio) is living in some hostel for Sailors, passing himself off as an able seaman & anxious to preserve this disguise. No comment on this, except that the country of the Queers, that of the non-Queers, & the no-man's-land between, are very perceptible territories here, more than I would have supposed. It's a temptation to speculate on the indefinable empire of the Queers.

Ngaio knew that overt homosexual references were marginalizing. Her letter suggests she had more to say on the subject, but chose not to. She was liberal and accepting of homosexuality yet vigilant in her efforts to remain distanced from its taint. Her ambition was to move mainstream audiences with her writing and theatrical productions, and in 1950 this did not happen from the margins.

Her own theatrical endeavours in London centred on manager Molly May's Embassy Theatre in Swiss Cottage, which had staged the *première* of Agatha Christie's first play, *Black Coffee*, 20 years earlier. The project that linked Ngaio to the Embassy was a dramatization of her *Surfeit of Lampreys* by semi-retired solicitor Owen Howell. Ngaio and Pamela Mann met Howell at his home to discuss the venture, and Ngaio gave it her backing. The play was to be directed by Daphane Rye and the setting designed by John Pemberton. Ngaio was not directly involved in script development, staging or production, which was probably detrimental to the overall result. The show opened on 24 October 1950 and closed on 5 November. It was not a success. The translation of a Ngaio Marsh novel into theatre required more skill and experience than Howell or the show's director possessed, and this point was made in a *Times* review. The novel's humour and visual and imaginative richness existed in language, and a literal translation of this into action on stage could be very static if it was not cleverly done. Ngaio felt that:

> Mr Howell's play might well have succeeded but it did not do so, largely I think because the Lamprey flavour, present in his dialogue, was sadly missing in the production, which was much too heavy-going. The set was extremely lugubrious.

It was not that a stage production of *Surfeit of Lampreys* or any of Ngaio's other novels was impossible, but it required a great deal of interpretative talent, and probably the best person to do it was Ngaio herself, yet she resisted the temptation. She was too involved in the Commonwealth theatre project and her next novel to take up a challenge that may have offered her new opportunities.

By 1950, two of the Queens of Crime were already heavily involved in writing for the theatre. Agatha Christie wrote *Black Coffee* in 1929 as a response to the disappointing portrayal of Hercule Poirot in Michael Morton's 1928 *Alibi*, based on *The Murder of Roger Ackroyd*. The first season of *Black Coffee*, which opened at the Embassy in 1930, was less than two weeks long, but it reopened in April 1931 and moved between theatres, before closing in June. Christie described it as a 'conventional spy thriller, and although full of clichés, was not, I think, at all bad'. The play was a modest success and she was encouraged to keep writing for the stage. In 1945, she produced *Appointment with Death*, based on her 1938 book of the same name; in 1946, *Murder on the Nile*, based on her 1937 *Death on the Nile*; and, in 1951, *The Hollow*, based on her 1946 book of the same name. *A Daughter's a Daughter*, written in the 1930s and based on a book Christie had written under her historical romance writing pseudonym, Mary Westmacott, was not staged until 1952. Her most famous play was given life as a short radio drama in 1947 called *Three Blind Mice*. It was rewritten for stage and renamed *The Mouse Trap*, and its world *première* was at the Theatre Royal in Nottingham on 6 October 1952. In November, the play shifted to the West End and it has been there ever since. It is the longest first run of any play in the world.

Christie's theatrical achievements were as outstanding as those of her novels. In Dorothy Sayers' case, the balance was less equal, but she was enamoured with the theatre. She began writing for the stage in 1935, when *Busman's Honeymoon* was adapted for stage and opened in December 1936 at the Comedy Theatre in London. Much of her other theatrical writing was associated with the church. In 1937, she wrote *The Zeal of Thy House* for the Canterbury Festival based on William of Sens's rebuilding of the cathedral's choir in 1174. This was followed by the 1938 radio play, *He That Should Come*, about the birth of Christ; another Canterbury Festival play, *The Devil to Pay*, presented in 1939; and the comedy *Love All*, staged without commercial success in 1940 at the Torch Theatre in Knightsbridge. Her greatest and most controversial achievement was *The Man Born To Be King*, a radio drama about the life of Christ commissioned by the BBC and broadcast as a cycle of 12 plays four weeks apart: the first episode began in December 1941 and the last in October 1942. The project created a storm of protest. Atheists, agnostics and ardent Christians all had an opinion and the debates were heated. Sayers was unmoved in her determination to make the life of Christ real and immediate for a contemporary audience. After it had aired, the play cycle was deemed a great success by all but those at the extreme ends of the spectrum.

In 1950 Val Gielgud, Sir John's brother and the producer of *The Man Born To Be King*, but now director of the BBC, approached Ngaio to write a play script for a new autumn radio series. He believed she easily had the talent and experience to write an excellent piece. In his generous letter, he said he was a great admirer of her work. But Ngaio was already committed in many perhaps too diverse directions and the invitation fell on fallow ground. She was too busy with her Commonwealth theatre commitments to follow up an opportunity that could have given her a new creative direction.

The work required with Molly May at the Embassy was familiar, and therefore less taxing — or so she thought. May had heard of Ngaio's successful 1949 tour of Australia with Pirandello's *Six Characters* and invited her to direct a season, beginning in late November and ending in December 1950. The Embassy was a club theatre that ran three-week seasons. There were to be just two intensive weeks of rehearsal before opening night. Ngaio wanted Biddy Lenihan to take the part of the Stepdaughter, and Lenihan was desperate to have it because, ironically, the picture Ngaio had painted of destitution in *Opening Night* was not far from her reality.

New Zealand playwright Bruce Mason met Lenihan in London, and with other student player friends he:

shared her huge disappointment over Ngaio's production of *Six Characters* . . . We were all in it somewhere; Robert Stead as Stage Manager winkled New Zealanders into it wherever he could. But Molly May insisted on a 'name' for the Stepdaughter, and Yvonne Mitchell finally played the part. As a consolation, Bid was given second lead in a piece of flimsy-whimsy called *Isle of Umbrellas*, a long series of poor jokes about the English weather.

Pamela Mann, who had finished course work at The Old Vic, was May's personal assistant, but there was nothing for Lenihan. Five years later, Rodney Kennedy met her in London. 'I shared the coldest winter of her life without work, her marriage to John Knight broken up. She was lost. The cold bitch theatre had no room for youth and beauty. I tried to persuade her to come back: the New Zealand Players needed her.'

Ngaio was facing her own crisis, cut down by a devastating dose of 'Asian influenza' that left her with a 'temperature of 102'. It was difficult at the best of times for an outsider to come in and lead a group of professional English players, but with ill health the task was daunting. Each day Ngaio woke up and wondered how she would get to the end of it. A friendly doctor kept her on her feet by prescribing 'M and B's at night and benzedrine by day'. Against the odds, she imposed her signature style of production on a recalcitrant English cast. She insisted on 'pace, attack and understanding', with good result. Reviews of the show were very pleasing. 'Ngaio Marsh, author of 16 detective stories, last night produced her first play in England,' wrote the critic for the *Daily Mail* on 22 November 1950. 'Under her guidance Pirandello's six characters came to life . . . Outstanding performances by Karl Stepanek and Yvonne Mitchell helped to realise an extremely difficult and fascinating entertainment.' According to *The Observer*, 'the piece turns strongly', and the *Evening Standard* beseeched audiences to 'to hie thee to the . . . Embassy'. *The Times* published rambling reservations, but about Pirandello's play, not the production. This was the success *Surfeit of Lampreys* had failed to be. Ngaio, however, hardly lingered long enough to appreciate its impact before she left for Brighton, and a 'wan recovery with Miss May', who had contracted the same bug.

The Festival of Britain was a huge national exhibition, due to open in London in May 1951, and many cultural events were planned to coincide with the celebration. Among them was a summer season of English comedy at the Embassy, which Molly May invited Ngaio to direct. There was also another possibility. Stage director Sir Tyrone Guthrie and Dan O'Connor were considering running a Shakespeare season during the festival in a Woolwich theatre bombed during the war, and Ngaio was to be involved if it went ahead. It was planned, in proper Elizabethan style, to move audiences down the River Thames by barge to the theatre. Guthrie, his wife Judy, Bob Stead and Ngaio took a memorable boat trip down the river, picked up the theatre keys from an old pub, and entered the derelict building. Unfortunately the theatre was too badly damaged for their purposes and the project was abandoned. A Shakespearian season in London would have delayed Ngaio's departure, but May's offer was not tempting enough to hold her. She turned down the comedy season and prepared to leave England with a group of Commonwealth players she and Stead had spent months getting together.

When she was not writing, broadcasting, or directing, Ngaio was poring over *Spotlight* magazines with Stead, looking for ideal actors. There were countless professional photographs and flattering biographies. Ngaio was realistic. She knew the plight of post-war actors, and that every time a new play was cast in Britain or the United States there were 30 or more unemployed actors perfectly capable of playing each role. But they had very particular criteria. They needed people prepared to be away from England for at least six months. They wanted actors who would be ambassadors for their countries, and who were versatile, good-looking and congenial.

Ngaio fell back on the familiar. Biddy Lenihan was given the Stepdaughter's part in *Six Characters*, Essie in Bernard Shaw's *The Devil's Disciple*, and Viola in *Twelfth Night*, all of which Ngaio planned to tour. There were other campaigners, including Bob Stead and his wife Mizzy, and Owen Howell's son Peter, who had been Prompter in Ngaio's production of *Six Characters* at the Embassy. She had worked with Peter Howell on *Hamlet* at her Knightsbridge flat, with a view to his taking a lead role. Other major players in the company were the openly homosexual John Schlesinger, later famed for his direction of the films *Midnight Cowboy* and *Sunday Bloody Sunday*, who was an 'enchanting' Feste; Frederick Bennet, who played Toby Belch with 'elegance and breeding'; and Peter Varley, who made 'a wonderful praying Mantis of Malvolio'. As individuals, Ngaio liked and admired each of them.

A fragile sun was dissolving early-morning mist on the Thames Estuary as Ngaio left London with her company of Commonwealth players, bound for Sydney. There were tensions among the actors. This was not a honed group of homogeneous young players, but a diverse collection of professional prima donnas with egos that pulled against each other. The boat trip was not a quick passage across the Tasman, but a prison sentence, if you were travelling with people you did not like. Ngaio would use her experiences travelling with this company in a later book, but in the meantime it was a nightmare to be endured.

The cast rehearsed onboard and opened in Sydney with *The Devil's Disciple* to mixed reviews. It was 'a play,' Ngaio wrote despairingly in *Black Beech*, 'that grew colder and colder in my hands the more I tried to blow some warmth into it'. She was criticized in the press for her dictatorial direction. The actors became 'wooden puppets' in her hands, according to *The Sydney Morning Herald*. The strains and stresses of the journey, and the disappointing reviews, brought out 'dissonances of all sorts . . . in the company . . . houses faded and gnawing anxiety and depression settled upon us'. Things were so clearly going wrong that Dan O'Connor was forced to join the tour in Sydney. He had chosen to stay in England with his wife Shirley, who was expecting a baby. Deirdre was only nine days old when he left to try to help Ngaio turn things around.

After eight weeks in Australia, they made the desperate decision to move to New Zealand, where *Twelfth Night* opened in Auckland to a more positive reception. This might have been sustainable, and Ngaio thought a national theatre could have been based there, but the plan was to tour, and tour they did, with treacherous consequences. The dynamic of the group was further challenged by poor attendances in Christchurch, where Ngaio had always received so much support. She was not a good financial manager, and the Commonwealth project was too demanding for the resources and infrastructure of a tiny country. Her vaulting ambition, not so much for herself, but for New Zealand, had 'o'er leaped itself' and the consequences were tragic. By August 1951, in spite of the knocks, Ngaio was still clinging to her dream. 'Yours is not a letter to be answered, according to my present habit,' she wrote to John Schroder from the Theatre Royal in Christchurch,

in staccato little chunks scribbled between rehearsals & performances & lasting over days & through towns & yet after hoping for a decent interval it is after all under those conditions that I am trying to write to you I can't wait any longer for a fair run.

Ngaio was tired, but still hopeful. 'I'm glad you liked our play,' she continued. 'This is a frightfully, exciting & rewarding adventure. I sometimes wonder if it all really *is* happening.'

The greatest challenges were yet to come. It was in the provincial theatres that the company was routed. In Dunedin, the theatre was next to a winter fair where wild screams from the chamber of horrors and the grinding noise of the helter-skelter punctuated each performance until they resorted to using sandbags to try to deaden the sound. They found 'once-pretty Victorian and Edwardian play-houses' filthy and neglected. Some had no running water; in others, vandalized lighting equipment was beyond repair. In Nelson, in a packed house the fuses blew 25 times. The company's last performance in Blenheim, after six long months, epitomized their struggle. 'Rats darted in and out of the dressing-rooms, and the rain, which was extremely heavy, found its way through the roof.' Ngaio watched John Schlesinger as Feste from the wings, in a lonely pool of light, singing 'Heigh ho, the wind and the rain', as the drips plopped in a growing puddle on stage.

It was an ignominious end to something that had promised and taken so much. Ngaio had worked and sacrificed, and Dan O'Connor had lost money. It would take time for them both to recover. After years of what seemed like an endless summer of successes, Ngaio experienced the winter of failure. There was nothing more to say than goodbye to the players, who mostly returned to England, get into her car and drive home.

Ngaio returned to the comfort of her old life. Stella Mannings and her husband, who had come down from Tauranga to look after Ngaio's house while she was away, stayed on for several years with their sons, John and Bear. Both boys had completed their schooling at Christ's College, and John had had a year at university before deciding he wanted to join the British Army; Bear chose the New Zealand Air Force. Ngaio used her contacts to help John get his wish and organized a farewell cocktail party for him and Bear at Marton Cottage. John, Bear and a friend called Snowy were responsible for serving drinks, but somehow the instructions went astray. John remembers the event well:

The first rounds [of drinks] were neat, really solid . . . that relaxed them and then you watered them down a bit [with soda] . . . that was the thing [Ngaio] always did . . . something really solid at the beginning to get things going and then ease off . . . but it was the people who were there like the Bishop of Christchurch . . . and the Dean . . . who got completely plastered . . . they left and it was a very dark night and they somehow got down the stairs and they lost each other, one went down the drive, and the other the path, and there was a hedge in between them so they couldn't see each other . . .

'Dean, where are you?'

'Here.'

'Yes, but where's here?' . . .

It was pitch black and they didn't know whether one was behind or in front of the other.

'Dean, who's taking Communion tomorrow?'

'You are, my Lord.'

'Dean, I think it would be a good thing for you to take Communion tomorrow.'

'But Bishop, people are coming just to hear you.'

The Dean was found later in a heap under a bush in the garden.

One of the ladies woke up semi-naked on the floor in a room with a telephone still in her hand . . . Somebody, I can't remember who, just slumped on to the floor and people stepped over her, as if that was natural and normal, to talk to somebody else . . . It was quite a party . . . We were supposed to add soda but . . . it all happened suddenly . . . as far as Ngaio knew it had been diluted.

Ngaio watched in horror as distinguished guests dropped like flies from the effects of alcohol. When she discovered the reason she was 'furious', but some years later 'she thought it was terribly funny'. In spite of the pitfalls of having two young men around, Ngaio was sorry to see the boys leave for overseas. 'They were immensely companionable and I think I may say that a bond, already established, was greatly strengthened during the three years that followed my home-coming.'

Early in 1953, Ngaio drove up to Auckland with Sylvia Fox especially to see the opening night of a Royal Stratford-upon-Avon season of *Othello*, *As You Like It* and *Henry IV, Part I* with Anthony Quayle (whom she knew), Leo McKern and Barbara Jefford. While she was there, she received the tragic news that, on Friday, 13 February, the Little Theatre had been gutted by fire. The wiring was blamed, but the blaze seemed to have started in the roof where the wardrobe was stored. Students smoked cigarettes in the area, which contained felt tunics painted in oil paint, and in summer, under a hot slate roof, this was a highly combustible combination. There were numerous possible causes, but the result was simply devastating. The fabric of a decade of Ngaio's work with student players was destroyed. Almost all of the costumes, scenery, props, lighting equipment, storage boxes, programmes, photographs and records were burnt. The evidence of so many wonderful experiences had gone forever.

> What phrases, what jetting sounds went roaring up that night: Othello's opulent agony, the ghost's booming expostulations, wings in the rooky wood, Clytemnestra's death cries, Puck's laughter . . . What a bonfire!

The cradle of Ngaio's theatrical dreams had gone, but characteristically she was not defeated. In November 1952 she produced Christopher Fry's *A Sleep of Prisoners*, and a few weeks later announced that the drama society would produce *Julius Caesar* in July.

The only accommodation the university could offer was the Great Hall: a cavernous wooden Victorian Gothic space that would drown the intimacy of theatre. Ngaio made her plans, which included the model for a structure within a structure, to be made by the New Zealand Army: a scaffolding auditorium was constructed around three sides of a temporary stage. This was the closest thing audiences had seen to an Elizabethan-style Globe Theatre in New Zealand. In the centre of her makeshift seating was a stage that was equally unique. She and sculptor Tom Taylor worked on the set design. The stage rose powerfully from the hall floor through three levels to a tower connected by a dramatic spiral staircase. The stage revolved, and the plan was to project the action upwards, to enhance the flow and speed of scene changes. It was a daring move, and one that captured the respect of critics and commentators.

Ngaio used the limitations of the space to enhance the play's dramatic impact. She had actors coming onto the stage from between the seats, and crowd scenes that mixed riotously with the audience. Rather than togas, the costumes were Italian Fascist uniforms. *Julius Caesar* had the immediacy of her modern-dress *Hamlet*, for similar reasons. War shortages had affected the earlier production; now it was dearth caused by fire.

At the end of the production, like Caesar, perhaps Ngaio glimpsed her future from the top of the tower. She had not achieved the national theatre she had hoped might come out of the Commonwealth players, and now the hub of the drama society had burnt down: 'We were in the wilderness.' What remained were her resources of experience and leadership, and these she would use. For the next 15 years Ngaio and her players were in a kind of exile. Rumblings about how the Great Hall was left after the scaffolding, stage and wiring were removed meant that they were never offered the space again. There was a regrouping. From now on, if the players produced avant-garde or contemporary theatre they found their own premises and sponsorship, and when Ngaio was in New Zealand she produced Shakespeare somewhere else. *Julius Caesar* was a turning point. It re-established her reputation as an innovator, it was a box-office success, and it rekindled her confidence and desire to see Shakespeare produced annually in Christchurch.

Ngaio moved quickly to complete her 17th novel before rehearsals began for *Julius Caesar*. *Spinsters in Jeopardy* was published in Boston in 1953, London in 1954, and as *The Bride of Death* in New York in 1955. After her theatre commitments were completed for the year, she began work on *Scales of Justice*, a novel commissioned by Collins to celebrate 25 years of its Crime Club label. Ngaio knew it needed to be good because of its significance. As she collected her thoughts, she contemplated the message of George Orwell's now famous essay on the 'Decline of the English Murder', published in 1946. Orwell began his treatise with the image of a patriarch, full of Sunday roast, settled on his sofa, with a cup of 'mahogany-brown' tea, reading the *News of the World*. His wife dozes in an armchair near the fire, the children are out for a walk, and what does he choose to read about but murder. Orwell argued that the murders which made books sell, and were rehashed in Sunday newspapers, followed a domestic pattern and were inspired typically by middle-class motives — sex, money, jealousy — and, of course, gaining social position or protecting one's position from scandal. These cases included the great poisoners like Dr Crippen, Dr William Palmer of Rugeley, Dr Thomas Neill Cream, and Mrs Florence Maybrick. These narratives were intriguing because the middle classes could relate to them and read about murder instead of committing it.

What disturbed Orwell was his detection of a new kind of killing. The Cleft Chin Murder, for instance, was a case where two people randomly thrown together maimed and murdered unknown people for no particular reason. 'The background was not domesticity, but the anonymous life of . . . dance-halls, movie-palaces, cheap perfume, false names and stolen cars.' How could this be memorable or pleasurable for a patriarch to read about? This was the kind of hard-boiled detective fiction that writers had been contemplating since the mid-1920s, a sub-genre that took the ambiguities and random violence of working-class street life and made stories that did not fit the tidy patterns of the Golden Age. It began with the work of Carroll John Daly and was refined in the writing of Raymond Chandler who, with Dashiell Hammett, became one of the great exponents of the American school. Philip Marlowe, Chandler's tough-talking, street-wise, stunt-pulling private eye, with the hint of a sensitive side, was the antithesis of the aristocratic super-sleuth. Chandler's commentaries on detective fiction such as 'The simple art of murder' (1944) were in part an advocacy of his own style, which he saw as more relevant to modern life.

Collins's Crime Club list had been dominated by the greats of the Golden Age, and a revolution, especially from Ngaio, was out of the question, but the old clichés would not stand and the challenge was to inject freshness into an iconic form. The story needed to be classic, but not rigid. So Ngaio began cogitating a fishy tale fit for Collins's 'silver-wedding', as the *New Statesman* called it. She had *Scales of Justice* half finished when she received an invitation from her friend Essie Malone to join her in a trip to England on a Norwegian wool freighter called the *Temeraire*, out of Adelaide and bound for the Russian harbour town of Odessa. Ngaio had been thinking of going away, and she liked the novelty of this unconventional mode of transport because, apart from Essie Malone and her, there were only 10 other passengers. In total there were 63 on board, including the crew. There was only a small passengers' common room with a bit of deck outside, a small games deck, and a narrow promenade. Their only other outdoor accommodation apart from this was hatch covers, on which they lay or sat.

This mixture of isolation and an odd degree of intimacy appealed to Ngaio. 'As soon as we were shown our cabins I knew I would like the *Temeraire*. She was old-fashioned, odd and good.' Ngaio enjoyed the soft-hearted Norwegian captain, who cried when he made birthday speeches and toasts to the English Queen. The people onboard and the ship itself became the material for *Singing in the Shrouds*. The concept of a few passengers travelling for weeks on a cargo vessel with a killer must have occurred to her as she moved around the ship or sat sunning herself on a hatch cover. She would brew the idea, but in the meantime she worked on her current novel. 'Essie had agreed to act as secretary for the duration,' she wrote in *Black Beech*, 'and we used often to work in the evenings at my current book: *Scales of Justice*.'

Ngaio was especially keen to see Odessa. She had arranged for a special visa and was looking forward to seeing the opera house. In the few years she had been back in Christchurch since her Commonwealth tour she had become increasingly involved with two Estonian immigrants, Vladimir or Val Muling and his wife, Anita. This was a 'new friendship-of-three' that rapidly assumed a great significance. They had talked animatedly into the early hours of Russia and its culture, and in Odessa Ngaio hoped to bring these conversations to life.

Instead, the *Temeraire* sailed into an Iron Curtain that had been made chillier by the Cold War. The ship and its passengers were searched and searched again. Ngaio was instructed to stay in her cabin to await customs officials. She was anxious for herself and the other passengers, and there was the book. It had been typed in triplicate. Would it be seized? Should she hide it? When the officers arrived, the experience was less sinister than she had anticipated, but while they were at anchor in the port they were never allowed to leave the ship. It was frustrating. For 12 days the *Temeraire* unloaded wool, and all she saw of the Great Russian Bear was a few bedraggled soldiers guarding the wharf. The passengers were flooded with relief when an official put their passports on the table and the ship was free to go.

They continued on to Spain, and then to a port in Wales where Bob Stead met them and drove them to London. Ngaio took a 'minute but beguiling house in Hans Road', three streets over from Beauchamp Place, off Brompton Road. This was her Knightsbridge neighbourhood again, and she adored it. She shopped for her groceries at Harrod's, saw Shakespearian plays at Stratford-upon-Avon and West End theatre, caught up with old friends like Pamela Mann and the younger generation of Rhodeses, and delivered *Scales of Justice* to her publisher.

Scales of Justice was edited through 1954, and came out in Britain and the United States in 1955. Ngaio had decided to celebrate the Crime Club's silver anniversary with an undiluted English cosy. The book was dedicated to her much-loved cousin Stella Mannings, who had typed sections of it, and in spite of its rural English setting it contained snatches of Ngaio and her private world. Nurse Kettle pushes her bike up to the top of Watt's Hill and surveys the pretty village of Swevenings with its meandering trout stream, trees, gardens, lanes, hedges, golf course, stately home, and quiet country cottages dripping with summer roses. She is one of a handful of brilliantly sketched characters. Another is the slightly soft-in-the-head cat fancier Octavius Danberry-Phinn, who is convinced that his feline family of nine are human (or perhaps, better). Ngaio adored cats herself. 'Just a scribble to give you my most heartfelt sympathy on the loss of dear Chris S,' she wrote to a friend on the death of her cat. 'It really is shattering when they reach their little span & the blackness that follows can only be understood by the true catty-fan . . . she was indeed a most exceptional person & you will find it hard to think of a successor.' Octavius Phinn's Thomasina Twitchett had a real-life namesake in Ngaio's portly tortoiseshell Tom Twitchet, who was being cared for at Marton Cottage by house-sitting friends Helen and Lyall Holmes. In the novel, one of Thomasina's progeny is a young male called Ptolemy.

Octavius Phinn's cats are an integral part of a plot based on the premise 'that the scales of no two trout are alike: I mean, microscopically alike in the sense that no two sets of fingerprints correspond'. Colonel Cartarette published this fact in his treatise, *The Scaly Breed*. He is the murder victim and, with the assistance of Roderick Alleyn and Thomasina Twitchett, it is this little-known scaly fact that helps to catch his killer.

Alleyn is brought into the case by Lady Lacklander, because she is concerned that her family's dark Nazi spy secret may be revealed to someone other than a 'gent'. Her husband, a traitor, in the topmost echelons of the Foreign Office, was responsible for the suicide of Ludovic Phinn, Octavius's son. The death of his only child, and his wife's of a broken heart soon afterwards, sent Octavius catty. The class system inevitably rears its cosy head in *Scales of Justice*, but it is modified. Kitty Cartarette, the colonel's unfortunate choice of a second wife, calls the snobs in Swevenings 'survivals from the Ice Age'. And when Lady Lacklander hypocritically says of Kitty Cartarette, 'You never know with that sort of people what they may do', Alleyn curtly replies, 'Nor with other sorts either, it seems.'

Many reviews were ecstatic. 'Excellently characterised English village murder mystery,' wrote the reviewer for *The Observer* in May 1955. 'Miss Marsh's best yet, I do believe. No-body is caricatured, not even the District Nurse; yet everybody is full of quirks . . .' The murder of the 'nice colonel' was 'pleasantly delayed' and there was a 'good surprise solution'. *The Sunday Times* agreed:

Miss Ngaio Marsh might be said to be now occupying the throne regrettably vacated by Miss Dorothy L. Sayers, in that she brings the true detective story closer to the straightforward novel than any other woman writer. Her work, in fact, is as nearly flawless as makes no odds. Character, plot, wit, good writing, sound technique: all are there, together with the final requirement of the detective-story writer, ability to bamboozle the reader.

This high praise was followed in 1956 by a special honour awarded on the strength of the new novel's popularity. Ngaio was back in New Zealand when it was bestowed, so Collins Crime Club editor George Hardinge sent it to her with a memo in December:

I am forwarding herewith the 'Scroll' awarded to you as a result of the ballot organised by the Crime Writers Association and the *Daily Mail*. This should have been presented to you at an immense banquet at the Piccadilly Hotel, but was accepted by Mr Smith on your behalf in your absence.

All is going well with OFF WITH HIS HEAD.

Ngaio began *Off With His Head* while she was living in Hans Road. Its inspiration was a freezing winter trip to stay with the Rhodeses who were living in the Kent village of Birling. Where *Scales of Justice* had been a light summery tale of angling assassination, *Off With His Head* was a chilling story of murder among Morris dancers in the village of Mardian.

At the book's beginning, the door is opened to a frozen world. 'The two Mardians were mentioned in the press and on the air as being the coldest spots in England.' It is four o'clock on the afternoon of the winter solstice. Snow and frost lie deep and impenetrable on the ground. The trees are shuddering in the north wind as middle-aged Mrs Bünz's tiny car makes its way through the bleakness. She is swaddled in homespun wool and wooden beads. 'Mrs Bünz was the lady who sits near the front of lectures and always asks questions . . . She weaves, forms circles, gives talks, handthrows pots and designs book-plates.' She is a fanatic folklorist in search of one of the richest remnants of pure pagan ritual left in England. In the distance, on a white hillside, she can see the ruins of an ancient Norman castle partly encircling a hideous Victorian mansion. This is where the Mardian Morris Dance of the Five Sons will take place. It is a fertility rite of death and resurrection handed down through generations of Andersens, who have been Mardian smithies as far back as human memory can recall.

Off With His Head is a cleverly written cosy that uses ancient English folklore as the fabric of a fabulous homicide: the old Guiser Andersen from the smithy, who plays the fool in the Mardian Morris Dance with his five sons, is found decapitated at the end of the solstice ceremony. To strains of traditional violin music, in full public view, he dances around the dolmen stone, on which he then lays his head. According to legend, the old fool had five sons among whom he divided his property and then they killed him. In the Mardian dance, the fool's five sons symbolically sever his head, and later he is miraculously restored to life. Dancing with the fool and his sons are 'Crack', a hermaphrodite man-woman figure in skirted dress, and 'Betty', an equine monster costumed in metal hammered at the forge. Both are personifications of fertility who chase onlookers, tagging them with brushes dipped in liquid tar.

When the time comes for the fool to stand up, nothing happens, and the Guiser's lifeless body is discovered behind the stone, with his head some feet away in a bloodied paper mask. His death shocks the small community. Everyone is involved in the event. The doctor plays the violin; the storekeeper is 'Betty'; the vicar's son, and heir of Mardian Castle, is 'Crack'. And this has been the pattern for centuries: the Mardian Morris Dance is an ageless ritual of unification in which classes meet and are galvanized in the heat of a midwinter bonfire. Ngaio's characterization is superb, and her knowledge of English folklore and dance is reinforced by meticulous research. The mystery of the decapitation whodunit is preserved cleverly to the end.

In a review of *Scales of Justice* published in the *New Statesman*, the critic wrote: 'Miss Marsh's style does not please everyone . . . and her books are often heavily loaded with crudely snobbish class-consciousness. But given the right plot, her workmanship can be magnificent.' This critic liked *Scales of Justice* and for the same reason would have endorsed *Off With His Head*, because Ngaio observed the nuances of the British class system with a critical eye. If she was blinded in places by Anglophile admiration in her earlier novels, after the war she became more searching. In *Off With His Head*, aging representatives of the class system are archaic:

To Dame Alice . . . class was unremarkable and existed in the way that continents and races exist. Its distinctions were not a matter of preference but of fact. To play at being of one class when you were actually of another was as pointless as it would be for a Chinese to try and pass himself off as a Zulu.

She is 94 years old, and like the Guiser, one of the 'survivals from the Ice Age'. The younger generation is different. It is Dame Alice's great-great-nephew and heir Ralph, who is set to marry the Guiser's granddaughter Camilla, who will ensure that future fertility dances take on a new aspect.

Ngaio worked on *Off With His Head* through the bitter English winter of 1954–55. Her next book, *Singing in the Shrouds*, consolidated her journey to England on the *Temeraire* and her trip home. It was begun in February 1956, on the boat back to New Zealand. She imagined what it would be like departing the Thames on a cargo freighter with a serial killer among its nine passengers. 'Silly cows,' the taxi driver mutters to PC Moir. He has waited an eternity on the wharf in the blackness and fog for his fare to come back. She is a shop girl with a huge box of hyacinths that she is delivering to celebrity Mrs Dillington-Blick, who is boarding the *Cape Farewell*. The flower girl never returns, and he steams in his taxi, as the night grows longer and colder.

It is almost midnight when PC Moir decides to look for the taxi's mysterious fare. There are many dark corners and cupboards of blackness along the wharf. Packing cases, dumps of equipment and cargo, piles of ropes and rotting canvas take on sinister form as he flashes his lamp over them. A rat scuttles across his boot and he starts. The light from his lamp lurches haphazardly along an alleyway, catching suddenly in its beam a 'high-heeled shoe with a foot in it'. The shaft of light 'crept from the foot along a leg . . . and came to rest at last on a litter of artificial pearls and fresh flowers scattered over the breast of a dead girl'. In her hand she clutches the tiniest shred of evidence, the torn corner of an embarkation card, which leads Roderick Alleyn — who in the fictional space between *Scales of Justice* and *Off With His Head* has been promoted to superintendent — to believe a serial killer is aboard the *Cape Farewell*. He joins the ship by pilot cutter after it has set sail.

This was Ngaio's first book with a serial killer, so it involved a new type of murderer with a different pathology. The killing could appear random, because the pattern existed in the murderer's mind and modus operandi. 'These sorts of criminals are often our worst headache,' Alleyn explains to two shipboard confidantes.

They have no occupational habits. They resemble each other only in their desire to kill for gratification. In everyday life they may be anything: there are no outwards signs . . . The thing one looks for, of course, is a departure from routine. If there's no known routine, if your man is a solitary creature as Jack the Ripper was, your chances lessen considerably.

The serial killer in *Singing in the Shrouds* has a routine, which is to strangle a victim every 10 days, while singing strains of songs and leaving a shower of flower petals over the victim. This is the killer's fingerprint that Alleyn works out, but not before a fourth murder has been committed.

Ngaio's real life and writing are linked in the novel's reference to a drunken episode of on-air spoonerisms by the character Aubyn Dale, who is a television talk-show host. 'He was going all springlike over a display of hyacinths and said that in arranging them all you really needed was a "turdy stable".' This relates to a joke Ngaio shared with John Schroder. 'My Chemist known as *Turdy Stable*,' she told him in December 1958, '[said] aren't you a dangerous person to know, Miss Marsh & would you care for our Xmas Calendar (cats in funny hats).' The chemist had recommended that Ngaio use a 'turdy stable' when taking indoor photographs with her Box Brownie and had become thus-named.

In this same letter, written after her return to New Zealand, Ngaio also appealed to John Schroder for a job for Val Muling.

Val (Vladimir) is an Esthonian [*sic*] who was exiled at the age of 19 & has spent the rest of his life in Paris & then in China where he was Commissioner for the Northern (I think) Territory . . . In Paris he studied the piano under Corteau (?) & played with the Paris Symphony Orchestra . . . Val speaks some eight languages & is quite astonishingly civilised & the nicest of chaps . . . He now wonders if by any chance there would be a dogsbody job at 3YA.

Val would become an arbiter of her detective manuscripts before they were sent off to the publisher, and the Mulings often accompanied her to all-important play rehearsals. They were colleagues in culture and close friends, mentioned in the dedication to *Spinsters in Jeopardy*. She was intimately connected to both of the Mulings, but her link to Val was perhaps the one she valued the most. When he was charged with soliciting sodomy in a Christchurch park toilet, Ngaio never faltered in her support or affection for him or Anita. Ngaio was never a prude. She accepted sexual diversity as a matter of course.

A return to Christchurch inevitably signalled a switch for Ngaio from her intense focus on detective novels to involvement in Shakespeare. In August 1956, she produced a season of *King Lear* at the Civic Theatre. The costumes were elaborate, with brilliantly contrasted heraldic patterns. Her stage set was simple and dramatic, and she used two portable aprons to bring the stage forward, extending the action into the audience to create a sense of intimacy and immediacy. Ngaio hated the venue. 'This great barn is rather like a theatrical joke in bad taste,' she wrote in *Black Beech*. It seated about 1,100 people, which was a huge capacity compared with the Little Theatre.

This was an ambitious play to tackle with young players. The issues were complex and sophisticated, and not all critics felt the cast had explored all the psychological nuances. But there were some rising stars who would establish themselves as Ngaio's protégés at home and abroad. There was Mervyn Glue (nicknamed Sticky), a young law graduate who had played Brutus in *Julius Caesar* and now tackled Lear. Ngaio had groomed him from the early days of Little Theatre productions and he was consistently good. 'Mervyn Glue's performance as the King was robust,' wrote a reviewer, 'a rash fiery voluntary it was hard to believe that he would ever bend before age or misfortune . . . even in the broken man this energy was manifest.'

Annette Facer's Cordelia was less emphatic. She played her part with 'grace and scrupulousness', but with her 'self-effacing' grey costume and subdued manner 'she tended to be lost in the spate of events'. Ngaio's King of France, Gerald Lascelles, and her Earl of Kent, David Hindin, would become stalwart players, and this was Elric Hooper's entrée in a major role as the Fool, whom he played to perfection. 'In his jester's suit with bells and bauble complete, this fool seemed to embody a spirit from time long past.' Ngaio had spotted him in student reviews and invited him to audition. She could see his potential and that of young Fine Arts student Jonathan Elsom, who played Oswald.

Ngaio was commended by commentators for her courage in taking on such a difficult play with untested amateurs. 'No praise can be too high for Miss Marsh's work as producer,' wrote one critic, who found in the play 'moments of pure and perfect beauty . . . giving an insight into the profoundest depths of drama. Kent in the stocks, or the lecherous Edmund eyeing Regan and Goneril at his first entrance.' Ngaio had worked tirelessly on preparation for the production. Before opening night, a reporter for *The Christchurch Star-Sun* visited her at home. 'On either side of her armchair on two low tables rested her working script of the play, "King Lear" — voluminous notes in loose-leaf folder — and a collection of small dolls, with which she works out the groupings and movements of her actors.'

Ngaio was as meticulous in her planning for the stage as she was with the research for her novels, and sometimes they overlapped. In *Off With His Head*, Ngaio had made references and links to Shakespeare's *Lear*. 'I began to see in these ritual dances a distillation of the Lear theme,' she explained to a reporter, 'the same characters always cropping up, with the protagonist an old man. All have the idea of resurrection — they are basically fertility dances.' She was aware of the sexual dynamics of the Lear theme and brought it out in both the book and the play. *Off With His Head*, which was dedicated to John and Bear Mannings 'with love', was released in the United States in 1956 (as *Death of a Fool*), and in Britain in 1957.

In July 1957, Ngaio produced her second *Henry V*. Her stable of leading actors took the key roles again. David Hindin, who had been Kent in *Lear*, was cast as the King, Elric Hooper as Chorus, Mervyn Glue as the comic Pistol, Jonathan Elsom as the Dauphin, and Annette Facer as Katharine. The show was a spectacle. Ngaio extended the aprons further into the audience, and the blaze of colour, crowd scenes and eruptions of dramatic action were dazzling. 'Pattern is enhanced and underlined by costume,' wrote the critic for *Canta* magazine, 'and in this production the costumes, designed by Jon Elsom, were superb, conforming to character, identifying the protagonist and gorgeous in colour.' Wardrobe mistress Doreen Sharp worked evenings and weekends and ran working-bees for months to translate the designs and '200 yards of material' into 43 lavish 15th-century period costumes.

Hindin played an animated and versatile King: 'the high point was perhaps his blunt English wooing — slightly burlesqued — of the sophisticated French princess Katharine. Annette Facer was a good foil for his wooing.' Hooper's Chorus was judged superb. Glue's portrayal of Pistol, with his characteristic skinful, was applauded, and Elsom's 'effeminate, and much-too-talkative Dauphin . . . was as subtle, polished, and odious as the role demanded'.

Reviews of the show were encouraging, but there were some nagging reservations. Not all of the acting was consistent or flowing, and in this patriotic demonstration of heraldic testosterone there was a dearth of women. Maybe this was why Ngaio, the next year, was working on a play with a stronger female lead. She wrote to her friend Lady Doris McIntosh in April 1958, after a particularly nasty tummy bug that was finally 'clearing up':

. . . just as my students at Canterbury College have decided to do *Hamlet* after I had done three weeks intensive work on *Antony & Cleopatra*. It appears that a request has come in from the schools for this play and also from the Arts Faculty within the university, so there is nothing for it but as rapidly as possible to exchange Egypt for Elsinore.

This was just the beginning of the battle.

Hamlet was relatively easy to find in the bristling talent of Elric Hooper. 'My Hamlet . . . arrived here yesterday at 2 & left at 11 exhausted. He can manage the reflective bits very well but the savage under-tones at the moment elude the boy. Still he's intelligent & a glutton for punishment so I hope all may be well.'

Casting a comparable Ophelia, however, was an ordeal. 'Rehearsals every day — two on Sunday — & a thousand & one crises & upheavals,' Ngaio told Doris McIntosh.

. . . a dearth of Ophelias has been the major worry but at last that one has been settled — not before a lot of time has been squandered in trying to squeeze the part out of a physically suited young lady who wouldn't be able to give a convincing performance of a deaf mute in the dark.

The Ophelia she was so thrilled to find was Annette Facer, who, like the rest of Ngaio's stable, had been warming with each role. Ngaio now plunged into what she described to Doris as the 'six week maelstrom of production'. Everything was shelved in favour of the production: 'correspondence, normal human intercourse & personal appearance suffer neglect'. There was also the tyrant in Ngaio that sometimes emerged to shape coarse students into fine players. 'Can it be true after all that we *are* the gentler sex? You wouldn't think so if you could hear me tearing the tights off the wretched footballer who is playing the role of Marcellus.'

Jonathan Elsom, now in his fourth year of Fine Arts, again designed the set and costumes. He worked closely with Ngaio to 'familiarise himself with her stage groupings and movements, and ensure that any characters likely to be on the stage together in clashing colours would never be close'. Instead of modern dress, Ngaio chose a Byronic style from the early 1800s. Once again the costuming was sumptuous, with the exception of Hamlet, who was in fitting black. A flurry of promotional activities preceded all of Ngaio's plays. Bob Scott, who had played Gower in *Henry V*, was publicity co-ordinator and there were promotional features in the *Listener* and *The Christchurch Star-Sun*. A full-page article in the latter introduced a facetious note that would amplify. 'Here is the recipe for play-acting perfection,' wrote Norman Scott Forrest.

Take the University of Canterbury Drama Society, stir in the script of 'Hamlet', then give the mixture to wonder-chef Ngaio Marsh to bake into a rich delicacy for Christchurch audiences. The final concoction should be entitled: 'Ngaio Marsh, as presented by "Hamlet".'

Ngaio had become the Garrick of Christchurch theatre, but neither she, nor the play, deserved the lashing they received in the *Star-Sun* review. The critic was galled by her oedipal reading of the play, and by Hooper's 'playing the role as it appeared to have been interpreted for him'. The costuming was effete and lacked nobility, and every actor seemed to have fallen short of their role except Ophelia, whose mad scene was 'delicate and tragic'.

The editor of the paper received a flood of irate letters and a retraction was published. Ngaio's stamp was indelible and pervasive, but she was a tall poppy of talent, ambition and dynamism in a country where jealous egalitarianism was the universal measure. Inevitably, she, and what she did, became targets. Other criticism was positive. The *Press* reviewer described Hooper's interpretation of Hamlet as 'truly artistic' and 'highly accomplished', and Facer's 'graceful and touching' Ophelia as the demonstration of a new level in her acting achievement. Mervyn Glue, David Hindin, Jonathan Elsom and Gerald Lascelles were all commended for their performances, and the costumes and set design deemed 'a considerable accomplishment by any standard'. In the end, Ngaio was exhausted but pleased, especially with the season's £200 profit and Hooper's news that he had won a bursary to the London Academy of Music and Dramatic Art (LAMDA). He left New Zealand three weeks after *Hamlet* closed.

Ngaio had put her three-quarters-finished novel aside to produce the play, and it was hard, after weeks, to come back and pick up the ends. 'I struggle in a debilitated manner with my book and loathe every word of it,' she wrote to Doris McIntosh. 'Can only hope that this reaction is due, as you hearteningly suggest, to the aftermath of the bug.'

Ngaio was always full of insecurities about her books. Rosemary Greene, her secretary in London during 1949–50, and in New Zealand from 1961, has testified to Ngaio's lack of confidence in her work. 'Whenever I posted off the finished typescript to Edmund Cork . . . or Dorothy Olding . . . she would be extremely thankful to be rid of it but she would then be in an absolute fever until she heard back to know what they thought of it. I used to feel quite disloyal during this waiting period that I wasn't also in a fever, but I'd seen this so often.'

When Ngaio began a book she started with a new set of characters and plot. The formula was a framework, but the challenge to be original within it was one she faced anew each time. Like an actor, she considered herself only as good as her last performance. The news about *Singing in the Shrouds*, published in the United States in 1958 and Britain in 1959, was very encouraging. On 21 January 1959, she received a memo from Richard Simon at Collins. 'The reviews this book has had are really wonderful. It looks like being the most successful Ngaio Marsh ever.' A transcript of reviews followed. George Millar of the *Daily Express* described it as:

. . . a book that, within its chosen limitations, is masterly . . . I admit to being amazed by Miss Marsh, she is astonishingly good. Moments of pure hilarity are perfectly set among moments of delicious fear. Writing, characterisation, even the sea background are as crisp and as welcome as new banknotes.

Maurice Richardson of the Sunday *Observer* said it was 'as good as a good Christie . . . I had not thought such an old familiar pattern could read so fresh'.

Ngaio struggled on with *False Scent*, which she found 'irksome, sticky & slow'. 'I refer to my "twenty-first little bastard", as some lady novelist is supposed to have said,' she wrote to John Schroder. The character of Mrs Bellamy was not hard for Ngaio to evoke, but the technicalities of death by a deluge of insecticide sprayed unwittingly from a perfume bottle needed expert advice. The plot centres on the 50th birthday party of a fading stage star who is a time-bomb of jealous possessiveness.

Mary Bellamy's temperaments were of rare occurrence but formidable in the extreme and frightening to behold. They were not those regulation theatre tantrums that seem to afford pleasure both to observer and performer; on the contrary they devoured her like some kind of migraine and left her exhausted.

Vivien Leigh's birthday at Marton Cottage may have been the inspiration for this cleverly characterized but, after Alleyn's investigation begins, rather inert novel. Mrs Bellamy, the female equivalent of *Final Curtain*'s Henry Ancred, is powerfully portrayed as a larger-than-life narcissist with bipolar tendencies. 'You're a cannibal Mary, and it's high time somebody had the guts to tell you so,' says Pinky Cavendish. But honesty like that with Mary is an invitation to dinner. 'But could she actually do you any damage?' Pinky later enquires of his friend, Bertie Saracen. 'Can the Boa-constrictor . . . consume the rabbit?' *False Scent* was dedicated to 'Jemima with love', who was really Eileen Mackay, the eldest Rhodes daughter.

Ngaio's consolation during 'irksome' hours of writing was the arrival back in New Zealand of John Mannings, who now hyphenated his middle and last names and was known as Dacres-Mannings, and his brother Bear. John had contracted tuberculosis while serving in Germany. 'In the British Army I experienced the greatest comfort and discomfort,' he later commented. 'The war did not end in Europe with peace.' Conditions there were grim and he became ill and was hospitalized for months. His return to New Zealand to stay with Ngaio was part of his convalescence. She was thrilled to have him back and he stayed with her in Christchurch.

In spite of his ill health he did a huge amount of work in Ngaio's garden, which was one of the city's finest. She loved flowers and plants, and gardening was one of her sustaining passions. Dacres-Mannings blasted rock and moved it from one part of the property to another to create space for a drive and garage, and landscaped terraces on the steep hillside. There was another consolation. 'News is that one of our three cats . . . Smokey Joe, developed gastro-enteritis coupled with septic wound on the tum,' Ngaio told Doris McIntosh. Ngaio dosed him half-hourly for nearly a week. 'One triumphant day a little grey skeleton took three laps of milk, since when he has never looked back.'

In March 1959, Ngaio began preparations for a new play. There were 'auditions, drawings-to-scale & the long, *long* job of planning moves and getting on terms with a play which the more I know of it the more I marvel at'. Elric Hooper was in London, and Jonathan Elsom now touring with the Southern Comedy Players and departing in August on a bursary to LAMDA. This left a hole in her constellation of stars, but any apprehension she may have had about talent was unfounded. In fact, selecting the best was the challenge. 'Agonisingly difficult auditions for A-&-C,' she wrote to Elsom, 'with Annette, finally & after some pretty hot competition, as the Serpent of Old Nile. Sticky [Glue] as Antony & David [Hindin] as Enobarbus. A newcomer, Jim Laurenson, very promising indeed as Scarus.' The cast also included Mervyn Thompson as Proculeius, or Proc as he became known.

Rehearsals were conducted in a condemned boatshed 'full of holes in the walls, (literally) through which the winter fogs & gales effect an uninterrupted entry'. She worked hard on models for the set. One was a Roman pavilion and the other Egyptian, 'all on the giant apron & in front of the house curtain. Phew!' It was an immense undertaking, so she was delighted with the response.

'ANTONY & CLEOPATRA really did go off very well and in particular got a very enthusiastic press,' she wrote ecstatically to Doris McIntosh. 'I never wish for a harder nut to crack.' The production had been 'fraught with difficulties' and the play was full of 'traps for young players'. There were moments, she admitted, when she wondered if they would ever make the mark. She put the success of the show down to a vintage year of talent and the 'students' capacity for gruelling hard work and brutal treatment from the producer'. Now it was all over and she could hardly believe it.

Surely there is no activity as ephemeral as that of a stage production? Half an hour after the last words of the play are spoken on the last night, the whole thing is vanished like Prospero's vision into the thinnest of thin air. This was particularly evident in a production of this sort, where the actual stage setting was massive and had an unusual air of permanence. One lives for a few days in a sort of vacuum, before finding oneself able to start off again on another tack.

The production was epic, and its end brought a sense of loss, but not for long because Ngaio had something in the wings. She was packing up the house for tenants and facing the awful fear of losing her passport in transit to Wellington for a Japanese visa: 'the *tax* clearance . . . the *Bank!* . . . the heat & the shops & THE PEOPLE'. On top of this, she planned to sell her car.

At 64 years of age, Ngaio was making arrangements for a marathon promotional tour of Japan, the United States and Britain early in the coming year. She had begun a new book and was about to set sail.

Katherine

CHAPTER SEVEN

Doyenne and Dame

What a hurly-burly it was at the gang plank,' Ngaio declared after she left New Zealand. Chaos reigned on the wharf in Sydney where she was convinced that they had neglected to teach the maritime workers their alphabet. 'With the natural results I found half my luggage under S & the rest under Z. One case still floating somewhere about dockland but said to be traceable.'

Ngaio delighted in catching up with John Dacres-Mannings and his new wife, Elizabeth, whom Ngaio described as an 'enchanting', 'delicate beauty' with a 'good brain'. After his convalescence, Dacres-Mannings had moved to Australia where he worked half-days with a Sydney stockbroker. He married not long before Ngaio arrived. His mother, Stella, had gone over for his wedding, then on 'for a passionately longed-for trip to England'; she and Ngaio planned to meet in London. In the meantime, Ngaio was thrilled to dine with the newly-weds and deliver a wedding present from Doris and Alister McIntosh. This was the cherished beginning to an amazing adventure.

Her promotional tour would prove exacting but immensely rewarding, and it would extend Ngaio's international reputation as a detective fiction writer and celebrity. The boat trips were a hiatus with rest mixed with a little writing in an itinerary that would otherwise have been overwhelming. Her ports of call, after Fremantle, included Djakarta, Singapore, Hong Kong, which was 'alive, grubby, beautiful & contradictory', and finally Yokohama.

'Japan was glorious,' she wrote enthusiastically to friends in New Zealand. Her advice to any of them visiting Japan was 'engage Miss Shinko Matsumoto to go with you'. She cost just £30 for three weeks, but Ngaio thought she was worth her weight in gold. Without such a guide, so much precious time could be wasted in misunderstandings and the confusion of being sent off to the wrong place or, worse still, to a dull one.

Once Shinko, a young graduate and translator of English books, realized that Ngaio was a truly curious and intrepid traveller, she proudly showed her the pageant of Japan. Ngaio was enthralled. They stayed in little inns, visited remote shrines, saw a Shinto wedding, watched a judo contest and a spring festival performance of geishas, wandered through narrow back streets filled with signs and superb traditional shopfronts, and ventured into the hills among the incredibly 'lovely farm houses'. Except for Western-style hotels, Ngaio hardly saw a European for days. One of her highlights was stopping at an island as they sailed down the Inland Sea, bathing, dining and walking through a gorgeous garden before re-embarking at midnight. Japan was an experience she commemorated by the 'wildly extravagant' purchase of an oriental screen and three pieces of decorative 'lacquer' she bought at a workshop, plus porcelain pieces and rugs.

Ngaio was a tourist, but between the sights and sounds of her trip she crammed an inventory of public functions, which included a formal dinner put on for her by the New Zealand ambassador J.S. Reid in Tokyo. There, she was introduced to eminent people and treated like visiting royalty. In three weeks, she went almost from one end of the country to the other. Her itinerary left just two full days free. 'It was extremely strenuous but I managed nicely except for one rather droll mishap,' Ngaio admitted to friends. 'I fainted on Tokyo railway station & came to, very cosily resting on the breast of the station-master who was quite charming.'

This she believed was the result of eating spoiled food on one of the trains. But as she got older, Ngaio's health was not always good. She began to have accidents. In Sydney, she partly crushed a bone in her toe and hobbled around the boat until it recovered. She also endured chronic stomach pains that were exacerbated by the heat and the constantly changing diet and drinking water. But Ngaio constantly pushed herself to perform.

The luxury food and facilities of the *Chusan* passenger liner from Yokohama to San Francisco provided a welcome respite. It was also an opportunity to people-watch. The ship was packed with Americans, and although she felt guilty about making generalizations, Ngaio could not help herself. 'They are an almost pathologically naive race,' she told Doris McIntosh.

> They are thoroughly nice & difficult to distinguish, the one from the other. Shrewd without being subtle, observant but not penetrating, immensely capable along acceptable lines, even their 'originals' are eccentric according to given patterns.

Ngaio loved 'characters' and the comfortable conveyor-belt conformity that she detected in the many American tourists she met in Japan and onboard the *Chusan* did not go unnoticed.

However, when she arrived in the United States she found it exciting, stimulating and 'at times beautiful'. Her tour included stays in 'vastly' expensive hotels, and she was picked up by an attendant and rushed around from one promotional event to another. At the Fairmont Hotel, 'The hospitality is all it's cracked up to be & was laid on like a Lord Mayor's Show.' She had many press and radio interviews 'but jibbed at television which would have eaten into too much time'. Before leaving San Francisco she enjoyed a dinner at Fisherman's Wharf, with a visit afterwards to a nightclub where they sang grand opera.

In mid-May, Ngaio boarded a train for New York, where she faced another round of celebrity interviews and events, and caught up with her American agent Dorothy Olding, whom she had first met in London in 1954. Their correspondence had warmed over the years and they were now firm friends. At a Little, Brown luncheon for Ngaio on 23 May, the guest list included key figures from the newspaper and publishing worlds. They sat among fern leaves and crimson roses and ate exquisite food in the wine room of Pierre's Restaurant on 53rd Street. While she was in New York, Ngaio did a radio interview with Martha Deane for *The World in Books*, and was interviewed by reporters for *The New York Times*, *Newsweek* and the *New York Herald Tribune*.

An unscheduled event, however, proved one of her most memorable experiences. 'The great white chief of the N.Y. police laid on a night tour in a plain car with one of his superintendents', and they drove through the Bronx. Home in prohibition days to bootleggers and then to waves of immigrant communities, the area had become a melting pot of social discontent, renowned for high-density housing and crime. This was the beat of hard-boiled writers like Dashiell Hammett. Ngaio and her escort arrived back at the precinct at 2am. She was thrilled to have been taken seriously by American law enforcement agencies, but this was foreign territory for her. 'My god what a lawless city it is & how proud, in a funny sort of inverted way, they are of their criminals.'

In New York, Ngaio saw 'exciting' opera, some 'revolting' theatre and was beguiled by the brilliant Vivien Leigh in *Duet of Angels*. There was another unofficial visit. 'Had a midnight prowl with my agent in The Village,' she admitted to Doris McIntosh. Ngaio struggled to convince Dorothy Olding that an excursion on a very wet, holiday weekend with few trains was worthwhile. Greenwich Village was a centre of bohemian culture and progressive thought. In the 1950s it was the focus of the Beat Generation, and through the 1960s it was known for its role in gay liberation. The district was largely residential, and at night there was not much to see, but Ngaio was pleased to savour, even if vicariously, New York's counter-culture. She managed a quick trip to Boston to see her editor Ned Bradford at Little, Brown, and was comatose with tiredness by the time she boarded the *Bremen*, bound for England. The surfeit on this week-long voyage was not American but German tourists, mostly millionaires, she observed, munching through food like 'boa-constrictors'.

Her arrival in Southampton on 8 June was 'bliss', and the first sudden sight of Big Ben brought tears to her eyes. After more than three months' travelling she was finally in the London she loved, but then came the shocking news that her luggage from Japan, containing her half-finished novel, had not arrived. It was a huge relief when it was finally traced and returned. Her first fortnight was consumed with media events — newspaper, radio and 'telly' interviews — and parties to promote *False Scent*.

Between, she snatched time to house hunt. The area that drew her, as it had so many times before, was Knightsbridge. At 29A Montpelier Walk she found a tiny, two-bedroom Georgian house close to the Brompton Oratory, set in a 'mewsy', 'pubsey' village of its own. In a Christmas card to her Cleopatra, Annette Facer, she described it as a fairytale house, borough fronted and black, with a scarlet front door. Here the traditional traffic of London passed by. There were street musicians, and the daily cries of a chair-mender, a knife-grinder, a flower-seller with a horse-drawn cart, and an 'any-old-rags-bones-or-bot-oools' man. These were centuries-old echoes that reminded her of a street scene from

Henry V. She would stash her impressions away for another novel.

Ngaio was fiercely proud of her student players who were living nearby. Elric Hooper had already begun to make an impact at The Old Vic, where he was appearing in an 'exciting' production of *Romeo and Juliet* by the Italian director Franco Zeffirelli. He sang the song in the ballroom scene and was understudy to Romeo. Jonathan Elsom, studying at LAMDA, quickly took up her offer of the attic bedroom in the Montpelier house at a nominal rent of £5 per week. It was a saving for him, and she enjoyed the young friends he brought home, his descriptions of LAMDA teaching, and his first-night student productions, to which they drove in the black XK150 Jaguar she bought not long after her arrival. The only drawback was how to explain their cohabitation. 'I think we'd better introduce you as my godson,' she suggested, and that was what she called him from then on.

They made an agreement to alternate the cost of going out together. One time she would pay for the show and he for the taxi, and then they reversed it. Ngaio cleverly engineered films on Elsom's night and expensive theatre tickets when she paid. On Sunday afternoons when they were both at home, they would watch television together. Ngaio's favourite recreational viewing was on-the-mat wrestling. They sat on sofas eating pieces of fruitcake topped with slices of cheese, and Ngaio would become engrossed in the action, leaning forward, leaping up, and occasionally shouting directions at the screen. A woman cleaned and cooked their evening meal, and they had a live-in family retainer, a black cat called Lucy Lockett, whom they adopted. She was a hunter, but not with good instincts. 'Lucy . . . has brought up here from Mr Raymond's abode of license, a small wooden fish which I found her tossing up & madly clutching on the carpet.' Ngaio missed her cats at home and almost always tried to find a feline in London to fill the gap. Ngaio's memories of Lucy Lockett would surface in a similarly character-filled cat in *Black As He's Painted*.

Not long after her arrival, Ngaio was asked by a theatre company to dramatize *False Scent*. It was a difficult prospect and she wrestled with what she believed was one of her weaker novels. 'I think the fault may well be that like so many of my books it falls between teckery [or detective fiction writing] and a comedy of manners.' She worked on the script in collaboration with Eileen Mackay.

In August, she took a break from their work to go to Oberammergau in Bavarian Germany for the Passion Play. She had been contemplating this trip with Jonathan Elsom since December 1959, and it was finally happening. The visit was fascinating. They travelled on the same Blue Train that Ngaio and Nelly Rhodes had embarked on years before. The play gave her a sense of continuity and tradition that she treasured. The crowds, the shops, and the merchandise were almost as interesting: Ngaio bought crucifixes, angels and figurines made into wine-bottle stoppers, all cleverly created by German woodcarvers. Some she kept and some she gave away as gifts.

When she returned to London, she picked up the threads of her play and, as the days shortened and the winter chill settled on London, she began writing with intense focus. It was the Third Act that presented the major problem, and, apart from buying food and making the occasional trip to the theatre, she watched London from her living-room windows. For more than three months of her precious time abroad, she was locked inside her Montpelier house.

She enjoyed an enchanting Christmas break with the Rhodeses, but the New Year of 1961 brought the 'sickening' news that Val Muling had died of thrombosis. His health had been precarious and she had just managed to get a last letter to him. She knew Anita would be devastated: 'brave, poor girl'. Ngaio felt numb and ill herself. Val was a unique individual in her life and it would seem strange returning to New Zealand, knowing he was not there. She struggled in the depths of winter to shake off the gloom of his death. Weekend stays with the Rhodes family and good friend, novelist and playwright J.B. Priestley were a respite. She found J.B., as she called him, very good company. '[He] is a man who has taken commonsense to a point where it almost becomes genius.' The Priestleys owned an immense mansion close to Stratford where she stayed and enjoyed the measured pattern of an English writer's life. After breakfast, each of them retired to one of the vast Georgian rooms and got 'down to it'.

When she had been in London for about a year, Ngaio decided to take a holiday in Devon. She loved watching the English countryside as it changed from the scoured earth of winter, with its tracery of black-branched trees, to land that was lush green and 'absolutely shouting itself hoarse with flowers' and foliage. She walked the moors and enjoyed the woods and wildflowers of lonely uplands that were 'so beautiful they almost hurt'. Why, she wondered, did the progression of England's seasons have so much more significance? Its rhythms turned 'slowly about the Heavens like the earth itself'.

Ngaio's September return to New Zealand had to be delayed because of the play. Edmund Cork loved the script she and Eileen Mackay sent, but she knew that the machinations of stage management were crisis-ridden and fickle. The theatre world in Britain and the United States was a 'jungle'. She had discussions with the Worthing Theatre Company about casting, and received a commitment from them that *False Scent* would be staged in October. The management wanted her around to keep an eye on rehearsals.

In the meantime she had abandoned her next novel, *Hand in Glove*, for the play script, and by June she still had 20,000 words to write, and her publisher was clamouring. It was hard to pick it up again after being 'so long in suspension'. She worked all hours of the day and night on the novel. After a late stint, Ngaio would leave her folio of handwritten pages downstairs on the dining-room table, and sometimes, before he left for LAMDA, Elsom took a peek. Later, when the book was published and she sent him a copy, he was amazed to see his name on the dedication page. *Hand in Glove* is a parody of upper-class English country life. Light humour ran through it like the flowing rhythms of alliteration and assonance in the names of its principal characters: Percival Pyke Period, Bimbo Dodds, Nicola Maitland-Mayne and Mary Ralston, nicknamed Moppett. And the feline *femme fatale* in *Scales of Justice*, Thomasina Twitchett, had a *Hand in Glove* canine equivalent. But not all animals in Ngaio's novels are equal, and Constance Cartell's Pekinese is a stinker. Li-chi is the kind of dog that insists on 'marrying your shoe', and when let out after being caught short will fly off to the nearest newly turned flowerbed and use it. Constance Cartell's brother, Harold, known as Boysie, has a half-breed Boxer called Pixie that is more trouble and even less attractive.

Hand in Glove is a story about good breeding; about the fake ancestral lineage of the sad Percival Pyke Period; and about Constance Cartell's adopted ward, Moppett's, instinctive attraction to the bullying cockney men of her origins, in spite of a genteel upbringing.

Harold Cartell's murder by being crushed in a ditch under an enormous concrete pipe seems incidental to the exploration of themes of foolish pride and unhealthy parental indulgence. This is another novel of manners rather than 'teckery'. Ngaio uses cameo romantic couples in almost all her novels; in *Hand in Glove* she has them in yin and yang opposites. There is Nicola Maitland-Mayne, painted by Troy for her 21st birthday, and her beau Andrew Bantling, from the right side of the tracks. Then there is Moppett with her slimy boyfriend Leonard Leiss, who slithers into this country cosy by virtue of Constance Cartell's affection for her ward. The feelings between Nicola and Andrew are full of promise, while those of Moppett and Leonard are fatefully twisted by innate dishonesty. But the point about these contrasting kinds of love is never laboured and the story remains a delicate and cleverly charactered spoof. The underlying message, though, is that good breeding counts, and pedigrees, with the exception of rampant Pekinese, are advantaged by the purity of their lineage. 'Having written the last word (I hope!) of my incubus of a book', Ngaio was relieved to hand the script into her publishers. After months of writing, she was free.

Ngaio enjoyed going to the theatre again with Pamela Mann. The 'kitchen sink' play was on its way out and high tragedy was making a return. Her taste in plays was relatively conservative: she found the 'shapeless, climaxless, plotless' modern plays unsatisfying. She enjoyed the palatable Existentialism of Pirandello, but not the more avant-garde or equivocal. 'I still cannot help thinking the whole [Existentialist] theory is a sort of convoluted glimpse of the obvious.' She was, though, willing to admit she might be at fault.

She enthusiastically tracked the careers of her star players. 'One of my boys', Elric Hooper, was Lorenzo in *The Merchant of Venice* at The Old Vic. His success was a matter of personal pride: he was her creation, one of a group of careers she launched that would have an international impact. For her young cousins, John and Bear, and her players, she wrote references and letters of introduction. When she was in England, she took them to weekend parties with the Rhodeses and to meet other friends. She liked having a select group of young men around as protégés and surrogate sons.

A number of Ngaio's key players were homosexual, although, in some cases, this was a matter of conjecture for Ngaio, because the subject was never discussed. Bob Scott was one of the few who openly talked about his sexuality as a young man. It puzzled her that he reconciled his Faith with his homosexuality, but she accepted his reasoning.

Incongruously, while Ngaio surrounded herself with handsome young men, her own persona was distinctly androgynous. She was lady-like, but often wore the trappings of femininity as an actor wears a costume. Elric Hooper was visiting her Montpelier flat one day when she answered the telephone. There was an awkward silence, then a frosty voice said sternly, 'That was *Miss* Marsh, thank you.' The unfortunate caller had mistaken her deep contralto voice for a man's, and it happened more than once.

In the theatre world, Ngaio was less conspicuous, and her eccentricities were regarded as dramatic flourish, rather than a deviation from the norm. This was her *milieu* and her great ambition was to have a West End hit with one of her detective stories. She waited anxiously for a response to *False Scent*, which was staged at the Connaught Theatre in Worthing on 23 October.

Ngaio's *False Scent* play programme, rating the actors' performances with handwritten annotations beside each name, suggests she thought the cast weak. Arthur Barrett as Roderick Alleyn was 'awful', Patrick Noble as Inspector Fox 'peculiar', and the director Guy Vaesen 'adequate but not imaginative & a bit weekly rep'. The outcome of the 'preliminary canter' was that not long before her departure for New Zealand she was asked to rewrite the last Act of *False Scent* for an anticipated London season the following March.

'This has not been a holiday,' she told Doris McIntosh flatly. There was the play, then the book, and she had not been 'inside a theatre for weeks & weeks'. Ngaio and Eileen Mackay took a two-week cruise around the Adriatic and Aegean before settling down for a final assault. The trip relaxed and refreshed her, and she was stunned by the beauty of Athens. With the rewrite completed, Ngaio made preparations to go home. It would be hard to leave London, but she felt settled about how things were left. Elric Hooper was doing well, and Jonathan Elsom had begun his career in Dundee with her old Hamlet, Jack Henderson, who was now head of Dundee Repertory. Recommended by Ngaio, Elsom arrived to find he had a major part. 'It's nice to see them so safely embarked as maybe in this precarious business'. Lucky Lockett was re-homed. 'The telly has gone & the desk & the pictures & my luggage,' she wrote to Elsom, '& as I look out on the lights over the little pub & hear people going past, I think of the last 18 months which have been so happy here.'

Ngaio left on 30 November 1961, and was shocked to find when she arrived back in New Zealand that her Jaguar was impounded on the wharf. They refused to release it and she was furious. 'I have done everything: but every *bloody* thing that *was* asked of me.' It seemed that tax laws had changed retrospectively while she was in transit. It took an age and a fortune to get the car back; and the house, depressingly, was not the way she had left it. The plumbing was leaking and the tenants had allowed taps to drip and the cats to claw the furniture.

But she was hardly home before a new project carried her off. Composer David Farquhar had been in touch by letter while she was overseas because both had been commissioned as a collaborative team to create New Zealand's first opera. Ngaio was to write the libretto based on *The Wyvern and the Unicorn*, her play script for children, and Farquhar was to write the music. Ngaio was excited about the project. In January she and Farquhar, who had come down from Wellington, worked on the opera 'from 9 am until, dizzy with fatigue' they retired to their 'various couches in the early hours of the morning'. Well into March, Farquhar was 'still hard at his Opera & is clamouring for a meeting SOON'. She had completed the libretto for the first and third Acts, but for the second, which was all singing, '[he] says he can't get on without me'. Ngaio begged him to come down to Christchurch again, because she was frantically busy.

She had been asked by the University of Canterbury to deliver the Macmillan Brown Lectures. This was an immense honour, because the series — founded by Professor John Macmillan Brown (1846–1935), a founding professor of the University of Canterbury — was one of the academic cornerstones in Christchurch. Ngaio picked a subject she knew well. 'The Three Cornered World: Shakespeare in the Theatre' was a detailed and more intellectual treatment of the themes of producer, actor, and audience which she had dealt with in *A Play Toward* in 1946 and also in *Play Production*, a booklet for schools that was published in 1948 and revised for the *Post-Primary School Bulletin* in 1960.

She began with a lecture on the Shakespearian producer, describing the role as being similar to that of a lens, which collects disparate light like the multiple elements of a play, and projects it through the actors onto the audience. The producer was a transparent filter through which a play passed before it came to life, and inevitably there were those shattering 'terrors of Shakespearian rehearsals' when nothing was in focus: 'Baleful nights and days when the play seems to come apart and fall to pieces,' she wrote. 'However careful his preparation, however great his own devotion and that of his company, he will, at one stage or another be visited by this nightmarish experience.' She imagined what it would be like for Shakespeare confronted by an actor such as Burbage. 'Look Will . . . what the hell am I meant to make of this one . . . what does it *mean*?' Ngaio used wit, intelligence and personal experience to illuminate Shakespearian production, not just for specialists, but for a wider audience. The lecture was funny, fresh and fascinating, especially for those who heard it delivered in person in the museum auditorium.

The actor was the subject of her second lecture. 'He must feel the character grow within himself and out of his own personality,' she observed, 'and must make it known, boldly and widely, to however many persons may be waiting on the other side of the curtain.' In essence, this was Constantin Stanislavsky in *An Actor Prepares* again. Ngaio knew what it was like to be a performer. She discussed the practicalities of breathing, of voice quality, control and projection. She identified the importance of the actor's movement through a part, with its rhythm and climaxes, and considered the intrinsic significance of the ebb and flow in Shakespeare's dramatic poetry. What was an actor? she asked. 'How can one define him? As a body, a voice and a mind that is occupied in the mass-transmission of a playwright's ideas? As a sort of pipeline between a dramatist and his public?' If the producer was the lens, then actors were light itself, with its qualities of immateriality and transformation. She talked about the simplicity of Shakespeare's most moving lines: 'a sequence of short, homely words that fall across a profound calm and are so explicit'. Her poignant example of this was the 'recognition scene' in *King Lear*. Maybe she was thinking of what had happened during rehearsals for *Lear* in 1956, when she took the part of the mad king to Annette Facer's Cordelia.

> Do not laugh at me;
> For, as I am a man, I think this lady
> To be my child, Cordelia.

Facer was so moved that she cried. Ngaio knew, from experience, that the power of Shakespeare's words to stir an audience lay not just in an actor's interpretation of their meaning, but also in the conveying of their emotion.

The audience, according to Ngaio's third lecture, was what Shakespearian play production was all about. It was the third estate of the theatre, the one that gave meaning to the others. 'Shakespeare's act of creation, the actor's changing attitudes over three hundred and sixty odd years', developments in theatre design, technology, and the 'whole accumulation of theatrical history' was all focused on bringing the plays 'to life before an audience'. The audience was like a giant fat cat, 'strange and wonderful', waiting in the dark to be fed. It was the consciousness in the blackness that absorbed the light. The audience was 'a group of individuals' that acted as one with different responses each night. At the end of her discourse on the audience, Ngaio tackled the thorny issue of funding assistance for professional theatre. She spoke of the cost to New Zealand of its most talented actors always having to go abroad to work, with little prospect of returning home. 'What is wrong with us that we can, and do support magnificently, our orchestras, chamber music and opera and yet cannot sustain the classic drama at the professional level?' It was a powerful way to end because it was less of a question than a challenge.

Ngaio's Macmillan Brown Lectures were delivered in April and broadcast by radio in May. What dated her 'Three Cornered' model, even in 1962, was its unequal weighting. Her triangle was really a pyramid with the power and control in the hands of a producer at the top. The actor was merely transformative material, and the audience a sometimes cruel, but nevertheless largely passive, beast waiting to be fed. She also presented Shakespeare's plays as if they were finite in their interpretation. This seemed reactionary to theatre renegades who were already deconstructing Shakespeare and the roles of producer, actor and audience. But in its practical suggestions, compelling logic and lively debate, especially about a New Zealand theatre company, the series made a valuable contribution to thinking about play production.

<hr>

Ngaio was relieved to have the lectures over, but like sand at the beach, the hole it left in her workload was rapidly filled with competing projects. 'One sits & wonders which in hell of these tasks one will tackle next & ends up going into a cross-eyed trance.' In March, she had already talked with students about the annual play production, which she thought would be *Macbeth*; the theatre company was demanding more changes to *False Scent* before a London launch, and she was receiving letters twice a week from her assiduous co-writer, Eileen Mackay; *A Unicorn for Christmas* was in the making, with David Farquhar desperate to see her; and thoughts of another novel, her bread and butter, were knocking at her conscience. 'I've simply got to get cracking on a new book before rehearsals begin.'

She began *Dead Water*, which was inspired by her recent trip to Devon and Cornwall. It was an odd story, and maybe some of its quirkiness came from the feeling she had to write and the inevitable interruptions that dogged its conception and development. 'It's been a snorter to control from the kick-off,' she later admitted to John Schroder. Ngaio dedicated the book to Alister and Doris McIntosh, who were becoming closer and closer friends.

Ngaio's relationship with the couple was interesting because Alister McIntosh was homosexual, as Ngaio knew and discreetly alluded to in her letters. She became a part of their marriage in a profound way, because for Doris she took on many of the roles of a partner. She was her confidante and her emotional support, and possibly more, although a physical dimension to this relationship was never suggested. But increasingly Ngaio wanted to share her special events with Doris, and Alister if he was available.

The plot of the new novel revolves around the mercenary activities of a cult that is marketing the healing properties of the spring waters of Portcarrow Island, where, allegedly, a young intellectually disabled boy's wart-covered hands have been washed clean in the spring. Desperate to escape tormenting children, he staggers into the pool, looks up directly into the sun and sees a Green Lady, who tells him: 'Say "Please take away my warts". Shut your eyes and do as I tell you. Say it again when you go to bed.' The next morning his warts are gone and word spreads rapidly. Soon tourists, along with the sick and the infirm, are coming to Portcarrow in Lourdes-like numbers. Racketeering becomes an economic strategy, and Portcarrow inhabitants organize package tours, turnstile entry into the spring enclosure, merchandising of magic water and painted plastic figurines of the Green Lady, and an annual commemorative festival run by the 'near-nymphomaniac', slightly unhinged Elspeth Cost.

Emily Pride, the new suzerain of Portcarrow Island, and coincidentally a great friend of Roderick Alleyn, decides to put her foot down. In a past life, she was Alleyn's wise old grasshopper, helping him with his French irregular verbs when he was a candidate for the Diplomatic Service. She was in the French Resistance and is staunchly moral. Any more spring-water swindling will be over her dead body. There are death threats and two attempts on Emily Pride's life before a body finally surfaces in the spring waters of the miraculous Green Lady grotto. But it is the wrong one: Elspeth Cost's, not Emily Pride's.

Although the storyline is farcical, and the murderer more predictable than most, the setting of Portcarrow Island is magnificently evoked, as is the crowd mentality of the miracle seekers. Memories of Oberammergau give vividness to Ngaio's writing: descriptions of rubbish-strewn pathways after spiritual tourists have passed by, busloads of anxious people desperate for a cure or an answer to their torments, and behind it all blind faith. Oberammergau's tourist shops sold wooden crucifixes and painted figurines; on Portcarrow Island, in Miss Cost's Gifte Shoppe, are bottles of magic water, pamphlets, handwoven jerkins, novelties and row upon row of painted plastic Green Ladies.

This is not one of Ngaio's best novels but it has some clever satire and startlingly vivid cameo characters, like the alcohol-addled Major Keith Barrimore, with the smell of whisky on his breath, purple veins in his face, and a tremor in his hand. The young New Zealand-born schoolmistress Jenny Williams is also convincingly evoked. Like Roberta Grey in *Surfeit of Lampreys*, she is a stand-in for Ngaio, and when asked whether she gets homesick she gives an answer that the writer might have given herself: 'A bit. Sometimes. I miss the mountains and the way people think.'

Rehearsals for *Macbeth* began in early June. Once again they were conducted in the most primitive conditions, but a warm sense of camaraderie among the student players made the cold crudeness less biting. Helen Holmes, who was to become a close personal friend, played an excellent Lady Macbeth, and Ngaio was thrilled with her thane, James Laurenson. 'The Macbeth himself has made a most impressive beginning & I have high hopes of him,' she told Doris McIntosh, whom she wanted to come down for the show. Finally, Ngaio had firm dates to send her. 'We open (now!) on July 27th (Friday) & play a week *missing* Monday 30th.' To enhance their barbaric marauding qualities, Ngaio dressed her Scottish thanes in the thonged sheepskins of the Highlands and put them against an unrelentingly metallic-grey set. The play oozed ambition, and the kind of sexual tension between the Macbeths that turned dreams into murder, and reality into a living nightmare.

Ngaio had called for an adjournment from her work on *A Unicorn for Christmas* with David Farquhar to produce *Macbeth*. There were words to write, but she could not concoct the rhymes while she was coming home from play rehearsals at 2am. Ngaio was always catatonic with nerves on opening night. 'If you were nervous,' Bob Scott remembers, 'you never looked at Ngaio. Her hands shook like a leaf.' As Alleyn says in *Dead Water*, 'one has to remember that all the first-night agonies that beset a professional director are also visited upon the most ludicrously inefficient amateur'.

Even after *Macbeth* closed, Ngaio was not free of commitments. In mid-September she told Doris McIntosh that she was on a regime of writing 'if possible 1500 words of "tekery" a day'. She had not been out of the house for about five weeks other than to buy food. 'I must finish this damned book by March & that's going to take some doing. How Agatha ever does it in 3 to 4 months I do not know.'

On 31 October 1962, another event pushed its way into her busy timetable, but this was warmly welcomed. Ngaio was presented with an honorary doctorate of literature by the now fully-fledged and independent University of Canterbury, in recognition of her services to literature and the theatre. Coming on top of the Macmillan Brown Lectures earlier in the year, it made her feel that there had been some acknowledgement of the huge contribution of time and money she had made to student theatre, and of her worldwide reputation for detective fiction writing. Ngaio was the first woman and the first non-academic to receive an honorary doctorate from Canterbury. She was delighted. University capping provided the kind of costuming spectacle that tickled her heart. More importantly, though, she wore her cap and gown with pride, knowing that the academic élite of Christchurch, who had often seemed aloof in the past, had made her their peer.

Ngaio did not bask long in the glory before she was writing to David Farquhar, arranging to be in Wellington in early December. '[I] would very much like to sit in the shadows of the dress-rehearsals, if I may.'

In late November, Ngaio's role shifted from the shadows to the limelight. One evening she received an urgent telephone call from the *Unicorn*'s production director, Donald Munro. Producer John Trevor had arrived at rehearsals drunk and had been reprimanded for his vicious verbal attack on one of the female cast members. Things were falling apart, and if something dramatic did not happen soon they would never open on time. 'There are unsettled arrangements for all sorts of ongoings. . . . [I] hold myself in readiness for whatever bombshells may fall.'

She was rocked by what she found. 'The acting . . . so bad,' she told Jonathan Elsom, 'that I made no bones about saying so.' The cast's improvement under her direction was enormous. They had three excruciatingly long rehearsals. John Hopkins, the conductor, came back after a few days in Sydney 'and . . . was amazed with the progress'. According to David Farquhar, 'Ngaio knew what she was doing and got it out of them.' Her feat was to transform singers into actors. The opera had been cast with the music rather than the acting in mind. Ngaio's libretto called for versatility in both acting and singing, and this she achieved with the cast in a production that opened on time and ran from 3 to 8 December 1962.

The initial reviews were very pleasing. 'Words trip from Miss Marsh's pen as notes dance from Farquhar's imagination,' wrote long-time *Evening Post* music critic Owen Jensen. But the same critic, a few weeks later, had acid second thoughts. It was little more than 'a cross between pantomime and farce,' he wrote. 'The story was naïve, the libretto corny . . . [and] David Farquhar's most attractive music seemed a squandering of his talent.' Ngaio shared at least some of his reservations. In a letter to her agents, she wrote: 'David's music is essentially sophisticated, adult & rather dry in character: extremely good musically but *not* of the light catchy sort. In a sense it is much too good for the libretto.' To some degree it was a mismatch. Ngaio had written light libretto for children, and Farquhar epic score for adults. After all her hard work Ngaio must have been disappointed, but she was remarkably resilient to criticism.

She returned home for Christmas. 'This past year has been an extraordinarily busy one for me. Not a let-up anywhere,' she wrote to Jonathan Elsom on Boxing Day, '& I now find myself landed with the whole production for the Royal Performance.' A second season of the *Unicorn* at the St James's Theatre in Auckland was planned for the New Year with a performance in front of the Queen and Duke of Edinburgh on 7 February 1963. This was exciting for Ngaio, who was an avid royalist.

Once again she found the rehearsals, held daily for two weeks, gruelling. Cuts were made to the dialogue of the wyvern and the unicorn, and Ngaio wanted further improvements in the acting. The gains were equivocal, because the final result depended on the cast on the day. 'One never knows when they will suddenly lose way & go flat. A strange phenomenon in singers but they don't apply the principles of singing to the techniques of acting.'

No one could have imagined the impact a royal performance of the *Unicorn* would have. A hundred thousand people packed the procession route. Hundreds struggled in a milling crush outside the theatre. As the Queen and Duke arrived, the police, in two lines, shouted 'Keep back! Keep back!' The barrier broke and the crowd surged around the official cars. For a moment some of the vehicles were separated from the entourage. At the entrance, police four deep could barely resist the push. 'Fifty people, most of them elderly, who fainted before the Royal couple arrived were treated inside the foyer,' wrote the reporter for the *Daily Telegraph*. 'St John Ambulance men sponged the straining faces of the police cordon.'

Inside, in the hush of the theatre, the royal visitors were treated to a performance that was very familiar in its symbols and storyline. Act One opened in the hall of Lacey Castle in Victorian times. Two heraldic figures in the family coat of arms, a wyvern and a unicorn, led the audience in a carol. The atmosphere was festive until it became apparent that the House of Lacey had fallen on desperate times. They had lost the Lacey Luck, a jewel with magical powers, and were on the verge of selling the castle. Act Two was a trip back in time to the Lacey family of the Tudor period. Here the lucky stone was lost when Barbara Lacey, betrothed to the horrible Lord Eustace Pinchbeck, tried to avoid her fate. Act Three returned to Victorian times and a dénouement that involved finding the jewel, saving the castle and some mistletoe romance. When the performance ended, the Queen and Prince Philip were ushered onto the stage to meet the cast and present the Queen Elizabeth II Arts Council charter to Prime Minister Keith Holyoake.

New Zealand's first opera was anything but indigenous. In essence, the *Unicorn* was a Euro-centric children's story about family history and inheritance, imbued with class-consciousness. Roger Savage described it as 'fiercely Colonial . . . a loving homage to home eleven thousand miles away, more English than the English'. The origin of its storyline was controversial, as were the exorbitant ticket prices. For a month before the opera opened, a battle raged over costs. David Farquhar was paid £25 to compose the musical score, and the cheapest seat was £10 2s and doubles £31 12s. The papers were vitriolic, and late in January prices were adjusted. Although it was contentious, the royal performance raised £7,100 for the new Arts Council and was a watershed in New Zealand's operatic history.

With limited resources of money, skill and experience, it was, as Peter Platt wrote in *Landfall*, 'a hazardous venture, a gamble which could have failed horrifyingly' but for the 'imagination and spirit' of those involved. The fervour of the crowds outside the St James's was proof of a continuing adoration for things British. The apron strings were still intact and, in 1963, the *Unicorn* was less of an odd choice than it would become. If it was not the future of New Zealand opera, it was a beginning that reflected the priorities of many in the present.

'I have a strong hunch which I scarcely dare write down, that it may go quite a long way,' Ngaio wrote to Jonathan Elsom. She was initially doubtful about the adaptation of a children's play for opera, but became swept up in the hope that something lasting would come of it. The genteel Farquhar saw it as an opportunity to write music and experiment with audience participation. Sadly, the opera was played on radio only twice, once live at the Royal Performance, and again in 1974 as a studio production in front of a select audience. No commercial recording of the opera was ever made. Added to this disappointment was a warehouse fire, which completely destroyed props and costumes six weeks after the opera finished. The production was lavish and the loss irreplaceable.

This was bad luck that certainly had an impact on future staging.

But for Ngaio the next commitment was already looming. She still had *Dead Water* to wade through before rehearsals began for *Henry IV, Part 1*. By January 1963 she had written about half of it, 'but will no doubt have to revise & re-write pretty drastically'.

When *Dead Water* was finished, she moved almost directly onto producing the play. It was a five-week task of working out the set and the costume designs, holding auditions, and then going through the production script. By April she had already had a preliminary meeting, 'lavishly attended by the usual callow but beguiling brew of freshers'. Through early autumn, Ngaio was laid low with what would become chronic problems: 'guts, digestion, neuralgia & strange pains'. But her focus was unfailing and she was undeterred by obstacles.

Three weeks before rehearsals began, there was no rehearsal room and she was having trouble casting the women. '*Why*, I wonder, out of some 2000 undergraduates is there never a better haul? Are they too anxiously involved in adolescent sex?' She was pleased with her Lady Mortimer, a pretty, delicate, hard-working woman of Welsh parentage with an 'Alice-in-Wonderland air'. The rehearsals rooms were finalized. A 'Dog Show at Addington,' she shuddered, in a letter to Doris McIntosh, 'an icy, vast, & filthy location'.

They had five instead of the usual seven weeks' rehearsal time, and this worried Ngaio because of the difficulties of Shakespearian comedy for students. They liked 'being funny' instead of understanding timing, '& waiting for the comedy to emerge of its own accord'. But she was quickly enamoured with their natural liveliness and verve. 'Gerry Lascelles shapes up not badly as Falstaff', Ian Kirk was a sensitive but not quite resolved Hal, and Huntly Eliott as King was excellent. 'The more we work, the more we are staggered by the genius of this play.' It was the language, the depth of understanding of human nature, of motive and impulse, communicated with 'terrifying economy of expression', that impressed her.

In February 1963, Ngaio wrote an extensive article on the arts in New Zealand for *The Times Supplement on New Zealand*. She talked about the emerging generation of New Zealand painters, writers and musicians who had begun to create 'with full authority, as New Zealanders'. These were painters like Colin McCahon, Toss Woollaston, Evelyn Page and Olivia Spencer Bower; writers A.R.D. Fairburn, Allen Curnow, R.A.K. Mason, Frank Sargeson, Denis Glover and Katherine Mansfield; and composers Douglas Lilburn and David Farquhar.

She saw these as the brightest lights in New Zealand's fine arts firmament, and Janet Frame as 'our most distinguished living novelist'. What she lamented again was that 'such talent constantly emerges and the opportunities presented in other countries are often irresistible'. Could New Zealand afford or be convinced to concentrate more of its resources on feeding the arts? 'Controlling interests are, on the whole, less sympathetic to the arts and to pure scholarship than to industrial expansion.' Ngaio had negotiated obstacles and slim opportunities by choosing popular fiction with a reader base overseas, but this meant that among her literary peers there was often little respect for what she did.

During the year she also worked intermittently on a book about New Zealand for American schoolchildren. She found it particularly frustrating because a personnel change in the middle of editing meant new priorities. A draft copy arrived back from the publishers requesting more writing, and the instructions from the copyeditor conflicted with those of the original brief. Outraged, she thought their observations were 'asinine'. 'Anything objective or critical was marked "too apologetic"; anything subjective was marked "make objective" ', while for the plainest of statements they asked her to 'explain this a bit more'. Ngaio was a professional writer. Because of her need for an income, even at the age of 68 she took almost every serious commission offered to her. 'Ten weeks vacillation . . . have set me back,' she wrote to Doris McIntosh in November. 'I mustn't miss a single day if I am not to lose a year's income . . . I never seem to save & really depend upon my job.'

Her taxation was exorbitantly high — so high, in fact, that she considered moving permanently to Britain to avoid double taxation. She felt exploited by New Zealand, a 'country that financially speaking treats me as an Aunt Sally'. In 1964 a new rule in Britain meant that if she stayed longer than six months her tax status altered and she had to pay more. She was hit by a whole lot of official questions: How long was she in Britain the time before last? How many books did she write 'A) here B) at sea C) in England. Awful lot of bull, but please the gods it gets us all somewhere.' Her tax was complicated, because she now had books selling in approximately 15 languages in at least that many countries. She was a limited liability company in the United States, where tax laws were different again. Ngaio was a freelancer. Her income was unpredictable and inconsistent, and she was not fit in her senior years to track its helter-skelter rhythms. So it became a vicious cycle. The more she earned, the more she paid in tax; and the more she lost in huge unexpected chunks, the more she had to earn. Tax was an unquantifiable fear that dogged her heels and occasionally bit hard.

It was Billy Collins who first approached Edmund Cork about Ngaio writing an autobiography. This was a significant commission. The agent broached the subject with his author, and Collins wrote to her in August confirming his interest. 'To show how keen I am on this book I have suggested an advance,' he explained. He had spoken to Ned Bradford of Little, Brown in Boston, who was equally keen. Collins was sure there would be 'no difficulty getting a signed contract from them'.

Ngaio responded with enthusiasm and warmth: 'how touched I am that you should think an autobiography worth doing: Believe me I am — never would such a notion have occurred to me of itself!' She was quietly delighted. It was a mark of her publishers' respect, and a money-generating project to keep the wolf from the door. She developed reservations, however, as she began to write. By the end of October she had 'shrinkingly' sent her agent a draft of the first chapter; he was encouraging. 'I have now gone into strict purdah & with considerable misgivings, am pressing on with it.' She allowed herself only one night off to see *Lawrence of Arabia*, which she thought superb for the photography alone.

She was chained to the task of a literary striptease, as Roderick Alleyn called it in *Died in the Wool*: 'you are using this room as a sort of confessional'. But this was not what Ngaio had in mind. She liked the idea of writing about her life, but the process of self-revelation was torturous. She felt unable to turn the prurient professional curiosity of the detective on herself. So writing the autobiography became a battle of balance between candidness and caution. What was acceptable as part of her public persona and what not? Which stories and relationships were part of the public domain, and which were private? For a woman who was Edwardian in her sense of propriety, getting it wrong was tantamount to a betrayal of friends and family. Ngaio even struggled with the book's name. 'Still undecided about the title,' she wrote to Doris McIntosh nearly two years later. 'What do you think of "Black Beech & Honeydew"?'

At the end of 1963, she was already planning the next year's drama production. She wanted to do a 'large scale Caesar in Modern dress with a huge crowd spilling into the Auditorium'. She intended to use a stylized setting with action on different levels and 'pooled lighting'. There was a vague plan to tour it, which would make the extra effort worthwhile. She wondered if this would not be her 'swan song with the kids'. The next year 'I shall *have* to catch up with my writing', and after that she hoped there would be a new theatre where students could produce their own plays. 'I am a great believer in leaving off *before* you begin to flag', and she intended to make her exit 'with as little fuss as possible'.

In the meantime she had a 'procession of boys' coming up to the house for auditions. A bout of flu laid her low and she missed four rehearsals. The only one still standing among the cast was Gerald Lascelles, her assistant producer, also cast as Artemidorus, who 'carried on nobly of course but couldn't do much more than mark time'. She was worried that they would not peak in time for opening night. 'Of course all dramatic dialogue must be orchestrated,' she wrote to John Schroder. Shakespeare's linguistic music was carried in the subtle inter-play between dialogue, in an 'overtone that is caught and carried on by another voice'. She found it in *Hamlet*, but also in 'Caesar, [in] the quiet little duets between Brutus and the boy Lucius'. She loved the moment of chemistry in a production when players captured the nuance of rhythm in the dialogue and 'suddenly the voices flow together & mingle & make one thing'. In spite of the flu, Ngaio felt her students achieved just that unified flow. She was thrilled with the production. All in all, she felt that they were the 'best lot' of players she had ever had. They worked wonderfully well, the houses were full and they made a large profit of £600.

Eleven years had passed since Ngaio's first staging of *Julius Caesar*. In 1953, it had been a symbol of her determination to continue in spite of the loss of the Little Theatre; in 1964, it might well be the final curtain on her career as a student producer. One *Julius Caesar* looked forward, the other back, but had there been any appreciable change in between? Theatre commentator Paul Bushnell argues quite rightly that they were very similar productions and there was 'little reworking of the original composition. Ideas might be elaborated, but they went largely unchanged, except for details.' This, he suggests, was because Ngaio saw her role as curatorial, and Shakespeare's plays as artefacts. She looked for essential meanings and saw play interpretations as finite. This was true, but it was also the thinking of her era, and on the eve of retirement, if her ideas had not changed, they had certainly matured.

Ngaio returned to her autobiography as soon as the production ended. '80,000 words,' she noted early in November, '& the end, I hope in view.' She was cutting everything after 1950 down to a minimum because she had 'no desire to drool' on about old age. But she needed earnings from a new book and was 'going eyes out' to finish her autobiography so she could take a Christmas break with friends in the Marlborough Sounds. 'I've been lumbering up the straight with my blasted book,' she told Doris McIntosh, and before Christmas she wrote the final sentence. She feared the rewrites would be extensive but was relieved to have it done, and left for Portage, in Kenepuru Sound, on Boxing Day with Anita Muling and her friend Marjorie Chambers. 'I shall go on tinkering for some time.' The manuscript was already too long, but if she wanted to add any more something must be cut. 'I find myself quite unable to see it in perspective & have moments when I think it a failure. Pity if I'm right after all the trouble.'

Her stay was an oasis of perfect weather and blissful long days of swimming and reading. 'We spent 10 days of utter, utter laziness — the hotel at Portage had been taken over by an Australian couple with gratifying results on the cuisine, which was excellent,' wrote Anita Muling to Olivia Spencer Bower. Ngaio had arranged for Val Muling to be buried in the Acland family cemetery at Peel Forest in South Canterbury. She had taken the Mulings there, and a friendship with the Aclands had begun. They had generously offered their cemetery, with its quaint stone chapel, as a final resting place for someone they knew Ngaio had loved. After her husband's death, Anita Muling shared a house, and what many people believed was a lesbian relationship, with Marjorie Chambers, matron at the Christchurch Public Hospital. The two women were regular guests at Marton Cottage, and Anita Muling still attended most Sundays while Ngaio's players rehearsed.

In the New Year, Ngaio was delighted to have John Dacres-Mannings staying with her. 'He doesn't change & is just the same affectionate, gentle, lethally absent-minded old thing.' In January, Ngaio began preparing for another trip to Britain. She and Crawsie launched themselves 'upon the hellish bosom of the cleaning-up-for-tenants tidal wave'. They carried things up the path to the whare at the top of the section that had been Ngaio's bedroom as a child. Blankets and precious objects were all stowed away. Her exact plans for the year were not settled, and she anxiously awaited her publishers' response to the autobiography: she expected 'some constructive observations'. A first draft had been sent to her American publisher and she hoped Billy Collins would read his copy of the manuscript in March.

In the meantime, Jonathan Elsom was over from London to play the role of Messiah in the York Cycle of Mystery Plays for the Pan Pacific Festival. It was 'lovely to see him again', and she proudly told Doris McIntosh that he had not had a week out of work in the past year. She was also delighted to play host to Maureen Balfour, Nelly Rhodes's second daughter, who was visiting her farm-cadet son. 'She & her brothers & sisters are "my family", & I couldn't be more happy to think she's coming.' In late February 1965, Ngaio saw the York Cycle, staged at night on the banks of the Avon River. She found the production patchy, especially the directing. Elsom's acting was 'a supremely sensitive solo in the middle of an insecure & *groping* ensemble'. The setting was superb and the mounting very good, but the co-ordination of crowd scenes incensed her. 'O! O! O! the lovely opportunities lost,' she wailed.

Her American publishers got back to her in early March to say they wanted illustrations for *Black Beech*. 'I am engaged in a slightly melancholy hunt through old photographs,' she told Doris McIntosh. Ned Bradford's response was 'gratifyingly drooling', but the photograph safari through a dusty savannah of drawers and albums seemed endless. Billy Collins and his son Pierre visited Ngaio in Christchurch that month. He was 'very pleased' with the biography. This was a relief.

Unchained from her 'gnawing misgivings', in April Ngaio became involved in another production. Jonathan Elsom and Brian Bell, production supervisor of local channel CHTV3, decided to put on a two-man show. Ngaio liked the material they were doing, and when they asked her to produce *Two's Company*, 'dived in boots & all & I must say with *great* satisfaction'. It was a medley of part-plays from Noël Coward, Anton Chekhov, John Mortimer, Luigi Pirandello and Marcel Achard, innovatively performed. 'The changes of make-up are effected at two side tables in view of the audience, & the whole thing runs like cream from the bottle.'

In April, Ngaio sent a desperate letter to Billy Collins. The new law, applied retrospectively to her last two visits to England, had left her with a tax demand of £1,700. 'This just about cleans out my savings & is a horrid blow.' She appealed to both her agent and her publisher for help, but double taxation seemed unavoidable and all she could hope for was a partial rebate when everything was settled in New Zealand. Collins was deeply concerned about the tax; he also discussed the autobiography. Jonathan Elsom's mother, Vy, had been commissioned to draw a portrait of Ngaio for the back cover. He told Ngaio this had been sent on from New York to Boston, where *Black Beech* would be published first. Collins in Auckland wanted a few changes, and Billy Collins himself asked for some additions, which he regarded as minor; for Ngaio, they were excruciating. The project soured in her hands, and by September she wrote to John Schroder: 'I've been having a gruelling time with my autobiography, unwillingly ventured upon (& I think perhaps unwisely, too).' Collins had been persistent. The autobiography was finished, but it was 'not the book I hoped it would be. I have been defeated by my own reticence.' She sent off the final manuscript with 'profoundest misgivings'.

Ngaio did not plan to produce a student play that year, but she still became involved in annual rehearsals. They were in the dog show shed in Addington: 'One wonders if billions of fleas are coming up for the fur orgy.' She turned down an opportunity to produce a play for the Wellington Repertory Company because she was at work on *Death at the Dolphin*, a new detective novel that once again drew on her passion for the theatre.

Somehow, though, in the latter part of the year she became caught up in the concept of a touring *Hamlet* or *Macbeth* with the New Zealand Theatre Centre, a 'pretty generously subsidised' organization intended to assist regional professional theatre. Ngaio was on the board and Dan O'Connor was tour manager, with Richard Campion assisting him. Ngaio was invited to direct their first major production. She delayed her departure from New Zealand, began organizing, spent all day with Raymond Boyce on set design, and talked to Douglas Lilburn about music, but by November the venture had fallen through. She was deeply disappointed, and seriously out of pocket, as she had to pay an additional £200 to travel on a large passenger liner 'which I dislike instead of a ship I know & love'. She had turned down an opportunity to launch *Black Beech* in the United States, and because of the tour had delayed the Collins launch in London until after Easter 'at great inconvenience to all concerned'. It was an upheaval and a waste of time. It was nobody's fault, she admitted: 'Just theatre where that sort of thing happens continuously. What a life.'

In the meantime, she stayed with Stella Mannings in Wellington in October. 'Our relationship is more like that of sisters than cousins.' She was looking forward to introducing Stella to Doris McIntosh. '[Stella's] a great dear but rather agonisingly shy . . . [with a] very good cranky sense of humour which pops up at surprising moments. I dote on the old tart.' While in Wellington, Ngaio presented the Katherine Mansfield Award. The event was not without incident. 'I had just been told I had to be televised canoodling with Frank Sargeson,' Ngaio explained to John Schroder. The problem was they lost Sargeson, so she had to lie on the lawn '& be photographed until he could be found'. The organizers neglected to tell Ngaio that he had won the award, which 'botched up my speech', and forgot to ask Sargeson 'to come & get his hundred smackers'.

Around speeches and public engagements, Ngaio packed and prepared to leave. There were permits, injections, tenants and cats to organize. She bought a new sewing machine for Crawsie, who was desolate after her 'old warrior' broke down. Ngaio rationalized the gift: 'instead of waiting till I pop off she might as well have something'. The parcel was duly delivered, accompanied by a note that said, 'with love from His Holiness the Pope'.

At the beginning of 1966, Ngaio was still 'packing & stowing', while an avalanche of *Black Beech* promotion rumbled in the background and began to pick up momentum. 'I've got T.V. chaps from Wellington tomorrow & Friday, all day, doing a programme in the house.' She also agreed to a 'whirlwind' of promotional events in Auckland. Ngaio departed Wellington aboard the *Arcadia* on 7 March, but on arrival in Auckland found that she had lost her luggage. 'I'm going pretty crazy as you can imagine.' A painting of Anita Muling's she was taking to Sotheby's, and a mink coat and precious camera, were all packed in her lost luggage. Her relief was palpable when, after a frantic telephone call, Gerald Lascelles managed to trace the luggage.

In Sydney and Melbourne she faced further 'book-shop-crawls' plus press, radio and television interviews. 'The Sydney T.V. gentleman would keep asking me why I had never married,' she wrote in her thank-you letter to Lascelles, '& how, in my surprise & exasperation, I answered him I tremble to conjecture.' Ngaio caught up with Elizabeth and John Dacres-Mannings and their young family, which included a toddler and a baby, Nicholas and Sarah. She was delighted to see them in their new house, still under renovation. Dacres-Mannings had visited her in the New Year. 'There we were: just as usual,' she explained to John Schroder. 'I couldn't like him better if he were my son & yet have no cluck-clucking desire to attach him to myself.' Perhaps that was the answer she could have given the Sydney 'T.V. gentleman' — that she cherished intimacy, but above all valued her freedom.

The journey was something of a *Marie Celeste* passage. The missing luggage was followed by disappearing galley proofs for her 'new tec', sent registered mail to Fremantle by her American publishers, and to be corrected and returned urgently. She was anxious that this would mean a delay in publication. In the end, a second set reached her in Gibraltar and she spent two 'hectic days &

nights in the Bay of Biscay O, correcting them' and returned them by airmail from London, which cost a small fortune. Ngaio was 'dreading the hullabaloo' of the London launch of her autobiography. 'I quite like the earlier bits, now,' she confessed to John Schroder, 'but shall never be reconciled to the thing as a whole.'

To her great delight, 'Jonathan and Elric were both down at the docks at the crack of dawn' to meet her. As soon as she arrived, she found her engagement book a 'thorny thicket' of events '& time's winged chariot, with a return ticket to N.Z. is hard on my heels'. Leisurely London stays were a thing of the past and she must make the most of her time.

The first three weeks vanished in a blur of press, television and radio interviews, followed by semi-business luncheons with publishers, Crime Club representatives, and her agent. A luncheon with Lady Freyberg made a pleasant interlude. She stayed at the Hyde Park Hotel until she found a flat at 5/51 Pont Street, Kensington. It was here that a 'bombshell' fell in the form of a commission from Alexander Cohen, 'the Eminence Grey of Broadway', to dramatize *Singing in the Shrouds*. Ngaio was staggered by this unique opportunity, but if she accepted 'I shall have my nose to the grindstone as usual'. It was a risk and she was not sure she could 'make a job of it'. In mid-May, Ngaio enjoyed a weekend stay with Billy Collins. She was stunned by the beauty of his 14th-century house, with its massively proportioned comfortable rooms 'smelling of applewood fires', and furnished with 'lovely' antiques. His library was in a huge silo separate from the house.

Work soon resumed. By the end of May, Ngaio had seen only five shows, and far less of her favourite family than she liked. This stay was shaping up to be another working holiday, with an emphasis on work. What theatre Ngaio did see, though, she enjoyed. 'YOU NEVER CAN TELL gets superb treatment at the Haymarket and the KILLING OF SISTER GEORGE, a terrifyingly funny play about lesbian ladies, is wonderful,' she told Gerald Lascelles. She also saw 'THE ROYAL HUNT OF THE SUN . . . [which was] superbly mounted and acted . . . TRELAWNY OF THE WELLS . . . an enchanting revival but the VOYSEY INHERITANCE' was not well done. Ngaio could not get in to see Sir Laurence Olivier's *Othello* and hesitated to write a private letter requesting a seat. She was always reluctant to push herself forward, even when it was justified.

In the midst of all this came responses to *Black Beech*, both personal and published, from readers and reviewers. The initial reaction was positive, but as the flurry of enthusiasm died down more critical voices emerged. One of those belonged to writer and publisher Dennis McEldowney, reviewing the book for *Landfall* in September 1966. In part his reaction was a statement of the obvious. There was not much about Ngaio Marsh 'except indirectly, in the latter part of her autobiography,' he stated in his opening sentence. 'Most of her adult life remains undisclosed.' He also observed that there was almost no discussion of her detective fiction. 'Followers of her criminal career may be disappointed to find so little of it.' There were none of the colourful Detection Club descriptions she had read out over the radio, and little revealing analysis of her theatrical work. What glowed brightly from an otherwise subdued fire were the coals of her youth. 'She recalls as convincingly as anyone I have read the unstable and extravagant emotions children are subject to, before they have grown wary of emotion.' Ngaio was less reticent about her early life and could recall it without embarrassment, McEldowney postulated, because time had elapsed.

These were reasonable comments, but there was a cruel barb to the review that must have stung Ngaio. McEldowney claimed she had only ever written about New Zealand 'as though she were a visitor, while believing she was a native'. He made cutting remarks about the way she handled the New Zealand accent in fiction as opposed to the cockney, implying that she was an Anglo-centric snob. And he ended with a diatribe against detective fiction. 'It is doubtful whether any New Zealand writer as ambitious as she was could now bring himself to write detective novels, even as a means of making a living.' He acknowledged that things were different when she began, and that detective fiction was 'then recreation of some respectable talent'. However:

It has never seemed to me . . . that Ngaio Marsh was a potential novelist wasting herself on detective stories. She has not been either passionate enough or detached enough. This doubt is strengthened by her autobiography, pleasant to read as it is. The reader can trace fascinating patterns but wonders if she knows they are there.

On the one hand, McEldowney admonished Ngaio for not offering more about her detective fiction; on the other he demonstrated the intellectual snobbery that had silenced her. Ngaio's reticence over her detective fiction writing had proved well founded. She had carried the weight of academic condescension for years.

It was an intense disappointment to her that what she sometimes slaved over was given so little respect in her own country.

Her discretion about her private life was probably equally well placed. She revealed her childhood because the people in it were mostly long dead, and among her more contemporary friends and associates, she easily mentioned those whose careers were already in public view: Dan O'Connor, Jack Henderson, Paul Molineaux, Elric Hooper and Jonathan Elsom. But she was more hesitant about the Rhodes family, whom she called the Lampreys in *Black Beech*, about her cousins, the Mulings, Doris and Alister McIntosh, and was almost completely silent about one of her closest friends, Sylvia Sibbald Fox. Although he was a major character in her novels, Ngaio never explained how Detective Inspector Edward Walter Fox got his name. His surname was that of her best and most faithful friend, Sylvia, and his middle name came from her father, Walter Sibbald Fox.

Their association began at Miss Ross's dame school. In *Black Beech*, Ngaio mentioned the boys who helped her adjust to the trials of her early school life, but never Sylvia. She was born on 5 December 1898, the eldest of three children, and the only girl. Her father, Walter Fox, was a surgeon and superintendent of Christchurch Public Hospital from 1914 to 1935. The family mixed in well-to-do circles and knew people of prominence in Canterbury, including the Aclands.

Sylvia Fox's was a genteel life of privilege and culture. She rode side-saddle and executed dressage as if the horse were an extension of her slim body. She was brought up to read widely, and loved art, music, theatre and ballet. In her youth, Sylvia was taken to cultural events that came to town, and there was always a horse to ride on one of her father's farms. Later, when the family fell on harder times, she mixed in circles where mounts were available and money for concerts was found regardless. Sylvia and Ngaio went to St Margaret's College together. One was poor and the other privileged, and although Ngaio was three years older they became firm friends. Sylvia went on the Marsh camping trips to Glentui, and discovered High Church Anglicanism with less fervour than Ngaio, although her Faith remained.

Beyond high-school years, their lives continued to overlap. Sylvia was a close friend of Evelyn and Frederick Page, Olivia Spencer Bower, Betty Cotterill, and many people Ngaio knew in art and theatre circles. Ngaio's imaginative, indulgent parents allowed her to follow her dream of studying art, while Sylvia's father had a more pragmatic path in mind. 'You must make yourself useful in life,' he told his daughter, 'so you need to get a qualification and I'm just setting up this cancer thing. You can be one of my first nurses.' Walter Fox was involved in establishing the first cancer clinic in New Zealand, which began as a crude system of radium treatment with needles. Aged about 20, Sylvia was among the first intake of five student nurses trained in the specialist procedure. They wore heavy lead aprons for protection, but after years of the work it seemed that they had been absorbing radiation along with their patients and were succumbing to cancer themselves. They were quickly pensioned off in their late 40s. 'Tipped out,' as Sylvia's nephew Richard Fox said, 'with a fairly useful pension.'

Sylvia Fox's passion was travel. She worked at the hospital until retiring in 1948 and nursed her parents for some years, but whenever she could she escaped overseas. Richard Fox estimates that she took four or five trips abroad with Ngaio, beginning possibly in the 1930s, but certainly from the 1949–51 trip onwards. She took the boat over to Britain with Ngaio and sometimes flew back independently.

Richard Fox remembers his stay with Ngaio and Sylvia in the mid-1950s, when Sylvia kept house at their Hans Road address in Knightsbridge. He stayed with them for 'five amazing weeks'. Ngaio, who liked to 'pin nicknames on people', announced his appearance at the door: 'the man-child has arrived'. Fox was 21 and his flight to Britain was a birthday present from an uncle. Sylvia showed him London on foot 'like a native'. They walked everywhere, and at night went to concerts and the theatre. Each morning, they sat in Ngaio's 'large bedroom [beside] her large bed and we would have a cup of tea, and she would have her breakfast, usually a hearty one . . . and expect us to give her a full briefing about what had happened the day before and a shorter briefing on what we were doing that day.' Ngaio was always interested.

They shopped for provisions at Harrod's. 'You're the housekeeper,' Ngaio would say to Sylvia, when a cheaper option was suggested, 'and you buy at Harrod's.' No money ever passed hands, but Ngaio kept Sylvia in a style her pension could not afford. She was part of Ngaio's everyday life, but also of a private world never mentioned in *Black Beech*. This was a decision they reached mutually. Sylvia was self-contained and very independent. It was this, along with her poise, pragmatism and delightfully dry sense of humour, that appealed to Ngaio. Public exposure went against the grain of this outwardly imposing, meticulously mannered, caring and humble woman. She wanted nothing more from Ngaio's notoriety than the pleasure of sharing her company.

'Sylvia has got her house on the hill just above Ngaio's and hopes to move in, in Spring — Overjoyed!' Anita Muling told Olivia Spencer Bower in July 1963. Sylvia took possession of 2 Sherwood Lane on 9 October 1963. The old friends were so pleased at the prospect of living close that a hole connecting the properties was quickly cut in the hedge. From then on, they dashed between houses and their lives became enmeshed. Even when separated, they were often in touch. 'Both houses had landscape windows looking out at the view', and Richard Fox remembers Ngaio ringing Sylvia to discuss the sunset. '"Isn't that splendid." "Yes. Yes, and did you see the next-door neighbour . . ." They just wanted to share it.'

Also missing from Ngaio's autobiography was the subject herself. There were few intimate psychological or emotional insights, and her sexual life was completely missing. A few unfulfilled and not entirely convincing liaisons were identified, and she never mentioned the fact that from an early age she had health problems. It appears that Ngaio had an operation when she was young, although her wider family were never exactly sure what it had been. It was understood, however, to have affected her sense of her own marriageability. This was private and she was understandably reluctant to share it, but along with other gaps it left readers feeling there was a riddle to be solved. When Collins was contemplating a reprint of *Black Beech* in 1980, memos went back and forth between the London and Auckland offices. New Zealand publisher David Elworthy explained that he had discussed the possibility of 'revising, extending and updating' her autobiography. Crime Club editor Elizabeth Walter's response was incisive. She thought 'the original book . . . pretty dull — largely because of her reticence. I have every sympathy with this, but if you are going to write an autobiography you have got to be prepared to let your hair down a little, and this she didn't do.'

In 1966, however, there were bigger things on the horizon. In the Queen's Birthday Honours List of 11 June, Ngaio was made a Dame Commander of the British Empire. Letters and telegrams of congratulation from across the world flooded into her London address and to Roses Greene, who was handling Ngaio's correspondence in Christchurch. It was not until the early hours of a July morning that Ngaio finally found time to write to Doris McIntosh: 'I have just been out to post today's lot (17) of acknowledgements'. This had been happening for three weeks at the rate of 30 letters a day. She found it 'touching & gratifying', but the volume was an ordeal. There were some special highlights among the correspondence. The former Prime Minister of New Zealand, Sir Walter Nash, wrote to convey his personal congratulations, and a telegram from the Australian Prime Minister, Sir Robert Menzies, declared him to be 'one of your most devoted readers'. Her achievements were celebrated in newspapers around New Zealand. *The Dominion* in Wellington announced her award with the comment: 'In a country where women play less than their due part in public life, it is refreshing to find a woman's name heading the Queen's Birthday Honours list.'

'The Damery was an enormous surprise & a great delight' for Ngaio, but the investiture was not until November, so she delayed her October return to New Zealand. She snatched time to work on the dramatization of *Singing in the Shrouds* and continued with her engagements, which included lunch with Bob Scott, an old university player now in London. He was one of her 'four liners', who had also handled marketing. For the 1958 production of *Hamlet*, he had advertised in the newspaper for a skull. Controversy and a flurry of disgusted letters to the editor brought in the crowds. He was now an Anglican minister, and at lunch he told her of a planned trip to the United States. 'How much money do you have?' she asked. He explained that he had $900 saved. '*What!* That's not enough for three months,' Ngaio exclaimed, reaching for her chequebook. He watched as she scrawled something and handed it to him. The cheque was signed and dated. 'But you haven't put anything in,' he said. 'You take it just in case,' she replied. She also gave him the name of her agent in New York. When he contacted Dorothy Olding, she said, 'Yes. Ngaio said you were coming.' She sent her chauffeur around to the YMCA and insisted he stay in her enormous penthouse apartment. No matter what honours she received, Ngaio's underlying humility kept her in touch with people's needs.

Before she arrived in England Ngaio had planned a barge trip, so in mid-July she took a five-day canal cruise on the Trent. She was looking for new material for a murder. Long experience had taught her that the most vivid and lasting impressions in her writing were her own, and her imagination was captivated by the idea of a body floating on the river. What would it feel like to look over the side of the boat and see the bloated face of an aging Ophelia bobbing below the surface with river weed in her hair billowing to the idle rhythms of the current? She would visualize the scene and the horror in *Clutch of Constables*, which she began writing towards the end of the year. Meanwhile she stashed her boating experiences away.

The story that was having an immediate impact when she arrived back in London was *Death at the Dolphin*, which was serialized in *Woman's Journal* before being released in the United States in the second half of 1966 under the title *Killer Dolphin*. She had handed the manuscript over to Edmund Cork as soon as she arrived in London.

The book plunges into a pocket of her memory and returns to her beloved theatre. It begins with director-playwright Peregrine Jay visiting a derelict dockside theatre that has been bombed during the war. He is hoping it might be restored. This is a reconnaissance trip like the one Ngaio had taken in 1951 with the Guthries and Bob Stead. Peregrine Jay, however, is alone. He picks up the key from a property agent's office, where there is something uncanny about the clerk's parting words. He warns Peregrine that there is considerable damage, especially on the stage. 'You *will* watch how you go. Underfoot.' Peregrine thanks him and promises to be careful.

Outside, the sun is starting to burn misty moisture off the damp cobblestones. Seagulls wheel above the Thames and he can hear the distant honk of barge horns. Inside the theatre portico, he finds a maze of peeling bills and agents' notices. Peregrine has difficulty turning the heavy key until the caretaker oils the lock, then disappears. He pushes the hefty door open to find a dark, dull world of 'rats, rot' and decay. The stench of old hobos who have dossed down here is almost overpowering. He makes his way to the stage and, stepping backwards, plunges into the filthy, freezing waters of a bomb shaft. It is 'nightmarish like a small death'. He struggles to lift himself out, but falls back feebly each time. After what feels like hours floating in the black, brackish water, he realizes that if he is not rescued soon he will certainly die.

Peregrine Jay's rescuer arrives in the form of mysterious millionaire, Vassily Conducis. What is he doing there? How can he have known? But Peregrine is soon seduced by his redeemer's offer. Conducis will bankroll his restoration of the Unicorn Theatre and the establishment of a company 'producing Shakespeare and other plays of high cultural quality'. This is Ngaio's dream, too: if only Tyrone Guthrie had seen more promise in the Woolwich theatre, her future as a director-playwright might have been different. Ngaio describes the Dolphin Theatre, 'high, square and unbecoming', as the object of Peregrine's 'greed and deep desire'. He is tempted as Faust was, and his desire is deepened by the discovery of a fragile cheverel glove, reputed to be that of Shakespeare's beloved son Hamnet, who died at the age of 11. This is in Conducis's possession, and Peregrine Jay decides to write a play about it and to help put it on display in the refurbished Dolphin.

In August, Ngaio took an Aegean cruise with Joan Pullen, the secretary she often used when she was in London. Ngaio described her as a heavy-set, jolly sort of woman who was congenial company. 'We only call for a day in Venice,' she reported to Doris McIntosh, 'so no chance of going to Rome.' Ngaio had just heard the 'exciting' news that Alister McIntosh had been made New Zealand High Commissioner in Rome. Already thoughts of visiting the couple began to whirl around in her head: 'I swear that somehow or another I *will* visit you there'.

Ngaio worried about her tax and how long she was spending in England. The extension of her stay for the investiture potentially put her over the time limit, so a second trip to County Cork in Ireland with her old friend Gwendoline Jellett gave her a two-week absence. Jellett was the daughter of the doctor with whom Ngaio had collaborated on *Exit Sir Derek* in 1935. Ireland had strange echoes of New Zealand, but the difference lay in its combination of stunning scenery with ruined castles and rustic thatched cottages, which were often as picturesque as they were primitive. The cottage she stayed in was particularly cold and archaic, but this did not detract from the experience.

Ngaio was back in London at the beginning of November. She described her long-anticipated investiture as being 'like a fairy-tale', but it was not without its bad magic. The Rhodes family were notorious for their practical jokes, and Denys Rhodes was on the staff at Buckingham Place. While he was staying at Balmoral he told the Queen that Ngaio preferred to be called 'Dame Edith' and was a semi-cripple. On the day of the investiture, as the cars swept down the driveway carrying their distinguished guests towards the main gates, a security man waved Ngaio's limousine out of the line and directed it around the back. The car stopped at a small side entrance. She stepped out and was greeted by an exquisitely groomed footman pushing a wheelchair. Ngaio was shocked, and not a little bit disappointed that she had missed her announcement and glamorous front entrance. She politely turned down the offer of wheelchair assistance, explaining that she could manage without help, but had the distinct feeling that the Queen, who 'was smiling broadly', was in on the joke. This was a pinnacle of achievement for Ngaio, and although she was never conceited or pushy about it, the honour meant a great deal because she felt it was deserved. She had worked hard.

The fairytale finished with an enchanting party two days later at Eileen Mackay's Knightsbridge flat. This was doubly exciting, because it also celebrated Bear Mannings's Queen's Commendation for Valuable Service in the Air, which was presented in the same list. He received his honour for the part he had played, during the 1960s, in training aircraft pilots in newly emerging African nations. It was a risky job that sometimes involved heart-stopping near-misses by inexperienced African air cadets. Bear was the adventurous, fun-loving cousin, whom Ngaio grew to appreciate more and more over the years. She was as thrilled with his achievement as she was with her own. This was a moment to take pride in one of her special surrogate sons.

Ngaio travelled back aboard the *Gothic*, arriving in Christchurch on 27 December 1966. 'I *hated* leaving Home this time,' she admitted to Doris McIntosh. 'This house, one or two friends & one or two of my student players are the only anchorage.' She felt disillusioned about what she had achieved while she was abroad, but had no time to dwell on it.

In March she announced: 'I'm about to direct *Twelfth Night* for the opening production in the new University theatre which they have very touchingly named after me.' Gerald Lascelles and Ngaio had begun corresponding the year before about the possibility of her directing the play. She was 'delighted' and 'touched', but hesitant about the rigours of the 'rehearsal marathon' on her health. She could not see herself standing up to midwinter 'show ground conditions'. In the end she was persuaded. The theatre itself, however, presented staging problems. After years of waiting for a student theatre to be built at Canterbury University's new Ilam site, there were functional difficulties, particularly with space and access. There was nowhere to move scenery to the side or to fly it in the ceiling. Access for heavy scenery onto the stage was through a door one storey up, which meant it had to be lowered. This was ultimately solved, two years later, by a hydraulic lift. A similar problem existed for the audience, who entered the theatre from the second storey, making access impossible for anyone with compromised mobility. In the future this would include Ngaio.

Coming back to *Twelfth Night* after a break of nearly 20 years was refreshing. She found it 'lovely, delicate & haunting' and wondered how her rough-and-ready band of players would 'shape up to it'. There were the usual hitches during rehearsal, and more. 'Every kind of pest & hindrance besets us . . . illness, non-arrival of essential properties, absenteeism owing to other obligations', and Gerald Lascelles, her production assistant, had 'stones in his waterworks'. 'I suppose we shall muddle through.' Ngaio wanted 'Sticky' Glue to play Sir Toby Belch, but he already had a major part in a review and could not rehearse properly until 18 days before opening night. 'I'm keeping my fingers crossed for Mr [Fred] Betts,' Ngaio told Lascelles in a note that accompanied get-well 'grapes from Crawsie for her lovely young gentleman'.

The inaugural production of *Twelfth Night* at the Ngaio Marsh Theatre opened in June 1967. Betts did play Sir Toby; Robin Alborn was Orsino; Vincent Orange, Sir Andrew Aguecheek; Barry Empson, Malvolio; David Hindin, Feste; Judie Douglass, Olivia; and Annette Facer, Viola. This was Ngaio's stable of players mixed with some emerging talent. Her formula for success combined experience with raw enthusiasm to bring both the dynamism and intellectual solidity of Shakespeare to life. The *Press* critic described the production as being like a full-bodied red wine, 'sometimes delicate with a bouquet of romance, sometimes intoxicating with mirth'. Vincent Orange as Sir Andrew 'elevated this silly sop to the peerage of clowns'; Fred Betts's Sir Toby 'kept the comedy driving forward'; Barry Empson's Malvolio 'had moments of inspired delight'; Judie Douglass's Olivia 'shone out like the rose she carried'; and Annette Facer 'was clear and pert and feminine and boyish and all the things a girl dressed up as a boy should be'. The main criticisms were technical issues to do with the theatre and lighting. Beyond the formal criticism, there were rumblings that Ngaio sometimes over-used her stable.

After the production closed, Ngaio settled down to serious work on her novel *Clutch of Constables*. She was tackling a new structure. 'It's all in flashback from a lecture Alleyn's giving to C.I.D. recruits & I can't tell you what pitfalls lurk in that seemingly straightforward formula.' She had more and more misgivings as she struggled on, but this was typical. The plot is, in fact, cleverly spliced with sections of Alleyn's talk counterpoised with Troy's involvement in the murder he is describing. *Clutch of Constables* is a pun, because the plot revolves around a gang of art forgers who are planning to plant a clutch of Constable paintings in the area where he painted, to be 'discovered' and sold for a fortune. The story is lulled along by the quiet rhythms of the river until the body of Miss Hazel Rickerby-Carrick is found tied to a weighted suitcase and floating. This novel achieves a retrospective telling of murder much more engagingly than *Died in the Wool*.

Ngaio's confidence in her work should have been bolstered by critical response to *Death at the Dolphin* when it was released in Britain in May that year. Collins Crime Club editor George Hardinge sent her a selection of reviews from leading newspapers. The book had gone down a treat. 'Of the several excellent theatre stories she has written, I count this easily the best — a first rate book,' wrote Edmund Crispin for *The Sunday Times*. Peter Philips for *The Sun* was effusive: 'The first writer in the English language of the pure, classical, puzzle whodunit . . . Among the Crime Queens, Ngaio Marsh stands out as an Empress.' The *Oxford Mail*, though, positioned what she was writing most accurately in the current climate of detective fiction writing: the novel 'differs very little in treatment from the stories, which made her famous so many years ago. Yet there is nothing threadbare about it — rather, it has worn wonderfully well.' In *Death at the Dolphin* Ngaio did what she did well, but it appealed to nostalgia rather than looked ahead. The new lead in detective fiction writing had been taken by a generation of writers that included figures like Ruth Rendell, and P.D. James, whose first novel, *Cover Her Face*, featuring Adam Dalgliesh of New Scotland Yard, was published in 1962. James's books were set against the backdrop of Britain's vast post-war bureaucracies, such as the criminal justice system and the health service. These were not cosily confined worlds where the ends were neatly tied up, but human zoos of power and corruption.

Ngaio remained determined to stay with the McIntoshes while they were in Rome, but *Clutch of Constables* needed to be 'in the bag' before she departed. She was still busy on the novel when she wrote to ask whether they would still be there in 1969. 'I long to come, especially as I am quite remarkably fit.' Ngaio was on a new diet: 'breadless, butterless, potatoless & fatless'. She had lost 10 pounds.

But there was a blight on her wellbeing. Sylvia Fox had been in England for Ngaio's investiture and had stayed on, arriving back in New Zealand in November. A week after her return she had been taken into hospital for an operation on her right breast. She had cancer. 'It's been caught in very good time & we pray all will be well.' This was Sylvia's second scare. In 1964, she had developed an infected thyroid which the doctors would not say was not malignant until they saw it. She had a five-week course of pills and an operation, which was a success. Sylvia did not appreciate a fuss. A doctor's daughter, she took her bouts of poor health in her stride. 'I do wish to heavens she'd consult a quack,' Ngaio had written in desperation to Doris McIntosh nearly a decade earlier. Sylvia was 'desperately tired & depressed' and Ngaio suspected anaemia. 'She's not an easy person to help & retires into a scratchy reticence if one tries to help or suggest.'

At the beginning of 1968, Ngaio wrote 'a hasty line' to Doris McIntosh: 'I put my name down for the 30 March sailing in the *Angelina*'. The booking was made on an impulse after walking past the McIntoshes' residence in Wellington. '[I] have yet to find out if I can afford this caper.' Her plan was to go straight to Rome and stay with her friends, then tour Italy by hire-car for two weeks with Pamela Mann, then spend five weeks in London before sailing for New Zealand at the end of August. She had 12 weeks to put her house in order before she left for Rome. This meant a huge rush to finish the book and take care of last-minute details. 'I've found tenants of a sort who will be nice to the cats.' To her great relief, Sylvia was making good progress and 'being wonderful about her beastly radium treatment. The after effects are really awful but should begin, now, to go off gradually.'

Then, just weeks before her departure, came the sad news that Nelly Rhodes had died, at the age of 72. 'It's a body-blow,' Ngaio told Doris McIntosh. She found her friend's death impossible to comprehend. 'I think scarcely a day went by without my having some reminder or thought of her.' For the first time in her life, Ngaio was leaving New Zealand and Nelly would not be at her journey's end. 'It's difficult indeed to believe she won't be there.'

CHAPTER EIGHT

Rome to Jubilee

Barnaby Grant sits alone at an outdoor café in the Piazza Colonna, in Rome. Above him, a black, brooding sky booms across the traffic noise with the thunderous promise of rain. It is noon, and the café, which pulsed with life just moments earlier, is deserted except for a table of three callused country yokels, a couple of young lovers, and an unkempt Englishman who hovers between tables and stares oddly at him. Grant reaches down to satisfy himself that his 'locked attaché case' is still there. '[It's been] a bit of a swine, this one, he thought. It's been a bit of a swine.'

Suddenly, as if the sluicegates of heaven have opened up, it begins to rain — just a handful of giant drops at first, but then a torrent that fills canopies in an instant and hits cars and the kerb so hard that it ricochets. Barnaby Grant leaps to his feet along with the others. There is a stampede, a collision, then a row between the three countrymen and the young lovers. Lightning flashes, thunder rolls, punches fly, and Grant emerges from the confusion stunned by a head-wound and with a nasty cut on his hand. He sits for a moment to recover, reaching habitually down for his comforter. There's nothing there. His hand claws the space frantically. He can hardly bear to look.

Edmund Cork had often warned Ngaio not to keep just a single handwritten copy of her novel; in *When in Rome* Barnaby Grant has done just this. This is writer's paranoia come to life. The sensation for Grant is like that of drowning, a powerless sinking into sensory nothingness. 'An impossible flood of thoughts crowded his brain . . . for instance, of how long it had taken him to write his book, of his knowledge that undoubtedly it was the best thing he had done, perhaps would ever do.' He is numb with desolation, but lingering will not bring it back, and reporting it to the British Consulate might. '*Blackmail*' is the consul's declaration. Then he corrects himself: perhaps 'Ransom' is a better word.

So the agonizing wait for a telephone call begins. On the third morning, a heatwave hits Rome. Barnaby Grant sits alone in the breathless shade of a hotel roof garden with his 'uneaten brioche, a pot of honey and three wasps'. He has been in a state of anxious exhaustion, and is now in 'a condition that he supposed must be that of Despair itself'. Then he vaguely realizes that the waiter is gesturing towards the door. Through it and onto the roof walks Sebastian Mailer, the enigmatic Englishman whom Grant had seen three days earlier at the café. As he moves towards the shade, the man draws an attaché case from under his jacket. 'I think you will be pleased to see me.'

Barnaby Grant returns to England and publishes his novel, *Simon in Latium*, to the acclaim he anticipated. It crowns a career which had had a rocky beginning. One of his early novels was very similar to someone else's. There were accusations of plagiarism, then a court case. He withdrew the book from sale himself. This was another writer's neurosis. Ngaio said that one of the reasons she never read detective fiction was that she was too frightened of discovering in print either the quintessence of the novel she was about to write or the one she had just written. Grant has lived in the shadow of public humiliation, even though he has long since become an internationally celebrated author. Less than a year later, he is back in Rome and, while sitting in the foyer of a hotel, he happens to see Sebastian Mailer standing at the reception desk, making arrangements for his tour party. Overtaken by a sense of repugnance, Grant hides behind his newspaper and escapes onto the street, where a battle ensues between his conscience and his instinct for self-preservation. His conscience wins and he returns to the foyer to thank Mailer once more for saving his novel.

If only his instincts had fought harder. Mailer ushers him into a private room where he threatens to expose him as a plagiarist. In the three days he kept Grant's novel, Mailing had written a novella with a similar theme, which he showed to people at the time claiming it was his own. He now tells Grant he will go to the press and say that the famous novelist has stolen his work. From this point he begins blackmailing the writer. His first request seems innocent enough: Barnaby Grant is to be the main attraction of Il Cicerone, a tour company Mailer has developed to fleece rich tourists.

Mailer is also a suspected drug boss in an international heroin and cocaine smuggling ring, which uses the route from 'Izmir [in Turkey] via Sicily to Marseilles and thence, through France or entirely by sea, to the U.S.A.'. Roderick Alleyn is tailing Mailer, and this is why he is on hand to take Mailer's tour of San Tommaso's in Pallaria. The party consists of wealthy Barnaby Grant fans, Alleyn incognito, plus Mailer and his Italian drivers. Down, down into the bowels of Rome's history they descend, until they reach the pagan remains that feature so 'vividly in Grant's novel'. This is the excavated remnant of a pagan house where the god Mithras was worshipped. There is a shrine with a statue of the god still in place.

Enthralled, Baroness Van der Veghel begs Barnaby Grant to explain the secrets of the cult and its setting. Grant casts a dagger-look at Mailer before suggesting, 'confusedly, that an author seldom reproduced in scrupulous detail, an actual *mise-en-scène* any more than he used unadulterated human material. "I don't mean I didn't start off with San Tommaso . . . Of course I did. But I gave it another name and altered it to my purpose."'

Barnaby Grant is reluctant to talk the writers' shop that Ngaio readily discussed with Doris McIntosh as she worked on the manuscript for *When in Rome* after she returned from her Italian trip. 'It will be clear enough that my S. Tommaso is based on S. Clemente,' she explained, 'but as you will see there are very wide divergences in architecture, lay-out etc.' Ngaio received her knowledge of heroin trafficking from Edmund Cork: 'my London agent got the gen for me'. Toni's drug den, where marijuana and hard drugs are supplied like soft drinks, was her own invention. 'I've had no prompting about drug pads & very likely have gone hopelessly off the beam.' Doris McIntosh helped Ngaio with the Roman police hierarchy. '[I] would be profoundly grateful for any stray gems that might trickle from your pen under the general heading of Roman Police Force.' Doris responded by sending Ngaio a comprehensive list. 'What an angel-child you are & what a superb resumé.' Doris also assisted Ngaio with the spelling of Italian words. As things got progressively more difficult to explain by letter, Doris suggested Ngaio send over a typed transcript so that she and Alister could proofread the Italian properly and check for inaccuracies.

Ngaio's publishers were 'rampant' for the manuscript. In the timeframe available, she could only supply a heavily annotated and changed carbon copy. This was sent and returned by airmail at vast expense, in just enough time for Ngaio to make the McIntoshes' amendments to the galley proofs. Even then, there were last-minute queries. 'I note that DEPUTI-QUESTURI is now to be VICE-QUESTORE — Change in spelling, O.K.?' Ngaio always worked hard to get the facts in her fiction correct. It was in her nature to do so, but if she failed her publisher received a barrage of mail correcting the fault. In *Final Curtain*, she used the 'trade-mark word' Thermos as a noun with a small 't' and received a stiff note from the manufacturer reminding her of the mistake. *When in Rome* was a minefield of potential hazards. 'I don't want Alleyn involved with any more Italians!'

The art historical and architectural references in *When in Rome* came from Ngaio's experiences on her trip, and so, interestingly, did the central clue that exposes the murder of Mailer and his estranged Sicilian wife, Violetta. One of Ngaio's key problems in writing the book was 'achieving structural union of Antiquities & story-line'. The linking needed to be seamless to avoid it becoming 'a sort of bastard thriller-guide'. Ngaio began collecting her Rome experiences when she arrived at the McIntoshes' apartment in the Via de San Pantaleo in early May 1968. Before leaving New Zealand, she had had her first bout 'of all filthy complaints gout!' — in her left foot. 'It now resembles a red-hot pumpkin stabbed by white-hot knitting needles.' The gout settled before her departure, but she sometimes needed the support of a stick. Ngaio's stay at the embassy was unforgettable. Her five weeks in Rome was 'the experience of a lifetime,' she told Gerald Lascelles, '& I still can't get over my luck in seeing it under such wonderful guidance & in such almost indecent luxury'. They had a driver to take them 'hither & thither' and the Pantaleo was just half a minute's walk from the piazza that Ngaio thought the loveliest in Rome.

'I am sitting on a balcony of a palazzo in Old Rome surrounded by the facades of other houses,' Ngaio wrote to Annette Facer. The houses near the Pantaleo were ochre- and terracotta-coloured, and some of them were very poor. People sang as they hung their washing out on balconies. 'The beauty & excitement & sheer warmth of the place is indescribable.' Ngaio and Doris McIntosh spent days in leisurely sightseeing, sitting beside fountains and at kerbside cafés and drinking in the city's enchantment. At night they wandered down ancient alleyways and through darkened streets, and one evening spent hours driving round just looking at the stunning lights. Ngaio was struck by the Colosseum, lit from inside. It seemed so alive she could almost hear the lions roar '& the multitude roaring still louder'. They saw a wealth of magnificent sculpture — 'I like the pagan & especially the Etruscan things best' — and among the architectural treasures the Basilica di San Clemente, where second-century worshippers built a temple to their god Mithras. Ngaio stored her impressions. 'Have you any idea how deep down the Mithraic house is at S. Clemente?' she enquired of Doris McIntosh after she returned to New Zealand.

When Pamela Mann arrived to pick Ngaio up for their road trip, 'I came away almost but not quite muttering with Macbeth: "No more sights".' The McIntoshes and driver Marcello escorted their hire-car to the edge of town and said farewell. The traffic was frightening, and there was nothing for it but complete immersion. 'Pammy is now a wizard at the wheel,' Ngaio reported. 'I no longer push out the floor boards which I must confess I was doing pretty vehemently in Rome.' Together they toured northern Italy, visiting Perugia, Assisi and Florence. At dusk, they walked along Perugia's ancient ramparts and 'looked across the Umbrian hills & plains towards Assisi'. There they were treated to Quattrocento painting and sculpture, 'my greatest delight', and 'went into the mountains to St Francis's little grotto which I found very touching'; and in Florence to 'the "unfinished" Michelangelo's. Also the Donatello David.' At Fiesole they found a 'retrospective season' of the film director Michelangelo Antonioni playing in the ruins of the Romano theatre, and when they dined at Mario's, Antonioni was at the next table. 'Great thrill for Pammy whose programme he autographed.' They arrived back in Florence by bus at one o'clock in the morning and walked to their hotel. The shady roof garden of their Pension Hermitage in Florence suggested the setting where Barnaby Grant sits in despair over his missing manuscript.

At the end of June, they took the train from Viareggio to Geno and then on to Paris, which was still in political turmoil after the student riots of May 1968. It was ironic that Ngaio was there at the very time when the intellectual unrest behind the writing of Roland Barthes' essay, 'The Death of the Author' (1968), with its Post-Structuralist implications, was being felt. This essay underpinned a shift in thinking that would have an impact on a new generation. What it promoted was the very antithesis of Golden Age detective fiction, where authors became serialized celebrities writing about male heroes, in closed worlds with absolute values and a universal truth.

Barthes challenged the author's authority to dictate an ultimate meaning of a text. He argued that language was so complex and the author's mind so unknowable that a single meaning was a Western bourgeois delusion. This viewpoint enfranchised the reader, because meaning was not implicit in the text, but in people's diverse readings of it. This perspective embraced flux, ambiguity, change, cultural and sexual diversity, and multiple realities and truths. More than just a student riot, May 1968 represented a revolution in cultural and social thinking that sealed a watertight door in history, making what came before it seem outmoded. Ngaio observed the stand-off between students and the authorities, just as her characters do in *When in Rome*:

> In the street a smallish group of young men carrying a few inflammatory placards shouted one or two insults. A group of police, gorgeously arrayed, pinched out their cigarettes and moved towards the demonstrators who cat-called and bolted a short way down the street.

Superficially it seemed that control had been reasserted, but the long-term impact of intellectual and political unrest could not be anticipated.

When she reached London, Ngaio was lucky to have the use of her secretary Joan Pullen's flat while Joan was away on a Mediterranean cruise. Her first weeks of a brief stay were taken up with 'publishers, agents & solicitors'. Her *Clutch of Constables* was expected to do well, and the publishers wanted her there for the promotion so they advanced the release date. She stayed briefly with Billy Collins in Kent, caught up with 'my three boys in the theatre' — Elric Hooper, Jonathan Elsom and James Laurenson — and with 'my dear, dear, family . . . They all miss their mama very grievously & wanted to talk over *very* many things.' She saw all but one of the Rhodes children, and found it more difficult than ever to leave after just five weeks. 'The old London enchantment is hard at it.'

She could not explain why she bothered to return home, but she did and, shockingly, it was without many of her precious Italian photographs. Harrod's had sent her slides back to Italy to be processed and they were lost. 'It's absolutely maddening . . . Can you beat it,' she exclaimed to Doris McIntosh. She stewed over her losses and decided to put them to work by using photographic prints as the clue to expose her murderer in *When in Rome*.

The photographs belong to the Dutch Baron and Baroness Van der Veghel. The couple remind Barnaby Grant of the Etruscan bride and bridegroom who

lie on a 'sarcophagal couch' at the Villa Giulia. They are similar in appearance —
heavy and large-framed like the terracottas with almond-shaped eyes and
timeless Etruscan smiles — and in their all-consuming passion for each other.
It is as if the sculptures have come to life. The tourists take photographs deep
down in the pagan excavations of the Mithras house under San Tommaso's. The
Baron calls the party together. He and his wife want a group photograph, with
Barnaby Grant in the middle. The Baron, because he is tall, stands at the back.
The Baroness is delighted: 'Good. Good. And so, all are ready? Freeze, please.
I shoot.' They stand crowded together in near-darkness and nothing happens.
Her bulb has blown. There is a frenzied search for a new bulb, and after much
delay the picture is finally taken. The Baroness then replaces the Baron in the
group and another photo is snapped that includes her. Kenneth Dorne has also
taken a group shot.

'It is a pity,' the photographic expert tells Roderick Alleyn, 'there has been
a misfortune. Light has been admitted.' All the Van der Veghels' photographs
taken under San Tommaso's are mysteriously blank. 'I cannot understand this,'
the Baron says to Alleyn, as he fingers the exposed prints. Nothing has survived
except Kenneth Dorne's single photograph, and the person missing from his
snap is Mailer's murderer. In the darkness, the killer has slipped away from the
group and murdered the blackmailing drug dealer. The evidence is there in black
and white; or rather the evidence of absence.

'I have no Roman [film] since the one Marcello's friend developed & only some
from Florence & Perugia which have somehow survived,' wrote a despondent
Ngaio. She had told Annette Facer that Rome and its treasures were impossible
to capture on film, never realizing Fate would take her literally. She left London
'feeling cheated'. There were many things she still wanted to do, but so much
of her time had been taken up with business and promotion.

Her trip back to New Zealand at the end of August was purgatory. After a
stopover in Naples, she became ill with food poisoning. It was not uncommon
for her to get stomach complaints, but this was a vicious attack of diarrhoea and
vomiting that left her so weak that she collapsed in her bathroom, coming to
badly bruised and with a bleeding nose. The food on the ship was awful. 'The
meat tastes of stables or nothing . . . the vegetables are sodden & sour. Even hard
boiled eggs taste like straw out of a wet mattress.' There was almost a mutiny
among the passengers.

But her spirits lifted when she arrived home to the news that her *Clutch of Constables* was doing exceptionally well. It had been chosen as book of the month in Britain and the United States. Ngaio was pleased, because they paid 'about a thousand quid (of which I get about a third)'. Her agent was thrilled, Collins was delighted, and Dilys Wynn writing for *The New Yorker* magazine topped everything by stating, 'It's time to compare Christie to Marsh instead of the other way round.'

In the New Year of 1969, Ngaio wrote excitedly to Doris McIntosh, 'I'm dug into a new one set . . . you will be flabbergasted to learn, in Rome.' Ngaio would dedicate *When in Rome* to 'the Ambassador and Mrs McIntosh and the Staff of the Residence, New Zealand Embassy in Rome who made it possible'.

By mid-February, Ngaio had written 16,000 words of the manuscript and was still developing ideas about how she would finish her 'complex plot'. For the moment, however, it was put aside. Ngaio thought coming back after a break might clarify her approach, and she was considering tackling *A Midsummer Night's Dream*: 'if we can stage & light the kind of job I'd like to make of it'.

At the end of February, she was making preparations. 'Sorry this is blotched with black,' she said of a letter to Doris McIntosh. 'I'm doing costume designs for the theatre & showcard colour abounds.' In the same letter she described fainting at a vice-regal buffet dinner, after standing too long in a small, stifling, crowded room. She came to with the Governor-General leaning over taking her pulse. He took her into a quiet side room and they talked while she recovered. 'Wasn't it *too* shaming & *awful*. Never, never, *never* again, a buffet dinner for this old girl.' Ngaio's health was fragile, yet she willingly took on the huge task of another student production. The theatre was her life-blood and young people a reminder of spring in her autumn years.

In March, when she began auditioning, 'a huge dirty, barefooted, filthy-jeaned, shoulder-length undergraduate' turned up to challenge her sensibilities. 'Yeah but Ah'ma not setting ma sights at a fairee,' he announced to her in a husky voice with a New Zealand twang. Ngaio was horrified. 'A brief and staggering vision of him as Oberon very nearly unseated me.' Collecting herself, she replied with gravity that perhaps it would be better if he tried for a mortal role. In the end, she decided he was 'a nice, intelligent chap' as long as you stood 'windward of him'.

Ngaio had been directing student productions for nearly 30 years, and over that time fashions and faces changed, but never the sense of camaraderie and respect that developed between a director and players. Ngaio changed her ideas. Directing students kept her contemporary. She accepted the challenge of working with a late 1960s–early 1970s generation, a fresh group of players accepted her guidance and authority, and once again they brought something magical to life. It was not vastly different from what Ngaio had done before, but more refined and sophisticated in its presentation.

The leading roles went to established players like Mervyn Glue, who was Nick Bottom, and David Hindin, who was Peter Quince, but also to a new group that included the future film and television actor Sam (Nigel) Neill as Theseus, Catherine Wilkin as Hippolyta, and Paul Sonne and Jane Thompson as Oberon and Titania. Ngaio had an instinct for a star when she chose Sam Neill.

Ngaio also had a wild card: Elric Hooper had put a 'west end engagement' aside to come out and play Puck. She was in negotiations with the Queen Elizabeth II Arts Council to raise money for his fare. He was perfect for the role with his boyish looks, irascible character and Puck-like humour, and she knew he would be a drawcard. Ironically, the Arts Council that she had done so much to launch had a short memory, and it was Ngaio who paid. 'Whether I get the cash back . . . is anyone's guess. I don't really care . . . it's splendid having him here & his Puck will be dynamic.' It meant that she could not afford a trip to meet Doris McIntosh in London.

The show was a massive undertaking for a 74-year-old. Elric Hooper and Annette Facer were Ngaio's assistant directors for *A Midsummer Night's Dream*, and this alleviated some of the stress, but performances were not without drama. Glue, a talented and well-seasoned actor, developed the practice of nipping down to the local Bush Inn for a quick drink between scenes. Ngaio, who, confoundingly for an agnostic, ritually crossed herself before curtain rise on first-night performances, would have done so more vehemently had she realized that Glue timed his expeditions to the last minute. On one occasion Gerald Lascelles, who had been anxiously pacing the theatre car park for Glue's return, threw him Bottom's donkey head seconds before he stepped onto the stage. Then one night the inevitable happened. Lascelles scanned the car park. No Glue roared up. After a frantic backstage consultation he flung on Bottom's head himself, and he and Annette Facer, who was hiding in the rude mechanics' hut as his prompt, took to the stage together. Stagehands shifted the hut with Facer still ensconced, badly gashing her heels, but this was the only blood spilt, because Lascelles had made a passable ass and saved Glue's Bottom.

This was one problem averted. *Fiddler on the Roof* and some 'very good concerts' were stiff competition for the production, and Ngaio complained that she only had to produce *A Midsummer Night's Dream* 'to bring about hideous snowstorms & floods. Last time . . . it coincided with the severest snowstorm in N.Z. history. This time — blizzards, snow, record low temperatures & flooding.' Against the odds, houses filled to capacity each night and 'we were turning them away by dozens at the end'.

Hooper was as dynamic a Puck as she had hoped, and a 'shot in the arm' for both the cast and the members of the public who attended his lectures and classes. This was the self-perpetuating artistic enrichment she longed for — New Zealanders teaching New Zealanders. She saw it as a sign of cultural maturity.

During the show she found time to see the Frances Hodgkins retrospective exhibition at the Robert McDougall Art Gallery. 'Wonderful!' she wrote ecstatically. She longed to own one of the works, as Doris McIntosh did. Hodgkins's drawings and still-lifes set in landscape were 'superb'. She was an expatriate whose work changed New Zealanders' ideas about art. This was what Ngaio wanted for the theatre.

A Midsummer Night's Dream finished with a huge cast party for 80, at Marton Cottage. 'It too was a howling success if somewhat exhausting.' In the end the production made a 'remarkable' $3,000 profit.

While she worked on the play, Ngaio kept writing to Doris McIntosh, checking details for *When in Rome*. Sometimes she forgot the answers. 'As always I destroyed your last two immediately,' she said of the most recent letters. Ngaio had a strict practice of destroying her correspondence with Doris and, it seems, assumed that her own was also being disposed of. But Doris McIntosh valued Ngaio's letters more than her privacy and stashed them away, so half of their detailed communication about *When in Rome* has survived. Both of the McIntoshes were a huge help, and Ngaio derived immense pleasure from working with them. She struggled with her writing, moving material backwards and forwards to get the right balance of clues, motive and narrative flow. At one stage she had Alleyn photographing a footprint under San Tommaso's twice because she had shifted the episode in the text and forgotten to eliminate the original.

Before Christmas, she sent the manuscript off to Edmund Cork in trepidation. An even-mannered man, his response was ecstatic. It was 'the best yet' and 'it made him want to pack his bags & take off for Rome at once'. As Cork predicted, it proved to be one of her most acclaimed late novels, coming out in London in 1970, and Boston in 1971.

'I had the usual tree & as always enjoyed it very much,' Ngaio wrote to Doris McIntosh in January 1970. 'So did everyone else, I think. The children did a lovely play with George & the Dragon lasting every second of eight minutes.' Since the mid-1940s, Ngaio had held a Christmas party at Marton Cottage with a tree and presents for her players, friends, family, when they were around, and their children. It went so far back in people's minds that it was like Christmas itself, a much-anticipated ritual. Ngaio staged the event as she did a production, with precision, the props, timing and parts all organized. This was her way of giving, but also of experiencing Christmas anew in the faces of children as they saw the tree, the lavish decorations, the piles of presents, the candles, and the table, all crystal, crackers and sumptuous food.

Ngaio's parties brought back the ghosts of Christmases past. As the long days of summer warmed the tussock-covered hills around Marton Cottage, her parents would move her bed onto the verandah so that she could sleep outside. A hot nor-west Christmas under the stars was what she remembered. She left notes for Father Christmas at the top of a solitary pine tree, which were collected, and kept a secret Christmas book containing her first 'attempt at descriptive writing'. On Christmas Eve, she scanned the skies for a sleigh. It was all part of the Marsh ritual, as was the fantasy and theatre created by her father, who became Old St Nick himself with a beard, 'red outfit with white facings' and a bag of presents. Henry, who was 'Bah humbug!' about organized religion, took great pleasure in bringing the spirit of Christmas to his daughter. 'Very c-o-o-o-ld in the chimney to-night,' he would announce in his deepest, gruffest voice, as he stepped onto the verandah. Then, hanging up Ngaio's stocking, he would consult his notes out loud to see whether she had been a good or a bad 'little girl'. He was thrilled to watch her expressions of delight as Christmas unfolded. Ngaio was convinced — or at least reluctant to disbelieve — until her mid-teens.

Sylvia Fox was there, 'of course', at Ngaio's Christmas tree parties, along often with Betty Cotterill, sometimes Anita Muling, with Val when he was alive and then with Marjorie Chambers, Crawsie and her husband Andy, and over the years many friends and players and their children. Memories stretched back. 'Do you remember bringing Mark when he was a Heavenly gruff little job of about 5?' Ngaio asked John Schroder. 'I remember you suggested that he should give me a kiss.' Young Mark, stabbed with embarrassment, had said that his father might like to do it instead.

The Christmas of 1969–70 gave her the idea that a Christmas tree party could be the genesis of a plot for a book. She began *Tied Up in Tinsel*, and by June was 'up to 22,000 words . . . & making heavy weather of it'. Her books became progressively harder to write and there was more editing for the publishers at the other end, but the fact that she was still writing successful sellers made the agonizing process worthwhile.

Tied Up in Tinsel is substantially autobiographical, but it opens in a very different Christmas world from that of Ngaio's childhood. The countryside around Halberds Manor is a barren picture of white snow and black fallow paddocks. On a hillside nearby, a sightless scarecrow swivels in freezing winds that cut and carry away bits of straw from its cuffs and collar. This is the romantic winter Christmas that young Ngaio had seen on Christmas cards and read about in books.

Troy is staying at Halberds, painting a portrait, while Alleyn is working on an extradition case in Australia. The subject of her commission, Hilary Bill-Tasman, has invited her to stay for his Christmas tree party, which he puts on for the children of local prison officers and their parents. Like Ngaio, he is an agnostic, but for him Christmas is a timeless tradition, reaching back through ancient pagan ritual to the earliest Druids. He spends days planning. There are rehearsals. His uncle, Flea, will be Father Christmas. Hilary's showpiece is a costume with a superb beard and wig, plus a long golden gown that the grand old man Flea wears as he delivers his presents. The plan is that he will come in through the french windows to the recorded strains of Christmas carols, drawing presents on a golden sleigh behind him. Hilary will oversee the present distribution, while Uncle Flea escapes back out into the snow. Thirty-one children are coming and a dozen or so adults.

In the 'long room' stands the tree, decorated all in gold. 'They hung golden glass baubles . . . [and] mounted a golden angel. There were festoons of glittering gold tinsel and masses of gilded candles. Golden stars shone in and out of the foliage.' The tree is a vision, completed when the children's presents arrive in large golden boxes, one for each family. There is even a 'Crib' that Hilary's Aunty Bed bought for him in Oberammergau when he was a child. Hilary is sensitive about his paganism. 'You think I'm effete and heartless and have lost my sense of spiritual values,' he says defensively to Troy as they survey the splendour. He has read her mind.

Would Troy have thought the same of her creator? Is Ngaio using a fictional character to test her own behaviour? Or is she just thinking out loud? Whatever the answer, Ngaio, like Hilary, was motivated more by festivity than faith, but her religious beliefs were conflicted. While she was writing *When in Rome*, she found that Roman churches were dedicated to saints or well-known biblical or historical figures. She decided on a cryptic dedication for San Tommaso's. 'Mine will be Doubting T. [Thomas],' she announced, 'for whom I have always entertained a considerable amount of sympathy.' Ngaio loved the theatre of religion and the magic of the Christmas story but, like her father, she could never entertain the idea of faith without doubt. Her scepticism, though, was fraught with her mother's superstition. Ngaio bought crucifixes and icons as gifts, 'prayed for' and 'blessed' people, and had an enquiring mind about the spiritual dimension of human existence. She read books on spiritualism, telepathy, faith healing and fortune telling, and, in 1967, paid to have her palm read.

By the end of 1970, she was a long way through the first draft of *Tied Up in Tinsel*, and her Christmas tree at Marton Cottage 'was a great success & really did look pretty stunning being all GOLD,' she told Doris McIntosh. 'The boxes [were] golden too.' She spent a hectic eight days getting ready for her 30 guests. Ngaio usually had Christmas and Boxing Days on her own. Sylvia would go and stay with her nephew, Richard, his wife Ginx, and their two children, while Ngaio enjoyed the stillness and liberty to do what she wanted. Her life was so full of people that she treasured the chance to pause and reflect. Being alone did not mean loneliness: it meant the space to potter around and do ordinary things and meditate. The year had been a busy one, but her major theatrical involvement, a production of Arthur Pinero's *The Magistrate* for the Canterbury Repertory in November, had been less taxing than working with students.

The year had begun with the sad news in January of the death of Allan Wilkie, at the age of 91. This was the end of an era for Ngaio, and for the theatre: he was one of the last actor-managers with a touring troupe.

In June, she received the shocking news that Brigid Lenihan, just 41 years old, had probably committed suicide in Melbourne. She had taken an overdose of sleeping pills and it was not clear whether this was accidental or deliberate. Her stage life had been dazzlingly brief and exotic. 'She was a brilliant and most loveable creature,' were Ngaio's closing words in a collection of tributes, organized by Bruce Mason and published in *Act* magazine in 1970. The fictional stage that Martyn Tarne walked onto so effortlessly in *Opening Night* had never been there for Lenihan. She had so much potential and talent, but it was a gargantuan undertaking to break into an English theatre world driven by class and networks. Ngaio saw her death as a tragedy.

The final bolt from the blue was news that Eileen Mackay had died. This death was immediate and personal because they had worked together so closely over the years, beginning with their collaboration on a children's book, and ending with the script for *False Scent*. It was the loss of a friend and a cherished history. Ngaio was devastated.

But there had been events and milestones to celebrate, too. In March, she had put on a luncheon at Marton Cottage for Lady Freyberg, the widow of former Governor-General and much-decorated soldier Lord Bernard Freyberg. Just 'a party of either 8 or 10' guests, Ngaio wrote in an invitation to Gerald Lascelles, 'so don't get yourself involved in a *cause célèbre* but do come & be the son of the house once more'. In the absence of family, Gerald was her surrogate son in New Zealand.

There had been her opening speech at Evelyn Page's retrospective exhibition at the National Art Gallery in Wellington, and, in September, Agatha Christie's 80th birthday had been celebrated around the world. Christie was still writing. In the early hours of the morning, Ngaio was linked by satellite to London and interviewed by the BBC. Unfortunately, the interviewer organized for the event failed to turn up at the studio and a technician was roped in. His first question was: 'So what do you think of Agatha Christie's Lord Peter Wimsey?' Ngaio gaped like a goldfish, not knowing quite what to say, and the interview went from bad to worse. But it was a technological undertaking that underlined the changes the world had seen in her lifetime. In the late 1920s she had taken a dilapidated coal-fired steamer to England; now she was being beamed there on radio waves.

There were now just two Queens of Crime left alive. In December 1957, Dorothy Sayers had died suddenly of a heart attack, at the age of 64. She was working on a translation of 'Paradiso', the third volume of Dante's *Inferno*. Sayers had been out shopping and was found at the bottom of her staircase surrounded by Christmas gifts. She had long since given up writing about Lord Peter Wimsey, but took the real mystery of her illegitimate son to her grave. Margery Allingham had died more slowly and sadly of breast cancer in June

1966. *A Cargo of Eagles*, the crime novel she was writing, was completed by her husband, Philip Youngman Carter, and published in 1968. He wrote two more Campion novels before stopping in 1970. Christie was still writing a novel a year. Ngaio's rate was a novel every 18 months to two years, but this picked up rather than diminished as she directed fewer plays in her last years.

Tied Up in Tinsel proved more difficult to finish than Ngaio expected. In February 1971, the 'new' book needed just '3,000 words & a week's hard concentration, but can I get into it? No: It will have to be finished during the voyage I fear.' She was planning another trip to England.

'I do wish that you could come to New York to enjoy our spring or even our autumn. It would be heavenly to see you again,' wrote Dorothy Olding. These words were the spur for Ngaio to try very hard to get a ship to England via New York, but this was impossible in the timeframe. 'I'm sorry you can't find a ship,' Olding responded. 'We would all love to have you here again, much more than you know.' They planned to meet in London anyway. Olding would be there on business, arriving just two days after Ngaio, and she was prepared to change her tickets to fit around her author's schedule. 'I most certainly will want to see you *very early* in my stay (at the Connaught),' she told Ngaio when their arrangements were more settled, 'preferably dinner and a nice long evening.' They planned to meet on the 17th, 18th or 19th of May, depending on Ngaio's availability.

Ngaio's friend Bessie Porter moved into Marton Cottage to look after the cats, and, after a week-long stay with the McIntoshes who had returned to Wellington, Ngaio left from Auckland on the *Orsoua* on 3 April. In Sydney, they picked up flood-contaminated water that began a gastric scourge of the ship. Ngaio was sick and on a 'dose of 6 antibiotic pills every 4 hours & a drench in a bottle that made one as sick as a cat'. She was not well again until after Cape Town, but the remainder of the journey was 'enchanting'.

She arrived in London in spring when the city sparkled and looked its best. Initially, she stayed at her favourite Basil Street Hotel. Once again she faced agents' and publishers' meetings, mixed with 'exhaustive flat-hunting' — and her rendezvous with Dorothy Olding. The chemistry between the women had lain dormant since New York in 1960, but their meeting again in London a decade later proved as memorable and dynamic as their last. 'I so much hated you going that I suddenly jibbed at walking out on the pavement & then thought how damn silly & made after you,' Ngaio wrote. But just at that moment she was called back into the hotel to take a telephone call, and when she returned to the street Olding had gone. Ngaio began plotting a longer encounter. She arranged to travel by ship with Dorothy from Nassau in the Bahamas through the Panama Canal, with stopovers in Acapulco and San Francisco.

In London, Ngaio headed for her stamping ground of the early 1960s, taking a three-room basement flat at 5 Montpelier Walk, in Knightsbridge. It was 'very small & like every last — hovel in this area — fiendishly expensive', but she delighted in the 'leafy little square & walking down the darling little streets to my old shops'. There was Capri, her Italian grocery, and a 'wine shop whose family greeted me as if I'd only been away for the weekend'. For the first time Ngaio noticed the difference in exchange rates and cost of living between New Zealand and Britain. 'There's no denying it's very *very* expensive here. Food, rents, fares — *everything* had spiralled like crazy.'

The year before, she had had another tax scare. Her tax was difficult to keep track of. In the United States, she paid an alien tax of 30 per cent in the dollar, and there were national differences in currency and tax laws. Agatha Christie had tax troubles, too, magnified by the same problem of worldwide sales. Ngaio Marsh Ltd paid for Ngaio's tickets to England and her upkeep, but costs were high and her income subject to flux. Ngaio felt financially vulnerable now and watched what she spent.

She was aware, too, of time slipping away. Her Danish publisher, Samleren, invited her to Copenhagen for a fortnight. This was 'another great chunk out of precious, *precious* time' that she had paid for in London. Ngaio wanted her Copenhagen visit shortened, but in the end thoroughly enjoyed her all-expenses-paid stay at one of the city's most exclusive hotels. There was a succession of television, radio and press interviews, but her trip to Kronborg Castle near the town of Helsingør, immortalized as Elsinore in *Hamlet*, was unforgettable. She left feeling her Danish sojourn had been 'a huge success'.

One of the tasks she returned to was *Tied Up in Tinsel*. The book had been a struggle. In mid-June, she promised Dorothy Olding she would look at it again and possibly 'shorten the 1st part a bit'. It was another month before she handed the finished manuscript to her agents. Reaction to the book was subdued, and she was asked to make revisions. Ned Bradford of Little, Brown in Boston was almost alone in his enthusiasm. He instantly offered her a contract on the usual terms of $10,000 advance against a royalty of 15 per cent. Collins also confirmed their commitment, and publication was set on both sides of the Atlantic for early 1972. The typescript was sent out to serializing magazines and distributing publishers. Serial rights were sold to the *Woman's Journal*, but the general response was that, in style and setting, it was too dated and English.

Ngaio worked on the revisions until early August, when Lord Ballantrae and his wife invited her to visit them in Scotland. Ballantrae was Sir Bernard Fergusson, Governor-General of New Zealand from 1962 to 1967, and later Baron Ballantrae of Auchairne and the Bay of Islands. Ngaio had met the Fergussons through Doris and Alister McIntosh and they became firm friends. 'Bernard & Laura were both in wonderful form. What a lovely, friendly, shabby old house it is & what dears they are.' In spite of his 30-year career as a soldier and the demands of public life, Lord Ballantrae was a published author, military historian and romantic, and this was his link to Ngaio. Her visit to Scotland consolidated their friendship, and in the future she would confide in him about her books. He was a talented man with a pedigree that appealed. This was a friendship she cultivated.

When Ngaio returned to London, she began work on yet another novel dramatization: of *When in Rome*. 'I must say I still think the book is an extraordinary choice . . . & I have many doubts about the outcome,' she explained to Doris McIntosh. This time Ngaio collaborated with travel book and script writer Barbara Toy. Hughes Massie, Ngaio's literary agents in Britain, initiated the project. Even when Ngaio departed for a 'double cruise' in the Mediterranean in mid-October, she took her secretary Joan Pullen so that she could work on the dramatization. 'Talk about a working holiday! I . . . worked on the play every morning [Joan] typed in the afternoon & I revised in the evening.' Back in London Toy worked, too, and when Ngaio returned they burned the midnight oil to bring it to completion.

On 8 December, Ngaio set sail from Southampton aboard the *Oronsay*, 'with more than the usual regrets' about a visit that had been rushed and frustrating. The voyage back that she had planned with Dorothy Olding had its wild moments of compensation. Olding was concerned about monopolizing Ngaio's time. 'All I can say to that,' she replied, 'is the more you monopolise it the better I shall like it.' Ngaio attempted to get a cabin closer to her friend's, and on one 'exhausting' but memorable evening together they went out to 'three parties in one night'. But Dorothy Olding, 15 years younger than Ngaio, noticed the age difference. A colleague wrote to Olding, hoping the trip 'wasn't all busman's

Holiday'. Privately, Olding admitted that the voyage was restful, but she was surprised to find Ngaio 'really quite frail & more than a little deaf. Also, she came down with the ship's chest and was laid low for several days.'

Ngaio was feeling her age and finding trips overseas increasingly demanding, but Anita Muling and Marjorie Chambers were on the wharf to meet her when she returned, and she had a 'happy arrival into the arms of my old Crawsie'. Sylvia Fox, who had been her housekeeper in England, flew back to New Zealand rather than taking the boat and 'arrived hot on my heels'. 'Syl looks a bit exhausted after her 3 day hop with only one stop at Los Angeles, but says she feels grand.'

On her first day home, Nekko-San, her cat, followed her constantly. Every time she sat down the cat leapt up, 'all 2 stone of him', and began kneading her lap with 'loud purrs & much dribbling'. Apart from the fact that Bessie Porter had eaten almost everything in the deep freeze — 'Gallons of steak. Several fowls', three curries, mulberries, casseroles, preserved fruit . . . and the list went on — it was good to be home. The weather in January was settled, and 'so one takes up the familiar routine'.

Almost immediately, there were discussions about Ngaio directing the inaugural production for the James Hay Theatre in the new Christchurch Town Hall. It was a tempting offer, but she decided to take her time and think about it. This would be a huge undertaking and she was not sure she was physically up to it. By April she had accepted the commission: 'Henry V is on in Sept. or Oct. God help us.' She agreed on the basis that Helen Holmes, a player of old and now her assistant, was able to carry much of the administrative weight. But, at 77, could Ngaio cope with the stresses and strains? This was not a student production but something approaching professional theatre, which required experienced repertory players. As auditions were organized, everyone wondered how Ngaio would hold up, but once in the director's chair she was 'again that vital, sensitive, determined, decisive, enthusiastic, joyfully intense force that we knew of old'. She was every bit as tireless and exacting in her search for best actor for the role as ever. 'I hope most ardently that Jonathan Elsom may come out to play Chorus,' she wrote to Doris McIntosh. In the meantime, she had 100 actors to audition for about 30 speaking parts.

Ngaio's old friend Olivia Spencer Bower was one of those who auditioned. She had been at Marton Cottage for lunch with Ngaio, who, out of the blue, asked her why she did not try for a part.

'Don't be so silly,' I said, 'I'm too old — I haven't acted for years.'

'Well, read the play again,' she replied.

Of course I did & I auditioned & got the part of Alice.

Because the James Hay Theatre was new, there were no costumes and props from previous productions, so these had to be purchased or hired and Ngaio 'hardly expected to break even'. The 1,000-seat theatre, however, looked 'more & more exciting' as it approached completion. As they rehearsed solidly for eight weeks, it was 'hectic beyond measure'. 'Rehearsals going reasonably well,' Ngaio wrote in a rushed letter to Doris McIntosh in August, 'but all sorts of side alarms almost continuous. Jonathan E. arrived & lovely to have him.'

Ngaio had a plan for the opening night. Stall seats were booked for the McIntoshes, who were flying down to see the inaugural performance. Ngaio urged them not to be late, as those who arrived after the beginning would not be admitted until Scene Three. 'I couldn't bear you to miss Jonathan's opening Chorus which is I hope going to pack a considerable surprise.' On opening night the curtain rose and out onto a misted blue stage walked William Shakespeare: the Bard himself would play Chorus. The audience gasped, clapped spontaneously, and as Jonathan Elsom stepped forward he could only hope there would be quiet for his opening lines. The applause died away, and for the first time in public on that new stage Shakespeare's words were spoken:

O for a Muse of fire, that would ascend
The brightest heaven of invention,
A kingdom for a stage . . .

The audience was captivated, the actors were electrified, the director had pulled off a coup: Ngaio's three-cornered world was working in perfect unison. 'I was lost in admiration of much of it,' wrote Bruce Mason in an ecstatic letter to Ngaio, 'the Droeshout idea [a reference to the famous portrait of Shakespeare] was inspired, and brilliantly executed by Jonathan . . . The opening was quite unforgettable: a brilliant idea, and astonishing and dazzling.' Mason was in the audience reviewing the inaugural performance for the *Listener*. This response was echoed in many of the other published reviews. As Olivia Spencer Bower told a friend, 'Every seat was taken for the full 2 weeks but the place was booked so we had to stop.'

The production was blighted by teething difficulties, however. 'All I can say is . . . the James Hay theatre must have the jaws and dental equipment of a dinosaur,' Ngaio told Mason, in response to his letter. Their achievement had been against technical odds. At each performance there were anxieties about the fire curtain, and one night the audience waited an hour for it to rise.

By mid-November the financial results of *Henry V* were available. 'We made a net profit of $12,000,' Ngaio announced to Doris McIntosh, 'a staggering result from a 10 day season & pretty hefty costs on the production.' This was a 'gratifying' outcome, and Ngaio was warm in her thanks to cast and crew. In October, she sent a 'round-robin' letter to those she felt had made it possible. Annette Facer's read: 'Throughout the rehearsal period, the very difficult and all too short preliminary days in the theatre and the season itself, you were the sort of company that a director dreams of but very seldom sees.' Ngaio saw their success as a 'corporate achievement' that had come out of their combined efforts and spirit.

As usual, Ngaio had stopped a book in mid-flow to direct the production. She had begun *Black As He's Painted* not long after she arrived back in Christchurch, but the novel had started ambivalently as she tossed up whether it should be set on a boat at sea or in London. In the end, London won. The setting was Knightsbridge, and more specifically Montpelier Walk, where she had lived with Jonathan Elsom in 1960–61 and on her most recent trip to England.

The basement flat had brought back memories of the little cat she and Elsom had adopted, so Lucy Lockett would become a central character in *Black As He's Painted*, and an agent in the murderer's undoing. The real Lucy had been given to Ngaio and Elsom by their housekeeper, 'a Miss Gordon-Lennox,' Elsom recalls, 'and, I think a member of the Cats Protection League'. Lucy had been discovered wandering round Westminster.

Lucy was black, sleek, and enchanting with a small white 'bib' under her chin, and when I was about to depart for an acting career in Southwold and then Dundee, and Ngaio was soon to sail off for NZ . . . I arranged . . . a new home with a little spinster, a Miss Clinch (retired Headmistress) friend of my 'adopted family' down in Burgh Heath (Surrey). Lucy lived on for many years after, and I'd renew acquaintance when I visited my 'family' in Surrey.

Lucy was named after a character in John Gay's *The Beggar's Opera*. 'Ngaio always said Lucy was "no better than she oughta be" — it seemed a suitable name for our little cat with loose morals.'

It is Mr Whipplestone who finds Lucy Lockett in *Black As He's Painted*: she is wandering around Capricorn Walk. Just before the book's publication, Ngaio received a memo from Collins publishers in London: 'I have a sneaking feeling that Capricorn stands pretty much for Montpelier, with the street, square, mews, etc., and that the Oratory is none other than the Brompton Oratory. Am I right? If so, we could make a rough map of that particular area substituting Capricorn for Montpelier.' The recently retired Mr Whipplestone is walking along Capricorn Mews and into Capricorn Place. As the traffic noise rages around him, he realizes 'that he himself must now get into bottom gear and stay there, until he was parked in some subfuse [*sic*] lay-by' and finally towed away. Suddenly a cat, thin and black, flashes in front of him, then there is the inevitable screech of brakes and a 'blot of black ink' on the pavement. A group of louts laugh at the neat little heap. Mr Whipplestone stops, leans down and, in a flash, the cat leaps into his arms and is 'clinging with its small claws and — incredibly — purring'. It has blue eyes and is black, except for the last 'two inches' of its tail, which are snow white.

When Mr Whipplestone shifts flats to No. 1 Capricorn Walk, Lucy Lockett moves in and life accelerates into a higher rather than lower gear. Astonishingly, he finds that his new cleaning lady and her husband, Mr and Mrs Chubb; Mr Sheridan, the man in Flat No. 1A downstairs; the Sanskrits, two morbidly obese sibling ceramicists living and working in a ceramics factory down the road; and his near-neighbours Colonel and Mrs Cockburn-Montfort are all involved in an attempted assassination of Alleyn's old school friend and the subject of Troy's latest portrait, His Excellency the President of the emerging African state of Ng'ombwana.

How is Lucy Lockett involved? The fictional and real Lucy Locketts share a dubious propensity: they are cat burglars. The real Lucy stole a wooden fish; its fantastic counterpart slips into the Chubbs' tiny apartment and disappears with a ceramic fish on a chain which is the emblem of this secret group of assassins. Lucy Lockett's light-fingered escapades help to connect the pieces. Mr Whipplestone, who once served in the Foreign Office in Ng'ombwana and, by a strange quirk of fate, is also a friend of Alleyn's, finds himself involved in stakeouts and international espionage, and Lucy Lockett becomes his batman.

There are three murders in *Black As He's Painted*. The Ng'ombwana ambassador is accidentally speared at a diplomatic function in London, and towards the end of the book the Sanskrits are found hideously murdered in their pig pottery. 'The Oratory dome looks bland upon us,' Ngaio had written to John Schroder in November 1960, '& in an old stable a strange girl sits modelling clay unicorns & firing them on the spot in an improvised kiln.' In fiction 12 years later, unicorns become pigs, and the ceramicists are double agents who came to a sticky end. *Black As He's Painted* is a well-written suspense-ridden murder mystery in the ilk of Ngaio's best. She agonized over it, as she so often did, but all the time probably had a sneaking suspicion that she had hit on something good. Her descriptions of the retired but far-from-redundant Mr Whipplestone and his cat are spare and incisive. She is writing about what she knows.

Ngaio continued to battle with *Black As He's Painted* leading up to Christmas 1972 and into the New Year. Her Christmas tree party, planned for 15 December, and for 48 guests, was a major interruption. Reviews for *Tied Up in Tinsel* had filtered through as she was organizing *Henry V* and, in spite of her agent's reservations, it had been very successful in the States, where it was picked up by Pyramid for a 'guarantee $9000 straight 10% royalty', along with three older titles: *Vintage Murder*, *A Man Lay Dead* and *The Nursing-Home Murder* at '$14,000 guarantee for the three . . . with 8% royalty'. Little, Brown, who sold them to Pyramid, was delighted.

But there was sadness, too, as Christmas approached. 'I'm afraid that poor little Nicola may very well have to have her amputation before then & will not be able to come.' Nicola, the daughter of Judie and Malcolm Douglass, had been diagnosed with bone cancer. Ngaio had offered the money to send her to a private school, which she thought would be less stressful. To be fair, she also helped to pay the fees for the Douglass's older daughter, Joanna. Ngaio's players were an extension of her family, and she quietly advised and helped many of them behind the scenes. 'Helen's Emily *has* got a hole in her heart . . . so we have two rather tragic little girls in one company this year,' Ngaio told Doris McIntosh. Helen Holmes's daughter was due for an operation at Greenlane Hospital the day after the Christmas tree party.

Annette Facer remembers the pattern of Ngaio's Christmas gatherings.

On the night we would arrive to be met at the door by Ngai or sometimes Crawsie and ushered in to the Blue Room (sometimes referred to as the

Long Room). The adults would be provided with deadly cocktails/drinks and the children would sort themselves out [for their play] . . . Each year a different theme evolved, sometimes written by the parents with references to the latest Drama Soc Shakespeare production and latterly by the children themselves . . . The audience was always most appreciative with Ngai clapping and cheering.

Then . . . the children were called to the dining table which was beautifully decorated with candles and Xmas things and name places and Ngai aided by Crawsie would enquire if each dish was to the child's liking. If the response was no they weren't served it. Most of Ngai's special older friends like Betsy, Sylvia, Marjorie and Anita (all childless) were delighted observers of this ritual . . . When all the littlies were fed they had to wait until they heard the bells chiming. This was Ngai playing an ancient record, which did not always respond immediately to her instructions. Then they were released into the Blue Room to discover that the screens had been removed and there stood The Tree ablaze with real lit candles. Such was the power of our elegant hostess that the tree never caught on fire. Family names were called out by Ngai and those so named came forward to collect their boxes which were often bigger than the recipients.

Nicola wrote the script for the play that year, and co-wrote it for a number of years to come. Emily was in charge of properties. Her health improved, but sadly Nicola's did not, and she died of cancer in her mid-teens.

Tied Up in Tinsel had been dedicated to Ngaio's godson, the Dacres-Mannings's older son, Nicholas. At Christmas the family visited from Australia. There were now three young children — 'They are such a happy family & Bet is such a splendid wife for him' — but Ngaio did not accept their invitation to visit Sydney. The youngsters were more than she felt able to cope with and she was under pressure with her writing of *Black As He's Painted*.

'The new book is giving me *utter* hell' and had been 'hideously difficult to pick up again'. She had no set structure, and was allowing the characters to evolve and interact, in the expectation that a pattern would emerge. This was not unusual, but when she was younger the structure had materialized earlier in the process. Ngaio had planned on taking a trip south with Doris McIntosh, but cancelled it in order to finish the book by midwinter, so it could reach her publishers in time for a Christmas release. The book presented some unexpected difficulties, which resulted in Ngaio taking professional diplomatic advice from Alister McIntosh. 'A murder takes place during a party on the occasion of the President's visit at a new African Independency Embassy in London. The suspect is an African body guard. Alleyn & Troy are guests.' The murder happens on Ng'ombwana soil. How would this affect Alleyn's investigation?

By April 1973, she had written 50,000 words and still did not know how it would end. There were other interruptions to the book's progress. Ngaio had taken a fall. '[I] flung up both feet to quite a *remarkable* height above my head while descending the concrete path on a gusty morning.' She had landed with all her weight on her right foot, which was twisted underneath. Her foot, which 'resembled that of an elephant', was badly bruised, and possibly broken. This was followed by a dose of flu. Ngaio admitted that things were much more difficult to get over when 'one is old'.

In the midst of her trials, she was visited by two of her oldest and dearest English friends, J.B. and Jacquetta Priestley. 'I pulled myself together' sufficiently to put on a dinner party in their honour. The Priestleys were anxious to see as much of New Zealand as they could in their limited time, and when an air strike grounded them in Dunedin they chartered a plane back to Christchurch to be there for the event. Helen Holmes took them all on a day-trip to Castle Hill, and the next day the Priestleys were gone. Ngaio wished she had been in 'better form for the occasion', but was delighted to see them. As soon as they had left, Ngaio was back into her book. With no plans to stage a production that year, she worked on in 'purdah'.

Her finger was still on the theatrical pulse, however, and she knew exactly what was said about the various productions in town. Some shows slipped by, but not the 'new professional Court Theatre's' production of *Home*, which she described as superb: 'no praise can be too high'. For years Ngaio had dreamed of a professional theatre in the city of her birth, and now it had happened.

After finishing *Black As He's Painted* in June and sending it off with a dedication to her cherished secretary, Roses Greene, and Roses' husband Mike, Ngaio took a three-week break with the McIntoshes in Wellington. She arrived back at Marton Cottage to find the 'South Pole whistling up through holes in the flooring, the sun-porch crammed to the ceiling with hardware & everything ground to a halt'. She was having underfloor heating installed and the workmen had created a gaping abyss, then disappeared.

Then came a brief visit from Stella Mannings's daughter, Jean. Her plane had circled a fog-bound Christchurch airport before diverting to Rangiora. 'I wish she could have stayed & been looked after,' Ngaio told Doris McIntosh. Jean's husband had died unexpectedly. 'She's very thin & worn poor child . . . It's tragic to see a still young & devoted wife left so desolate. But she has immense character & the heart of a lion.' But Ngaio's house was far from a warm refuge. After work recommenced, she moved into the attached flat.

While she was still in renovation limbo, she received wonderful news from England: Edmund Cork was ecstatic about the new book. She had also sent off a short story that Dorothy Olding had asked her to write. Her relief was palpable. It was more of an incident than 'murder & teckery', but if they were not interested she was sure it would come in handy somewhere else. Ngaio did not enjoy the short-story form. She needed a substantial canvas on which to exercise her skills of character development, scene setting and the investigation of social mores. The short story, by definition, was a vignette, dependent on a tight and cleverly delivered conceit.

It was mid-August before heating was restored to Marton Cottage, and it would have been bliss if only she could have worked the controls. 'I'm getting myself trained to manage the manipulation & avoid plunging from the tropic of Capricorn to the Antarctic Circle at irregular intervals all day.' She was sick of workmen. Nothing was returned to the kitchen, they slopped tea and coffee on the carpet, and broke her bedroom window, but as far as she could 'make out they haven't stolen anything'. But the heating was worth the wait. 'It makes a noise rather like a tiger purring but that I don't mind.'

She was pleased to hear in September that the *Woman's Journal* had bought the pre-production rights of *Black As He's Painted* for £2,000, 'which is better than a poke in the kisser with a wet rag, isn't it?' She worked on proofs for her American short story, which she found harrowing because of a new editing process. Ngaio lightened the burden by going out with Sylvia to see English comedian Frankie Howerd live in concert. 'We laughed ourselves sick at his deep blue jokes,' she admitted. Sylvia's recovery from cancer had been nothing short of miraculous. It was years since her radiation treatment, and she continued to do an immense amount for Ngaio, welcoming guests and cooking for people who visited when the semi-retired Crawsie was not available. 'Syl is marvellous & does an amazing amount but we all tremble a bit,' Ngaio admitted. 'She does have bad days . . . but her tests are still in the clear.' When Ngaio went out to shows, films or the theatre, it was usually with Sylvia. She was Ngaio's most constant companion.

But Ngaio was restless again for a change of scene. Before her Christmas tree party — '40 this year, ye, Gods!' — she made plans to leave in March the following year, on the *Oriana*. After some disappointments, 'I've found a tenant — my little hairdresser!' The process of packing began. What was ordinarily an ordeal turned into a nightmare. Her health was patchy and she had a massive reaction to a series of injections. 'Over the past three decades vaccination has been a mere formula', but now her left arm blew up like 'a glowing purple tennis ball'. Writing was a 'non-starter & I a semi-cot-case'. In February she began 'phase 2' of house and personal packing, with a nasty throat virus that lingered. She did manage to see some of the 1974 Commonwealth Games in Christchurch, 'which were a howling success', and to have dinner aboard HMS *Britannia*, where she enjoyed 'a long & very hilarious conversation with Prince Philip'.

She asked if Alister and Doris McIntosh had been involved with the opening of Parliament fiasco. 'It was agony watching it on T.V. "Ourpin the dor-ers" commanded a hidden voice.' Then there was the ceremonial bang, bang on the door. ' "It looks as if there's a hitch" observed the commentator & there sat the Royals, splendidly po-faced, but seething, I dare say, with repressed giggles.' To the horror of government officials, the doors had jammed.

Ngaio stayed with the McIntoshes at the end of February, and her ship departed on 1 March 1975. 'Yours is a second home to me in N.Z. my dear,' she wrote to Doris, once onboard the *Oriana*. 'At the moment [I] am seated at an open-air tavern by a swimming pool with a glass of lager on a glorious morning.' The *Oriana* was fun but incredibly hard to navigate. 'There is a migrant band of us wanderers. We pass & re-pass, giving each other . . . misdirections.' It was little wonder. There were no maps, the signage was poor and the ship was huge: there were three shops, four swimming pools, five bars and three restaurants.

'Dear Jonathan Elsom was on the wharf at Southampton & has been like an attentive son ever since,' she wrote after her arrival in early April. She was immediately involved in promotional activities. *Black As He's Painted* was receiving great reviews and was 'on the *Sunday Times* best seller list'. Ngaio was delighted. Instead of taking her usual flat in London, she stayed with Maureen (*née* Rhodes) and John Balfour at Walnut Tree Farm in Birling, Kent. Ngaio was relieved not to be thrown on her own resources. 'Thank the Lord, the cost of living being what it is — astronomical!' She commuted to the various Collins events, and to a lunch at the BBC, followed by a stint on *Woman's Hour*.

There were IRA bombs in London. She could not believe how calm people were. 'Nobody mentions bombs', yet their reality faced people in the newspapers every morning. It did nothing to dampen her ardour for the city. London flourished with spring tulips and the 'Mall is vivid with banners & one gets the old up lift in the old way'. She saw as much theatre as she could: John Aubrey's *Brief Lives*, Pirandello's *Henry IV*, John Gielgud in *The Tempest*, a Jacobean masque called *The Aerial*, all of which she liked, plus *The Califon*, which she found disappointing.

She interrupted her theatre fest with a trip to Laura and Bernard Ballantrae's new residence in Auchairne, Scotland. 'Hollywoodhouse was something out of a fairytale,' she told Doris McIntosh. At dinner a pipe major in full regalia 'played his way in through pair after pair of folding doors until there he came in full blast', to be offered a whisky, which he 'downed at one draught', and then continued at full steam. She went up to Edinburgh and spent four days walking through the magnificent streets. The Ballantraes offered her their flat in London, but she had the use of a friend's Chelsea flat over summer. Ngaio noticed the price of rents with horror. A basement flat in Montpelier now cost three times more than a whole house in 1961.

In July, she took a cruise through the Worcestershire canals with Mizzy and Bob Stead, who owned their own houseboat; for them this was a weekend pastime. Bob, who had been in commercial television for 25 years, had gained considerable seniority as an administrator and editor. 'At the moment he's editing *The World at War* for distribution overseas.' Not many months before Ngaio arrived, the couple were involved in a serious car accident, which left Bob 'scalped, (literally) & hurt in the leg' and Mizzy with permanent head injuries. She became desperate to return home, and Bob Stead was under pressure to repatriate and take work at New Zealand television. The position of director general was mooted but he wanted to know more about the job.

While she waited for the Chelsea flat to become available, Ngaio stayed at the Basil Street Hotel. 'I'm amusing myself trying my hand at an episode for "Crown Court" on Thames Television,' she explained to Doris McIntosh. 'My Jonathan Elsom has a leading role in the series & is very keen that I should, but it may come to nothing.' She found the series concept fascinating. The jury was recruited from people on the street so the actors never knew the verdict. It necessitated an excellent knowledge of the script because the proceedings could not easily be halted, and actors were required to ad lib.

Ngaio visited the Priestleys, 'saw the current repertoire' at Stratford-upon-Avon, which she thought too Symbolist, and in August moved back to stay with the Balfours at Walnut Farm. She was to have tests. 'I've got to pop into King's College Hospital this week to be plumbed by a gynaecologist,' she casually told Doris McIntosh. Her specialist, one of Britain's leading gynaecologists, suspected polyps on the neck of the uterus. Ngaio thought she would be back at the end of the week, and was planning trips to New York, and to Jersey in the Channel Islands. This was far from what happened. Her minor surgery turned into a complete hysterectomy for cancer of the uterus. She was four weeks in hospital. 'But [it] has been dealt with so promptly & was so well enclosed, that the likelihood of a recurrence is remote.' Ngaio was confident about her prognosis. The Balfours, Jonathan Elsom and the Steads visited her regularly in hospital, and she asked Bob to ring the McIntoshes to give them a fuller picture.

Her trip to North America was off, but she still hankered after a Jersey excursion before the depths of winter hit. Ngaio returned to Walnut Farm to convalesce. She was resilient in spite of her ordeal, and expected that life would continue unchanged. 'Will have to begin thinking about a book before too long.' Jersey might be a perfect place to start.

Before Christmas, Ngaio, Maureen Balfour and her sister-in-law hired a car to take them into London to shop for presents. Because Ngaio was frail, Maureen Balfour assigned her Dorothy, a sewing maid who had been a family retainer for years. Dorothy travelled with a medicinal flask of brandy, which she flourished whenever Ngaio wilted. 'She also accompanies me to hospital for my check-ups, similarly & quite un-necessarily equipped.' Walnut Farm was full of family for Christmas. Before festivities began they decorated the house with evergreen branches and white chrysanthemums. On Christmas Eve, they went to a carol singing and communion service. 'We came out to a brilliant night sky & a sleeping village' and Ngaio was overwhelmed by the sense of continuity and history 'that pervades this countryside'.

As her health improved, life became busier. One of the highlights towards the end of her stay was Granada Television's recording of her episode of *Crown Court*. 'Jonathan Elsom has a big part which will be fun for both of us.' A television strike interrupted rehearsals and shooting, and she thought she might have to sail before she saw it produced, but shooting of 'Evil Liver' began just in time. Her second stay with the Ballantraes had to be cancelled: 'too much involved with the making of my Crown Court play on television'. She was delighted with the result. 'They did it *very* well indeed & I do hope it finds its way out to N.Z.'

Preparations for the trip home on the *Oronsay* were exhausting, 'which is not surprising at my age after what I've been through'. But her final tests in England were clear and, amazingly, while she convalesced she had half-written a new book called *Last Ditch*, which she had begun on a brief excursion to Jersey. She dedicated the book to 'the family at Walnut Farm', to whom she was deeply grateful for their care and support. Ngaio was a surviving friend from Nelly and Tahu Rhodeses' generation and they had cared for her as if she were a parent.

'I shall leave [England] with sorrow,' she told Doris McIntosh, but there was little time to dwell on it. Almost as soon as she was back in New Zealand, Ngaio found herself involved in another production. She only just had time for the Christmas tree party, which had already been 'announced to the children & couldn't be unpicked'. Her friends were divided into two groups: those who received Christmas cards before she embarked on the show, and the remainder who received nothing at all and were 'cross'.

Jonathan Elsom had asked her to help him write and direct a show they would call *Sweet Mr Shakespeare*. Ngaio dropped everything to write and produce it in the two-week timeframe. 'It *was* worth doing. He enriched & developed his performance quite wonderfully & on the last night had his audience — including me — in tears & completely enthralled.' She was amazed at the sheer feat of memory. In 14 days he absorbed a vast script and delivered it with the intense focus of a solo performance. The show was positively reviewed at the Court Theatre, and in March 1976 it moved to Wellington for a season at Downstage. Ngaio was keen to see it travel beyond New Zealand and hoped it might tour American university campuses. She approached Dorothy Olding to help her place it with a suitable agent, but the difficulty of finding representation was an obstacle, and Elsom was already committed to Tom Stoppard's *Dirty Linen*, which was drawing good crowds in the West End. *Sweet Mr Shakespeare* was filmed for Norwegian television in 1985.

Last Ditch 'went overboard' for *Sweet Mr Shakespeare*, and its retrieval in the New Year was rocked by news of Bob Stead's suicide. Ngaio could hardly believe it. They were such close friends and she had had no inkling of what he was contemplating. Since the car accident, he had been under 'an intoxicating pressure of anxieties', but this was completely unexpected.

In spite of interruptions and shocks, the manuscript for *Last Ditch* was sent off, and she received responses in February. Edmund Cork hailed it as 'the best', and Ned Bradford's cable began 'Ngaio how you improve with age'. In reality, the manuscript had problems that required closer editing than ever before. The reader's report for Collins began, 'It's marvellous how the old campaigners keep it up', then continued to weigh up the pros and cons. At its worst it was a 'self-indulgent conversation-piece . . . Although the idiom here is resolutely modern in some ways there are fossilised relics of older days.' The plot was thin, the end anti-climactic, and murderer predictable. In its favour, the reader 'emphasised the entertainment value of an extremely accomplished performance. It is witty and civilised and amusing . . . [and] never ceases to be thoroughly enjoyable.'

Collins went ahead with publication because *Last Ditch* contained the ingredients that sold books. Ngaio had to make numerous changes, many of them the result of errors that had crept into the typescript owing to her own rewriting. In June, she received a 'very-up bucking letter from Billy Collins saying he likes "Last Ditch" as much as anything I have ever written'. She told Doris McIntosh that she was walking on air.

The book focuses on a now-adult Ricky Alleyn, who is a writer. He has escaped to one of the Channel Islands, as Ngaio had, to write a novel, and, like her, he battles insecurities.

At half past nine on that same morning, Ricky chucked his pen on his manuscript, ran his fingers through his hair and plummeted into the nadir of doubt and depression that from time to time so punctually attends upon dealers in words.

'I'm no good,' he thought, 'it's all a splurge of pretension and incompetence. I write about one thing and something entirely different is trying to emerge. Or is there quite simply nothing there *to* emerge?

But it is dealers in drugs, not words, who get Ricky into trouble. If he had stuck to his writing instead of staking out a suspected drug-dealer's hideout, he would not have been kidnapped to secure the traffickers' escape. But this is not his only lesson. Ricky also learns about infatuation when he falls for Julia Pharamond, a woman not unlike Nelly Rhodes. He is completely captivated. When they dance, he is overwhelmed by her presence. 'The stars in the sky had come reeling down into the ballroom and the sea had got into his eardrums and bliss had taken up its abode in him for the duration of the waltz.' He is in love, but Julia is a mother and a married woman.

Immediately after submitting *Last Ditch*, she wrote 'Morepork' for a collection of short stories published for the International Crime Century Year. She disliked the prospect in principle, but 'this was at the request of Julian Symons — he's a personal friend, one I like very much . . . so I felt I had to give it a go'. Symons was a doyen of murder, thriller and detective fiction, and that seems to have made her strive for something extra. 'Morepork' has a clever twist in the end. It is set in the New Zealand bush that she loved so passionately, and in her descriptions of the primal forest she finds a voice as pure as the bird songs that are being recorded by fanatic Caley Bridgeman. While he is in the forest he is murdered, and his death is made to look like an accident. Bridgeman's tape-recorder captures the voice of his killer, along with the mournful cry of the owl, or morepork, which according to Maori legend is a harbinger of death. The story was published in *Verdict of Thirteen: A Detective Club Anthology* by Faber and Faber in 1978, and by Harper and Row, in the United States, the following year.

After Ngaio sent off 'Morepork', she was free to do nothing for the first time since she returned from England, 'which is heaven'. Ngaio was an avid reader, and she and Doris McIntosh often discussed and swapped books. 'At the moment I'm re-reading Michael Holroyd's biography of Lytton Strachey.' This she followed up with Virginia Woolf's letters. Holroyd's book was 'well done', but 'Homosexuals seem to live in such a state of hectic misery & to get so little fun out of whatever antics they employ . . . one wonders they don't give it up as a bad job.' This comment undoubtedly had a real resonance for Doris, in relation to her husband, and Ngaio may have been tailoring her words for her friend's sake, but it was a statement she made at regular intervals to different people in different ways. If Ngaio were a lesbian, she could not see the point in living openly as one.

In May, she continued her respite by taking a 10-day vacation in Wellington with the McIntoshes. When she got back her cats were delighted to see her. 'Lieut. Pinkerton is on my chest with loud manifestation of approval'. Earmes Catte Esquire was delighted, too. 'Syl is in good heart & already a slave to her adopted puss — Mrs Millimant Mieux', who was known on occasions to play with Ngaio's 'two hard-case items'.

In July, Ngaio began another book. She had a 'mass of desultory notes' around her and 'about 3000 words of the first chapter'. She did not have a firm idea about how it would develop, but 'the setting (surprise, surprise) is a Kentish village'.

That same month she heard that Bernard Ballantrae had cancer of the throat and Crawsie's husband Andy had had a serious stroke. It was also around this time that she heard more sad news: Billy Collins and then Agatha Christie had died. 'I'm sure you were saddened by Agatha's death but I gather it was a blessed relief for her,' wrote Dorothy Olding. Friends were ill and dying and she herself was becoming increasingly infirm. Her cancer tests were still clear, but she had developed a cataract in the right eye. This was diagnosed immediately before the proofs for *Last Ditch* arrived. She wondered how she would manage, because she already knew these would be more demanding than usual.

Her TV appearance for the New Zealand *Encounter* programme complicated the editing process by opening a floodgate of fan mail. 'Which ranges from one lady who doesn't care for Shakespeare but is keen on me to another who merely tells me she lost (literally it seems) her husband.' The proofreading process for one book could cost her in excess of $100 just for postage. She had to shelve her new book at 18,000 words, and she found sitting over the proofs hard on her eyes.

In November a hernia was diagnosed, but Ngaio decided not to go ahead with an operation unless it was necessary. The Christmas tree party that year followed a new pattern. 'The parents are kindly getting the presents for me which saves a tiring trek around the shops.' Friends stepped in to help — parents and players like Annette Facer and Helen Homes, and old friends such as Roses, Crawsie, and Sylvia. The tree looked magnificent with its candles blazing and an Angel on top 'from Oberammergau'. 'Freddie & Eve Page's daughter [Anna Wilson] brought her little girl [Charlotte] dressed in the frock she had worn herself to the First Tree, 30 years ago.' A young Teddy Tahu Rhodes was also in attendance.

After the Christmas tree party she put herself in 'purdah' to finish her book, which was more troublesome than most. She considered abandoning it, but the idea of beginning again was more daunting than carrying on. In January 1977, Annette Facer encouraged her to participate in the South Canterbury Festival. As part of the celebrations there was a stage show, and Ngaio was convinced to read an excerpt from *David Copperfield*. 'I must say I thoroughly enjoyed myself.' Ngaio stayed at Mount Peel with her friends Kit and Jack Acland, and 'revisited old haunts'.

In April, copies of *Last Ditch* arrived from the publishers 'clad in a ridiculous jacket on which the woman in question is depicted as galloping backwards . . . having successfully cleared the ditch in which she was found dead. Honestly!' This was disappointing and so was progress on her new book. 'All things conspire against it.'

It was not long after this that Ngaio was admitted to Princess Margaret Hospital with angina and a life-threatening thrombosis. The combination was almost fatal. Someone informed the media 'with the result that this little room is a cross between a horticultural side-show & a regional post-office . . . too kind but an awful problem for poor Roses', who had to write the mountain of thank-you letters. At the end of June Ngaio was feeling better, but knew she would never have a full recovery. 'I shall have to learn to "live with it" which is better than dying of it.' Ngaio was on heavy medication that included the blood-thinning drug warfarin. It was more than a month before she was home.

After her return, she was taken to the filming of *Vintage Murder* at the refurbished Theatre Royal. It was a great thrill. 'George Baker who has been brought out to play Alleyn came to call & is a nice chap with a good voice & bags of English experience in theatre & studios'. When she saw *Vintage Murder* — along with *Colour Scheme*, *Died in the Wool* and *Opening Night*, made-for-television movies in a *Ngaio Marsh Theatre* series — she decided that they were 'thoroughly professional' in acting and production, but that 'the direction was often mistaken when it came to humour'. The humour that permeated her writing was an essential ingredient because it made what she did unique and brought it alive, but it proved elusive when conveyed dramatically. Even she found it difficult to preserve its subtleties in the stage adaptations she wrote of her own novels.

She struggled on with her health and a 'stand-up fight' with the book, while the central heating sent out volumes of 'black oily smoke' and the new 'astronomically expensive decromastic' roof leaked. 'I've had to give up my Christmas Tree Party for this year which I hate doing & cancel any other activities until I'm in the clear.' But she had finished the 'bloody book', which was with a doctor friend of Anita Muling's and Marjorie Chambers' being 'vetted for medical blunders'. The manuscript for *Grave Mistake* was duly sent off, and almost immediately Ngaio found herself committed to another short story for Julian Symons, this time for an important Crime Club compendium. With not much confidence in her short-story writing ability, she was casting around for a plot.

Bob Scott, her player turned vicar and now associate priest at St Peter's Church in Wellington, came to dinner at Marton Cottage and told her that Doris McIntosh's knees were too bad for her to attend services. Ngaio had not realized how incapacitated her friend was and begged her to come and stay for a break, or perhaps Ngaio could 'come up & hold the fort for a week', but this did not happen. She was planning a trip to England the following year, if she could find good tenants. 'I'm prepared to lend it — central heating, colour-telly, gardener & cats . . . to anybody who will be kind to the last named.'

Ngaio, who had provisionally booked a passage for March 1978, was still at Marton Cottage in April, and her attitude to 'the last named' — Lieutenant Pinkerton and Earmes Catte Esquire — was no less benign, even though they had been prime suspects in the case of a missing piece of meat. Ngaio had placed a small roast of beef in a syrupy marinade under a lid to soak for 24 hours. Later in the day she went into the kitchen, 'did a spot of figure-skating, threw my feet up towards the ceiling & crashed on the floor with sickening emphasis'. She banged her head and bruised her coccyx, but broke no bones. Thoroughly shaken, she took herself off to bed. The next day, when the housekeeper asked where the meat was, Ngaio explained that it was in marinade on the table. The mystified woman plumbed the bowl, but there was no beef to be found. A closer examination of the crime scene revealed a trail of oily marinade leading out of the kitchen into the yard. 'A BIG DOG — the Hound of the Baskervilles, presumably,' people jokingly suggested, but Ngaio suspected an inside job, until a week or so later when there was a sequel. Ngaio heard a huge crash in the kitchen. As quickly as she could, she rushed to the door 'just in time to see an enormous red Irish setter lolloping down the garden path with my delicious leg of Prime Canterbury in its maw'. The setter was caught and the cats were acquitted.

The physical jolt of her fall possibly precipitated Ngaio's next bout of illness, because not long after this she was back in Princess Margaret Hospital. Sylvia Fox wrote a reassuring note to Doris McIntosh: 'Ngaio has a delightful room & every care & attention. She likes Mr [David] Hay her heart man very much.' Ngaio was in considerable pain with her leg, and was expected to be in hospital at least another two weeks. Once again, it was a combination of thrombosis, heart problems and getting the balance of her medicine right. She was back home towards the end of May and 'ploughing' through the English proofs for *Grave Mistake*.

She was encouraged in this laborious task by the thrilling news that, along with Daphne du Maurier, she had been awarded one of crime fiction's highest awards. Elizabeth Walter wrote to her in March 1978: 'Many congratulations from us all on becoming a Grand Master of the Mystery Writers of America — an honour which I am sure is long overdue.' Ngaio was invited to collect her prize, a ceramic bust of Edgar Allan Poe, at an awards dinner in Los Angeles, but poor health made travel impossible so she received it by post. The recognition spurred her on to produce her last books under gruelling circumstances.

On both sides of the Atlantic, her publishers thought *Grave Mistake* lacked a convincing motive for the murder. 'I feel this is probably a case of you as a writer knowing exactly why,' wrote Collins's Robert Knittel, 'but having inadvertently forgotten that the poor reader doesn't have your inside knowledge.' Ngaio's response was less diplomatic and closer to the truth. She knew there were problems, but thought the trouble stemmed from the fact that the book had 'been interrupted so often by illness'. '[It] hung round my neck like the Ancient Mariner's Albatross,' she admitted to Edmund Cork. Apart from the technical problems, *Grave Mistake* was an old English cosy with the thinnest new paint job. What worked best were the parts written from experiences closest to Ngaio's heart. 'Obviously there is more than a nodding acquaintanceship between Upper Quintern & Birling,' she wrote to Maureen and John Balfour. Her descriptions of the village of Upper Quintern were richly evocative, her night scenes written as freshly as if she were stepping out again into that crystal-clear Christmas Eve.

Elizabeth Walter congratulated Ngaio on the cleverly drawn character of Verity Preston, and on the unrequited sexual static between her and suitor Nikolas Markos. 'They linger in my mind in the way that the best characters in a book so often do,' she wrote. Walter thought Ngaio had made a wise choice in leaving Verity and Nikolas buzzing but unbedded. Verity is a successful West End playwright. At the time of the murder 'she was engaged in making extremely tricky alterations to the last act of a play which, after a promising try-out in the provinces, had attracted nibbles from a London management'. This was what Ngaio had wanted first for *False Scent*, *Singing in the Shrouds* and then *When in Rome*, but her stage plays remained in the provinces. Ngaio could make it happen in fiction, however, where the destiny of a play was in the hands of the author, not a fickle English theatre management. Ngaio increased the murderer's share of the will, made his relationship with the victim knotty, and resubmitted the manuscript, with a dedication to criminal lawyer Gerald Lascelles.

For many in Christchurch, Lascelles was as mysterious and intriguing as one of Ngaio's characters. He moved in cultural circles that were theatrical and musical and therefore often fringe and bohemian, and his work as a barrister involved dealings with shady criminal characters; in conservative and suspicious Christchurch, rumours circulated. Ngaio was a fierce supporter of friends, and Gerald Lascelles was one of her best. Her dedication to him was as much a statement of solidarity as of thanks.

She had 'trudged through' proofs unwell and with reduced eyesight, so the outcome was cause for celebration. '*Grave Mistake* seems to be beating all records in the U.S.A.,' she wrote to Maureen Balfour the following year. 'It has sold 22,000 copies . . . & [is] still going strong.' The book was also taken up by the English and American Mystery Guilds, which delighted both Collins and Little, Brown — and Ngaio. Her Golden Age detective fiction had a momentum that was still going strong.

Success would have been sweeter, though, if not for family worries. Stella Mannings's second husband, after just four years together, had a series of life-threatening strokes, and she was 'very sad' to hear that Jean's second husband had died. Ngaio had helped pay for Jean's son to go to school and was distressed to think the family might be disrupted by tragedy again. Both women took respite stays with Ngaio. There was also the disturbing news that Bruce Mason had been diagnosed with cancer. Her generation was suffering, and every good moment must be cherished.

In August, Doris McIntosh sent Ngaio and Sylvia two dozen mussels. They replied in a joint thank-you note; Ngaio's contribution is in italics:

We write to thank you *jointly* for a luncheon *binge* the like of which *has never been* surpassed *or indeed equalled*. Firstly, soup *made by* Syl *of unparalleled* richness. *Next, with* brown bread & butter. *With these,* a light lager. *Being now*, up to our gunwales *& incapable* of more *we close* this effusion *repeating over* [sic] *warmest* & fullest and most grateful thanks *& blessings.*
Sylvia
Ngaio

Ngaio and Sylvia did things as a couple. They entertained, often had Anita Muling and Marjorie Chambers over for lunch or dinner, and their favourite pastimes were going out to films, the theatre or concerts. Sylvia drove at night so that Ngaio would not be housebound with her cataract.

They became stalwarts of the Court Theatre. Ngaio was particularly thrilled with Elric Hooper's directorship, and his work was a draw for them both. In private she called him the 'infant phenomenon', and thought of him as, at times, difficult and demanding, but brilliantly talented. She believed he had 'lifted the level of The Court out of all sight'. It was something she had desperately wanted to do herself, but she was generous enough to recognize, and delight in, the achievement of another.

Hooper's success at the Court was part of a blossoming of professional theatre companies in New Zealand. The demise in 1960 of Richard and Edith Campion's touring New Zealand Players had proved that the cost of moving a professional company around the country was prohibitive. As a result, the concept was largely abandoned. Wellington's Downstage opened in 1964, Auckland's Mercury in 1968, and in Christchurch the Court was established in 1971. It was the realization of Ngaio's dream of professional opportunities and standards of production in New Zealand theatre. She had hoped it could be achieved through a national theatre company, but accepted now that this was more likely to be achieved through independent urban-based professional companies.

Directing was Hooper's 'true metier & Jonathan has had shining notices for his performance in *The Millionairess* . . . & Jimmy Laurenson goes from strength to strength. So all this old bird's chicks prosper,' she told Bruce Mason.

Less pleasing was the news that a rogue American publisher had pirated 23 of her novels and was selling them illegally. She was informed of the fraud by the American Mystery Writers Association. The distressing episode became a lengthy saga of lawyers and to and fro correspondence with little resolution. 'It may turn out to be an operation of the stable-door kind,' she wrote to Doris McIntosh, and she was right.

A highlight of 1978 was a last trip in July to stay with the Dacres-Mannings family in Sydney. 'My visit to Johnny and Bet in Sydney was great fun. They are such darlings & the children are Heaven.' The purpose of the visit was to see her godson Nicholas confirmed. The trip back to New Zealand realized all of Ngaio's fears of flying. In anticipation of turbulence, before they took off the pilot warned passengers not to be concerned when the wings 'wobbled'. This was the entrée to a flight from hell. Ngaio had gastro-enteritis, which added to her difficulties. 'Drawers opened of their own accord, china crashed, everything was bouncy-bouncy', and when she arrived she was almost blown off the tarmac.

Not long after her return to Christchurch, Ngaio began a new novel. Her mobility was limited. 'One begins to wonder which bit of one is *going* to be left in something like working order.' Writing, however, was something she could do successfully. In October she wrote to Doris McIntosh: 'I'm glued to my work & see & think of little else than how to pin a plot to a group of characters . . . It's a worrying & disagreeable phase.' She hoped the novel would emerge from its misty beginnings. *Photo-Finish* proved almost as difficult to write as its predecessor. For only the fourth time in a career spanning almost 50 years, Ngaio set the story in New Zealand. She worried about the 'danger of letting it degenerate into a sort of travelogue with a crime theme pinned on to it', but she continued to write in spite of her 'usual doubts'. She planned to dedicate the book to Fred and Eve Page.

Ngaio celebrated her Christmas tree: 'Presents, visits innumerable from all my old "children" of the Shakespeare days. I find it impossible to believe that the earliest ones are approaching the 50 mark.'

Collins requested changes to the manuscript of *Photo-Finish* — they wanted four keys instead of three — but these alterations were superficial. A reader's report extolled the book's virtues, although exchanges between Alleyn and Fox were described as 'distasteful' and Alleyn's relationship with Troy 'dowsed with customary treacle':

The which said, the story is an astonishing achievement by a woman of 80 [actually, 84], and it shows her to have kept her vitality and control much longer than Agatha did. It is witty, the setting is impressive, the plot is tidily organised and the solution is dramatic. What more? . . . This is a rich and engrossing story by a professional who has not lost her cunning.

Collins wanted to publish the book as part of their Crime Club's jubilee celebrations. Ngaio's *Scales of Justice* had featured in their silver anniversary celebrations and this was a remarkable demonstration of publishing continuity. There was to be an honorary dinner on 23 April 1980, which was Ngaio's and Shakespeare's birthday and St George's Day. Fifteen senior police officers were invited, along with Crime Club authors and a heavy contingent of media. 'We had an enormous white iced cake with a huge Crime Club Gunman on it, and the words: "Collins Crime Club, 1930–1980" embossed on it in gold lettering,'

Elizabeth Walter wrote to Ngaio. Ian Chapman of Collins made a speech, Julian Symons replied, and Walter cut the cake with a huge sword. She offered to send Ngaio a slice. 'Fossilized or not,' Ngaio replied, 'I shall give my piece of cake a hearty, nostalgic munch.'

Photo-Finish was a return to better form for Ngaio. The structure was tighter, and the setting fresher for its change of air. The New Zealand outdoors provides an epic backdrop to the murder of world-famous opera singer Isabella Sommita. Television presenter Max Cryer, who visited Ngaio at Marton Cottage at this time, said she told him Isabella Sommita was based on Maria Callas, and the soprano certainly comes across as a similarly larger-than-life character. 'The lady has the temperament of a wild cat and the appetite of a hyena,' says her singing master, Signor Lattienzo.

The conventions are Golden Age — a house party at a luxurious island lodge in the middle of a fictitious South Island lake — but some of the issues are contemporary, especially that of a stalking member of the paparazzi who makes Isabella Sommita's life unbearable. She is followed relentlessly — Milan, Paris, London, New York, Sydney — and ugly gratuitous snaps were taken and published with ridiculous captions. 'The general effect [of one of the published photographs] was that of a gargoyle at the dentist's: an elderly and infuriated gargoyle. The photograph was signed Strix.' Alleyn is dispatched from England to relieve Isabella Sommita of her pursuer and, by an astonishing coincidence, Troy is commissioned to paint a portrait of the diva's benefactor, Montague V. Reece. This will be another busman's holiday.

Photo-Finish was released in September 1980, to warm reviews and pleasing sales. 'My memory is deteriorating but fortunately not, so far, in the matter of writing books & I am a happy old girl by & large,' she told John Balfour. Writing gave Ngaio purpose and kept her vital.

One of the literary challenges of 1980–81 was a revision of *Black Beech*. David Elworthy in Auckland broached the subject with Ngaio and Elizabeth Walter. Ngaio's response was that 'her life since the early fifties had been singularly dull', but she would make an attempt, and Walter replied: 'it would give me great personal pleasure to do the book, but it does need to be something more than the original modest memoir'. Ngaio tackled the gaps by adding material about her crime fiction writing and aging. She completed the 30,000-word extension in January 1981. 'It's been tricky work,' she admitted to Maureen Balfour, 'sandwiching new bits into old ones & the end result is anyone's guess.'

The additions were more revealing about Ngaio as a writer and an older woman, but did not illuminate the private psychological life that Elizabeth Walter had hoped to read more about. Ngaio had still not let her hair down.

Ironically, at the same time as she was making additions to *Black Beech*, she was systematically destroying papers. Each day her housekeeper, Joy Carter (now Wilkinson), was given piles of documents — letters, notes, handwritten manuscripts and even photographs — to take down to the incinerator to burn: 'I took arm loads each afternoon.' It was a practical endeavour that coincided with extensive renovations to the house, but it was also an expunging of the private Ngaio. She had destroyed correspondence throughout her life: this was a final purge.

It was during this time that two important records of Ngaio in her late years were saved: one was her interview for a *Kaleidoscope* television programme; the other was a series of interviews conducted by a young student, Bruce Harding, for his master's thesis in English at Canterbury University.

Harding first met Ngaio in 1977, but because of her ill health it was not until April 1978 that he began recording their conversations. He had difficulty being taken seriously. 'I certainly ran into quite a lot of academic snobbery and disdain for wishing to do a project . . . on an author who dared to dirty her hands in the commercial world of popular writing,' he recalls. He went with his topic proposal to the Head of the English Department, Professor John Garrett, 'who was originally appalled at the idea. I think I actually remember him saying: "Ngaio Marsh! After I've taught you: Keats, Wordsworth, Shelley!" ' In the end, Professor Garrett was persuaded to write a letter of introduction to Ngaio's secretary, Rosemary Greene, and an appointment was made. Harding asked Ngaio many questions about her life, and particularly her writing, which she answered candidly. The one taboo subject was the Rhodes family and their relationship to the Lampreys. Always the privacy of her intimates was paramount.

He canvassed her frustration at being marginalized by the New Zealand literati because she wrote detective fiction. She was cautious not to generalize, because significant people such as John Schroder, Allen Curnow, Maurice Shadbolt, Mervyn Thompson and Bruce Mason had supported her writing over the years. But she did think there was a prevailing provincial snobbery in New Zealand that was largely absent overseas. In Britain and the United States, academics like Ronald Knox wrote detective fiction to demonstrate their flexibility and as a diversion from their usual mode of writing. The academy's disdain of her books was a matter of contention for Ngaio. Ironically, those who dismissed her work as Anglo-centric often had a misplaced sense of superiority born of English-based academic élitism. As Harding explains: 'New Zealand literary academia was . . . I would now say, too provincial, too Neo-colonised — acting as though the concrete quadrangles of Ilam [Canterbury University] was still somehow Oxbridge'. Harding's research anticipated a scholarly interest in New Zealand popular culture, fostered by Post-Structuralism and already blossoming overseas.

Ngaio's friends were succumbing to old age. Sylvia had a frightening reoccurrence of cancer. 'She's as brave as a lion & makes nothing of it but I'm afraid things don't look at all good,' Ngaio told Doris McIntosh. Sylvia received radiation treatment in 1979, and miraculously went into remission. News of Ned Bradford's death reached Ngaio in October 1979; and sadly, less than a year before, a friend of the McIntoshes called to tell her that Alister had died. Doris was now too frail to write, so Ngaio rang instead. 'I was so happy to hear your voice sounding exactly as of old.' But she worried that her telephone calls were tiring. 'Unless you say "don't" I shall go on [ringing] from time to time.'

In the midst of disruptive renovations to add a new study and lift to her house, Ngaio began thinking about another novel. The renovations would be at 'awful expense' and she had received a crippling tax bill of $28,000 that cleaned out her savings. She needed the money and the distraction, and what she had in mind was almost a date with destiny. 'It's been in my head for years and I've always shied off it realising how difficult it would be,' she explained to Elizabeth Walter. Ngaio planned to set *Light Thickens* at her fictional Unicorn Theatre in London, with the now mid-career director Peregrine Jay and his sidekick, set designer Jeremy Jones. The murder would occur during a production of *Macbeth*. It would bring together the worlds she loved, literature and the theatre, and draw on the idea that staging *Macbeth* was bad luck.

With this in mind, she tackled her ultimate challenge.

Pistol

CHAPTER NINE

Dénouement

Peregrine stood with his back to the curtain, facing the company with whom he was about to take a journey. Always it felt like this.' This is his opportunity to direct a perfect *Macbeth*. It needs to be compact and drive quickly through to the end. It must be remorseless, like Macbeth's own slide into evil. He has cut out 'spurious' parts of the play to reveal its structure and economy. He has chosen his cast carefully and without bias. Some of them he does not like, but they are actors not friends. His Lady Macbeth oozes the sexual allure that might steel a man to murder, and his thane seems infinitely capable of it. Jeremy's set is perfect. 'It's so *right!* It's so bloody *right,*' Peregrine exclaimed when he saw the sketches.

The witches are right, too: two women and a Maori man called Rangi, who understands the mysticism of the tribe and brings the power of his ancestors to the stage. Peregrine is not superstitious, but Rangi has presence. What Peregrine wants is authenticity: to capture the essential forms and linguistic magic of the Bard. His costuming is accurate, down to the detail of the black sheepskin tunics. His fight scene, in which Macbeth is decapitated off stage, has been choreographed by an expert swordsman, Gaston Sears, who carries a real *claidheamh-mòr* on stage.

The rehearsals are exacting. Peregrine expects the best from his players, but is clear about what he wants. He talks the characters through with the actors who play them. It is as if he momentarily merges with the characters himself, and his insights are profound. He is good; they are good. He feels it, that moment in rehearsal when 'the play flashes up into a life of its own and attains a reality so vivid that everything else fades'. The life of a brilliant production is there, and all would be perfect — if it were not for the sequence of hoaxes that blister concentration and send his superstitious actors into a frenzy of crucifix kissing. There is the fake decapitated head mysteriously suspended in the king's room, then planted under a dish on the banquet table; there is the real rat's head in Rangi's witch's shopping bag; and the anonymous note that reveals nine-year-old William, who plays the son of Macduff, as the real son of a serial killer.

The play is to start on 23 April, Shakespeare's birthday, and royalty will be there on opening night. Peregrine can only pray that the prankster will take a night off, and miraculously this happens. 'AT LAST! A FLAWLESS MACBETH' sing the praises of the press: 'the best Macbeth since Olivier's and the best Lady Macbeth in living memory'. When he receives his review copy, William the child prodigy shouts, 'Mum! What's an Infant Phenomenon? Because I've avoided being one.'

How long can perfection survive the bad luck of *Macbeth*? The company plays for a month to full houses. The tension builds, foreboding and ominous, until the murder of Macbeth in *Light Thickens* seems as inevitable as Duncan's. For one last time, a murder will happen while Alleyn sits in the audience. At the end of the final duel between Macbeth and Macduff, there is a cry off stage, more action, then Gaston Sears appears with Macbeth's head held aloft on the end of his *claidheamh-mòr*. It is supposed to be a fake, but this time it drips real blood. 'The ambulance men came in and put the body into a plastic bag and the bag on a stretcher.' It is an ignominious exit for Sir Dougal Macdougal, playing the thane.

It was the most difficult book Ngaio had ever written. 'The play closes in on him. And on us,' Peregrine tells the cast. 'Everything thickens.' The same thing was happening for Ngaio. As she told John Balfour, 'It was extremely difficult & has the form of a fugue, really, with sophistications woven through the growth of the play . . . It was hell to write.' She thought, in the end, that if it appealed to anyone it would be to theatre lovers and academics rather than to her stalwart detective fiction readers.

Before she completed the manuscript, she heard the sad news that Denys Rhodes had died. Now there were only two left 'out of that most lovable family', Maureen and Teddy. Her own health was a delicate balance of cautious living and complex medication. She could not be alone at night, and, after a succession of live-in housekeepers, she had found Mrs Berens, a 'magnificent Dutchie, terribly expensive but a godsend'. Then Sylvia broke her ankle on a treacherous visit through the hedge. 'She skidded down hill on her bottom into my garden where she remained for some time wailing to us,' Ngaio explained to Maureen Balfour. As soon as she was out of hospital, on crutches and mobile, Sylvia moved in with Ngaio and they were both cared for by the devoted Mrs Berens. It was like old times. They laughed together and entertained each other with their private jokes. Sylvia spent the winter with Ngaio, then moved back to her house behind the hedge.

The Christmas tree party was at Roses and Mike Greene's that year. Just a small one, with Helen Holmes and her second husband Hamish, Marjorie Chambers and Anita Muling, Jean Esquilant (a friend of Ngaio's and the Rhodeses), Olivia Spencer Bower, and Sylvia. 'Ngaio was in great form & looking marvellous in her Chinese coat.'

She battled on with *Light Thickens* until it was finished and in the post on 7 January 1982. She dedicated the book to James Laurenson, the thane, and Helen Thomas (Holmes), his lady, in 'the University Players' third production of *Macbeth*'. The manuscript was sent with the most diffident note that had ever accompanied one of her scripts. She was not sure she had pulled it off. 'I don't know what you will think of the result,' she wrote to Elizabeth Walter. 'If you feel it really is unsatisfactory may be we just scrap it?' For the first time, Dorothy Olding considered turning it down, but in the end decided she could not. 'I've had a cable from my U.S. agent: "Little Brown very pleased with *Light Thickens* same terms as last . . . congratulations & much love".'

Ngaio was delighted, but still hovered for a response from Collins. It was a relief, though, to know that publication would go ahead in the States. The renovations had cost her '$40,195'. She needed to pay the bill, but did not 'begrudge a penny'. Marton Cottage now had the perfect study lined with books, and a lift, which meant she could stay in the house. She began organizing her diary for the year. John Dacres-Mannings was planning a visit at Easter — and Jonathan Elsom, too. 'Well, my sweetie-pie, I *do* hope you will be walking in, come April, & will like to stay here,' she wrote. The aerogramme was sealed and sent by a friend. It was probably the last letter she wrote.

On 18 February, 'Helen Holmes rang up to say Ngaio had died, which was a terrible shock,' recalls Gerald Lascelles. She had lunch, then vomited. Mrs Berens and Helen Holmes called the doctor, who could see that the end was near and decided not to admit her to hospital; he called ambulance men to help carry her to her room. She died peacefully in her own bed two hours later. Lascelles arrived soon afterwards and rang the undertaker: 'I thought, God, after a life of distinction, to end up in a black plastic bag', but this was the only way of carrying her out of the house and safely down the precipitous steps.

'The days leading up to the funeral were very demanding . . . particularly for Helen who did a magnificent stage managing job,' wrote Jean Esquilant to Jonathan Elsom. It was a sad, but strangely wonderful, experience of friends together remembering old times: Helen, Jean Esquilant, Roses Greene, Gerald Lascelles, Simon Acland, who was to take the funeral service, and Sylvia. 'There is going to be a very big gap for many of us,' Roses Greene wrote to Elsom. 'I realise it very physically everyday I sit at the desk with the empty armchair opposite.' The funeral was delayed until 26 February so that John Dacres-Mannings and his son could travel from Sydney. Jonathan Elsom was in England, and work commitments meant that he was unable to attend.

Christchurch Cathedral was packed, and Simon Acland began a eulogy that would have warmed even the blustering, dyspeptic heart of proud atheist Henry Marsh. He talked of the paradox of Ngaio Marsh, of a private, shy woman with a 'chaste reticence' who had become a public figure and touched so many lives. He talked of her contribution on the world stage and to literature, and to theatre in New Zealand, to which she had given vast amounts of time and money. The detective fiction she wrote allowed her to do this. Her gift was unstinting. 'Publicly, in her own right, Ngaio Marsh was a great person. Privately I believe she was an even greater one.' She was overwhelming in both generosity and loyalty to friends. Acland also spoke of the mystery of Ngaio's age. It was only when she died that it was discovered she was four years older than most people cconsidered her to be. But this was not Ngaio's only secret. There were others she would almost certainly take to her grave.

She spent her life writing cosy whodunits, but there is no criminal in the frame or detective to tidy up the ends in her story. Her private life remained private. Who she was physically intimate with and how she constructed and expressed those relationships will remain a mystery. The consummate crime writer is the best person in the world to destroy incriminating evidence, to litter their life with red herrings and escape detection. Ngaio wrote according to the rules of Detection Club fiction, but she lived a richly complex life that is open to diverse interpretations or readings, and embraced flux, cultural diversity, sexual ambiguity and multiple truths.

Only one person had an overview of Ngaio, and that was Sylvia Fox. She knew and loved Ngaio as no one else did. The people of Ngaio's own generation in her intimate circle were women: Nelly Rhodes, Doris McIntosh, Anita Muling, Marjorie Chambers, Olivia Spencer Bower — and Sylvia. Her private world was female, and many of the men she felt particularly drawn to were homosexual. But although Ngaio was constant in her affections and friendships, she was never exclusive. She moved between hemispheres, cultural mores, passionate relationships, artistic, literary and theatrical circles, giving something of herself to everyone, but never enough for anybody to put her in a cosy and close the book.

A typed copy of *Light Thickens* arrived at Collins on the day she died, so Elizabeth Walter never had time to respond. Perhaps that was a good thing, because as it stood the manuscript was unpublishable. Embedded in the text was an essay on the direction of *Macbeth*, which needed to be cut so that it was less intrusive. Walter worked hard to reshape it and offered her revisions to Little, Brown. 'I'm just delighted to be able to take advantage of your fine work,' the senior editor, William Phillips, responded. 'Lord knows, the book can use it. I think we all agree this is one of Ngaio's least efforts, but ironically it may be the most commercially successful.' He urged Walter to send the changes immediately because there was 'already a major book club interest'. Ironically, he was right.

Light Thickens came out in England in September 1982, to excellent reviews and record sales. 'I am delighted about this and feel the hard work on the book was well justified,' Walter wrote to Pat Cork at Hughes Massie, 'although I would have done it anyway for Ngaio Marsh.'

Light Thickens was Ngaio's final curtain.

Epilogue

After the funeral arrangements for Ngaio were made, Sylvia Fox never went inside Marton Cottage again. Deborah Walton, who lived in the still-furnished house as a tenant, used to invite her over, but she never came and Walton went through the hedge to visit her. There were too many memories that Sylvia wanted to keep untouched, and of course there was the empty armchair opposite the desk. Sylvia sold her house in December 1985, and moved into a flat at Karitane Mews in Cashmere.

About a week before Sylvia died, Richard and Ginx Fox received a telephone call from Jean Esquilant to say that the end was close and that they needed to come down to Christchurch if they wanted to be with her. She died with her family around her on 6 October 1992.

Sylvia's funeral was held at St Augustine's Anglican church in Cashmere, and Elric Hooper gave a moving and amusing tribute. He told them how he used to say to his actors in rehearsal: 'Now, remember, that seat in the front is Miss Fox's, and she will be sitting there watching you.' Sylvia's nieces Sarah and Amanda were among her pallbearers, and as they carried the casket down the aisle they saw 'a beautiful black cat sitting in one of the pews and the cat got up and led Sylvia out'.

'She was really worried about where she was going to be buried . . . It was Simon [Acland and his sister-in-law Rosemary] who reassured Sylvia that yes, of course, when she died, she could be buried where Ngaio was out at the little church at Peel Forest.' Sylvia's ashes were carried out to Peel Forest by Richard, Ginx and a group of old friends, and Rosemary Acland took the committal service.

Sylvia's headstone is beside Ngaio's in the graveyard of the Church of the Holy Innocents. They were the closest of friends, companions and neighbours in life and will be for eternity.

Play Productions

1913 Sep   *The Moon Princess* by Ngaio Marsh, and directed by Helen Burton, at the
            St Michael's School Hall, Christchurch

1922   *Little Housebound* by Ngaio Marsh. Toured to Hastings and Havelock North
            (performed in Christchurch in 1924 and 1931)

1923 Sep   *Belinda* by A.A. Milne, and *The Little Stone House* by George Calderon at Coral Hall

1924 Oct   *Bluebell in Fairyland* by Seymour Hicks for Unlimited Charities at Theatre Royal

1924 Oct   *Little Housebound* by Ngaio Marsh for Wauchop School of Drama at the Caledonian
            Hall

1925 Jul   *The Sleeping Beauty* for Unlimited Charities at Theatre Royal

1935 Oct   *Exit Sir Derek* by Ngaio Marsh and Henry Jellett for Canterbury University College
            Drama Society (CUCDS) at the Little Theatre

1938 Sep   *A Man's House* by John Drinkwater for Dunedin Repertory at His Majesty's Theatre
            in Dunedin and in Christchurch at Radiant Hall

1938 Nov   *The Late Christopher Bean* by Emlyn Williams for Dunedin Repertory at His
            Majesty's Theatre in Dunedin

1939 Mar   *The Anatomist* by James Bridie for Dunedin Repertory at His Majesty's Theatre in
            Dunedin

1940 Aug   *The Last Hour* by Charles Bennett for Ashburton Repertory at Radiant Hall

1941 Jul   *Outward Bound* by Sutton Vane for CUCDS at Little Theatre

1941 Nov   *The Soul of Nicholas Snyders* by Jerome K. Jerome for Ashburton Repertory at
            Radiant Hall

1942   *Blithe Spirit* by Noël Coward for Canterbury Repertory at Radiant Hall (Aug) and
            Wellington Repertory Theatre Society, Wellington (Dec)

1943   *The Corn is Green* by Emlyn Williams for Wellington Repertory, Wellington

1943 Aug   *Hamlet* by Shakespeare for CUCDS at Little Theatre

1943 Nov   *Hamlet* by Shakespeare for CUCDS at Little Theatre

1944 Jul   *Othello* by Shakespeare for CUCDS at Little Theatre

1944 Oct   *Distant Point* by Alexander Afinogenev for Canterbury Repertory at Radiant Hall

1944–1945   *Hamlet* and *Othello* toured by Dan O'Connor

            1944 Dec   His Majesty's Theatre, Dunedin

            1945 Jan   Town Hall Concert Chamber, Auckland

            1945 Jan   Town Hall, Wellington

            1945 Feb   Radiant Hall, Christchurch

1945 Jul   *A Midsummer Night's Dream* by Shakespeare for CUCDS at Radiant Hall

1945 Dec   *Henry V* by Shakespeare for CUCDS at Little Theatre

1946 Jul   *Macbeth* by Shakespeare for CUCDS at Radiant Hall

1947 Jan   *Macbeth* toured by Dan O'Connor

              Jan   Concert Chamber, Auckland

              Jan   Concert Chamber, Wellington

1947 Sep   *The Anatomist* by James Bridie for CUCDS at Radiant Hall

1948 Sep   *Six Characters in Search of an Author* (Act One) by Luigi Pirandello for CUCDS (private performance for The Old Vic Company at Little Theatre)

1949   *Six Characters* and *Othello* toured Australia by Dan O'Connor

              Jan   Conservatorium, Sydney

              Jan   Albert Hall, Canberra

              Feb   Union Theatre, Melbourne

1950 Nov   *Six Characters* at Embassy Theatre, Swiss Cottage

1951   British Commonwealth Theatre Company tour of Australia and New Zealand (*The Devil's Disciple* by G.B. Shaw; *Twelfth Night* by Shakespeare; and *Six Characters*)

1952 Nov   *A Sleep of Prisoners* by Christopher Fry for CUCDS at Repertory Theatre

1953 Jul   *Julius Caesar* by Shakespeare for CUCDS in the Great Hall

1956 Aug   *King Lear* by Shakespeare for CUCDS at Civic Theatre

1957 Jul   *Henry V* by Shakespeare for CUCDS at Civic Theatre

1958 Jul   *Hamlet* for CUCDS at Civic Theatre

1959 Jul   *Antony and Cleopatra* by Shakespeare for CUCDS at Civic Theatre

1962 Jul   *Macbeth* for CUCDS at Civic Theatre

1963 Jul   *Henry IV, Part 1* by Shakespeare for the CUCDS at Civic Theatre

1964 Jul   *Julius Caesar* by Shakespeare for CUCDS at Civic Theatre

1965 Apr   *Two's Company* for Canterbury Repertory at the Provincial Council Chamber

1967 Jun   *Twelfth Night* for CUCDS at the Ngaio Marsh Theatre

1969 Jun   *A Midsummer Night's Dream* for CUCDS at the Ngaio Marsh Theatre

1970 Nov   *The Magistrate* by Arthur Pinero for Canterbury Repertory

1972 Oct   *Henry V* inaugural production in the James Hay Theatre for the opening of Christchurch Town Hall

1975 Dec   *Sweet Mr Shakespeare* by Ngaio Marsh and Jonathan Elsom at the Court Theatre

Selected Bibliography

ATL   Alexander Turnbull Library

Works by Ngaio Marsh

NOVELS

A Man Lay Dead, London, Geoffrey Bles, 1934;
New York, Sheridan, 1942.

Enter a Murderer, London, Geoffrey Bles, 1935;
New York, Sheridan, 1942.

The Nursing-Home Murder (with Henry Jellett),
London, Geoffrey Bles, 1935; New York,
Sheridan, 1941.

Death in Ecstasy, London, Geoffrey Bles, 1936;
New York, Sheridan, 1941.

Vintage Murder, London, Geoffrey Bles, 1937;
New York, Sheridan, 1940.

Artists in Crime, London, Geoffrey Bles, 1938;
New York, Furman, 1938.

Death in a White Tie, London, Collins, 1938;
New York, Furman, 1938.

Overture to Death, London, Collins, 1940; New
York, Furman, 1940.

Death at the Bar, London, Collins, 1940;
Boston, Little, Brown, 1940.

Death of a Peer, Boston, Little, Brown, 1940;
published as *Surfeit of Lampreys*, London,
Collins, 1941.

Death and the Dancing Footman, Boston, Little,
Brown, 1941; London, Collins, 1942.

Colour Scheme, London, Collins, 1943; Boston,
Little, Brown, 1943.

Died in the Wool, London, Collins, 1945;
Boston, Little, Brown, 1945.

Final Curtain, London, Collins, 1947; Boston,
Little, Brown, 1947.

Swing, Brother, Swing, London, Collins, 1949;
published as *A Wreath for Rivera*, Boston,
Little, Brown, 1949

Opening Night, London, Collins, 1951;
published as *Night at the Vulcan*, Boston,
Little, Brown, 1951.

Spinsters in Jeopardy, Boston, Little, Brown,
1953; London, Collins, 1954; published as
The Bride of Death, New York, Spivak, 1955.

Scales of Justice, London, Collins, 1955; Boston,
Little, Brown, 1955.

Death of a Fool, Boston, Little, Brown, 1956;
published as *Off With His Head*, London,
Collins, 1957.

Singing in the Shrouds, Boston, Little, Brown,
1958; London, Collins, 1959.

False Scent, London, Collins, 1960; Boston,
Little, Brown, 1960.

Hand in Glove, London, Collins, 1962; Boston,
Little, Brown, 1962.

Dead Water, Boston, Little, Brown, 1963;
London, Collins, 1964.

Killer Dolphin, Boston, Little, Brown, 1966;
published as *Death at the Dolphin*, London,
Collins, 1967.

Clutch of Constables, London, Collins, 1968;
Boston, Little, Brown, 1969.

When in Rome, London, Collins, 1970; Boston,
Little, Brown, 1971.

Tied Up in Tinsel, London, Collins, 1972;
Boston, Little, Brown, 1972.

Black As He's Painted, London, Collins, 1974;
Boston, Little, Brown, 1974.

Last Ditch, London, Collins, 1977; Boston,
Little, Brown, 1977.

Grave Mistake, London, Collins, 1978; Boston,
Little, Brown, 1978.

Photo-Finish, London, Collins, 1980; Boston,
Little, Brown, 1980.

Light Thickens, London, Collins, 1982; Boston,
Little, Brown, 1982.

SHORT STORIES

Death On the Air: And Other Stories, (foreword by Susan Howatch), London, HarperCollins, 1995.

'Moonshine', in *Yours and Mine: Stories by Young New Zealanders*, ed. W. Lawrence, New Plymouth, N.Z., 1936.

'Morepork', in *Verdict of Thirteen: A Detective Club Anthology*, ed. Julian Symons, London, Faber & Faber, 1978; New York, Harper & Row, 1979.

The Collected Short Fiction of Ngaio Marsh, ed. Douglas G. Greene, New York, International Polygonics, 1989.

NON-FICTION

A Play Toward: A Note on Play Production, Christchurch, N.Z., Caxton Press, 1946.

Black Beech and Honeydew: An Autobiography, Boston, Little, Brown, 1965; London, 1966; revised edition, Collins, Auckland, 1981; London, 1982.

New Zealand (with R.M. Burden), London, Collins, 1942.

Perspectives: The New Zealander and the Visual Arts, Auckland Gallery Associates, 1960.

Play Production, Wellington, N.Z., School Publications Branch, Education Department, 1948; revised 1960.

ARTICLES

'A New Canterbury Pilgrim: Outward', *The Press*, 1 September 1928, p. 13.

'A New Canterbury Pilgrim', *The Press*, 22 September 1928, p. 13.

'A New Canterbury Pilgrim: Durban', *The Press*, 20 October 1928, p. 13.

'A New Canterbury Pilgrim: Cape Town', *The Press*, 17 November 1928, p. 13.

'A New Canterbury Pilgrim: Last Stages', *The Press*, 1 December 1928, p. 13.

'A New Canterbury Pilgrim: Vignettes of London', *The Press*, 15 December 1928, p. 17.

'A New Canterbury Pilgrim: Meandering at Monte', *The Press*, 22 December 1928, p. 13.

'A New Canterbury Pilgrim: More London Vignettes', *The Press*, 26 January 1929, p. 15.

'A New Canterbury Pilgrim: Overture and Beginners Please', *The Press*, 13 April 1929, p. 13.

'A New Canterbury Pilgrim: A Church, A Market, and a Dinner Party', *The Press*, 20 April 1929, p. 15.

'A New Canterbury Pilgrim: Pictures, Broadcasting and the Great Cold', *The Press*, 27 April 1929, p. 13.

'A New Canterbury Pilgrim: Houses, People, and Lanes', *The Press*, 18 May 1929, p. 15.

'A New Canterbury Pilgrim: Some First Impressions', *The Press*, 25 May 1929, p. 15.

'A New Canterbury Pilgrim: Oddments and Marionettes', *The Press*, 6 July 1929, p. 13.

'A New Canterbury Pilgrim: Soldiers and Politicians', *The Press*, 17 August 1929, p. 13.

'A New Canterbury Pilgrim: The Old Canterbury Pilgrimage', *The Press*, 31 August 1929, p. 13.

'A New Canterbury Pilgrim: Vignettes of Paris', *The Press*, 28 September 1929, p. 13.

'A New Canterbury Pilgrim: More Parisian Vignettes', *The Press*, 19 October 1929, p. 13.

'A New Canterbury Pilgrim: Paris: Final Vignettes', *The Press*, 9 November 1929, p. 17.

'The Background: The Novelist's Problem', *The Press*, 22 December 1934, p. 19.

'The Canterbury Pilgrim Again: Before the Coronation', *The Press*, 29 May 1937, p. 14, Reference No: 91-051, ATL, Wellington.

'The Canterbury Pilgrim Again: Departure . . . and Sydney', *The Press*, 18 September 1937, p. 13, Reference No: 91-051, ATL, Wellington.

'The Canterbury Pilgrim Again: Call at Hobart', *The Press*, 25 September 1937, p. 18, Reference No: 91-051, ATL, Wellington.

'The Canterbury Pilgrim Again: Vignettes of Melbourne', *The Press*, 2 October 1937, p. 18, Reference No: 91-051, ATL, Wellington.

'The Canterbury Pilgrim Again: Colombo', *The Press*, 9 October 1937, p. 18, Reference No: 91-051, ATL, Wellington.

'The Canterbury Pilgrim Again: More of Colombo', *The Press*, 16 October 1937, p. 18, Reference No: 91-051, ATL, Wellington.

'The Canterbury Pilgrim Again: Journey into the Past', *The Press*, 29 January 1938, p. 18, Reference No: 91-051, ATL, Wellington.

'The Canterbury Pilgrim Again: Across Belgium', *The Press*, 12 February 1938, p. 20, Reference No: 91-051, ATL, Wellington.

'Detective Fiction: "It's Tough That's What It Is," Says Ngaio Marsh', *New Zealand Listener*, 16 August 1940, p. 15.

'Commentaries: Ngaio Marsh, Theatre, A note on the status quo', *Landfall*, No. 1, March 1947, pp. 37–43.

'Shakespeare in New Zealand', *Education*, No. 1, 1948, pp. 226–30.

'National Theatre', *Landfall*, No. 3, March 1949, pp. 66–69.

'A Note on a Production of "Twelfth Night"', *Shakespeare Survey*, No. 8, 1955, pp. 69–73.

'Achievement in Fine Arts', *The Times Supplement on New Zealand*, 6 February 1963, p. vi.

'The Quick Forge', *Landfall*, No. 18, 1964, pp. 32–40.

'Stratford-on-Avon', *The Atlantic Monthly*, February 1967, pp. 116–18.

'Birth of a Sleuth', *The Writer*, April 1977, pp. 23–25.

'Roderick Alleyn', in *The Great Detectives*, ed. Otto Penzler, Boston and Toronto, Little, Brown, 1978, pp. 3–8.

'Portrait of Troy', in *Murderess Ink*, ed. Dilys Winn, New York, Workman, 1979, pp. 142–43.

'Women on Women', *Landfall*, No. 130, June 1979, p. 101.

'Remembering John Schroder 1885–1980', *Landfall*, No. 136, December 1980, pp. 406–07.

PLAYS PUBLISHED

The Christmas Tree, London, SPCK, 1962.

PLAYS UNPUBLISHED

Little Housebound, New Zealand, 1922.

Exit Sir Derek (with Henry Jellett), New Zealand, 1935.

The Wyvern and the Unicorn, 1955. The libretto for *A Unicorn for Christmas*, produced in New Zealand in 1962, was based on this play.

False Scent (with Eileen Mackay), produced 1961, United Kingdom.

Murder Sails at Midnight, produced 1972, United Kingdom.

Sweet Mr Shakespeare (with Jonathan Elsom), produced 1975, New Zealand. Produced for Norwegian Television in 1985 as *Gentle Master Shakespeare*.

TELEVISION SCRIPT

'Evil Liver', part of the *Crown Court* series, first broadcast 1975, Granada, United Kingdom and published in *The Collected Short Fiction of Ngaio Marsh*, ed. Douglas G. Greene, New York, International Polygonics, 1989.

BROADCASTS

Radio and televsion broadcasts of Ngaio Marsh are held in the archives of the BBC London, Alexander Turnbull Library Oral History Centre, Radio New Zealand Sound Archives, and New Zealand television.

UNPUBLISHED MATERIAL

St Margaret's College exercise book titled: 'Ngaio Marsh, Form V, Composition', Reference No: MSX-4075, ATL, Wellington.

Handwritten speech in exercise book entitled 'The Queerest Party: a meeting of the Detective Club', Reference No: 77-067-3/4, ATL, Wellington.

Handwritten speech in exercise book entitled 'Detective Fiction', Reference No: 77-067-3/4, ATL, Wellington.

Secondary Works

BOOKS

Acheson, Carole and Carolyn Lidgard (eds), *Return to Black Beech: Papers from a Centenary Symposium on Ngaio Marsh 1895–1995*, Christchurch, University of Canterbury, 1996.

Allingham, Margery, *The Crime at Black Dudley*, London, Heinemann, 1929, this edition, 1967.

Bowen, Stella, *Drawn from Life: A memoir*, 1940, this edition (introduction by Julia Loewe), Sydney, Picador, 1999.

Brabazon, James, *Dorothy L. Sayers: A biography*, New York, Charles Scribner's Sons, 1981.

Brown, John Russell (ed.), *The Oxford Illustrated History of Theatre*, Oxford and New York, Oxford University Press, 1995.

Capote, Truman, *In Cold Blood: A true account of multiple murder and its consequences*, Australia, Penguin, 2006.

Christie, Agatha, *Agatha Christie: An autobiography*, London, HarperCollins, 1993.

Christie, Agatha, *Death on the Nile*, London and Glasgow, Fontana, 1978.

Christie, Agatha, *The Murder at the Vicarage*, London and Glasgow, Fontana, 1963.

Coleman, Terry, *Olivier: The authorized biography*, New York, Henry Holt, 2005.

Conan Doyle, *The Complete Sherlock Holmes*, New York, Gramercy Books, 2002.

Curnow, Allen, *Look Back Harder: Critical writings 1935–1984*, (ed. Peter Simpson), Auckland, Auckland University Press, 1987.

Gatrell, V.A.C., *The Hanging Tree: Execution and the English people 1770–1868*, Oxford and New York, Oxford University Press, 1994.

Grayland, Eugene, *More Famous New Zealanders*, Christchurch, Whitcombe & Tombs, 1972.

Hale, Kathleen, *A Slender Reputation: An autobiography*, London, Frederick Warne, published by the Penguin Group, 1994.

Haycraft, Howard, *Murder for Pleasure: The life and times of the detective story*, London, Peter Davis, 1942.

Haycraft, Howard (ed.), *The Art of the Mystery Story: A collection of critical essays*, New York, Biblo & Tannen, first published 1946, 1976.

Herbert, Rosemary (ed.), *The Oxford Companion to Crime & Mystery Writing*, New York and Oxford, Oxford University Press, 1999.

Hill, Reginald and H.R.F. Keating (eds), *Crime Writers: Reflections on crime fiction*, London, BBC, 1978.

Holmes, Richard, *Footsteps: Adventures of a romantic biographer*, London, Flamingo, 1986.

Holmes, Richard, *Sidetracks: Explorations of a romantic biographer*, London, HarperCollins Publishers, 2000.

Holroyd, Michael, *Works on Paper: The craft of biography and autobiography*, London, Little, Brown, 2002.

Hume, Fergus, *The Mystery of a Hansom Cab* (introduction by Simon Caterson), Melbourne, Text Publishing, 1999.

Keating, H.R.F., *The Bedside Companion to Crime*, London, Michael O'Mara Books, 1989.

Kirker, Anne, *New Zealand Women Artists: A survey of 150 years*, Sydney, Craftsman House, 1993.

Lewis, Margaret, *Ngaio Marsh: A life*, Wellington, Bridget Williams Books, 1991.

Malcolm, Janet, *The Silent Woman: Sylvia Plath and Ted Hughes*, London, Picador, 1994.

Mann, Jessica, *Deadlier Than the Male: An investigation into feminine crime writing*, Newton Abbott, David & Charles, 1981.

Modjeska, Drusilla, *Exiles at Home: Australian women writers 1925–1945*, Sydney, Sirius and Angus & Robertson, 1981.

Norman, Philip, *Douglas Lilburn: His life and music*, Christchurch, Canterbury University Press, 2006.

Olivier, Laurence, *Confessions of an Actor: An autobiography*, London, Weidenfeld & Nicolson, 1982.

Orwell, George, *Decline of the English Murder: and other essays*, London, Penguin (first published 1946), 1965.

Poe, Edgar Allan, *Forty-Two Tales*, London, Octopus Books, 1979.

Poe, Edgar Allan, *Great Short Works of Edgar Allan Poe*, (ed. G.R. Thompson), New York, Harper & Row, 1970.

Poe, Edgar Allan, *The Fall of the House of Usher and Other Writings*, (ed. David Galloway), London, Penguin, 2003.

Rahn, B.J. (ed.), *Ngaio Marsh: The woman and her work*, The Scarecrow Press, New Jersey and London, 1995.

Sayers, Dorothy, *A Matter of Eternity: Selections from the writings of Dorothy L. Sayers*, (ed. Rosamond Kent Sprague), London, A.R. Mowbray, 1973.

Sayers, Dorothy, *Creed or Chaos? Why Christians must choose either dogma or disaster (or, why it really does matter what you believe)*, London, Hodder & Stoughton, 1940.

Sayers, Dorothy and Robert Eustace, *The Documents in the Case*, London, Victor Gollancz, 1935.

Sayers, Dorothy, *The Greatest Drama Ever Staged*, London, Hodder & Stoughton, 1938.

Sayers, Dorothy L., *Whose Body?* New York, HarperCollins, 1995.

Seager, Madeleine, *Edward William Seager: Pioneer of mental health*, Waikanae, The Heritage Press, 1987.

Slate McDorman, Kathryne, *Ngaio Marsh*, Boston, Twayne, 1991.

Strachey, Lytton, *Eminent Victorians*, London, Bloomsbury, 1988.

Strange, Glyn, *The Little Theatre: Golden years of the New Zealand stage*, Christchurch, Clerestory Press, 2000.

Symons, Julian, *Bloody Murder — From the Detective Story to the Crime Novel: a history*, London, Faber & Faber, 1972.

The Listener: Bedside Book, (ed. Mary Crockett, Paul Little and Terry Snow), Auckland, Wilson & Horton, 1997.

Thompson, Mervyn, *All My Lives*, Christchurch, Whitcoulls, 1980.

Wagstaff, Vanessa and Stephen Poole, *Agatha Christie: A reader's companion*, London, Aurum Press, 2006.

Winn, Dilys (ed.), *Murderess Ink: The better half of the mystery*, New York, Bell Publishing, 1979.

ARTICLES

Acheson, Carole, 'Cultural ambivalence: Ngaio Marsh's New Zealand detective fiction', *Journal of Popular Culture*, 19(2), 1985, pp. 149–73.

Chandler, Raymond, 'The simple art of murder', *The Atlantic Monthly*, Vol. CLXXIV, July–December 1944, pp. 53–59.

Dart, William, 'A Unicorn for Christmas: A right royal opera', *Music in New Zealand*, 1988/89, Summer, pp. 6–13, 41.

'Edward Seager — pioneer therapist', *New Zealand Heritage*, Vol. 2, pp. 623–26.

Greener, Leslie, 'Rhona Haszard', *Art in New Zealand*, No. 17, September 1932, pp. 18–21.

Harding, Bruce, 'In memoriam: Dame Ngaio Marsh 1899–1982', *Landfall*, No. 142, June 1982, pp. 242–45.

Harding, Bruce, 'Ngaio Marsh', in *Mystery and Suspense Writers: The literature of crime, detection, and espionage*, Vol. 2, (ed. Robin W. Winks), New York, Charles Scribner's Sons, 1998.

Harding, Bruce, 'The New Zealand stories of Ngaio Marsh', *Landfall*, No. 144, December 1982, pp. 447–60.

Hearnshaw, Vickie and Julie King, 'Ngaio Marsh painting', *Art New Zealand*, No. 78, Autumn 1996, pp. 76–79.

Hill, Richard S. 'Worthington, Arthur Bently 1847–1917', *Dictionary of New Zealand Biography*, updated 22 June 2007, URL: http://www.dnzb.govt.nz/

James, P.D., 'A life of crime', *Independent Magazine*, September 1989, Vol. 56, pp. 50–53.

James, P.D., 'From puzzle to novel', from Reginald Hill and H.R.F. Keating (eds.), *Crime writers: Reflections on crime fiction*, London, BBC, 1978.

Mason, Bruce, 'In memoriam: Dame Ngaio Marsh 1899–1982', *Landfall*, No. 142, June 1982, pp. 241–42.

Mason, Bruce (ed.), 'Brigid Lenihan', *Act*, Wellington, Downstage Theatre, Nov/Dec 1970, pp. 6–9.

McCredie, Paul, 'A literary life', *NZ House & Garden*, April 1998, pp. 73–81.

McEldowney, Dennis, '*Black Beech and Honeydew: An Autobiography.* Ngaio Marsh', *Landfall*, No. 79, September 1966, pp. 294–96.

Norman, Julie, 'Mystery writer shifts to *Othello*: portrait of Ngaio Marsh', *Christian Monitor*, 26 March 1949, p. 12.

Shadbolt, Maurice, 'Dame Ngaio Marsh: Shakespearian Queen of Crime', *Reader's Digest*, Vol. 101, January 1973, pp. 34–39.

Stevens, Joan, 'Ngaio Marsh: artist in crime', *New Zealand Listener*, 8 May 1972, p. 13, Reference No: 77-067-3/4, ATL, Wellington.

Thompson, Mervyn, 'On the death of Ngaio Marsh', *Landfall*, No. 144, December 1982, pp. 442–46.

Watt, J.O.P., 'Ngaio Marsh novelist with versatile gifts', *The Sunday Times*, 25 January 1947, n.p., Reference No: 77-067-3/4, ATL, Wellington.

W.G.S., 'Descended from pirates: Ngaio Marsh', *Books and Bookmen*, June 1960, pp. 7–9.

UNPUBLISHED MANUSCRIPTS

Catchpole, Julie, 'The Group', MA thesis, University of Canterbury, 1984.

Greene, Rosemary, 'Ngaio, the Writer — As Seen From a Secretary's Viewpoint', speech given at the 'Return to Black Beech: Centenary Symposium on Ngaio Marsh 1895–1995', Christchurch, 1995, n.p.

Gibbs, Rowan and Richard Williams, 'Ngaio Marsh: A bibliography', Scunthorpe, 1990.

Harding, Bruce, 'The Janus Problem: A search for patterns in life and fiction of Dame Ngaio Marsh', MA thesis, University of Canterbury, 1979.

James, P.D., 'P.D. James on Ngaio Marsh', an address given by the Baroness James of Holland Park on the centenary of Ngaio Marsh's birth, London, 27 April 1995.

Pitts, Pricilla with Evelyn Page, extract from an interview conducted at the artist's home in Thorndon, Wellington, May 1982.

INTERVIEWS

Bell, Brian, interview with author, Sydney, 3 October 2007.

Crabtree (*née* Mannings), Jean, interview with author, Tauranga, 26 August 2007.

Dacres-Mannings, John, interview with author, Sydney, 4 October 2007.

Douglass, Malcolm and Judie, interview with author, Christchurch, 14 July 2007.

Elsom, Jonathan, interview with author, Sydney, 6 October 2007.

Facer, Annette, interview with author, Warrington, 16 July 2007.

Farquhar, David, interview with Douglas Munro, Wellington, 25 May 2001.

Fox, Richard and Ginx, interview with author, Turangi, 9 December 2007.

Greene, Rosemary, interview with author, Christchurch, 11 July 2007.

Harding, Bruce, interview with author, Christchurch, 21 March 2007.

Harding, Bruce, voice recording, 'Reflections on Ngaio Marsh (and interviews with Ngaio Marsh, 7 and 24 April 1978)', Christchurch, 23 December 2007.

Hooper, Elric, interview with author, Christchurch, 21 March 2007.

Lascelles, Gerald, interview with author, Christchurch, 19 December 2007.

Laurie, Alison, interview with author, Paikakariki, 10 February 2008.

Mannings, Roy, interview with author, Tauranga, 8 February 2008.

McVeigh, Cilla, interview with author, Christchurch, 12 July 2007.

Munro, Donald, interview with author, Wellington, 22 November 2007.

Scott, Bob, interview with author, Auckland, 27 February 2007.

Walton, Deborah, interview with author, Renwick, 9 July 2007.

Webb (*née* Reay), Barbara, interview with author, Christchurch, 23 March 2007.

Wilkinson [Carter], Joy, interview with author, Golden Bay, 7 July 2007.

Wilson, Charlotte, interview with author, Wellington, 12 July 2006.

PERIODICALS

New Zealand Listener, 1940–1982.

Art in New Zealand, 1928–1947.

INTERNET WEBSITES

http://www.ccc.govt.nz/Christchurch/Heritage/ChristchurchOverviewHistory

Project/Christchurch Overview History Draft Report, Part 06.pdf

http://library.christchurch.org.nz/Heritage/Chronology/Year/1897.asp

Notes

AAG   Auckland Art Gallery

AF   Annette Facer

ATL   Alexander Turnbull Library, Wellington

BB   *Black Beech and Honeydew*

CAG   Christchurch Art Gallery

DM   Doris McIntosh

DO   Dorothy Olding

EW   Elizabeth Walter

GL   Gerald Lascelles

HC   HarperCollins

JB   John Balfour

JE   Jonathan Elsom

JS   John Schroder

MB   Maureen Balfour

NCP   New Canterbury Pilgrim, articles for *The Press*

NM   Ngaio Marsh

NZL   *New Zealand Listener*

Chapter One

A Cradle in a Grave

13 **[smell] of damp newsprint** NM, 'Birth of a Sleuth', *The Writer*, April 1977, p. 23.

14 **I couldn't put it down** *BB*, p. 217.

16 **Graham's became the world's** Haycraft, *Murder for Pleasure*, pp. 3–4.

17 **After 18 years** Ibid, p. 29.

17 **In fact, crime writer** Symons, *Bloody Murder*, p. 54.

18 **Taking everything into consideration** Haycraft (ed.), *The Art of the Mystery Story*, p. 89.

18 **I tried to get it published** Quoted in Hume, *The Mystery of a Hansom Cab*, p. vii.

19 **It is my belief, Watson** Conan Doyle, *The Complete Sherlock Holmes*, p. 138.

21 **When I was dissatisfied** Quoted in Mann, *Deadlier Than the Male*, pp. 84–85.

25 **the Fairy Godmother** Haycraft, *Murder for Pleasure*, p. xxi.

25 **I thought it would be fun** 'Dame Ngaio: Detective fiction writer', 10 Mar 1978, BBC, British Sound Archives, British Library, London.

25 **attractive, civilised man** NM, 'Birth of a Sleuth,' p. 24.

26 **When the moralists** Mann, *Deadlier Than the Male*, p. 209.

26 **perfect specimen** 'A Passionate Affair: Ngaio Marsh', 29 May 2001, BBC, British Sound Archives, British Library, London.

26 **she exemplifies** Mann, *Deadlier Than the Male*, pp. 221, 224, 226.

26 **a looker on** 'Ngaio Marsh: London revisited', 26 Sep 1949, BBC, British Sound Archives, British Library, London.

27 **I guess I fell in love** 'Dame Ngaio: Detective fiction writer'.

27 **We were bewilderingly gay** *BB*, p. 200.

28 **bandwagon . . . 'rebore' and fresh 'coat of paint'** *BB*, pp. 166, 197.

29 **I know of no experience** NCP, 1 Sep 1928, p. 13.

29 **a queer little backwater** Bowen, *Drawn from Life: A memoir*, Sydney, Picador, 1999, p. 4.

29 **They are brilliantly painted** NCP, 1 Sep 1928, p. 13.

30 **The audience at the opera** NCP, 22 Sep 1928, p. 13.

30 **Australians who wanted** Ibid.

31 **I remember Mr J H Curle's contention** NCP, 20 Oct 1928, p. 13.

31 **aboriginals who have seen** NCP, 22 Sep 1928, p. 13.

31 **a grinning kaffir boy** NCP, 20 Oct 1928, p. 13.

32 **There seems to have been no thought** BB, p. 189.

32 **old Curfew bell** NCP, 17 Nov 1928, p. 13.

32 **Just before dawn** BB, p. 195.

32 **There is the same fascination here** NCP, 15 Dec 1928, p. 17.

33 **This, Londoners say** Ibid.

33 **As we gathered way** NCP, 18 May 1929, p. 15.

33 **A domestic roulette** BB, p. 204.

33 **grey and nasty** NCP, 22 Dec 1928, p. 13.

34 **baby blues and pinks,** BB, p. 206.

34 **Roulette in extremis** NCP, 22 Dec 1928, p. 13.

34 **I usually start with a group of people** 'Dame Ngaio: Detective fiction writer'.

34 **She is over middle-age** NCP, 22 Dec 1928, p. 13.

35 **entirely new to me** BB, p. 208.

35 **We chose a table** Ibid, p. 207.

35 **We separated** Ibid.

35 **[Christchurch . . . rumours]** Information from conversations with Bruce Harding (21 Mar 2007) and Gerald Lascelles (22 Mar 2007).

35 **[They] called us** NCP, 22 Dec 1928, p. 13.

35 **I suddenly found** BB, p. 209.

36 **We are in the middle** NCP, 27 Apr 1929, p. 13.

36 **thin morning mist** NCP, 25 May 1929, p. 15.

36 **crammed with rich cars** NCP, 27 Apr 1929, p. 13.

36 **some extremely humble job** BB, p. 25.

36 **The verger** NCP, 20 April 1929, p. 13.

37 **richly turned-out automaton** NCP, 6 Jul 1929, p. 13.

37 **The Sultan of Zanzibar** NCP, 17 Aug 1929, p. 13.

37 **environs of Paris** NCP, 28 Sep 1929, p. 13.

37 **is the biggest room** NCP, 9 Nov 1929, p. 17.

38 **I have become a shopkeeper** NCP, 'Shops, Houses and Theatres', [undated cutting, c. 1930], MS-Group-1635, ATL, Wellington.

38 **In respect of dogs** BB, p. 211.

38 **We became slightly less amateurish** Ibid, p. 212.

39 **raked by a cold wind** NCP, 20 Apr 1929, p. 13.

39 **I saw a dramatization** BB, p. 202.

39 **students, labourers** Ibid.

40 **demand that the drama** Brown (ed.), *The Oxford Illustrated History of Theatre*, p. 390.

40 **smell of the West End** BB, p. 196.

40 **'Uncles' was the smart** Ibid, p. 202.

40–41 **Sometimes the Prince of Wales** Ibid, p. 201.

42 **a number of secretaryships** Ibid, p. 213.

43 **at the top of his formidable** Ibid, p. 133.

43 [Tokareff's death] Peter Tokareff, J 46, cor1919/1272, Archives New Zealand, Wellington.

Chapter Two

The Theatre of Death

44 cruelly and as excruciatingly *BB*, p. 220.

45 The roof leaked 'Edward Seager — pioneer therapist', *New Zealand Heritage*, Vol. 2, p. 625.

45 Puck-like *BB*, pp. 28–29.

47 'They aren't really fighting Ibid, p. 32.

47 [International Exhibition] The International Exhibition was held at Hagley Park, the venue costing £90,000 to construct, and the event attracting 1,900,000 visitors over a six-month period. The site included an art gallery, concert hall, machinery hall, fernery, and Maori pa complete with fortifications.

47 [Dickens books] Harding, 'The Janus Problem', unpubl MA thesis, University of Canterbury, 1979, pp. 16–19.

48 From the beginning *BB*, p. 49.

49 How superb Ibid, p. 37.

49 We bought a tin Ibid, p. 53.

49 had a poor ear Ibid, p. 62.

50 To say that I took Ibid, p.71.

50 Eng. Lit. Ibid, pp. 74–75.

51 To my amazement Ibid, p. 76.

51 I showed it to my friends Ibid, p. 81.

52 Is there such a thing Ibid, p. 173.

52 Whatever I may write Ibid, pp. 32–33.

52 on a warm evening Ibid, p. 219.

52 Most of us Ibid, p. 220.

53 with his hand shaking Ibid, p. 220.

54 Mr. Marsh's manipulation Quoted in Bruce Harding, 'Ngaio Marsh', *Mystery and Suspense Writers: The literature of crime, detection, and espionage*, Vol. 2, (ed. Robin W. Winks), Charles Scribner's Sons, 1998.

54 trying to get the smell *BB*, p. 220.

56 If you long above everything Ibid, p. 215.

57 [When] we built a hut Ibid, p. 221.

58 [The Canterbury Society of Arts] Kirker, *New Zealand Women Artists*, p. 64.

58 [fellow pupils] Canterbury College School of Art: Evelyn Page enrolled in 1915, Rata Lovell-Smith in 1917, Rhona Haszard in 1919.

58 Life at an Art School *Southland Girls' High School Magazine*, 1921.

59 a lithe, slim figure Greener, 'Rhona Haszard — her tragic death: youth at the threshold of fame', *New Zealand Free Lance*, 4 Mar 1931, E. H. McCormick Research Library, AAG.

59 It had never occurred to me *BB*, p. 98.

59 [Ngaio's awards] Canterbury College School of Art Records, School of Fine Arts Library, University of Canterbury.

59 [Ngaio's exhibitions] Hearnshaw and King, 'Ngaio Marsh painting', *Art New Zealand*, No. 78, Autumn 1996, p. 79.

59 It was a *tiny* room Extract from an interview conducted by Pricilla Pitts with Evelyn Page in May 1982 at the artist's home in Thorndon, Wellington.

60 There [was no] deliberate attitude Catchpole, 'The Group', unpublished MA thesis, University of Canterbury, 1984, p. 5.

60 **We invited** Pitts interview with Page, May 1982. Quoted in Catchpole, 'The Group', p. 3.

61 **[Ngaio's exhibitions]** Hearnshaw and King, 'Ngaio Marsh painting', p. 79.

62 **I spent three months** *BB*, p. 221.

63 **startlingly realistic** Ibid, p. 222.

63 **An actress** Ibid, p. 223.

64 **the imposing Temple of Truth** Richard S. Hill, 'Worthington, Arthur Bently 1847–1917', *Dictionary of New Zealand Biography*.

65 **To this day** *BB*, p. 14

65 **Death is never** James, 'P.D. James on Ngaio Marsh', an address given by Baroness James of Holland Park on the centenary of Ngaio Marsh's birth, London, 27 Apr 1995, p. 3.

67 **The opening night of** *Hamlet* *BB*, p. 123.

68 **I obtained the address** Ibid, pp. 127–28.

68 **Your father** Ibid, pp. 134–35.

69 **On a warm autumn morning** Ibid, p. 136.

69 **I learnt how actors** Ibid, p. 142.

69 **Without knowing it** Ibid, p. 153.

69–70 **I, however, persisted** Ibid, p. 147.

70 **On a wet night** Ibid, p. 154.

70 **It wasn't easy** Ibid, pp. 155–56.

70 **I heard myself saying** Ibid, p. 156.

70 **She was unable to discover** Ibid, p. 157.

71 **My mother must have** Ibid, p. 161.

71 **Jimmy discovered** Ibid.

71 **There were to be other tours** Ibid, p. 154.

71–72 **[Susan Max]** 'Dame Ngaio: detective fiction writer'.

73 **Readers in the golden years** James, 'P. D. James on Ngaio Marsh', p. 2.

73 **On my return** Ibid, p. 228.

Chapter Three

Companions in Crime

76 **It started off rather grandly** 91-051, ATL, Wellington.

78 **I get a feeling** 'A Passionate Affair: Ngaio Marsh', 29 May 2001, BBC, British Sound Archives, British Library, London.

78 **talk about 'well-written' mysteries** Wilson, 'Who cares who killed Roger Ackroyd?', *The New Yorker*, 20 Jan 1945; quoted in Haycraft, *The Art of the Mystery Story*, p. 395.

78 **There must be no** Wright, 'Twenty rules for writing detective stories', *The American Magazine*, Sep 1928; quoted in Haycraft, *The Art of the Mystery Story*, pp. 189–90.

80 **I always tried** Winn (ed.), *Murderess Ink*, p. 142.

80 **I wanted to be told flatly** *BB*, p. 99.

82 **I enjoyed best the nights** Ibid, pp. 100–01.

83 **Mr Wallwork was pushing** Olivia Spencer Bower Papers, Archives, CAG Te Puna o Waiwhetu.

84 **On the road outside Camberley** NM, 'The Canterbury Pilgrim Again: Before the Coronation', *The Press*, 29 May 1937, p. 14.

86 **Where Conan Doyle** Hume, *The Mystery of a Hansom Cab*, pp. xiii–xiv.

88 **[execution information]** Gatrell, *The Hanging Tree*, pp. 589–611, 618–19.

89 *Death in a White Tie* might have been called Winn, *Murderess Ink*, p. 143.

90 this officer is keen Edward Griffith Bristed, WW1 6/1786, Archives New Zealand, Wellington.

91 We said at the beginning [and following] 'The Canterbury Pilgrim Again: Journey into the Past', *The Press*, 29 Jan 1938, p. 18.

92 It is difficult to order [and following] 'The Canterbury Pilgrim Again: Across Belgium', *The Press*, 12 Feb 1938, p. 20.

95 They even bathed to orders Manuscript for radio broadcast, St Margaret's College Archive, Christchurch.

96 Miss Marsh is a novelist [and following reviews] MSX-2741, ATL.

97 a terrible bore [and following quotes] Ibid.

97 a series hero Mann, *Deadlier Than the Male*, p. 109.

99 She has excelled herself Wagstaff and Poole, *Agatha Christie: A reader's companion*, p. 137.

101–02 Although I would have considerable difficulty [and following reviews] MSX-2741, ATL.

103 not Miss Marsh's metier MSX-2741, ATL.

103–104 Fox represents Slate McDorman, *Ngaio Marsh*, p. 92.

104 For days on end *BB*, p. 232.

105 The itch for travel Manuscript for radio broadcast, St Margaret's College Archive, Christchurch.

Chapter Four

Death Down Under

107 There can be no doubt *BB*, p. 164.

108 'Poor lassie! Seager, *Edward William Seager*, p. 27.

108 carriages and gigs *BB*, p. 36.

108–09 After the final performance Ibid, p. 166.

109 lived on a scale Ibid, p.167.

109–10 While the Lampreys Ibid, p. 169.

114 Her strongest card MSX-2741, ATL.

115 Her own personal performances 'Lords of lethal weapons: Ngaio Marsh meets the Detection Club,' *NZL*, 29 Mar 1940, p. 55; 'Detective fiction: "It's tough, that's what it is," says Ngaio Marsh', *NZL*, 16 Aug 1940, p. 15.

115 Miss Marsh is Detected 'Miss Marsh is Detected . . .', *NZL*, 9 Aug 1940, p. 31.

115 Not only will this detective novel 'Ngaio Marsh to read her new thrill at 2YA,' *NZL*, 7 Feb 1941, p. 9.

115 *Surfeit of Lampreys* was played to 2YA: 'Around the Nationals', *NZL*, 27 Jun 1941, p. 24.

115 a new series of talks 'Crime is her subject: a parlour game began it', *NZL*, 4 Dec 1942, p. 13.

117 She was a strong woman Crabtree interview with author.

118 Although the puzzle is intricate [and following reviews] MSX-2741, ATL.

119 there are no dull Chandler, 'The simple art of murder', *The Atlantic Monthly*, vol. CLXXIV, Jul–Dec 1944, p. 57.

119 It is the same careful Ibid., p. 56.

120 Hammett took murder Ibid., p. 58.

120 ran about the hills *BB*, p. 234.

120 I could see Ibid, p. 235.

120–21 Why have they left NM with Burden, *New Zealand*, p. 13.

121 When white-skinned men Ibid., p. 16.

121 The strong have Ibid., p. 27.

121 In some ways Ibid., pp. 7, 30.

121 New Zealand stands Ibid., p. 34.

122 but Pohutukawa Ibid., p. 47.

123 I experienced . . . absolute happiness *BB*, p. 90.

123 the girls could rid Ibid, p. 94.

123 I do not know Ibid, p. 95.

124 our presence here Ibid, p. 94.

125 We were plunged Ibid, pp. 106–07.

125 a straggle of huts Ibid, p. 108

125 I did a painting Ibid, p. 114

125 We learned about the behaviour Ibid, p. 115.

126 very pretty woman Ibid, p. 120.

126 To find such a slice NM and Burden, *New Zealand*, p. 8.

126–27 I confess it was [and following review] MSX-2741, ATL.

130–31 marvellous sense of comedy Ibid.

133 [Hers] was very much the Edwardian psyche Crabtree interview with author.

133 Anyone could take her down Ibid.

134 When you took literature Dacres-Mannings interview with author.

135 the multiple role Carole Acheson, 'Cultural ambivalence', p. 170.

136 Well I can't keep on lugging 'Dame Ngaio: detective fiction writer', 10 Mar 1978, BBC, British Sound Archives, British Library, London.

136 *Died in the Wool*, though competent MSX-2741, ATL.

Chapter Five

A Stage Set for Tragedy

139 at the end of each line Strange, *The Little Theatre*, pp. 79–80.

140 'Hamlet' — in modern dress MSY-2397, ATL.

141 open on a Monday night Norman, *Douglas Lilburn*, p. 118.

141 The good Ngaio Quoted in Strange, *The Little Theatre*, p. 87.

141 the very breath MSY-2397, ATL.

142 This was the beginning *BB*, p. 243.

143 I wasn't very good at reading Webb (*née* Reay) interview with author.

143 coterie of young men Webb interview.

144 Just imagine Quoted in Strange, *The Little Theatre*, p. 91.

144 We had three acting 'Acting in self-defence: New Zealand makes its own plays', *NZL*, 8 Sep 1944, p. 11.

144–45 seats for the whole [and following reviews] MSY-2397, ATL.

145 submissive to the meaning Ibid.

145 I was walking through town Ibid.

145 he stepped up the tempo Quoted in Strange, *The Little Theatre*, pp. 9–10.

145 the G.O.M. 'Acting in self-defence', p. 11.

146 Some friends are coming Ibid, p. 11.

147 Miss Marsh's imagery [and following review] MSY-2397, ATL.

148 He could be a tyrant Dacres Manning interview with author.

148 It was the first of many such occasions BB, p. 147.

149 For fully five minutes [and following reviews] MSY-2397, ATL.

149 an enormous contribution Strange, The Little Theatre, p. 106.

149 I was put in the Railway Hotel Webb interview.

150 it was done in like manner [and following letters] MSY-2397, ATL.

151 Miss Ngaio Marsh's Hamlet MSY-2397, ATL.

152 For who in the cast MSY-2397, ATL.

154 Great green eyebrows Ibid.

154 As before, in the Drama Society's Ibid.

155 [Max McGlashan and screwdriver] Strange, The Little Theatre, p. 119.

156 Settings almost stark in their simplicity [and following material] MSY-2397, ATL.

156 These notes, too slight for dedication NM, A Play Toward, n.p.

157 series of spoken movements Ibid, p. 12.

157 infinitely variable Ibid, pp. 26–27.

157 The producer's script Ibid, p. 20.

157 Don't snap Ibid, p. 25.

157 If you can't make Ibid, pp. 8–9.

158 the kind . . . on which Hooper, 'Ngaio Marsh: A life for the theatre', Return to Black Beech, Acheson and Lidgaurd (eds), p. 12.

158 real objects possessing Bushnell, 'The most ephemeral of the arts', Return to Black Beech, p. 87.

161 Another of Ngaio's delightful who-dun-its [and following reviews] MSY-2397, ATL.

162 It would be impossible Wilson, 'Who cares who killed Roger Ackroyd?', The New Yorker, 20 Jan 1945; quoted in Haycraft, The Art of the Mystery Story, p. 395.

162 The local colour in these books 'Great critics have their allergies: a defence of the detective story', NZL, 19 Oct 1945, p. 13.

162–63 I think that the character 'Is the detective story dying?', NZL, 17 Oct 1947, p. 8.

164 I fairly took to the country [and all following Henry Marsh memoir quotes] MS-Group-1635, ATL.

165 children, unreproved BB, p. 60.

166 was keen on detective stories Margaret Fox, 'Ngaio Marsh', The Press, 30 Nov 1955, p. 15.

166 Ngaio left me in charge Crabtree interview with author.

167 Why are you, Coleman, Olivier, p.191.

167 the tour was a grand gesture Ibid, p. 191.

167 Over, God be praised Ibid, p. 200.

167 You may not realise it Ibid, p. 200.

168–69 The entire power Email from Alistair Johnson to author, 20 Dec 2007.

169 At the end [of the performance] Email from Harry Atkinson to author, 3 Dec 2007.

169 I soared into the sky Coleman, *Olivier*, p. 201.

169 She has star quality NM, in Mason, 'Brigid Lenihan', p. 7.

170 the right air MSX-2741, ATL.

171 far more interesting and compelling Ibid.

171 People sat in Collins Street Quoted in Strange, *The Little Theatre*, pp. 157–58.

Chapter Six

The Marsh Million Murders

172–73 I am always asked *BB*, pp. 252–53.

173 They guarantee 175,000 copies Memo to NM, 21 Jul 1943, Box: UGD 243-1-11-6, Glasgow University Archives, Scotland.

173 I have read your new MS Letter from William Collins to NM, 1 Aug 1944, Box: UGD 243-1-11-6, Glasgow University Archives, Scotland.

173 Here in New Zealand Letter from NM to William Collins, 30 Oct 1944, Box: UGD 243-1-11-6, Glasgow University Archives, Scotland.

174 What can a New Zealander 'London revisited', Sep 1949, CDA 14383, BBC Sound Archives, British Library, London.

174 An entire year may pass Haycraft, *Murder for Pleasure*, pp. 260–61.

176 an absurd 97.5 per cent Coleman, *Olivier*, p. 205.

176 one pound and seven pence Harding, *The Star*, 24 Feb 1982, NM File, HC, Glasgow.

176 [We] are sharing this flat Letter from NM to Winsome and John Schroder, 15 Jan 1950, MS-Papers-0280-29, ATL.

176 I could hear minuscule *BB*, pp. 251–52.

177 sixty-two productions Lewis, *Ngaio Marsh*, p. 128.

177 director and instructor Advertisement, *NZL*, 17 Oct 1947, p. 9.

177 She was late NM, in Mason, 'Brigid Lenihan', p. 8.

181 We've invited a few people Hooper interview with author.

181–82 [Nelly] and I joined *BB*, p. 252.

183 We breakfasted at her flat *BB*, p. 252.

184 sent down to the shop Greene, 'Ngaio, the writer — as seen from a secretary's viewpoint', speech given at the 'return to Black Beech: Centenary Symposium on Ngaio Marsh 1895–1995', Christchurch, 1995, n.p.

184 With a group of fellow art-students MS-Group-1635, ATL.

185 She is talent-scouting Letter from Allen Curnow to JS, 13 Dec 1949, MS-Papers-0280-29, ATL.

186 D'Arcy Cresswell turned up Letter from NM to Winsome and John Schroder, 15 Jan 1950, MS-Papers-0280-29, ATL.

186 It struck me as strange Letter from Allen Curnow to JS, MS-Papers-0280-29, ATL.

187 Mr Howell's play *BB*, p. 254.

187 conventional spy thriller Christie, *Agatha Christie*, 1993, p. 448.

189 shared her huge disappointment NM, in Mason, 'Brigid Lenihan', p. 9.

189 I shared the coldest winter Ibid., p. 8.

189 Ngaio Marsh, author of 16 [and following reviews] Marsh File, Theatre Museum Archive, Victoria and Albert, London.

191 It was 'a play' *BB*, p. 256.

191 **dissonances of all sorts** Ibid, p. 256.

191 **Things were so clearly going wrong** Shirley O'Connor, in conversation with the author, Wellington, 17 Nov 2007.

191–92 **Yours is not a letter** Letter from NM to JS, 27 Aug 1951, MS-Papers-0280-29, ATL.

192 **Rats darted** *BB*, p. 258.

192–93 **The first rounds** Dacres-Mannings interview with author.

193 **They were immensely** *BB*, p. 258.

194 **What phrases** Ibid, p. 260.

195 **The background was not** Orwell, *Decline of the English Murder: and other essays*, pp. 12–13.

196 **As soon as we were shown** *BB*, p. 265.

196 **Essie had agreed** Ibid, p. 268.

198 **Just a scribble** Letter from NM to DM, 22 Jul 1963, MS-Papers-1946, ATL.

198–99 **Excellently characterised [and following reviews]** MSY-2395, ATL.

199 **I am forwarding** MS-Papers-1397, ATL.

200 **Miss Marsh's style** MSY-2395, ATL.

202 **My Chemist known as** Letter from NM to JS, c. 29 Dec 1958, MS-Papers-0280-29, ATL.

202 **Val (Vladimir) is an Esthonian** Letter from NM to JS, c. 29 Dec 1958, ibid.

203 **In his jester's suit** Unidentified review entitled '*King Lear*: Canterbury College Production: noteworthy achievement', AF's private papers.

203 **No praise can be too high** Unidentified review entitled 'The essential Lear finely brought out in brave production,' JE's private papers.

203–04 **On either side [and following quote]** Unidentified article entitled 'Connection between *King Lear* and ritual dances "more than feasible" ', JE's private papers.

204 **Pattern is enhanced** ' "Henry V" not so great', *Canta*, 7 Aug 1957, JE's private papers.

204 **the high point was perhaps** 'Ngaio Marsh scores brilliant success with play "Henry V" ', *The Christchurch Star-Sun*, 20 Jul 1957.

205 **just as my students** Letter from NM to DM, 9 Apr 1958, MS-Papers-1946, ATL.

205 **My Hamlet** Letter from NM to DM, 19 May 1958, ibid.

205 **Rehearsals every day** Letter from NM to DM, Jun 1958, ibid.

205 **Can it be true** Letter from NM to DM, Jun 1958, ibid.

205 **familiarise himself** 'Ngaio Marsh has a re-dressed "Hamlet" in production', *Freedom*, 17 Jun 1958, JE's private papers.

206 **Here is the recipe** 'This "Hamlet" is a Marsh recipe', *The Christchurch Star-Sun*, 11 Jul 1958, AF's private papers.

206 **playing the role as it appeared** 'Production of "Hamlet" loses tragic spirit', *The Christchurch Star-Sun*, 12 Jul 1958, p. 7.

206 **truly artistic** 'University Drama Society's "Hamlet" ', *The Press*, 12 Jul 1958, JE's private papers.

206 **I struggle** Letter from NM to DM, 28 Aug 1958, MS-Papers-1946, ATL.

207 **Whenever I posted** Greene, 'Ngaio, the writer — as seen from a secretary's viewpoint', n.p.

207 **The reviews this book [and following reviews]** Memo from Richard Simon to NM, 21 Jan 1959, MS-Papers-1397, ATL.

207 **I refer to my** Letter from NM to JS, 13 Jan 1958, MS-Papers-0280-29, ATL.

208 **In the British Army** Dacres-Mannings interview with author.

208 **News is that** Letter from NM to DM, 15 Oct 1958, MS-Papers-1946, ATL.

208 **auditions, drawings-to-scale** Letter from NM to DM, 3 May 1959, ibid.

208–09 **Agonisingly difficult auditions** Letter from NM to JE, 3 May 1959, JE's private papers.

209 **full of holes in the walls** Letter from NM to DM, 3 May 1959, MS-Papers-1946, ATL.

209 **all on the giant apron** Letter from NM to JE, 3 May 1959, JE's private papers.

209 **I never wish** Letter from NM to DM, 31 Jul 1959, MS-Papers-1946, ATL.

209 **the** *tax* **clearance** Letter from NM to DM, 22 Dec1959, ibid.

Chapter Seven

Doyenne and Dame

210 **What a hurly-burly** Letter from NM to DM, 6 Mar 1960, MS-Papers-1946, ATL.

210 **enchanting, delicate beauty** Letter from NM to DM, 29 [?] 1959, ibid.

211 **alive, grubby, beautiful** Letter from NM to DM, 10 May 1960, ibid.

211 **Japan was glorious** Letter from NM to 'Syl[via Fox], Bet [Cotterill] & Girls' 5 May 1960, ibid.

211 **It was extremely strenuous** Ibid.

212 **They are an almost pathologically** Letter from NM to DM, 10 May 1960, MS-Papers-1946, ATL.

212 **The hospitality is all** Letter from NM to DM, 17 Jul 1960, ibid.

212 **The great white chief** Ibid.

214 **Lucy . . . has brought** Letter from NM to JE, 13 Aug 1961, JE's private papers.

214 **I think the fault** Letter from NM to DM, 2 Nov 1960, MS-Papers-1946, ATL.

215 **[He] is a man** Letter from NM to DM, 16 Jul 1961, ibid.

215 **absolutely shouting** Letter from NM to DM, 1 Jun 1961, ibid.

215 **slowly about** Letter from NM to DM, 28 Jun 1961, ibid.

216 **so long in suspension** Letter from NM to DM, 16 Jul 1961, ibid.

217 **Having written the last** Letter from NM to DM, 16 Jul 1961, ibid.

217 **shapeless, climaxless** Letter from NM to DM, 3 Feb 1961, ibid.

217 **I still cannot help thinking** Letter from NM to DM, 6 Aug 1958, ibid.

217 **That was** *Miss* **Marsh** Hooper interview with author.

218 **This has not been a holiday** Letter from NM to DM, 7 Nov 1961, MS-Papers-1946, ATL.

218 **It's nice to see** Letter from NM to DM, 1 Jun 1961, ibid.

218 **The telly has gone** Letter from NM to JE, 28 Nov 1961, JE's private papers.

218 **I have done everything** Letter from NM to DM, 9 Jan 1962, MS-Papers-1946, ATL.

219 **from 9 am** Letter from NM to DM, 9 Jan 1962, ibid.

219 **still hard at his Opera** Letter from NM to DM, 19 March 1962, ibid.

219 terrors of Shakespearian rehearsals [and following quotes] MS-Papers-1397, ATL.

221 I've simply got to get cracking Letter from NM to DM, 19 Mar 1962, MS-Papers-1946, ATL.

221 It's been a snorter Letter from NM to JS, 8 Nov 1963, MS-Papers-0280-29, ATL.

223 The Macbeth himself Letter from NM to DM, 6 Jun 1962, MS-Papers-1946, ATL, Wellington.

223 We open (now!) Letter from NM to DM, 1 Jul 1962, ibid.

223 If you were nervous Scott interview with author.

223 if possible 1500 words Letter from NM to DM, 18 Sep 1962, MS-Papers-1946, ATL.

224 [I] would very much like to sit Letter from NM to David Farquhar, [undated], MS-Group-1635.

224 Things were falling Munro interview with author.

224 There are unsettled arrangements Letter from NM to DM, [c. Nov 1962], MS-Papers-1946, ATL.

224 The acting Letter from NM to JE, 26 Dec 1962, JE's private papers.

224 Ngaio knew David Farquhar, interview by Douglas Munro, Wellington, 25 May 2001.

224 Words trip from Quoted in Dart, 'A Unicorn for Christmas', p. 7.

225 David's music is essentially Letter from NM to Edmund [Cork], Jill or Pat, undated, private collection.

225 This past year Letter from NM to JE, 26 Dec 1962, JE's private papers.

225 One never knows Letter from NM to DM, 3 Jan 1963, MS-Papers-1946, ATL.

225 Fifty people 83-011-19, ATL.

226 fiercely Colonial Quoted in Dart, p. 8.

226 a hazardous venture Platt, 'A Unicorn for Christmas', *Landfall*, 65, Mar 1963, p. 64.

226 I have a strong hunch Letter from NM to JE, 26 Dec 1962, JE's private papers.

227 but will no doubt Letter from NM to DM, 3 Jan 1963, MS-Papers-1946, ATL.

227 lavishly attended Letter from NM to DM, c.5 Apr 1963, ibid.

227 guts, digestion Ibid.

227 *Why*, I wonder Letter from NM to DM, 9 May 1963, MS-Papers-1946, ATL.

227 Dog Show at Addington Letter from NM to DM, 28 Jun 1963, ibid.

227 with full authority NM, 'Achievement in Fine Arts'.

228 Anything objective or critical Letter from NM to DM, 30 May 1965, MS-Papers-1946, ATL.

228 Ten weeks vacillation Letter from NM to DM, 16 Nov 1963, ibid.

228 country that financially Letter from NM to DM, 19 Oct 1962, ibid.

228 A) here B) at sea Letter from NM to DM, 2 Nov 1964, ibid.

229 To show how keen Letter from William Collins to NM, 30 Aug 1963, Box: UGD 243-1-11-13, Glasgow University Archives.

229 how touched I am Letter from NM to William Collins, c. 30 Aug 1963, ibid.

229 I have now gone Letter from NM to DM, 30 Oct 1963, MS-Papers-1946, ATL.

229 **Still undecided** Letter from NM to DM, 21 Mar 1965, ibid.

229 **large scale Caesar** Letter from NM to DM, 30 Oct 1963, ibid.

230 **I shall *have* to catch up** Letter from NM to DM, 29 Mar 1964, ibid.

230 **carried on nobly** Letter from NM to DM, 31 Jun 1964, ibid.

230 **overtone that is caught** Letter from NM to JS, 7 Aug 1964, MS-Papers-0280-29, ATL.

230 **little reworking** Bushnell, 'The most ephemeral of the arts', p. 87.

230 **80,000 words** Letter from NM to DM, 2 Nov 1964, MS-Papers-1946, ATL.

231 **I've been lumbering** Letter from NM to DM, 7 Dec 1964, ibid.

231 **I find myself** Letter from NM to DM, 17 Dec 1964, ibid.

231 **We spent 10 days** Letter from Anita Muling to Olivia Spencer Bower, 1 Mar 1963, Olivia Spencer Bower Papers, Archives, CAG Te Puna o Waiwhetu.

231 **[Anita Muling and Marjorie Chambers]** Marian Minson, in conversations with author, Wellington 2007–2008.

231 **He doesn't change** Letter from NM to DM, 25 Jan 1965, MS-Papers-1946, ATL.

231 **some constructive observations** Letter from NM to DM, 1 Feb 1965, ibid.

232 **She & her brothers** Ibid.

232 **a supremely sensitive** Letter from NM to DM, 4 Mar 1965, ibid.

232 **I am engaged** Letter from NM to DM, 4 Mar 1965, ibid.

232 **dived in boots & all** Letter from NM to DM, 22 Apr 1965, ibid.

232 **This just about cleans** Letter from NM to DM, 22 Apr 1965, ibid.

233 **I've been having a gruelling time** Letter from NM to JS, 29 Sep 1965, MS-Papers-0280-29, ATL.

233 **Just theatre** Letter from NM to DM, 8 Nov 1965, MS-Papers-1946, ATL.

233 **Our relationship** Letter from NM to DM, 23 Sep 1965, ibid.

233 **I had just been told** Letter from NM to JS, 17 Nov 1965, ibid.

234 **instead of waiting** Letter from NM to DM, 24 Sep 1965, ibid.

234 **I've got T.V. chaps** Letter from NM to DM, Feb 1966, ibid.

234 **I'm going pretty crazy** Letter from NM to DM, 10 Mar 1966, ibid.

234 **The Sydney T.V. gentleman** Letter from NM to GL, 23 Mar 1966, GL's private papers.

234 **There we were** Letter from NM to JS, 27 Feb 1966, MS-Papers-0280-29, ATL.

234–35 **hectic days & nights** Letter from NM to DM, 23 May 1966, MS-Papers-1946, ATL.

235 **I quite like the earlier bits** Letter from NM to JS, 27 Feb 1966, MS-Papers-0280-29, ATL.

235 **Jonathan and Elric** Letter from NM to AF, 10 May 1966, AF's private papers.

235 **thorny thicket** Letter from NM to DM, 23 May 1966, MS-Papers-1946, ATL.

235 **I shall have my nose** Letter from NM to DM, 23 May 1966, ibid.

235 **YOU NEVER CAN TELL** Letter from NM to GL, 29 May 1966, GL's private papers.

236 **except indirectly** Dennis McEldowney, *'Black Beech and Honeydew'*.

238 **with a fairly useful pension [and following quotes]** Ginx and Richard Fox interview with author.

239 **Sylvia has got her house** Letter from Anita Muling to Olivia Spencer Bower, 17 Jul 1963, Olivia Spencer Papers, Archives, CAG Te Puna o Waiwhetu.

239 **Both houses had** Fox interview.

239 **[operation]** Dacres-Mannings interview.

239 **revising, extending** NM File, HC, Glasgow.

239 **I have just been out** Letter from NM to DM, 1 Jul 1966, MS-Papers-1946, ATL.

240 **In a country** *The Dominion*, 12 Jun 1966, AF's private papers.

240 **The Damery** Letter from NM to DM, 7 Jan 1967, MS-Papers-1946, ATL.

240 **How much money** Scott interview.

242 **I swear that** Letter from NM to DM, 1 July 1966, MS-Papers-1946, ATL.

243 **[Bear Mannings]** Roy [Bear] Mannings interview with author.

243 **I *hated* leaving** Letter from NM to DM, 7 Jan 1967, MS-Papers-1946, ATL.

243 **I'm about to direct** Letter from NM to DM, 6 Mar 1967, ibid.

243 **lovely, delicate & haunting** Letter from NM to DM, 3 May 1967, ibid.

244 **I'm keeping my fingers** Letter from NM to GL, undated, GL's private papers.

244 **sometimes delicate** 'Full-bodied Shakespeare', *The Press*, [details unknown], AF's private papers.

244 **[criticisms re over-using stable]** Minson conversation.

244 **It's all in flashback** Letter from NM to DM, 2 Dec 1967, MS-Papers-1946, ATL.

245 **Of the several excellent [and following reviews]** Memo from George Hardinge to NM, 1 Mar 1967, MS-Papers-1397, ATL.

245 **I long to come** Letter from NM to DM, 30 Oct 1967, MS-Papers-1946, ATL.

245 **It's been caught** Letter from NM to DM, 2 Dec 1967, ibid.

245 **[1964 scare]** Letter from NM to DM, 2 Nov 1964, ibid.

245 **I do wish to heavens** Letter from NM to DM, 23 Mar 1959, ibid.

246 **I put my name down** Letter from NM to DM, 5 Jan 1968, ibid.

246 **being wonderful about** Letter from NM to DM, 23 Jan 1968, ibid.

246 **It's a body-blow** Letter from NM to DM, 11 Mar 1968, ibid.

Chapter Eight

Rome to Jubilee

249 **It will be clear enough** Letter from NM to DM, 14 Oct 1969, ibid.

249 **I've had no prompting** Letter from NM to DM, 24 Nov 1969, ibid.

249 **[I] would be profoundly grateful** Letter from NM to DM, 18 Sep 1969, ibid.

249 **What an angel-child** Letter from NM to DM, 14 Oct 1969, ibid.

250 **I note that DEPUTI** Letter from NM to DM, 1 Dec 1969, ibid.

250 **I don't want Alleyn** Letter from NM to DM, 24 Nov 1969, ibid.

250 **achieving structural** Letter from NM to DM, 10 Feb 1969, ibid.

250 **of all filthy complaints** Letter from NM to DM, 11 Mar 1968, ibid.

250 **the experience of a lifetime** Letter from NM to GL, 14 Jul [1968], GL's private papers.

250 **I am sitting on a balcony** Letter from NM to AF, 20 May 1968, AF's private papers.

251 **& the multitude** Letter from NM to GL, 14 Jul [1968], GL's private papers.

251 **Have you any idea** Letter from NM to DM, 10 Feb 1969, MS-Papers-1946, ATL.

251 **I came away** Letter from NM to GL, 14 Jul [1968], GL's private papers.

251 **Pammy is now** Letter from NM to DM, [Jun 1968], MS-Papers-1946, ATL.

251 **my greatest delight** Letter from NM to DM, [Jul 1968], ibid.

252 **my dear, dear, family** Letter from NM to DM, 7 Aug 1968, ibid.

252 **It's absolutely maddening** Letter from NM to DM, 8 Aug 1968, ibid.

253 **I have no Roman [film]** Letter from NM to DM, 8 Aug 1968, ibid.

253 **The meat tastes** Letter from NM to DM, 5 Sep 1968, ibid.

254 **It's time to compare Christie** Lewis, *Ngaio Marsh*, p. 201.

254 **I'm dug into a new one** Letter from NM to DM, 3 Jan 1969, MS-Papers-1946, ATL.

254 **if we can stage** Letter from NM to DM, 10 Feb 1969, ibid.

254 **Sorry this is blotched [and Governor-General quote]** Letter from NM to DM, 28 Feb 1969, ibid.

254 **a huge dirty** Letter from NM to DM, 14 Mar 1969, ibid.

255 **Whether I get the cash** Letters from NM to DM, 9 Apr, 12 May 1969, ibid.

256 **to bring about hideous** Letter from NM to DM, 23 Jun 1969, ibid.

256 **It too was a howling** Letter from NM to DM, 17 Jul 1969, ibid.

256 **As always I destroyed** Letter from NM to DM, 18 Sep 1969, ibid.

256 **the best yet** Letter from NM to DM, 15 Jan 1970, ibid.

257 **I had the usual tree** Ibid.

257–58 **Do you remember** Letter from NM to JS, 27 Dec 1967, MS-Papers-0280-29, ATL.

258 **up to 22,000 words** Letter from NM to DM, 9 Jun 1970, MS-Papers-1946, ATL.

259 **Mine will be Doubting T.** Letter from NM to DM, 10 Feb 1969, ibid.

259 **was a great success** Letter from NM to DM, 28 Dec 1970, ibid.

260 **so don't get yourself** Letter from NM to GL, 22 Jan 1970, GL's private papers.

261 **3,000 words** Letter from NM to DM, 2 Feb 1971, M-S-Papers 1946, ATL, Wellington.

261 **I do wish that you** Letter from DO to NM, 3 Apr 1970, MS-Group-1635, ATL.

261 **I'm sorry you can't find** Letter from DO to NM, 20 Jul [1970], ibid.

261 **I most certainly will** Letter from DO to NM, [c. 16 Feb 1971], ibid.

261 **dose of 6 antibiotic** Letter from NM to DM, 22 May 1971, MS-Papers-1946, ATL.

262 **very small** Letter from NM to DM, 8 Jun 1971, ibid.

262 **There's no denying** Letter from NM to DM, 25 Jun 1971, ibid.

262 **another great chunk** Letter from NM to DM, 25 Jun 1971, ibid.

263 **Bernard & Laura** Letter from NM to DM, 14 Aug 1971, ibid.

263 **I must say I still** Letter from NM to DM, 29 Nov 1971, ibid.

263 **Talk about a working** Letter from NM to DM, 20 Dec 1971, ibid.

263 **All I can say** Letter from NM to DO, 4 Aug 1971, MS-Group-1635, ATL.

263 **exhausting but memorable** Letter from DO to NM, 23 May [1972], ibid.

264 **really quite frail** Letter from DO to Nora [?], 15 Feb 1972, ibid.

264 **happy arrival** Letter from NM to DM, 26 Jan 1972, MS-Papers-1946, ATL.

264 *Henry V* **is on** Letter from NM to DM, 1 Apr 1972, ibid.

264 **again that vital** MS-Group-1635, ATL.

264 **I hope most ardently** Letter from NM to DM, [c. May–Jun] 1972, MS-Papers-1946, ATL.

265 **Don't be so silly** Olivia Spencer Bower Papers, Archives, CAG Te Puna o Waiwhetu.

265 **Rehearsals going** Letter from NM to DM, [Aug] 1972, MS-Papers-1946, ATL, Wellington.

265 **I couldn't bear you** Letter from NM to DM, 19 Sep 1972, MS-Papers-1946, ATL, Wellington.

265 **I was lost** Letter from Bruce Mason to NM, MS-Group-1635, ATL, Wellington.

265 **Every seat was taken** Olivia Spencer Bower Papers, Archives, CAG Te Puna o Waiwhetu.

266 **We made a net profit** Letter from NM to DM, 16 Nov 1972, MS-Papers-1946, ATL, Wellington.

266 **Throughout the rehearsal** Letter from NM to AF, 18 Oct 1972, AF's private papers.

266 **Lucy was black, sleek** Email from JE to author, 2 Dec 2007.

267 **I have a sneaking feeling** NM File, HC, Glasgow.

268 **The Oratory dome** Letter from NM to JS, 25 Nov 1960, MS-Papers-0280-29, ATL, Wellington.

268 **$14,000 guarantee** Letter from DO [?] to Edmund Cork, 10 Apr 1972, MS-Group-1635, ATL, Wellington.

268 **I'm afraid that poor little Nicola** Letter from NM to DM, 16 Nov 1972, MS-Papers-1946, ATL, Wellington.

268–69 **On the night** Email from AF to author, 26 Feb 2008.

269–70 **The new book is giving** [and following quotes] Letter from NM to DM, 10 Apr 1973, MS-Papers-1946, ATL.

[I] flung up both feet Ibid.

I pulled myself together Ibid.

new professional Court Theatre's Ibid.

South Pole whistling up Letter from NM to DM, 2 Jul 1973, MS-Papers-1946, ATL.

271 **I wish she could have stayed** Letter from NM to DM, 2 Jul 1973, ibid.

271 **She's very thin & worn** Letter from NM to DM, 8 Aug 1973, ibid.

271 **I'm getting myself trained** Letter from NM to DM, 11 Aug 1973, ibid.

271 **It makes a noise** Letter from NM to DM, 21 Aug 1973, ibid.

271 **which is better** Letter from NM to DM, 25 Sep 1973, ibid.

271 **We laughed ourselves sick** Ibid.

271 **Syl is marvellous** Letter from NM to DM, 1 Apr 1972, MS-Papers-1946, ATL.

272 **I've found a tenant** Letter from NM to DM, 20 Dec 1973, ibid.

272 **Over the past three decades** Letter from NM to DM, 14 Jan 1974, ibid.

272 **which were a howling success** Letter from NM to DM, 7 Feb 1974, ibid.

272 **Yours is a second home** Letter from NM to DM, 9 Mar 1974, ibid.

272 **Dear Jonathan Elsom** Letter from NM to DM, 15 Apr 1974, ibid.

272 **Thank the Lord** Letter from NM to DM, 5 May 1974, ibid.

273 **Hollywoodhouse was something** Letter from NM to DM, 9 Jun 1974, ibid.

273 **At the moment he's editing** Letter from NM to DM, 15 Jul 1974, ibid.

273 **scalped, (literally)** Letter from NM to DM, 19 Aug 1974, ibid.

273 **I'm amusing myself** Letter from NM to DM, 15 Jul 1974, ibid.

274 **I've got to pop into** Letter from NM to DM, 19 Aug 1974, ibid.

274 **Will have to begin** Letter from NM to DM, [c. Nov] 1974, ibid.

274 **She also accompanies me** Letter from NM to DM, 9 Jan 1975, ibid.

274 **Jonathan Elsom has a big part** Letter from NM to DM, 1 Aug 1975, ibid.

275 **I shall leave [England]** Letter from NM to DM, 27 Jun 1975, ibid.

275 **It *was* worth doing** Letter from NM to DM, [c. Dec] 1975, ibid.

276 **the best** Letter from NM to DM, 3 Feb 1976, ibid.

276 **It's marvellous** NM File, HC, Glasgow.

276 **very-up bucking letter** Letter from NM to DM, 2 Jun 1976, MS-Papers-1946, ATL.

277 **this was at the request** Letter from NM to DM, 3 Feb 1976, ibid.

277 **At the moment I'm re-reading** Letter from NM to DM, 3 Feb 1976, ibid.

277 **Lieut. Pinkerton** Letter from NM to DM, 2 Jun 1976, ibid.

277 **two hard-case items** Fox interview.

278 **mass of desultory notes** Letter from NM to DM, 23 Jul 1976, MS-Papers-1946, ATL.

278 **I'm sure you were saddened** Letter from DO to NM, 9 Mar 1976, NM File, HC, Glasgow.

278 **Which ranges from one lady** Letter from NM to DM, 14 Sep 1976, MS-Papers-1946, ATL.

278 **The parents are kindly** Letter from NM to DM, 19 Nov 1976, ibid.

278 **Freddie & Eve Page's** Letter from NM to DM, 24 Jan 1977, ibid.

278 **I must say I thoroughly** Ibid.

279 **clad in a ridiculous** Letter from NM to DM, 10 Apr 1977, MS-Papers-1946, ATL.

279 **with the result that this little room** Letter from NM to DM, 20 May 1977, ibid.

279 **I shall have to learn** Letter from NM to DM, 26 Jun 1977, ibid.

279 **thoroughly professional** Christopher Moore, 'When Wexford was Alleyn', *New Zealand Memories*, No. 62, Oct–Nov, p. 50.

279 **stand-up fight** Letter from NM to DM, 24 Nov 1977, MS-Papers-1946, ATL.

280 **come up & hold the fort** Letter from NM to DM, [c. Dec] 1977, ibid.

280 **did a spot of figure-skating** Letter from NM to DM, 6 Apr 1978, ibid.

280 **just in time to see** Letter from NM to MB and JB, 8 May [1978], MS-Group-1635, ATL.

280 **Ngaio has a delightful room** Letter from Sylvia Fox to DM, [May] 1978, MS-Papers-1946, ATL.

281 **Many congratulations** Letter from Elizabeth Walter to NM, NM File, HC, Glasgow.

281 **I feel this is probably** Letter from Robert Knittel to NM, 23 Feb 1978, ibid.

281 **been interrupted so often** Letter from NM to RK, c. 23 Feb 1978, ibid.

281 **[It] hung round my neck** Letter from NM to Edmund Cork, 3 Jan 1978, ibid.

281 **Obviously there is more** Letter from NM to JB, 23 Oct 1978, MS-Group-1635, ATL.

281 **They linger in my mind** Letter from EW, 6 Mar 1978, NM File, HC, Glasgow.

282 *Grave Mistake* **seems to be beating** Letter from NM to MB, 27 Mar 1979, MS-Group-1635, ATL.

282 *We write* **to thank you** Letter from NM and Sylvia Fox to DM, 8 Aug [c.1978], MS-Papers-1946, ATL.

283 **lifted the level** Letter from NM to JE, 14 May 1979, JE's private papers.

283 **true metier** Letter from NM to Bruce Mason, 20 Feb [1978], MS-Group-1635, ATL.

283 **It may turn out to be** Letter from NM to DM, 10 Aug 1978, MS-Papers-1946, ATL.

283 **My visit to Johnny** Letter from NM to MB, 22 Jul 1978, MS-Group-1635, ATL.

283–84 **Drawers opened** Ibid.

284 **One begins to wonder** Letter from NM to DM, 29 Oct 1978, MS-Papers-1946, ATL.

284 **I'm glued to my work** Letter from NM to DM, 26 Oct 1978, ibid.

284 **danger of letting it** Letter from NM to DM, [c. Nov] 1978, ibid.

284 **Presents, visits** Letter from NM to DM, 7 Jan 1979, ibid.

284 **The which said** Memo from M. Reese, 21 Jan 1980, NM File, HC, Glasgow.

284 **We had an enormous** Letter from EW to NM, 9 May 1980, ibid.

285 **Fossilized or not** Letter from NM to EW, 20 May 1980, ibid.

285 **[Max Cryer comment]** Email from Max Cryer to author, 28 Jun 2007.

285 **My memory is deteriorating** Letter from NM to JB [c. 1981], MS-Group-1635, ATL.

285 **her life since the early fifties** David Elworthy to EW, 11 Apr 1980; EW to David Elworthy, 18 April 1980, NM File, HC, Glasgow.

285 **It's been tricky work** Letter from NM to MB, 29 Jan 1981, MS-Group-1635, ATL.

286 **I took arm loads** Wilkinson interview with author.

286 **I certainly ran** Voice recording: 'Reflections on Ngaio Marsh (and interviews with Ngaio Marsh, 7 and 24 April 1978)', Bruce Harding, 23 Dec 2007.

287 **She's as brave as a lion** Letter from NM to DM, 7 Jan 1979, MS-Papers-1946, ATL.

287 **I was so happy** Letter from NM to DM, c. Dec 1978, ibid.

287 **It's been in my head** Letter from NM to EW, 2 Feb 1982, NM File, HC, Glasgow.

Chapter Nine

Dénouement

289 **It was extremely difficult** Letter from NM to JB, 5 Feb 1982, MS-Group-1635, ATL.

290 **magnificent Dutchie**, Letter from NM to JE, 26 Sep 1981, JE's private papers.

290 **She skidded down hill** Letter from NM to MB, 30 Jun 1981, MS-Group-1635, ATL.

290 **Ngaio was in great form** Letter from Rosemary Greene to JE, c. 9 Mar 1982, JE's private papers.

290 **I don't know what** Letter from NM to EW, 2 Feb 1982, NM File, HC, Glasgow.

290 **I've had a cable** Letter from NM to JB, 5 Feb 1982, MS-Group-1635, ATL.

290 **Well, my sweetie-pie** Letter from NM to JE, 16 Feb 1982, JE's private papers.

291 **Helen Holmes rang up** Lascelles interview with author.

291 **The days leading up** Letter from Jean Esquilant to JE, 3 Mar 1982, JE's private papers.

291 **There is going to be** Letter from Rosemary Greene to JE, c. 9 Mar 1982, JE's private papers.

291 **chaste reticence** Simon Acland, public tribute to Ngaio Marsh, delivered Christchurch Cathedral, 26 Feb 1982.

292 **[Copy of manuscript arriving]** Mannings interview with author.

292 **I'm just delighted** Letter from William Phillips to EW, 4 Mar 1982, NM File, HC, Glasgow.

292 **I am delighted about this** Letter from EW to Pat Cork, 8 Jun1982, ibid.

Epilogue

293 **[Deborah Walton memories]** Walton interview with author.

293 **Now, remember** Fox interview with author.

293 **a beautiful black cat** Fox and Walton interviews with author.

293 **She was really worried** Fox interview with author.